THE MASTER AND THE DEAN

THE MASTER AND THE DEAN

The Literary Criticism of Henry James and William Dean Howells

ROB DAVIDSON

University of Missouri Press   Columbia and London

Library of Congress Cataloging-in-Publication Data

Davidson, Rob, 1967–
    The master and the dean : the literary criticism of Henry
James and William Dean Howells / Rob Davidson.
            p. cm.
        Summary: "Comparative study of Henry James's and
William Dean Howells's literary criticism. Examines the inter-
relationship between the men, emphasizing their aesthetic
concerns and attitudes toward the market and audience, and
their beliefs concerning the moral value of fiction and the
United States as a literary subject, and writings about each
other"—Provided by publisher.
        Includes bibliographical references (p.   ) and index.
        ISBN 0-8262-1579-3 (alk. paper)
    1.   James, Henry, 1843–1916—Knowledge—Literature.
2.   Howells, William Dean, 1837–1920—Knowledge—
Literature. 3.   American literature—History and criticism—
Theory, etc. 4.   Criticism—United States—History—20th
century. 5.   Criticism—United States—History—19th
century.   I. Title.
        PS2127.L5D34 2005
        810.9'004—dc22
                                                    2005006498

∞ ™ This paper meets the requirements of the
American National Standard for Permanence of Paper
for Printed Library Materials, Z39.48, 1984.

Designer: Kristie Lee
Typesetter: Crane Composition, Inc.
Printer and binder: Thomson-Shore, Inc.
Typeface: Galliard

This book is published with the generous assistance of the
Office of the Dean of Humanities and Fine Arts at California
State University, Chico.

for Linda

Contents

III. The Literary Criticism of Henry James and
     William Dean Howells, 1898–1920

Acknowledgments

First and most important, I thank my wife, Linda Rogers, for her constant support and encouragement. She continues to help in every important way, and I am grateful for her patience, love, and good graces.

I wish to express deep thanks to Robert Paul Lamb for his many close readings of this text. His comprehensive knowledge of the field, teamed with his unerring skill as an editor and his keen sense for the language, have greatly improved the quality of my scholarship. I thank Wendy Stallard Flory, John N. Duvall, and William J. Palmer for their work on my behalf. John W. Crowley offered helpful suggestions and encouragement, for which I am grateful. And I thank the Purdue Research Foundation and the Purdue University Department of English for extending research grants to me during the completion of this book.

Portions of Chapters 1 and 3 were originally published in *American Literary Realism* 36, no. 2 (2004): 120–47. The author wishes to thank the University of Illinois Press for permission to reprint this material.

Abbreviations

The following abbreviations refer to works cited parenthetically in the text. Full references to these editions are also located in the bibliography.

ES   William Dean Howells, *Editor's Study*
HoF   William Dean Howells, *Heroines of Fiction* (2 vols.)
HSL   William Dean Howells, *Selected Letters of William Dean Howells* (6 vols.)
ImI   William Dean Howells, *Imaginary Interviews*
JL   Henry James, *Henry James Letters* (4 vols.)
LC   Henry James, *Literary Criticism* (2 vols.)
LFL   Michael Anesko, *Letters, Fictions, Lives: Henry James and William Dean Howells*
SLC   William Dean Howells, *Selected Literary Criticism* (3 vols.)

THE MASTER AND THE DEAN

Introduction

The Undiscovered Country

I

In July of 1869, a gushing William Dean Howells wrote to his good friend Henry James Jr., "There seems to be a general waking-up to your merits; but when you've a fame as great as Hawthorne's, you wont forget who was the first, warmest and truest of your admirers, will you?" (*HSL* 1:331). The two men did not forget one another. In a friendship that spanned over fifty years, they regularly corresponded, read and criticized each other's work, argued over aesthetics and literary history, and shared in the personal triumphs, crises, and tragedies of their lives. No biography of the one can be written that does not give serious attention to the other; in a very real sense, the two friends have been forever joined.

James, of course, has enjoyed the larger posthumous success, both among practicing fiction writers and in the academy, and his fiction continues to be republished, read, and critically explored. In the case of Howells, however, relatively few of his many fictional texts receive significant critical attention, though scholars agree that his place as a critic and champion of American realism remains secure. Definitive biographies of each have been written; scrupulously edited volumes of their literary criticism have been produced; their letters have been picked over, published, then picked over and published again. Copious secondary material exists for each author.

It is indeed baffling, then, to discover a relative paucity of book-length studies on the literary criticism of either author. One reason may simply be ease of access. Until the publication of Leon Edel's invaluable two-volume set of James's literary criticism in 1984, James's enormous critical output was dispersed among the various volumes produced in his lifetime and the hundreds of reviews he authored in dozens of magazines—some of it hard to locate. This is not to suggest the criticism has been ignored. Quite to the contrary; ever since the publication of Percy Lubbock's *The Craft of Fiction*, James's critical writings—particularly the Prefaces to the New York Edition— have been carefully pored over. Early interpretations of James's criticism were written in an attempt to systematize and "clarify" James's frequently oblique critical pronouncements. Critics such as Lubbock, R. P. Blackmur, Leon Edel, and James E. Miller cataloged, structured, and rigidly codified James's criticism, imposing elaborate formalist schemas to assess the sprawling body of work. It is not the purpose of this current study to deny these critics an essential point: that James did treasure and return to various critical axioms, often employing oblique and highly esoteric language to define his views. Indeed, one may be hard-pressed to decide if New Criticism invented James, or if James invented New Criticism.

Interest in James remains unabated. Every major critical school of the twentieth century had its say on James's fiction and criticism; in this sense, his work remains vital at the beginning of the twenty-first century. But while certain areas of James's work as a critic have been carefully examined—seminal essays such as "The Art of Fiction" and the Prefaces, for example—there is, simply stated, a dearth of recent scholarly studies devoted exclusively to James's literary criticism. Indeed, I know of only two: Sarah B. Daugherty's *The Literary Criticism of Henry James* and Vivien Jones's *James the Critic*. Despite its strengths, Daugherty's volume sidesteps James's Prefaces to the New York Edition and is therefore an incomplete study. And while Jones's study remains a valuable text, it antedates a range of critical and theoretical approaches employed by recent scholars, most notably culturally and historically centered scholarship. In part, then, this study is an attempt to fill a serious gap in the field of James studies.

But it is also an attempt to reconfigure the dominant critical paradigm concerning James's development as a critic. From Lubbock's *The Craft of Fiction* and F. O. Matthiessen's *Henry James: The Major Phase,* and up to the present, there has existed in James studies an unstated assumption that the latter half of James's career as a critic is the period most worthy of deep study. Clearly, in his "major phase," James produced some of his most engaging, complex criticism. But the unintended consequence of focusing principally on the later years of James's career is to deny his earlier work its due. Regarding edited selections of James's criticism, one need only peruse the table of contents of such volumes as Morris Roberts's *The Art of Fiction and Other Essays* and Leon Edel's *The House of Fiction: Essays on the Novel by Henry James* to see that the most influential editors have typically favored

James's middle (1884–1898) and late (1899–1916) critical work in their edited selections. Blackmur's *The Art of the Novel* collected James's Prefaces, while for Lubbock's *The Craft of Fiction* James's Prefaces are clearly the ur-text. One noteworthy exception is James E. Miller's excellent edited volume *Theory of Fiction: Henry James,* which, if it presents mostly brief excerpts of James's essays arranged in an overly insistent formalist scheme, nevertheless samples an impressive range of the criticism.

Following the examples of Sarah Daugherty and Vivien Jones, this study attempts to embrace the whole arc of James's career as a critic, from his earliest reviews to the Prefaces, and attempts to identify the concepts, themes, and argumentative strategies that James employed throughout the whole of his career. In contrast to Daugherty and Jones, however, it does so in a relational context: James's criticism is read intertextually with the criticism written by his friend, editor, and publisher, William Dean Howells.

II

If James scholars have benefited from a uniform, comprehensive, and rigorously edited edition of the Master's criticism, the same, sadly, cannot be said for Howells. Indiana University's edition of Howells's selected literary criticism appeared in 1993, and while these carefully chosen texts are a welcome addition to Howells studies, the three-volume set gathers but one-third of Howells's output during his long career. The insufficiency is perhaps most egregious in respect to Howells's "Editor's Study" columns from *Harper's* (1886–1892), without question his most important critical contribution to American letters. Howells's output in the "Study" was tremendous—some 375,000 words spread over seventy-five monthly columns. Donald Pizer reprints less than one-third of the "Study" in *Selected Literary Criticism Volume II: 1886–1897,* and his decision to use parts of columns, cutting and pasting as he sees fit, only complicates the matter. Needless to say, the situation is less than ideal. Howells scholars are in need of a rigorously edited edition of the full "Editor's Study." The only complete scholarly edition of the column—*Editor's Study by William Dean Howells,* edited by James W. Simpson—is out of print. So long as the bulk of Howells's criticism remains uncollected and unread, it will be difficult for the field to develop.[1]

1. In addition to the Indiana University Press volumes and *Editor's Study,* ed. James W. Simpson, the standard edited collections of Howells's criticism are *Criticism and Fiction and Other Essays,* ed. Clara Marburg Kirk and Rudolf Kirk, and *W. D. Howells as Critic,* ed. Edwin H. Cady.

Recently, John Crowley has argued convincingly for the careful reassessment of Howells's overlooked fiction.[2] In a sense, I would like to argue the same for Howells's frequently overlooked criticism. The need for such a study seems self-evident: no full-length study of Howells's career as a literary critic exists, despite the fact that nearly all scholars of nineteenth-century American literature grant that Howells was the preeminent theoretical voice of American realism in his day.[3] When one considers Howells's role as an editor, publisher, and advocate for a long list of important American authors—a list that includes James, Mark Twain, Stephen Crane, Frank Norris, Charlotte Perkins Gilman, Paul Laurence Dunbar, Abraham Cahan, and Charles W. Chesnutt, to name but a few—and when one considers the fact that a significant part of Howells's influence was enacted in his literary criticism and book reviews, then a careful examination of the whole of his career as literary critic seems long overdue and of no small significance to the field of nineteenth-century American literature.

Indeed, one might wonder why no such study currently exists. The answer comes, perhaps, in the familiar narrative of Howells's legacy in American literature. After enjoying tremendous success as an author and critic in his own lifetime, Howells's reputation suffered an onslaught of posthumous abuse from which it has arguably never recovered.[4] After a brief "Howells Revival" in the mid-twentieth century, Howells's stature has continued to undergo reevaluation, but the legacy remains something of an open question. Recent critical studies have continued to explore the thesis that Howells suffered from a nervous hysteria that somehow restricted or impeded his creative output (a variation, perhaps, on Brooks's original claim that Howells was timid).[5] Other critics have suggested that Howells's culturally nor-

2. See three books by John W. Crowley: *The Black Heart's Truth: The Early Career of W. D. Howells; The Mask of Fiction: Essays on W. D. Howells;* and *The Dean of American Letters: The Late Career of William Dean Howells;* Crowley's trilogy of works constitute a valuable contribution to Howells studies.

3. In retrospect, many critics might argue that James was the superior critic. Nevertheless, Howells was more popular, more widely read, and more immediately influential during their lifetimes. James's enormous influence has mostly been posthumous; much to his chagrin, he never occupied a position equaling Howells's social or theoretical influence in his own lifetime.

4. The main culprits here include Van Wyck Brooks, whose study *The Ordeal of Mark Twain* both introduced and cemented, for many scholars, the perception of Howells as timid, genteel, and intellectually shallow. H. L. Mencken and Sinclair Lewis corroborated Brooks's account, the latter famously attacking the Dean in his 1930 Nobel Prize acceptance speech ("The American Fear of Literature"). Brooks would revise some of his opinions on Howells in *Howells: His Life and World.*

5. See Crowley, *Black Heart's Truth* and *Mask of Fiction.* In his acknowledgments for *Black Heart's Truth,* Crowley notes his debt to Edwin Cady's influential 1946 essay "The Neuroticism of William Dean Howells."

mative values—and his close ties to the world of publishing—thwarted whatever radical social potential he voiced in his criticism and personal correspondence (a variation, perhaps, on the charge that Howells was overly genteel and patrician).[6] While not disputing the validity of such claims or the work of scholars who have, without question, added to our knowledge of Howells, it goes without saying that there is still much undiscovered country in Howells studies. This study is an effort to open up the Dean's work as a literary critic for closer examination.

Of particular importance are the final two decades of Howells's life. While the early and middle periods of his career as a critic have received moderate attention over the years, the work written after 1898 has been all but ignored, even by Howellsians. Generally speaking, Howells did move away from expressly "literary" criticism. But that does not mean the Dean went soft. Rather, he explored an impressive range of rhetorical styles and critical voices, frequently blurring the boundaries between the "literary" essay and other genres, including fiction and sociocultural reportage. And, of course, he continued to write fine literary criticism, much of it in the "Editor's Easy Chair." In Part III of this study I address a wide range of Howells's later criticism—including the frequently overlooked *Heroines of Fiction*—in an effort to open up this vital but overlooked area of Howells studies.

III

If the literary criticism of both James and Howells deserves such close re-examination, the questions might legitimately be asked: Why not study the work of each author on its own terms? Why undertake a comparative study?

As any reader of the biographies, letters, or some of the recent biographically oriented scholarship knows, these two friends wrote regularly to, for, and of one another throughout the breadth of their careers. Certain seminal essays like Howells's "Henry James, Jr.," or James's "William Dean Howells" quickly come to mind. Such literal examples are, however, relatively few in number. As I shall demonstrate, James and Howells more frequently wrote their criticism as an indirect response to one another. James's "The Art of Fiction," for example, is, in part, a delicately worded response to the transatlantic conundrum surrounding Howells's "Henry James, Jr." Likewise,

6. See Daniel H. Borus, *Writing Realism: Howells, James, and Norris in the Mass Market;* Amy Kaplan, *The Social Construction of American Realism;* and David E. Shi, *Facing Facts: Realism in American Thought and Culture, 1850–1920.*

Howells's "Novel-Writing and Novel-Reading" is clearly indebted to "The Art of Fiction." And while one can read James's "The Science of Criticism" on its own terms, an understanding of James's rhetorical strategies in the essay is deepened when one positions it in relation to Howells's concurrent "Editor's Study" columns on the same topic; James's essay reads, in one sense, as a riposte to Howells. These intertextual occurrences—be they deliberate or inadvertent—deserve careful scrutiny, for it is quite obvious that each author exerted a profound influence on the other. This question alone—as it pertains to the literary criticism of James and Howells—remains largely unexamined by current scholars familiar with either author.[7]

Admittedly, the bulk of James's and Howells's criticism was not written consciously or deliberately in response to the work of the other. Cross-referentiality and overt intertextual connections aside, there is still ample justification for a comparative study of the literary criticism. James and Howells generated, between 1859 and 1920, a substantial body of critical work that unquestionably changed the course of American literature, and that continues to exert a serious influence today. Scholars generally agree that James and Howells were the two most important American literary critics of their period. Their achievements, it is well known, are major. Between them, they convincingly defined the connections between Continental realism and its younger American counterpart. Few scholars or critics have ever been as well-versed or articulate in contemporary literary trends as were James and Howells. Howells vigorously defended realism in the "Editor's Study" (and elsewhere), promoting what he considered to be the genre's inherent social and moral issues. In "The Art of Fiction," James not only defined fiction as a fine art, he also subtly introduced French aesthetics to a hostile Anglo-American audience. His Prefaces to the New York Edition still stand today as some of the most engaging and fascinating meditations on creative writing. For these important reasons the criticism of James and Howells deserves to be examined comparatively.

But there are other, less frequently cited connections between the criticism of James and Howells that deserve to be explored. Each author addressed shared topics of interest such as the definition of the literary critic and the question of how to view postbellum America as a literary subject. Also, both James and Howells continuously examined the practice of writing (both fiction and literary criticism) and its relationship to the market.

---

7. On the other hand, the fiction has been read in light of the work of other authors. For instance, Hawthorne's influence on James's fiction has been examined quite cogently and thoroughly by Richard Brodhead, in *The School of Hawthorne*. And Michael Anesko charts a fascinating pattern of mutual influence between James's and Howells's fiction in *Letters, Fictions, Lives: Henry James and William Dean Howells*.

Each author was keenly aware of the market forces that, at times, shaped his work as a critic. Sometimes, they addressed the issue directly, as in James's "The Science of Criticism" or Howells's "The Man of Letters as a Man of Business." More often, they approached the matter indirectly, as in James's Prefaces or in a range of Howells's contributions to the "Editor's Study." Their attitudes on this topic alone reveal a wealth of valuable data for culturally and historically centered scholars interested in the relationship between authors and marketplace forces during the time period. For all of these reasons, then, it seems natural to position the literary criticism of James and Howells beside the work of the other. Hence this study: the first comprehensive comparative examination of James's and Howells's respective critical oeuvres. The results are anything but predictable: a rigorous, intertextual reading of their work as critics reveals both deeper rifts and more intimate similarities between the two writers than have hitherto been recognized.

It bears noting that, for the sake of brevity, this study intentionally avoids extensive biographical information or an extended consideration of each writer's creative output, though careful consideration of each would be of unquestionable value. Similarly, a treatment of James's important work of cultural criticism, *The American Scene,* is beyond the scope of the present study. Finally, this book is not the place for an extended discussion of the American literary marketplace of the late nineteenth and early twentieth century, though I regularly refer to the marketplace and print culture of the era. The reader is humbly directed to the many excellent studies of the literary marketplace, the history of the publishing industry, and the construction of authorship.[8] Rather, the focus here is restricted to a consideration of the literary criticism, and critical aesthetic, of each author. It is my hope that this study will not be taken as a final word on these topics, but only as the opening argument in a discussion that will continue to develop and grow with time.

---

8. A selected list of titles on this topic includes Ellen Ballou, *The Building of the House: Houghton Mifflin's First Half Century;* Borus, *Writing Realism;* Eugene Exman, *The House of Harper: One Hundred and Fifty Years of Publishing;* J. Henry Harper, *The House of Harper: A Century of Publishing in Franklin Square;* Ellery Sedgwick, *The Atlantic Monthly, 1857–1909: Yankee Humanism at High Tide and Ebb;* and Jennifer Wicke, *Advertising Fictions: Literature, Advertisement, and Social Reading.*

I

The Literary Criticism of Henry James and William Dean Howells, 1859–1884

1. A Horror of Dogma

James, Howells, and the Roots of American Realism

Henry James published three unsigned book reviews in the January 1865 edition of the *North American Review*. In one, he criticizes Harriet Elizabeth Prescott Spofford's novel *Azarian* for its "incoherent and meaningless" verbal pictures. "Words," James declares, "possess a certain inherent dignity, value, and independence, language being rather the stamped and authorized coinage which expresses the value of thought." He goes on to ridicule Spofford's overcontrolled, thin characters, which are "more than an offence against art. Nature herself resents it." An accurate depiction of a character's "humanity," as opposed to her physical characteristics, ought to be the writer's aim. The novel's "foremost claim to merit, and indeed the measure of its merit, is its *truth*." James discriminates between Spofford's "descriptive manner" and "the famous realistic system" currently coming into vogue, in which to be "real" is not merely to "describe" but to "express" or "convey" (*LC* 1:604–7). James demands emotive, real people as characters, not flat caricatures. A few pages later in that same January issue, James addresses the charge of immorality in Anne Moncure Crane Seemüller's novel *Emily Chester*. James argues Seemüller's novel is not immoral because it depicts a young wife tempted by adultery, but rather because the novel itself is guilty of a "false representation" of human nature (*LC* 1:592).

These early reviews demonstrate a young, cocksure James. His prose is witty and acidic. But what is perhaps most striking is the rhetoric James employs in these early reviews; both Spofford and Seemüller fail miserably, in his view, but that view is expressed in explicitly moral terms. This raises the question: what did morality mean to Henry James? It is easier to begin with what it was not: it was not sentimentalism, realism, didacticism, or history. Rather, morality was, for James, most often related to questions of form and execution in art. From his earliest work as a critic, he viewed writing as a moral practice—not so much in terms of what a given work of art depicted (though, to be sure, he addressed this issue), but in the manner of the depiction itself: the language, the sense of verisimilitude, the overall accuracy of the portrait, and the greater purpose of the portrayal.

In the Spofford review, James turns to Balzac for a counterexample. In contrast to Spofford's flat characterization, loose form, and description for its own sake, Balzac's work "was clearly done because it was *scientifically* done." Balzac rendered things "as they stood. He aimed at local color; that is, at giving the facts of things." In this important passage, we see first mention of topics fundamental to James's literary aesthetic, which would always serve as the basis for his critical judgments: descriptions of things are warranted *"only in so far as they bear upon the action"*; "the soul of a novel is its action"; and the principle that a novelist should "only describe those things which are accessory to the action." Selection—a Jamesian buzzword if there ever was one—is the principle at the heart of this aside on Balzac, and selection is really at the heart of his critique of Spofford. Linking revision and excision to morality—"A true artist should be as sternly just as a Roman father"—James concludes the review by suggesting the novel could be trimmed by half. Sounding not a little like an impatient schoolmaster, he preaches the virtues of careful revision and selection and warns against sloppy, loose writing (*LC* 1:608–9, 611–13).

If the early James comes across as hotheaded and prescriptive, one ought not mistake his overearnestness—such dogmatism would lessen with the years—for a sincere attempt at identifying the objective criteria by which one may judge art. Invariably, James's criteria were subjective, and he frequently admitted as much.[1] Yet throughout his career as a critic, James sought tirelessly to articulate, to reshape, and to problematize these very criteria.

His first significant effort came in July 1865, again in the *North American Review*, with a review of Matthew Arnold's *Essays in Criticism*. In Arnold, James discovered a model that would fundamentally shape his sense of the critic's role. James finds Arnold "sensitive and generous" as a critic, and, most importantly, "sympathetic." James confesses to having a "keen relish"

---

1. One thinks of James's 1884 essay "The Art of Fiction," in which he declared that "Nothing . . . will ever take the place of the good old fashion of 'liking' a work of art" (*LC* 1:57).

for "the science and the logic" of Arnold's method and muses openly on the critic's proper role: "It is hard to say whether the literary critic is more called upon to understand or to feel. It is certain that he will accomplish little unless he can feel acutely." Yet James remains unsure; unwilling, perhaps, to let go completely of his traditional sense of the critic: "The best critic is probably he who leaves his feelings out of account, and relies upon reason for success. If he actually possesses delicacy of feeling, his work will be delicate without detriment to its solidity." James notes that some of Arnold's critics find his work too sentimental; but for James, Arnold's sentiment provides "his greatest charm and his greatest worth" (*LC* 1:712–13). Clearly, James is wrestling with this new sense of what roles a critic can and should perform.

James was deeply impressed by Arnold's didactic aims as a critic. In his review, James cites a lengthy passage from Arnold, in which the English critic argues that the business of criticism is "simply to know the best that is known and thought in the world, and, by in its turn making this known, to create a current of true and fresh ideas" (*LC* 1:715). Sarah B. Daugherty has observed that James learned from Arnold to be not a "narrow formalist" but a "cultural, social, and moral critic," and to consider an author's purpose when criticizing her work.[2] In Matthew Arnold, James found an English critic worthy of emulation; but James was also an observant student of French literature and criticism, and two French critics in particular—Edmond Schérer and Charles Augustin Sainte-Beuve—played crucial roles in helping James to develop his nascent sense of moral criticism.

In October 1865, James published a review of Edmond Schérer's recently published *Nouvelles études sur la littérature contemporaine*. Here one finds James elaborating on his Arnoldian principles. Schérer, notes James, has "no doctrines, and that in default of these he is prompted by as excellent a feeling as the love of liberty." The Frenchman has "plenty of theories, but no theory. We find—and this is the highest praise, it seems to us, that we can give a critic—none but a moral unity: that is, the author is a liberal." James goes on to praise the "intellectual eclecticism" of Schérer's work:

> The age surely presents no finer spectacle than that of a mind liberal after this fashion; not from a brutal impatience of order, but from experience, from reflection, seriously, intelligently, having known, relished, and appropriated the many virtues of conservatism; a mind inquisitive of truth and knowledge, accessible on all sides, unprejudiced, desirous above all things to examine directly, fearless of reputed errors, but merciless to error when

---

2. Sarah B. Daugherty, *The Literary Criticism of Henry James*, 4.

proved, tolerant of dissent, respectful of sincerity, content neither to reason on matters of feeling nor to sentimentalize on matters of reason, equitable, dispassionate, sympathetic. M. Schérer is a solid embodiment of Mr. Matthew Arnold's ideal critic. (LC 2:803)

James sees in Schérer an example of a critic who, despite rejecting external, prefigured notions of truth, maintains a degree of intellectual integrity, and, most importantly, it is Schérer's *independence* that cultivates such integrity. This is notable because, to put it simply, James's description of Schérer's virtues represents the type of critic he wished to become (and eventually became). James saw in the example of Schérer an articulation of the essential moral *practice* of criticism. (For James, notes Vivien Jones, a critic's "internal standard[s]" are "inevitably a moral phenomenon.")[3] From this, he extrapolated a paradigm of the relationship between author and critic:

[Schérer's] competency to the treatment of a given subject rests entirely upon his intellectual independence or irresponsibility. Of all men who deal with ideas, the critic is essentially the least independent; it behooves him, therefore, to claim the utmost possible incidental or extrinsic freedom. His subject and his stand-point are limited beforehand. He is in the nature of his function *opposed* to his author, and his position, therefore, depends upon that which his author has taken. If, in addition to his natural and proper servitude to his subject, he is shackled with a further servitude, outside of his subject, he works at a ridiculous disadvantage. This outer servitude may either be to a principle, a theory, a doctrine, a dogma, or it may be to a party; and it is against this latter form of subordination, as most frequent in his own country, that Mr. Arnold more especially protests. But as a critic, quite as much as any other writer, must have what M. Schérer calls an inspiration of his own, must possess a *unit* of sincerity and consistency, he finds it in his conscience. It is on this basis that he preserves his individuality, or, if you like, his self-respect. It is from this moral sense, and, we may add, from their religious convictions, that writers like Schérer derive that steadfast and delicate spiritual force which animates, coordinates, and harmonizes the mass of brief opinions, of undeveloped assertions, of conjectures, of fancies, of sentiments, which are the substance of this work. (*LC* 2:803–4)

In this passage one finds the roots of an argument James would return to (and revise) in his important 1893 essay "The Science of Criticism." James sees the relationship between author and critic as one of subservience; the critic is necessarily constrained: "His subject and his stand-point are limited

3. Vivien Jones, *James the Critic,* 11.

beforehand" to the text presented by the primary author. The creative *act* of criticism thus becomes the effort to assert one's independence from this paradigm by "resisting" both author and preconceived critical principles. The critic must necessarily rely on an "inspiration" mediated by one's conscience and "moral sense." In essence, James sought to assert the critic's intellectual freedom despite what he saw as the necessarily restricted playing field for the exercise. He would always resist the idea that a critic was completely subservient to an author, text, or critical principle; the virtue of criticism, for James, was in the resistance to that kind of thinking. He aspired to regard the critic as the equal to the writer, not a mere follower. The practice of criticism was therefore a kind of artistic act: a creative, open-ended form that ultimately afforded the critic the means to articulate his own personal viewpoint. What kept a critic from missing the mark or treating an author unfairly was the critic's conscience and moral sense.

But James felt that what held true for the creative artist also held true for the critic: namely, a critic's morality must never be explicitly or dogmatically asserted. Again, James lauds Schérer "because his morality is positive without being obtrusive; and because, besides the distinction of beauty and ugliness, the aesthetic distinction of right and wrong, there constantly occurs in his pages the moral distinction between good and evil; because, in short, we salute in this fact that wisdom which, after having made the journey round the whole sphere of knowledge, returns at last with a melancholy joy to morality" (*LC* 2:806). The "melancholy joy" James celebrates here reinforces one's sense of a crucial Jamesian paradox—the idea that, as we shall see below, while James always felt compelled in principle to grant an artist the freedom to address any topic, he found subjects like sex difficult to treat explicitly (or to accept) in fiction. James is only too happy to note that while Schérer has liberally looked into every topic, his own moral compass remains true. One might grant an author the right, theoretically, to treat any topic, but it is with both melancholy (sadness at the loss of an ideal) and joy (reaffirmation of one's own conscience) that one returns to morality—a particular and consistent stand on the topic.

James's thoughts on Schérer point to the development of one of James's richest and, perhaps, most paradoxical critical criteria: first, that one's critical axioms are irrefutably linked to one's moral sensibilities; and second, that a critic must trust and develop his moral sensibilities, rather than rely on preestablished critical standards. In other words, one's moral sensitivities create one's critical standards. And, of course, James would always argue that a critic should read deeply and with great sensitivity—indeed, as James would later pronounce, with "perception at the pitch of passion" (*LC* 1:98). Early in his critical career, he insisted morality—in the form of a generous, compassionate attempt to understand a writer on her own terms—would be the wellspring of any critical endeavor.

The influence of James's developing critical aesthetic is further demonstrated in his 1868 review of Rebecca Harding Davis's *Dallas Galbraith:*

> The day of dogmatic criticism is over, and with it the ancient infallibility and tyranny of the critic. No critic lays down the law, because no reader receives the law ready made. The critic is simply a reader like all the others—a reader who prints his impressions. All he claims is, that they are honest. . . . Public opinion and public taste are silently distilled from a thousand private affirmations and convictions. No writer pretends that he tells the whole truth; he knows that the whole truth is a synthesis of the great body of small partial truths. But if the whole truth is to be pure and incontrovertible, it is needful that these various contributions to it be thoroughly firm and uncompromising. (*LC* 1:223)

In this passage, James clearly lays out his developing sense of criticism and its relationship to morality. First, he asserts that the critic is unique, a free agent independent of preexisting critical theories. Second, he asserts that if true criticism is inherently subjective or personal, it is nevertheless morally rigorous: the critic's practice is variously described as "honest," "pure and incontrovertible," and "thoroughly firm and uncompromising." These thoughts illustrate James's developing sense of what one might call the "democracy of criticism" James promoted throughout his career: James would always define criticism, like art, as a personal endeavor, and he would always value the individual's subjective contribution to the larger practice. Also, James would always labor to remove all constraints on critics, asserting, as we have already seen, the independence and freedom of the critic.

Schérer's influence on James was profound, but James's conception of the ideal critic would ultimately be found in the example of Charles Augustin Sainte-Beuve. In an 1872 review of Hippolyte Taine's *History of English Literature,* James uses Sainte-Beuve as a counterexample to Taine; the comparison points to the issues James valued most in him:

> Now Sainte-Beuve is, to our sense, the better apostle of the two. In purpose the least doctrinal of critics, it was by his very horror of dogmas, moulds, and formulas, that he so effectively contributed to the science of literary interpretation. The truly devout patience with which he kept his final conclusion in abeyance until after an exhaustive survey of the facts, after perpetual returns and ever-deferred farewells to them, is his living testimony to the importance of the facts. Just as he could never reconcile himself to saying his last word on book or author, so he never pretended to

have devised a method which should be a key to truth. . . . [F]or Sainte-Beuve [truth] was a diffused and imponderable essence, as vague as the carbon in the air which nourishes vegetation, and, like it, to be disengaged by patient chemistry. His only method was fairly to dissolve his attention in the sea of circumstance surrounding the object of his study, and we cannot but think his frank provisional empiricism more truly scientific than M. Taine's premature philosophy. (*LC* 2:844)

In Sainte-Beuve, the young James found the most fully developed sense of the ideal critic: the disinterested yet sympathetic reader who, avoiding prepackaged critical formulas, acknowledged the deeply personal and always provisional nature of a critical response. Perhaps most importantly, James learned from Sainte-Beuve that truth is always relative.[4]

James's early criticism demonstrates a gradual movement from sarcasm, arrogance, and prescriptiveness toward a more sympathetic and flexible critical practice. His reading of Arnold, Schérer, and Sainte-Beuve—among others—prompted him to rethink and reshape his critical method and his notions of the critic's role. And, as his critical faculties deepened and matured, so too did his understanding of morality in art and criticism. Morality was always at the heart of James's critical endeavors, though its terms and the implications of his arguments became increasingly subtle and subjective.

Yet there were always limits to James's sympathies, limits as to how open he could be. Invariably, it was in his study of French literature that he most frequently demonstrated his critical and aesthetic boundaries. His reviews of Théophile Gautier present a striking case in point. On the one hand, James saw in Gautier's criticism much to be admired, much in the vein of Arnold, Schérer, and Sainte-Beuve. In 1873, James wrote of Gautier:

Rigid critic he was none; it was not in his nature to bring himself to fix a standard. The things he liked he spoke well of; of the things he disliked, a little less well. His brother critics, who would have preferred to count on him to substantiate their severities, found him unpardonably "genial." We imagine that, in the long run, he held a course nearer the truth than theirs, and did better service. His irresistible need for the positive in art, for something describable—phrasable, as we may say—often led him to fancy merit where it was not, but more often, probably, to detect it where it lurked. He was a constructive commentator; and if the work taken as his text is often

---

4. I leave aside any consideration of James's reading of Taine. For more on the topic, as well as James's debt to Sainte-Beuve, see Jones's useful work in *James the Critic*. For more discussion of James's early critical foundations, see Van Wyck Brooks, "Henry James as a Reviewer"; Daugherty, *Literary Criticism;* Cornelia Pulsifer Kelley, *The Early Development of Henry James;* and Morris Roberts, *Henry James's Criticism.*

below his praise, the latter, with its magical grasp of the idea, may serve as a sort of generous lesson. (*LC* 2:371)

A year earlier, in a review of *Théâtre de Théophile Gautier,* James had noted that "a man's supreme use in the world is to master his intellectual instrument and play it in perfection." Gautier is therefore to be praised for what he accomplished. James bluntly echoes this notion in an 1874 review: "In his own way, Gautier was simply perfect" (*LC* 2:356, 376).

And yet James's appreciation for Gautier the fiction writer, as opposed to the critic, had strict limits. James accuses a "grossly unillumined" Gautier of "moral aridity" and "a moral levity so transcendent and immeasurable as to amount to a psychological curiosity." He finds "the human interest in [Gautier's] tales . . . inferior to the picturesque. . . . Gautier's figures are altogether pictorial; he cared nothing and knew nothing in men and women but the epidermis." In fact, James frankly notes, "Nothing classifies Gautier better . . . than the perfect frankness of his treatment of the human body. We of English speech pass (with the French) for prudish on this point." Gautier's "unshrinking contemplation of our physical surfaces" obviously presents a challenge to James's nascent critical openness. "Flesh and blood, noses and bosoms, arms and legs were a delight to him," James observes, "and it was his mission to dilate upon them" (*LC* 2:355, 366–67).[5]

Interestingly, James is prompted to articulate a kind of synthesis, or middle ground between his obvious affection for Gautier's art and his own Anglo-American prudishness. If, on the one hand, Gautier "had an extraordinary intellectual simplicity" and his work was "so unweighted with a moral presence, so unstirred by the breath of reflection," James could also admit "This almost helpless-looking moral simplicity and benignity in Gautier . . . is the source of that part of our good-will for our author. . . . In one's admiration for him . . . there is something of compassion" (*LC* 2:376–77).

The reviews of Gautier mark a new phase for James as a critic, and they effectively serve as a kind of transition between his earlier, harsher criticism and the more sympathetic, mature criticism that followed. On the one hand, Gautier's frank, objective depictions of whores and starving dogs in Paris represent fictional material that James simply cannot embrace, and his praise for Gautier's work as both critic and artist is always tempered with reservation. On the other hand, James finds a kind of integrity in Gautier's example as both critic and writer; he values the geniality and eclecticism in Gautier's criticism, and he admires the artist who, in James's condescending

---

5. This criticism is of a piece with his earlier criticism of Spofford: not only description for its own sake, unconnected to the unfolding of action or understanding of character, but also tasteless.

opinion, never tried to do more than his faint intellect and modest talents allowed. In short, it is in the Gautier reviews that James first gropes toward the principle that a critic must grant a writer his donnée—one of several ideas he would develop in greater detail in "The Art of Fiction." And, as James's critical aesthetic developed and matured in the mid-1870s, new sorts of critical ambiguities emerged—the fertile dualities and paradoxes that define the mature James.

The "True" and "Honest" Critic

Henry James begins his 1865 review of *Our Mutual Friend* bluntly: "'Our Mutual Friend' is, to our perception, the poorest of Mr. Dickens's works. And it is poor with the poverty not of momentary embarrassment, but of permanent exhaustion. It is wanting in inspiration." If the novel is "so intensely *written*," it is also "so little seen, known, or felt." At the heart of James's vehement dislike is Dickens's characterization: "every character here put before us is a mere bundle of eccentricities, animated by no principle of nature whatever." And while James recognizes that Dickens's characters are grotesques, or types, he refuses to grant them any credence whatsoever. Dickens's world in *Our Mutual Friend* is simply unbelievable because it is so shallow; ultimately, Dickens is "the greatest of superficial novelists" because "one of the chief conditions of his genius [is] not to see beneath the surface of things" (*LC* 1:853–56).

William Dean Howells's review of *Our Mutual Friend* is decidedly more generous. Howells, à la Hawthorne, begins by distinguishing between the novel and the romance.[6] The former is "a portraiture of individuals and affairs," while the latter is "a picture of events and human characteristics in their subtler and more ideal relations." Based on this simplistic rubric, Howells pronounces that "Mr. Dickens is not at all a novelist but altogether a romancer. The novelist deals with personages, the romancer with types." Howells's sketchy definitions may lack depth and rigor, but they do afford him a certain critical generosity lacking in James's patronizing dismissal.[7]

6. Nathaniel Hawthorne's well-known definitions come from "The Custom-House" (*Novels*, 121–57) and, more specifically, the preface to *The House of the Seven Gables* (*Novels*, 351–53).

7. James's unwillingness to distinguish between the novel and the romance is not merely a youthful critical opinion; as late as 1884, in "The Art of Fiction," the distinction seems a moot point to him: "The novel and the romance, the novel of incident and that of character—these clumsy separations appear to me to have been made by critics and readers for their own convenience" (*LC* 1:55). James would not publicly revise this opinion until the 1907 Preface to *The American*.

Indeed, Howells seems to answer James quite directly: "We have slight patience, and less sympathy, with the criticism which accuses Mr. Dickens of exaggeration; and we have no blame for his last book because most of its people are improbable. So long as they are not moral impossibilities, we cannot think them exaggerations" (*SLC* 1:55).

While the difference in tone between the two essays is itself noteworthy, there is a deeper and more significant divergence between them, and that concerns critical practice. As noted above, James's early reviews were frequently sharp-edged, overly judgmental dismissals of writers he found inferior, as in Gautier, or with whom he disagreed regarding methods of characterization, as with Dickens.[8] It would take several years before James's tone would mellow and he would adopt the critical practice of granting an author her donnée, an act of critical generosity learned from his self-appointed European mentors. Not so with Howells. As his early review of Dickens demonstrates, Howells was, from the outset of his career, more willing to grant a writer his premises and then proceed from there.

Another early case in point concerns the poetry of Walt Whitman. James's sole review of Whitman came with the 1865 publication of *Drum-Taps,* which he reviewed one month prior to reviewing *Our Mutual Friend.* The Whitman review is possibly James's single sharpest dismissal of any writer. "We look in vain," he complains, "for a single idea. We find nothing but flashy imitations of ideas. We find a medley of extravagances and commonplaces. We find art, measure, grace, sense sneered at on every page, and nothing positive given us in their stead." Whitman's "spurious poetry" is not only pretentious, it is "an offense against art" (*LC* 1:629–34).[9]

Howells's first lengthy review of Whitman (March 1860) begins not with the poet but with a statement concerning critical practice itself: "Swift denunciation comes always from either ignorance or prejudice, or passion—no less in literature than in any other living affair; and it carries no force with it except to the ignorant, the passionate, and the prejudiced." A sober Howells continues: "It is a pity that criticism should ever forget this; but criticism does." He goes on to praise *Leaves of Grass* as a "wonderful" book, though he admits much of it baffles him. His generosity—and ultimate ambivalence—

8. James's response to Dickens is a more complex example; one senses, perhaps, the anxiety of influence: a young author eager to "kill off" the most esteemed novelist of the preceding generation. James seems to have had a certain reverence for Dickens, and the apparently second-rate nature of *Our Mutual Friend* seems, in part, to have disappointed him. Indeed, in his first published book review, an 1864 response to Nassau W. Senior's *Essays on Fiction,* James had identified Dickens as a writer of "genius" (*LC* 1:1201).

9. James would eventually regret his harsh dismissal. In a 1903 letter to Manton Marble, he refers to his review of *Drum-Taps* as "the little atrocity I . . . perpetrated (on W. W[hitman]) in the gross impudence of youth" (*Henry James: Selected Letters,* 348).

toward Whitman is even more evident in a July 1860 review of *Leaves of Grass.* If "there are passages in the book of profound and subtle significance, and of rare beauty," he notes, there are also "passages so gross and revolting" that they are essentially unreadable. In the final instance, "Whitman is both overrated and underrated. It will not do to condemn him altogether, nor to commend him altogether. —You cannot apply to him the tests by which you are accustomed to discriminate in poetry" (*SLC* 1:9, 12). Howells's response to Whitman is telling and points to certain tendencies that would mature in Howells's critical aesthetic over time. Namely, despite a degree of vulgarity in the work, Howells can recognize elements of beauty, if not genius, in Whitman's poetry. There is no all-encompassing dismissal. Second, and more importantly, Howells can frankly admit that if Whitman baffles him, he himself is partly at fault. Whitman is sui generis, and for all that Howells fails to grasp, he does understand that "You cannot apply to him the tests by which you are accustomed to discriminate in poetry." Today, Henry James is remembered as the critic whose practice was predicated on sympathy and generosity, and who would articulate his vision of that critical aesthetic in decidedly moral terms; "The Art of Fiction" and other essays secured his place in this regard. But as these early reviews of Dickens and Whitman demonstrate, Howells actually put the concept into practice—albeit it in a less frequent and systematic manner—well before James.[10]

In addition, Howells articulated what he viewed as the moral dimensions of literary criticism well in advance of James. The topic is at the heart of his first major essay on the subject, "Literary Criticism," published in 1866, three months before James T. Fields would hire Howells as assistant editor of the *Atlantic.* In "Literary Criticism," Howells establishes the foundation for his own particular vision of criticism's project: "True criticism, indeed, is the function and the natural habit of every intelligent and candid mind. . . . Criticism implies in its very derivation and signification judgment, discernment, sifting, separating good from bad, the wheat from the chaff. True criticism, therefore, consists of a calm, just, and fearless handling of its subject, and in pointing out in all honesty whatever there is hitherto undiscovered of merit, and, in equal honesty, whatever there has been concealed of defect" (*SLC* 1:60). Howells distinguishes between "true" literary criticism and the "mere trade-puff of the publisher, the financial comments of the advertiser, or the bought-and-sold eulogium of an ignorant, careless, or mercenary

---

10. Howells's third lengthy review of Whitman came in 1865, with the publication of *Drum-Taps;* Howells is closer to James in his assessment of Whitman's second volume, labeling the book "unspeakably inartistic." Its author "cannot be called a true poet." While Howells does praise certain aspects of the book, on the whole this review is more hostile to Whitman (*SLC* 1:48–51).

journalist." Book notices and literary reviews do not deserve "The dignified title of criticism."[11] "Honest criticism," Howells loftily declares, "is at once the attribute and the indication of an educated and refined literary taste." Men of "accomplished mind" are all but obligated to offer intelligent criticism. "And when such almost unconscious and certainly unavoidable exercise of discernment between the good and bad, the false and the true, the sincere and the sham, is honestly and loyally put into print for general perusal . . . pray is not the public the gainer?" (*SLC* 1:60–61).

Howells accomplishes two things in this important essay. First, he defines the critic as the intellectual aesthete, the elitist. Second, he outlines for the first time what he sees as the didactic function of criticism. He reiterates the point in the essay's conclusion; literary criticism is "honest, painstaking labor." The critic's job is "finding what is faulty in a book, and pointing it out to the author and to all authors and readers, for the benefit of all" (*SLC* 1:62). A young Howells felt strongly that "true" and "honest" literary criticism played a vital and important educative role in society, and that it was properly practiced by the intellectual elite who, by right of their "educated and refined" tastes, were capable of identifying good and bad literature. According to this elitist scheme, the largely ignorant reading public will surely benefit from the patronizing critical largesse of the few.

Here one notes a crucial difference between the early criticism of James and Howells. James emphasized the moral value of criticism, but rarely in a socially educative or didactic manner. His criteria were more idiosyncratic, more personal. For James, a moral critic reads closely and well, following the examples of Arnold, Schérer, and Sainte-Beuve. Moral criticism is really a question of aesthetic appreciation: recognizing and accepting an artistic form; granting a writer his donnée; reading and feeling deeply. Criticism, in this sense, was itself an act of creation as difficult and personal as any artistic process. As practiced by James, the process became increasingly ruminative, contemplative, eclectic—and subjective. Broadly speaking, James's critical aesthetic is self-serving, and thereby inwardly directed: as numerous scholars have noted, James ultimately wrote criticism for himself, or, at best, to create and sustain an audience for his own fiction.

In contrast, Howells's early critical aesthetic may broadly be characterized as outwardly directed, or concerned with definitions of the critic's social and

11. Interestingly, James would articulate a surprisingly similar viewpoint in "The Science of Criticism," vehemently distinguishing criticism from book reviews and notices. Obviously, both Howells and James perceived some confusion among the public concerning the mission of each. Or, perhaps each was keen to distinguish his own brand of serious, thoughtful literary criticism from the mass-media book review, toward which both James and Howells would become increasingly hostile.

educative roles. While there are surely many reasons for the marked differ-ence, one does well to keep this fact in mind: Howells, as an up-and-coming editor, was in a very different position than the freelancing James. Howells always had to keep his magazine's best interests in mind, and the concerns of its audience. As critics have noted, the readership of the *Atlantic* in the mid-nineteenth century was largely feminine and "family oriented." This is not to suggest that Howells kowtowed to the popular opinion. He could, at times, be controversial and take risks that deeply alienated his reading pub-lic.[12] Rather, Howells was acutely aware of his position as a writer and edi-tor in the marketplace. As Edwin H. Cady has noted, Howells "wrote to be paid by journals which maintained theories of their readership and expected him to appeal to their subscribers. As a professional, Howells obliged."[13] An aspiring Howells, in the 1860s, quietly accepted whatever constraints came with his editorial positions. But in his criticism he sought to redefine the na-ture of the critic and to promote his own sense of the avant-garde. As scholars have shown, he used his position to change radically the literary establish-ment. And this forward-thinking critical practice has its roots in Howells's earliest work.

Upon assuming his first editorial position at the *Atlantic* in March 1866, Howells began to explore, revise, and sharpen his own sense of the critic's role. In an 1867 review of Thomas Purnell's *Literature and Its Professors,* Howells complains that "many who write reviews have not formed opinions and have not *felt* at all, and have rather proceeded upon a prejudice, a sup-posed law of aesthetics applicable to every exigency of literary develop-ment." More importantly, Howells backs off from the lofty pretensions he had articulated in "Literary Criticism," humbly acknowledging literary crit-icism's limitations: "A sense of the inadequacy of criticism must trouble every honest man who sits down to examine a new book; and it might al-most be said, that no books can be justly estimated by the critic except those which are unworthy of criticism." In language reminiscent of James's 1865 review of Arnold's *Essays in Criticism,* Howells openly questions whether criticism is a science (relatively objective) or an art (relatively subjective), de-ciding that "criticism is almost purely a matter of taste and experience, and there is hardly any law established for criticism which has not been over-thrown as often as the French government" (*SLC* 1:98–99). Clearly, How-ells—now in charge of the *Atlantic*'s prestigious "Reviews and Literary Notices" department—sounds quite Arnoldian, not to mention Jamesian.

---

12. Howells's decision, in 1869, to publish "The True Story of Lady Byron's Life" by Harriet Beecher Stowe—an essay accusing Byron of committing incest with his half-sister—cost the *Atlantic* some fifteen thousand subscriptions (*LFL,* 119n7).

13. Cady, *W. D. Howells as Critic,* 2.

For both James and Howells, the writing of fiction and literary criticism was essentially a moral *practice*. Each stated as much—sometimes directly, more often indirectly. But what this moral practice meant, what it entailed, what its sociocultural implications were, and, ultimately, how an awareness of this moral practice influenced the writing of each—here one finds radical differences between the two. Questions of morality were central to the critical and aesthetic practices of both writers from the first instance and would remain so throughout their respective careers. And the roots of each writer's early opinions on the topic are most frequently and cogently expressed in literary reviews—particularly reviews of European writers.

Curious Meditation

The bulk of James's early literary criticism exists in the form of critical reviews and career-spanning assessments of European writers, most notably the French. His first major volume of criticism was, of course, *French Poets and Novelists*. A careful examination of James's earliest work on selected French authors demonstrates his developing sense of moral criticism—and morality in art—at work.

In his 1876 essay on Charles de Bernard and Gustave Flaubert (tellingly entitled "The Minor French Novelists"), James flatly declares that de Bernard "had no morality. . . . I mean that he had no moral emotion, no preference, no instincts—no moral imagination, in a word. . . . He doesn't care, he doesn't feel, and his indifference is not philosophic." In contrast, James found Flaubert a "potent moralist" and went on to explain that "Every out-and-out realist who provokes curious meditation may claim that he is a moralist, for that, after all, is the most that the moralists can do for us." In essence, it is a question of form. In moral fiction, James argues, "the tale and the moral" must "[hang] well together." This requires "a definite intention" on the part of the author, "that intention of which artists who cultivate 'art for art' are usually so extremely mistrustful." According to these criteria, James declares that "Realism seems to me with 'Madame Bovary' to have said its last word" (*LC* 2:166–71).

Reports of realism's death may have been greatly exaggerated in James's review, but his criteria for what constitutes moral fiction is worth noting. If the point of moral fiction is to promote "curious meditation"—not to provide answers or interpretations—then the onus is, James implies, on the reader to determine the meaning of what he reads. Such a strategy demands a readerly participation in the work; it demands a total investment in the process of reading. And so here, I think, one finds the roots—or perhaps one of the tendrils—of James's creative aesthetic. As a fiction writer, James would move toward increasingly indeterminate story structures and open-ended conclusions, from, say, *The Portrait of a Lady,* to *The Turn of the Screw,* to *The Wings of the Dove,* and other works. James's fiction poses questions, not answers. And it is in his early critical work on French realists and naturalists that one finds James first thinking through these aesthetic questions in their various dimensions.

Nevertheless, James did have strong opinions on Flaubert's depiction of an adulterous Frenchwoman drowning in romantic illusions—and its moral implications. In his earlier 1874 essay on Flaubert, James bluntly states

> "Madame Bovary," we confess, has always seemed to us a great work, and capable really of being applied to educational purposes. It is an elaborate picture of vice, but it represents it as so indefeasibly commingled with misery that in a really enlightened system of education it would form exactly the volume to put into the hands of young persons in whom vicious tendencies had been distinctly perceived, and who were wavering as to which way they should let the balance fall. (*LC* 2:290)

Clearly, James saw the didactic possibilities of realist fiction, even if, with the passing years, he infrequently nodded in this direction. The comment, in fact, points to a powerful tension running through all of James's French criticism. On the one hand, James sought to ally himself, theoretically, with the freedom and frankness of the French authors he read and criticized. On the other hand, he could never completely let go of his Anglo-American sense of morality and decency.

James was rarely more prudish, for example, than in his 1877 overview of George Sand. James notes an unspoken agreement among English novelists to refrain from explicitly depicting "passion" in fiction (i.e., sexual content): "We have agreed among our own confines that there is a certain point at which elucidation of it should stop short." James lists several notable English-language writers (Austen, Scott, Dickens, Thackeray, Eliot, and Hawthorne) who, in not writing sexually explicit material, "have spared us much that we consider disagreeable." In contrast, "George Sand has not spared us" (*LC* 2:724).

At his most liberal, however, James repeatedly stressed that "intelligent realism, in art, is sure to carry with it its own morality" (*LC* 2:271). As I have noted, James saw morality in art chiefly as questions of execution and of form. The artist's goal was twofold; first, a scene must be established. "The new fashion of realism has indeed taught us all that in any description of life the description of places and things is half the battle," he wrote in

1882. The artist must demonstrate both "the faculty of feeling as well as seeing" (*LC* 2:217). Second, the scene must be peopled with accurately drawn characters. In an 1868 review, James criticizes Octave Feuillet's "decidedly thin and superficial" characters and states that "Men and women, in our conception, are deeper, more substantial, more self-directing; they have, if not more virtue, at least more conscience; and when conscience comes into the game human history ceases to be a perfectly simple tale." Feuillet's book fails—James is reviewing a translation of *Camors*—because its author does not possess the "freedom and generosity of mind" required "to write with truth and eloquence the moral history of superior men and women" (*LC* 2:285).

This combination of accurately depicted places, and vivid and complex characters, must then be joined with a fully blooming aesthetic form in which the reader can sense the author's depth of feeling. Again, the moral and the tale must hang together and create "curious meditation." And while the author shouldn't necessarily judge overtly in his work—Flaubert's objective portrayal in *Madame Bovary* would always remain a high point of realism for James—James nevertheless felt an author should have subjective moral opinions on the subjects he treats, and that those opinions will inform a work and be "felt" by the attentive reader. It is on the basis of such subjective and imprecise criteria that James suggests *Madame Bovary* is rich in didactic possibilities.

James's early work on George Sand offers an excellent case study of how he employed these critical criteria. James takes issue first with the depiction of character. Sand's novels, James states, "contain no living figures, no people who stand on their feet." Her novels "are not exact nor probable; they contain few living figures; they produce a limited amount of illusion. . . . [Sand's] people are usually only very picturesque, very voluble, and very 'high-toned' shadows." Thin characterization points to a larger problem, in James's opinion. Sand "lacks exactitude—lacks the method of truth. . . . She was contemplative; but she was not, in the deepest sense, observant. She was a very high order of sentimentalist, but she was not a moralist. She perceived a thousand things, but she rarely in strictness judged" (*LC* 2:713, 707, 733).

One notes the distinction James employs between the sentimental writer and the moral writer; he continues, noting that Sand was, in his opinion, a mix of optimist and romancer, a mix that is "not the making of a moralist." Her writing was beautiful for many reasons but ultimately lacked "that tender appreciation of actuality which makes even the application of a single coat of rose-colour seem an act of violence" (*LC* 2:734). Sentimental optimism, an impediment to realist fiction, is a fault ultimately manifested in aesthetics: "It has been said that what makes a book a classic is its style. We should modify this, and instead of style say *form*. Madame Sand's novels have plenty of style, but they have no form" (*LC* 2:730). James finally resents Sand's optimistic didacticism, arguing that faulty characterization weakens the total effect of her work and prevents it from being moral in the truest sense. James could neither recognize nor grant her moral agency when her novels were, in his opinion, all style and no form. For if a novel lacks proper form, in James's view, it cannot be moral.

In Turgenev, it seems, James found the perfect counterpoint. Turgenev's fiction "takes its starting-point in character"; Turgenev "*feels* the Russian character intensely." The emotional tone of Turgenev's fictional vision is anything but sentimental: "his temper is that of a devoutly attentive observer, and the result of this temper is to make him take a view of the great spectacle of human life more general, more impartial, more unreservedly intelligent, than that of any novelist we know." But such a tone does not preclude emotional investment in the work:

> He has an eye for all our passions, and a deeply sympathetic sense of the wonderful complexity of our souls. . . . He has a passion for shifting his point of view, but his object is constantly the same—that of finding an incident, a person, a situation, *morally* interesting. . . . He believes in the intrinsic value of "subject" in art; he holds that there are trivial subjects and serious ones, that the latter are much the best, and that their superiority resides in their giving us absolutely a greater amount of information about the human mind. . . . In a word, he is universally sensitive.

James continues to heap praise on the Russian author; Turgenev "almost invariably appeals at the outset [of a story] to our distinctively *moral* curiosity, our sympathy with character." In a mature artist, James notes, one looks for "some expression of a total view of the world they have been so actively observing. This is the most interesting thing their work offers us" (*LC* 2:972–92).

There is no higher praise for an author in the rubric of Henry James. Turgenev offers a decisive and vivid vision of the world, something unique—something, as James would phrase it famously a few years later, direct and personal. And this vision convinces James for two principal reasons. First, Turgenev's focus is on vivid and believable characters, the rendering of whom constitutes the dramatic center of his fiction. Second, James values the skill with which Turgenev conjoins form and moral meaning. For example, James praises the inconclusive, oblique ending of *A Nest of Noblemen* (alternately titled *Liza*): "The moral of his tale . . . is that there is no effective plotting for happiness, that we must take what we can get, that adversity is a capable mill-stream, and that our ingenuity must go toward making it grind our corn." This picture of the lovers "accepting adversity" demonstrates how the story's "moral interest" outweighs whatever sentimental potential the scene has (*LC* 2:981–82). In James's opinion, the open-endedness of the work's form reinforces the work's moral meaning. Again, it is a lesson James took deeply to heart.

James, however, is ultimately uncomfortable with what he sees as the excessive melancholy of Turgenev's style. "His sadness has its element of error," James declares, though "it has also its larger element of wisdom." In the final instance, "we hold to the good old belief that the presumption, in life, is in favour of the brighter side, and we deem it, in art, an indispensable condition of our interest in a depressed observer that he should have at least tried his best to be cheerful. . . . We value most the 'realists' who have an ideal of delicacy and the elegists who have an ideal of joy" (*LC* 2:997–98).

The passage is quite simply stunning when one recalls James's critique of George Sand as excessively optimistic and sentimental. (Incidentally, both essays were included in *French Poets and Novelists.*) James, of course, frequently strode a "middle course" when assessing an author, and this paradoxical stance really typifies the whole of his work on French authors. For instance, James's comment on Turgenev's excessive melancholy is similar to his celebration of Schérer's "return to morality": James values a realist who looks fearlessly into every topic, but whose vision nevertheless settles on "delicacy" and "joy." In short, James always finds himself torn between, on the one hand, wanting to grant the European writers their theoretical and artistic freedom, and, on the other hand, defending his Anglo-American sense of taste and decorum. Nowhere is this tension more palpable, or more glaringly obvious, than in his 1880 review of Zola's *Nana*.

James begins his review by noting that the French naturalist novel doesn't bother with distinctions between "Decency and indecency, morality and immorality, beauty and ugliness." But if Zola believes he is offering a truthful depiction of "nature," James begs to differ: "On what authority does M. Zola represent nature to us as a combination of the cesspool and the house of prostitution? On what authority does he represent foulness rather than fairness as the sign that we are to know her by? On the authority of his predilections alone. . . . [N]ever surely was any other artist so dirty as M. Zola!" Despite these reservations, James finds "Zola's attempt is an extremely fine one; it deserves a great deal of respect and deference." James quarrels not with Zola's naturalist theory, but with his "application" of it. Nevertheless, in a passage reminiscent of his final reservations on Turgenev, James frames his critique of Zola in terms of realism's moral credibility: "Reality is the object of M. Zola's efforts, and it is because we agree with him in appreciating it highly that we protest against its being discredited. In a time when literary taste has turned, to a regrettable degree, to the vulgar and the insipid, it is of high importance that realism should not be compromised. Nothing tends more to compromise it than to represent it as necessarily allied to the impure" (*LC* 2:866–67). The telling word here is *necessarily,* for although James is, in this part of the essay, principally addressing questions of taste, the thrust of his critique is that Zola has done as a novelist what James had warned critics not to do—namely, to import a prefigured theory and to insist upon it, rather than remaining open to the material. James, as critic, novelist, and critic of critics, is an antitotalist, always preferring multiplicity and endless possibility. The idea of a novel being written according to a formula—and Zola believed his work was "scientific" in its observation of human nature—was anathema to James.

In a fascinating conclusion, James directly addresses the particular concerns of the Anglo-American author: the writing of English fiction "is mainly in the hands of timid (even when very accomplished) women" and the English novel "is almost always addressed to young unmarried ladies. . . . [It] may be said that our English system is a good thing for virgins and boys, and a bad thing for the novel itself. . . . But under these unnatural conditions and insufferable restrictions a variety of admirable works have been produced." Should the French accuse the English novel of not being "serious" (i.e., lacking verisimilitude), James primly responds, "There are many different ways of being serious." Clearly, James has wandered from his original claim—that "the matter reduces itself to a question of application"—and, quite uncharacteristically, concludes as an apologist for the English novel, which he ultimately believes offers "a deeper, more delicate perception of the play of character and the state of the soul" (*LC* 2:868–70).

Despite the paradoxical conclusions to his essays on Turgenev and Zola, it remains clear that James valued several things about each author. And at the heart of each critique is James's evasive, esoteric sense of the moral quality of the work. In both instances, James is willing to set aside—or to attempt to set aside—certain hesitations on his own part: for Turgenev, it is the problem of excessive melancholy; for Zola, a question of poor taste in subject matter. James seeks to extract and to articulate some clean, hard, indissoluble essence; in each case, the search leads him to an appreciation of the overwhelming force and power of each author's vision. But if "some expression of a total view of the world" is "the most interesting thing" in fiction, no writer holds a higher place in James's pantheon than Balzac, an author to whom James would often turn at important moments in his career.

In his 1875 overview of Balzac, James characteristically mixes praise with blame. He finds Balzac "morally and intellectually . . . superficial. . . . The moral, the intellectual atmosphere of his genius is extraordinarily gross and turbid; it is no wonder that the flower of truth does not bloom in it." Balzac wrote not with a great conscience but with a "great temperament—a prodigious nature. . . . He had no natural sense of morality, and this we cannot help thinking a serious fault in a novelist." Yet this weakness is also the source of Balzac's greatest strength: "In place of a moral judgment of conduct, . . . Balzac usually gives us an aesthetic judgment," which James naturally respects. Balzac's "magnificent" (read graphic or picturesque) portrayals are powerfully rendered. And, in keeping with James's earliest conceptions of realist fiction, both place and character are the essential areas of focus. As regards place, "The place in which an event occurred was in his view of equal moment with the event itself; it was part of the action; it was not a thing to take or to leave, or to be vaguely and gracefully indicated; it imposed itself; it had a part to play; it needed to be made as definite as anything else." As for characters, Balzac's are unsurpassable: "behind Balzac's figures we feel a certain heroic pressure that drives them home to our credence—a contagious illusion on the author's own part. . . . [T]hey seem to proceed from a sort of creative infinite and they help each other to be believed in. . . . This is altogether the most valuable element in Balzac's novels; it is hard to see how the power of physical evocation can go farther" (*LC* 2:47–50, 53).

Clearly, what James loves about Balzac is the weight and density of the illusion, the "irresistible force" of the prose (*LC* 2:53). For James, this irresistible force is in and of itself a moral quality: a measurement of the total effect of the art. In Gautier, in Zola, and again in Balzac, James notes but ultimately looks beyond the graphic depiction of controversial subject matter to articulate his sense of the aesthetic moral value of the work. James promotes such readerly openness—a willingness to submerge one's self in the world of a writer regardless of "distasteful" subject matter—for one simple reason: he desires the same from the readers of his own fiction.

Howells and Europe

"No one invented realism; it came," William Dean Howells wrote to T. S. Perry in 1886. "It's perfectly astonishing that it seems to have come everywhere at once, and yet not in England. They always had it there, though" (*HSL* 3:153).[14] For Howells, realism came from the same place as

---

14. Howells's comment that England "always had" realism is probably a nod to Jane Austen and George Eliot; as he would make clear in *Heroines of Fiction*, he saw those women as early exemplars of the realist aesthetic.

it did for James: Europe. Like James, Howells used his early literary reviews as opportunities to explore and articulate his developing critical aesthetic. Apart from his work on James, two of Howells's most important early essays concern Norwegian author Björnstjerne Björnson and Ivan Turgenev.

Howells's lengthy review of Björnson, published in the *Atlantic* in 1870, afforded the editor an early opportunity to articulate a number of important realist tenets. Howells praises Björnson's "singular simplicity . . . reticence and self-control." Indeed, Björnson is "the reverse . . . of all that is Trollopian in literary art." Howells goes on to praise Björnson's understatement as it applies to characterization. Character is hinted at, suggested, shown: "All the processes of [a character's] thought are clearly suggested, and then almost as much is left to the reader's fancy." Actions speak louder than narrative explanation: "People are shown without effort to account for their presence further than it is explained in their actions." Character is at the heart of the novel's dramatic form: "the action is principally in a world where the troubles are from within, and inherent in human nature, rather than from any artificial causes." Accordingly, Björnson's understatement also affects his descriptions of place, which "are brief, incidental, and strictly subordinate to the story" (*SLC* 1:154–60).

Howells concludes by praising Björnson's stripped-down prose, which

> is always direct, unaffected, and dignified, expressing nothing of the author's personality, while fully interpreting his genius, and supplying no intellectual hollowness and poverty with tricks and caprices of phrase. . . . From him we can learn that fulness exists in brevity rather more than in prolixity; that the finest poetry is not ashamed of the plainest fact; that the lives of men and women, if they be honestly studied, can, without surprising incident or advantageous circumstance, be made as interesting in literature as are the smallest private affairs of the men and women in one's own neighborhood; that telling a thing is enough, and explaining it too much; and that the first condition of pleasing is a generous faith in the reader's capacity to be pleased by natural and simple beauty. (*SLC* 1:164–65)

The essay on Björnson offers one of Howells's earliest and clearest articulations of the realist aesthetic he would go on to trumpet so powerfully in the coming years. And the review, published prior to the bulk of James's work on French authors, demonstrates that Howells identified, articulated, and valued key traits of European writers. And, in some instances, Howells got there first.

Turgenev is an important case in point. Howells's twin 1873 reviews of Turgenev predate James's first lengthy essay on Turgenev by a year, and one notes that the terms of Howells's assessment clearly prefigure some of James's more frequently cited points. Howells praises Turgenev's spare style—"Everything is unaffected and unstrained"—and the moral quality of *Liza:* "It is hard to reconcile the sense of this artistic impartiality with one's sense of the deep moral earnestness of the author's books." And though Turgenev appears "impassive in respect to his characters . . . one feels the presence, not only of a great genius, but a clear conscience in his work" (*SLC* 1:207). For both Howells and James, Turgenev offers an early example of a powerfully emotive writer whose fiction was both morally charged and written in a relatively spare, understated realist mode. Also, as James would a year later, Howells appreciates the oblique endings in Turgenev's fiction. In his review of *Dimitri Roudine,* Howells notes that if the reader does not wholly understand the eponymous protagonist at the conclusion, "in the mean time we are taught a merciful distrust of our own judgments, and we take [a] forgiving and remorseful attitude towards him. It may be safely surmised that this was the chief effect that Turgénieff desired to produce in us" (*SLC* 1:219).[15]

Howells's posited reaction to Turgenev—a "forgiving and remorseful attitude"—sounds surprisingly similar to the "curious meditation" James felt Flaubert inspired in his readers, a reaction James ultimately felt had didactic potential. Clearly, then, there is strong agreement between James and Howells concerning both the moral principles concerning realist fiction in these admittedly limited (and early) examples. Furthermore, both authors agree on the aesthetic issues at stake: the need for true-to-life fictional characters situated in vividly drawn locations. For each writer, form was an issue from early on.

But by no means did the two author-critics agree on all counts. Terms like "form" and "style" came to mean different things for each. Ultimately, James would shy away from pointing out the didactic potential in fiction, whereas Howells would return to the topic frequently. Form and vision—the overall dramatic impact of a work—would come to be the ultimate criteria for James; Howells would never take his formal concerns for narrative that far. If there were occasional areas of similarity and overlap early on, it was the differences between the two writers that would emerge more potently in the years to come. And the seeds of these differences are perhaps most evident in their mutual criticism of and correspondence with one another.

15. As William Alexander has noted, in this passage we see an important early step toward the humanism that would define much of Howells's mature criticism, particularly the optimism that prompted Howells to note the "more smiling aspects" of American life. For more on the roots of Howells's early humanism, see Alexander, *William Dean Howells: The Realist as Humanist,* 1–10.

Conclusion

As young critics, Henry James and William Dean Howells shared a number of important critical sympathies, chief among them a high regard for
European realism and its influence over what both writers saw as a new
phase in American literature. On broad aesthetic points—such as the need
for vivid, believable characters in fiction—the two friends were in solid
agreement. Both authors felt a need to articulate aesthetic and critical standards commensurate with this new phase, and both set about their projects
with diligence and zeal. But the differences between James and Howells in
this early period are profound and highlight some of the most crucial questions facing American authors in the postbellum period.

In James one finds a struggle to move from an early critical stance predicated on sharp wit and haughty dismissal of inferior work toward a more
sympathetic, disinterested viewpoint. James's early essays on Arnold, Sainte-
Beuve, and Schérer demonstrate this evolution at work. And his reviews of
French and European authors afforded him an opportunity to practice these
critical theories. Like Howells, James was intensely concerned with the moral
values of the literature he read, but not in a didactic sense. Rather, James
struggled in his early criticism to articulate a kind of reader-centered model
of interpretation and valuation. Morality is crucial to this scheme, but James
was principally concerned with justifying his own esoteric tastes and articulating his sense of the overall quality of a given writer's work. Morality in art
was, for Henry James, primarily an aesthetic question, and it would largely
remain so for the rest of his career.

Many of the seeds of Howells's later critical aesthetic are also in clear view
from early on. More importantly, there is, to quote Ulrich Halfmann, "a
fundamental unity of outlook and continuity of development" in Howells's
early work.[16] While it would be several more years before Howells would
clearly and cogently articulate the critical and aesthetic principles for which
he would become so famous, still, in essays like "Literary Criticism" and the
Purnell review, one finds key elements of his developing critical aesthetic:
one that would, in contrast to James, increasingly stress the didactic aims of
fiction. And in his reviews of Björnson and Turgenev we see the roots of his
aesthetic preferences taking hold with increasing force and clarity.

Another big difference between the two concerns the question of audience. Both James and Howells were professional—and successful—writers
actively seeking an audience, but their early work shows just how diversely
each man felt about his readership. James, a fiercely independent and proud

16. Ulrich Halfmann, introduction, *SLC* 1:xx.

artist, developed an increasingly esoteric, private rhetoric in both his fiction and his criticism. To the consternation of many, he deliberately sought out paradox, in-between spaces, and doubleness. In essence, he sought not to find but to create his audience, and in this regard his literary criticism was always an attempt to claim new turf. In James's literary essays and criticism one senses a deliberate effort to educate the reader, to teach her how to read difficult work; his essays on controversial authors like Gautier, Zola, and Balzac demonstrate this principle. In this respect, James's prose is always self-serving, or inwardly directed.

Howells also wrote out of a deep conviction to educate his readers, but his purpose could not have been more different from James's in this regard; as an up-and-coming editorial assistant, and then as editor of the *Atlantic,* Howells sought clarity in his prose. He did so by forging what Arthur O. Lovejoy has called an "intellectual anti-intellectualism": a studious, careful rhetoric that was nonetheless easily digestible for the audience of the day— an audience that happened to be predominantly female.[17] In contrast to James, Howells employed a less pretentious tone. And, with his audience in mind, he deliberately employed a more didactic approach, articulating and reinforcing the values he prized both personally and those he felt his audience demanded.

17. Lovejoy, quoted in Cady, *W. D. Howells as Critic,* 17.

2. Young Americans

Criticism and Correspondence I

Henry James was a restless young man. His father, Henry James Sr., moved the family nearly a dozen times during Henry Jr.'s childhood, shuttling back and forth between various residences in New England, Great Britain, and continental Europe. James's education was eclectic, including tenures at W. C. Leverett's Berkeley Institute (where he met lifelong friend Thomas S. Perry); Institution Rochette, a pre-engineering school in Geneva; and, eventually, a hapless stab at Harvard Law School. Perhaps because of this cosmopolitan upbringing, James decided in his early thirties to reside abroad permanently; in 1876 he moved to London, and from that date forward England became his adopted homeland. He would die a British subject in 1916.

William Dean Howells could not have had a more different upbringing. The son of a small-town newspaper editor and printer, Howells labored long hours on his father's newspapers, learning to read as he set type. A relentless autodidact, Howells taught himself to read Spanish, German, and Italian and introduced himself to the history of English and American literature. By the time he left Ohio for New England, he had given himself a first-rate education. In contrast to James, Howells would always consider himself American. As he would phrase it in a 1903 letter to Charles Eliot Norton, he always felt proud that his fiction was "wrought in common, crude material . . . that is the right American stuff" (*HSL* 5:54).

The question of America as a literary subject remained central to both

James and Howells throughout their lives. Of the two, James had the more quarrelsome literary relationship with his native country. As this chapter will demonstrate, he labored to distance himself as a writer from his American literary forebears. Yet, as both creative writer and literary critic, he was always fascinated, troubled, and inspired by America. For Howells, the question was somewhat simpler: he embraced an impressively broad range of American authors in his lifetime. And in his various (and highly influential) capacities as editor, publisher, and book reviewer, he helped put many new writers on the literary map—among them Henry James.

James and Howells met in Boston in 1866, and from that point forward the two remained lifelong friends as well as keen readers and critics of each other's work. A careful study of the early criticism and correspondence between James and Howells makes clear that the two friends read and commented on each other's work regularly, continuing their ongoing debates and discussions about aesthetics. Both authors could be either generous or frankly critical of each other, and the criticisms offered by one on the work of the other frequently reveal as much about the person pronouncing judgment as they do of their purported subject. This chapter will examine the criticism and correspondence that James and Howells wrote to, for, and of one another. This chapter will also consider each critic's very different conception of his readership, or audience, and it will address the larger question of how each writer viewed postbellum America as a potential literary subject.

A Somewhat Melancholy Spectacle

James began the public show of mutual support with an 1868 review of Howells's travel volume *Italian Journeys,* declaring Howells "a man of the world, who is not a little a moralist,—a gentle moralist, a good deal of a humorist, and most of all a poet," and "a descriptive writer in a sense and with a perfection that, in our view, can be claimed for no American writer except Hawthorne." Strong praise, to be sure, but one notes the gently patronizing tone of the conclusion: Howells, "the master of certain refinements of style," offers "a real masterpiece of light writing. . . . Howells's touch is light, but none the less sure for its lightness" (*LC* 1:475, 478–79). One recalls James's pronouncement, made but a year prior to the review of *Italian Journeys,* that "what makes a book a classic" is not style, but form (*LC* 2:730). It was a judgment that, in James's studied opinion, relegated George Sand to a secondary tier of literary eminence.

James, in fact, frequently referred to Howells's works as "light" literature.[1] In 1875, he published two reviews of Howells's novel *A Foregone Conclusion*. In the first, one finds copious, if sugar-coated, criticism carefully woven amid generous lines of praise: "Mr. Howells's story . . . is simple in the extreme,—is an air played on a single string, but an air exquisitely modulated. Though the author has not broken ground widely, he has sunk his shaft deep. . . . [O]n its limited scale it is singularly complete. . . . Mr. Howells's touch is almost that of a miniature-painter; every stroke in 'A Foregone Conclusion' plays its definite part, though sometimes the eye needs to linger a moment to perceive it" (*LC* 1:487–88). The tone seems clear; James can, at best, praise the style of the book, for he finds the subject small and predictable.

To be fair, this initial review of *A Foregone Conclusion* does contain its share of genuine praise.[2] James lauds Howells's depiction of the hapless Italian priest, Don Ippolito, as "vivid, complete, and appealing. . . . He is in every situation a distinct personal image." The American protagonist, Florida Vervain, is a "complex personage." Furthermore, James praises the "unfailing cohesion of all ingredients" in the novel. Nevertheless, one senses that, for James, Howells's "little masterpiece" cannot rise above the status of "light literature" (*LC* 1:486–93).[3]

In his private correspondence with others, James could be even more frank concerning what he perceived as Howells's shortcomings. "What a pity," James writes of *A Chance Acquaintance* to his sister, Alice, "that with such pretty art, [Howells] can't embrace a larger piece of the world" (April 25, 1873; *JL* 1:373). Concerning Howells's novel *Their Wedding Journey*, James admits to Grace Norton,

> Poor Howells is certainly difficult to defend . . . ; make any serious demands and it's all up with him. He presents, I confess, to my mind, a somewhat melancholy spectacle—in that his charming style and refined intentions are so poorly and meagerly served by our American atmosphere. . . . Thro' thick and thin I continue however to enjoy him—or rather thro' thinner and thinner. There is a little divine spark of fancy which never quite

1. James, reviewing the "light lyrics" of Howells's *Poems* in 1874, declares that "whatever [Howells] writes, *style* somehow comes uppermost" (*LC* 1:479). Again, the innuendo seems clear.

2. James's second review of *A Foregone Conclusion* is more generous. James fondly pronounces Howells "intensely American in the character of his talent" and, in contrast to the "ponderous, shapeless, diffuse piece of machinery" that has become the English novel, praises Howells's "studied compactness" and "polished composition" (*LC* 1:494, 497).

3. Interestingly, James was not necessarily alone in such assessments. In an 1870 letter to James, Howells himself comments on his volume *Suburban Sketches*, confessing that "these things seem rather small business to me," and "I have an impression that they're to lead me to some higher sort of performance" (*HSL* 1:352).

goes out. He has passed into the stage which I suppose is the eventual fate of all secondary and tertiary talents—worked off his less slender Primitive, found a place and a routine and an income, and now is destined to fade slowly and softly away in self-repetition and reconcilement to the common-place. But he will always be a *writer*—small but genuine. (November 27, 1871; *JL* 1:264)

James faults Howells's early range as a critic, too, writing to Charles Eliot Norton that Howells's

talent grows constantly in fineness, but hardly, I think, in range of application. I remember your saying some time ago that in a couple of years when he had read Sainte-Beuve etc. he would come to his best. But the trouble is he never will read Sainte-Beuve, nor care to. He has little intellectual curiosity; so here he stands with his admirable organ of style, like a poor man holding a diamond and wondering how he can use it. It's rather sad, I think, to see Americans of the younger sort so unconscious and unambitious of the commission to do the *best*. (August 9, 1871; *JL* 1:262)

Clearly, James seeks to distinguish himself and his European tastes from those of Howells, which in this instance he views as distinctly "American" and thus "unconscious and unambitious." This "Americanness" is at the heart of one of James's most frequently cited criticisms of Howells, articulated in an 1871 letter to Charles Eliot Norton. James notes that Howells "seems to have resolved himself . . . into one who can write solely of what his fleshly eyes have seen; and for this reason I wish he were 'located' where they would rest upon richer and fairer things than this immediate landscape. Looking about for myself, I conclude that the face of nature and civilization in this our country is to a certain point a very sufficient literary field. But it will yield its secrets only to a really *grasping* imagination. This I think Howells lacks. (Of course *I* don't!)" (*JL* 1:252).

In each of James's letters one senses a pattern of complaints: Howells may be a promising writer of style and talent, but his range is remarkably small. This is inevitably tied to his "Americanness," a label that, for James, is often synonymous with "provincial." But James was far too tactful ever to say as much directly to Howells. First, the two men were friends; in his published reviews and in his private correspondence with Howells, James tried to put things in the best of lights—though he did not, as we have shown, back away from offering specific criticism. Second, Howells was James's editor and publisher. And, as recent critical work has shown, James—who spent the bulk of his career as a freelance writer, negotiating his own contracts and publishing agreements—was acutely aware of the need to finesse and manage professional working relationships with his editors.[4] In contrast, James's private opinions were precisely that—hardly written, one imagines, with an eye for posterity and its curious critics.

Strange Flavors

The larger question concerning whether or not America offered a writer a sufficiently deep field for art was frequently at the heart of the criticism of both James and Howells. Personally, of course, James voted with his feet; yet his great fictional subject was, without question, the "international" theme of the American confronting Europe. Howells zeroes in on this element in an 1875 review of James's first volume of stories, *A Passionate Pilgrim:*

> The American who has known Europe much can never again see his country with the single eye of his old ante-European days. For good or for evil, the light of the Old World is always on her face; and his fellow-countrymen have their shadows cast by it. This is inevitable; there may be an advantage in it, but if there is none, it is still inevitable. It may make a man think better or worse of America; it may be refinement or it may be anxiety. . . . More and more, in any case, it pervades our literature, and it seems to us the mood in which Mr. James's work, more than that of any other American, is done. (*SLC* 1:249)

Howells is characteristically astute here, both with regard to the specific example of James as well as to the larger questions confronting American writers of the day. And while Howells believes that James's tone "is not that of a mere admirer of Europe and contemner of America," he openly wonders for whom James writes. James appears to address himself "less to men and women in their mere humanity, than to a certain kind of cultivated people, who, well as they are in some ways, and indispensable as their appreciation is, are often a little narrow in their sympathies and poverty-stricken in the simple emotions; who are so, or try to be so, which is quite as bad, or worse" (*SLC* 1:249, 255).

The comment points to the important questions of tone and audience.

---

4. Recent volumes addressing these complex relationships include Michael Anesko, *"Friction with the Market": Henry James and the Profession of Authorship;* Anesko, *Letters, Fictions, Lives;* Borus, *Writing Realism;* and David McWhirter, ed., *Henry James's New York Edition: The Construction of Authorship.* For similar recent assessments of Howells, see Kaplan, *Social Construction,* and Crowley, *Dean of American Letters.*

Howells senses measurable disdain in James for the common readers of the day; he senses that James writes to an insular audience of initiated, educated readers—sophisticated readers. And Howells is largely correct. James, in an 1872 letter to his brother William, candidly confesses that he will never be "a free-going & light-paced enough writer to please the multitude. The multitude, I am more & more convinced, has absolutely no taste—none at least that a thinking man is bound to defer to. To write for the few who have is doubtless to lose money—but I am not afraid of starving" (*LFL*, 33).[5]

James's sharp tone is both telling and familiar, calling to mind the scathing reviews of his early career as a critic. Michael Anesko has suggested that James's early reviews "served only as a pretext for him to deride the imbecility of the novel's usual audience and the conventional expectations it presupposed" (*LFL*, 33). Other critics agree. Vivien Jones points out that "A desire to make an audience for his own novels always underlies James's criticism." Leon Edel argues that "The critical act, in the case of James, was essentially an enlargement of his action as a novelist," and that James's essays "are not mere literary opinion . . . they offer us the vision of a theorist of fiction appraising, in the light of his aesthetic, the work" of others.[6]

Howells was the first to recognize that James refused to meet an audience on its own terms. "If we take [James] at all we must take him on his own ground, for clearly he will not come to ours," he insightfully noted in 1882. The "flavor" of James's fiction is "so strange" that readers must "'learn to like' it" (*SLC* 1:318–19). As Howells so clearly understood, James was engaged in creating an audience for his work both in his fiction and in his criticism. James's criticism—both public and private—was frequently an extension of this largely self-serving, inwardly directed act.

If Howells was James's most sympathetic contemporary reader, he was nevertheless his friend's keenest critic. In his response to *French Poets and Novelists,* Howells suggests that James's "reviews of other writers are not precisely criticism, but they possess a pleasant flavor of criticism, agreeably diffused through a mass of sympathetic and often keenly analytical impressions." Howells's recognition of the "sympathetic" nature of James's work suggests that he is quite aware of the distinctly Arnoldian flavor of the essays, and he even notes that James "reminds us more of Sainte-Beuve than any other English writer" (*SLC* 1:280). If nothing else, Howells proved

5. Michael Anesko cites this 1872 letter from Henry James to William in *The Correspondence of William James,* ed. Ignas K. Skrupkelis and Elizabeth M. Berkeley (Charlottesville: University of Virginia Press, 1992), 1:170.

6. Jones, *James the Critic,* 53; Leon Edel, introduction to *The House of Fiction: Essays on the Novel,* 10, 12.

James's 1871 prediction ("he never will read Sainte-Beuve, nor care to") wrong.

At the heart of Howells's critique of *French Poets and Novelists* is a debate concerning the very nature of literary criticism. One recalls James's question, in his 1865 essay on Arnold, of whether a critic should "feel or understand" (*LC* 1:713). For Howells, there is no question. He labels James "less a critic in the systematic sense," and jumps right to James's major essay on Balzac, lamenting its "exasperating inconclusiveness" and "somewhat too paradoxical summary." It is a problem for most of the essays in the volume, Howells complains: "In general, there is a want of some positive or negative result clearly enunciated; and the presence of such results is what, to our mind, distinguishes the systematic critic like Sainte-Beuve or Matthew Arnold from the highly suggestive, charming talker like Mr. James." It is not, for Howells, an idle point. Howells clearly privileges "systematic" literary criticism. He values clarity of judgment and decisiveness: "If we are speaking of criticism, the question is whether we are to approach as nearly as possible to an equation of conflicting views, or whether we are to work out a problem to some conclusion on one side or the other. As a matter of definition we are inclined to say that pure criticism has for its aim the latter task" (*SLC* 1:280–81).

In 1878, of course, Howells was in a wholly different position from James. He was the editor of the *Atlantic* and an internationally recognized authority on American literature. And to a large extent, his criticism was shaped principally by his audience; he frequently assessed texts in terms of their appropriateness for family reading, and so forth. And while Howells would always be a keen and perceptive reader whose standards would broaden impressively with time, he had both a need and a desire to be clear, to be declarative, to come down firmly on one side or another. Of course, he perceived a didactic aim in his criticism, and didacticism relies on a firm sense of judgment. In this respect, then, Howells was quite different than James. James's criticism was ultimately a project intended to create a space for his own creative works to be appreciated. Howells's early critical work was more outwardly directed and socially engaged. He perceived and pursued a didactic aim in his criticism, and these convictions would harden in the coming "Realism War," as Edwin Cady has termed it.

James and Howells appear not to have corresponded regarding the review of *French Poets and Novelists,* nor, perhaps significantly, did James discuss the review in any of his extant correspondence. But the two authors would soon square off over Howells's 1880 review of James's *Hawthorne,* and their conflicting opinions regarding Hawthorne's legacy would again point to the very different positions James and Howells occupied by 1880.

The Question of Hawthorne

In an 1872 review of Hawthorne's *Notebooks,* James complained that "They are a record of things slight and usual" and serve only to "diminish our impression of his general intellectual power. . . . They represent him, judged with any real critical rigor, as superficial, uninformed, incurious, inappreciative" (*LC* 1:307–8). These charges would be repeated in *Hawthorne;* the notebooks, a "minute and often trivial chronicle," are possessed of "an extraordinary blankness—a curious paleness of colour and paucity of detail. . . . For myself, as I turn the pages of his journals, I seem to see the image of the crude and simple society in which he lived. . . . [O]ur foremost feeling is that of compassion for a romancer looking for subjects in such a field" (*LC* 1:350–51). Such provocative assessments were carefully calculated on James's part: "The little book was a tolerably deliberate & meditated performance," he wrote Howells in 1880, "& I should be prepared to do battle for most of the convictions expressed" (*LFL,* 146; *JL* 2:266).[7] Furthermore, one suspects James enjoyed ruffling a few feathers, even if he underestimated the amount of negative criticism *Hawthorne* would receive. The project was, for James, an important exercise; it gave him an opportunity, in his mind, to escape from Hawthorne's considerable shadow, as well as a chance to articulate some of the reasons why he chose to live in Europe for most of his writing life.[8]

Howells simply had to disagree with James. Regarding the charge that Hawthorne's notebooks were filled with meaningless trivia, Howells suggests that Hawthorne copiously recorded quotidian things "because he loved them, and as a great painter, however full and vast his world is, continues to jot down whatever strikes him as picturesque and characteristic" (*SLC* 1:294). Howells believes the question of how to read the notebooks is an example of James's "defect, or his error," throughout much of *Hawthorne,* and cites two reasons for James's misreading. First, he points out that James fails to distinguish clearly the mission of the romance writer from that of the novelist. Early in his review, Howells declares:

> No one better than Mr. James knows the radical difference between a romance and a novel, but he speaks now of Hawthorne's novels, and now of

7. In certain instances, there are minor discrepancies between Edel's *Henry James Letters* and Anesko's *Letters, Fictions, Lives.* When textual variations are evident, I privilege Anesko's text (see Anesko's introduction for a detailed explanation of some of the problems with Edel's edited selections of James's letters), though, for the sake of scholarly convenience, I cite both volumes.

8. For more on James's problematic relationship to Hawthorne, see John Carlos Rowe, *The Theoretical Dimensions of Henry James,* 30–57; and Richard Brodhead, *School of Hawthorne.*

his romances, throughout, as if the terms were convertible; whereas the romance and the novel are as distinct as the poem and the novel. . . .
Hawthorne's fictions being always and essentially, in conception and performance, romances, and not novels, something of all Mr. James's special
criticism is invalidated by the confusion which, for some reason not made
clear, he permits himself. (*SLC* 1:293)

By 1880, this was an old bone of contention for Howells; one recalls his
efforts to distinguish between the two genres in his 1865 review of Dickens,
in which he'd declared he had "slight patience, and less sympathy" for critics who failed to recognize the essential differences between the genres
(*SLC* 1:55).

Howells's second explanation for why James misreads Hawthorne is even
more substantial and centers around a point James makes in the provocative
first paragraph of *Hawthorne,* in which he labels Hawthorne's New England
both "a small and homogenous society" and "provincial."[9] James notes
Hawthorne's "limited scale" and questions "the importance of the literature" before suggesting that Hawthorne is preeminent only because of an
"absence of competitors" and "the general flatness of the literary field that
surrounds him." James is even so bold as to suggest it unfair to compare
Hawthorne to European writers: "we render him a poor service in contrasting his proportions with those of a great civilization." The moral of Hawthorne's example, James declares, is that "it takes a great deal of history to
produce a little literature, [and] that it needs a complex social machinery to
set a writer in motion" (*LC* 1:319–20). It is not hard to understand why
Howells and several other American readers were incensed by James's study.[10]

James's Eurocentric disregard for America peaks in the most famous passage from *Hawthorne,* a catalog of everything James felt America lacked
and, conversely, a list of everything he prized in Europe:

The negative side of the spectacle on which Hawthorne looked out, in his
contemplative saunterings and reveries, might, indeed, with a little ingenuity, be made almost ludicrous; one might enumerate the items of high civilization, as it exists in other countries, which are absent from the texture of
American life, until it should become a wonder to know what was left. No
State, in the European sense of the word, and indeed barely a specific

9. James employs the term *provincial* abundantly throughout *Hawthorne.* "The provin-
ciality strikes us as somewhat over-insisted upon," Howells quietly counters (*SLC* 1:292).

10. In an 1880 letter to Elizabeth Boott, James comments on the U.S. reaction to *Hawthorne,* noting that critics have responded with "vanity, vulgarity & ignorance. I thought they
would protest a good deal at my calling New England life unfurnished, but I didn't expect
they would lose their heads and their manners at such a rate. We are surely the most-thin-
skinned idiots in the world, & I blush for my compatriots" (quoted in *LFL,* 43).

national name. No sovereign, no court, no personal loyalty, no aristocracy, no church, no clergy, no army, no diplomatic service, no country gentlemen, no palaces, no castles, nor manors, nor old country-houses, nor parsonages, nor thatched cottages nor ivied ruins; no cathedrals, nor abbeys, nor little Norman churches; no great Universities nor public schools—no Oxford, nor Eton, nor Harrow; no literature, no novels, no museums, no pictures, no political society, no sporting class—no Epsom nor Ascot! (*LC* 1:351–52)

Howells's response is telling: in the place of everything James says America lacks, Howells believes "we have the whole of human life remaining, and a social structure presenting the only fresh and novel opportunities left to fiction, opportunities manifold and inexhaustible" (*SLC* 1:294). James's hardheaded counterresponse, in an 1880 letter to Howells, is equally telling:

It is on manners, customs, usages, habits, forms, upon all these things matured & established, that a novelist lives—they are the very stuff his work is made of; & in saying that in the absence of those "dreary & worn-out paraphernalia" which I enumerate as being wanting in American society, "we simply have the whole of human life left," you beg (to my sense) the question. I should say we had just so much less of it as these same "paraphernalia" represent, & I think they represent an enormous quantity of it. I shall feel refuted only when we have produced (setting the present high company—yourself & me—for obvious reasons, apart) a gentleman who strikes me as a novelist—as belonging to the family of Balzac & Thackeray. (*LFL*, 147; *JL* 2:267)

Never were the differences between the two writers more aptly and concretely summarized, for at the heart of this debate over Hawthorne is the larger question of how to view America. Clearly, for James, it is a limited field best left behind. Biographically, this makes a kind of sense, as James had only recently emigrated to Europe in what would become a permanent exile. But the mention of Balzac is especially noteworthy. Balzac, one of James's self-appointed mentors, represented several things to James, not the least of which was a man who claimed a new social identity: it is common knowledge, James notes in his 1875 essay, that Balzac's honorific "de" was "as fabulous (and quite as ingenious) as any that he invented for his heroes." Furthermore, Balzac, in his love for the Catholic Church and the monarchy, was an "elaborate conservative" who, in James's opinion, willingly allied himself with these conservative social institutions. "A monarchical society is unquestionably more picturesque, more available for the novelist than any other, as the others have as yet exhibited themselves," notes James, "and therefore Balzac was with glee, with gusto, with imagination, a monarchist." The reader of Balzac "constantly encounters the handsomest compliments to the Catholic Church as a social *régime*" because, James believes, a "hierarchy is as much more picturesque than a 'congregational society' as a mountain is than a plain" (*LC* 2:36, 43, 45). Such comments, together with James's comments in the exchanges over Hawthorne, reinforce the notion that, as a writer, James saw little potential for himself in the American social and political landscape. His decision to emigrate concerned, to a large extent, the question of affording himself the proper milieu to create art.

Howells's relationship to America is just the reverse. His appreciation for Europe was, at best, decidedly ambivalent during his lifetime. As Olov W. Fryckstedt has noted, Howells's four-year stint in Venice as consul was composed of equal parts appreciation for Italy and poignant homesickness for America, and he returned to New England harboring a "serious disappointment" with the corruption and harsh class distinctions he had witnessed in Europe. In contrast, Howells saw America as a land ripe with potential to be all that he felt Europe was not. For a self-educated printer's apprentice from Ohio who rose to become the biographer of presidents, a consul to Italy, an internationally acclaimed author, and the editor of the nation's most prestigious literary magazine, such idealistic dreams of freedom and social equality were quite real. America, for Howells, was the most fertile site for an artist intent on exploring those topics in his work—which Howells obviously did, in novel after novel.[11]

It was Howells's opinions on Europe that would, in fact, shortly garner him a mountain of attention when he published an 1882 essay entitled "Henry James, Jr." Howells's overview begins with a powerful, concise list of James's strengths: "the finished workmanship in which there is no loss of vigor; the luminous and uncommon use of words, the originality of phrase, the whole clear and beautiful style." James offers "a splendor and state which is wholly its own." In James, Howells sees numerous lessons. First, "that it is the pursuit and not the end which should give us pleasure." Second, regarding character, Howells notes that "it is the character, not the fate, of [James's] people which occupies him; when he has fully developed their character he leaves them to what destiny the reader pleases" (*SLC* 1:318–19). This, Howells suggests, is the proper way to interpret the open-ended *Portrait of a Lady,* James's most recent novel.

But the largest and most provocative lesson Howells derives from the example of James concerns the state of literary realism itself, and in a passage that caused nothing less than an international conflagration, Howells announces that

---

11. Olov W. Fryckstedt, *In Quest of America: A Study of Howells' Early Development as a Novelist,* 18, 37. See Kenneth S. Lynn, *William Dean Howells: An American Life,* 14–28.

> The art of fiction has, in fact, become a finer art in our day than it was with Dickens and Thackeray. We could not suffer the confidential attitude of the latter now, nor the mannerism of the former, any more than we could endure the prolixity of Richardson or the coarseness of Fielding. These great men are of the past—they and their methods and interests; even Trollope and Reade are not of the present. The new school derives from Hawthorne and George Eliot rather than any others; but it studies human nature much more in its wonted aspects, and finds its ethical and dramatic examples in the operation of lighter but not really less vital motives.

Howells goes on to note that if American realism "is largely influenced by French fiction in form," it also "has a soul of its own which is above the business of recording the rather brutish pursuit of a woman by a man, which seems to be the chief end of the French novelist." Howells pronounces realism the school "of the future as well as the present" and Henry James "its chief exemplar . . . ; it is he who is shaping and directing American fiction" (*SLC* 1:322).

While nearly all of Howells's essays on James, like his essays on Björnson and Turgenev, are crucial milestones in an ongoing aesthetic development, "Henry James, Jr." is an important step forward because Howells draws a clear line in the sand, publicly trumpeting, for the first time, a changing of the aesthetic guard. Howells did not set out to produce such an international firestorm; in fact, when the negative reactions to his essay appeared, he wrote Edmund Gosse to request a copy of the *Century* so he could review what he had written (*HSL* 3:40–41). But Howells never issued an apology or explanation for the essay; he stood by his words.

"Henry James, Jr." became, quite by accident, the opening salvo of the "Realism War" that would fuel so much of Howells's work in the "Editor's Study" in the coming years. As Edwin Cady notes, "Howells himself was forced by the outcry against ideas he had quietly taken for granted to accept more boldly the fact that he had become a literary radical and that the need to formulate his creed for it might soon be imperative."[12]

Conclusion

Of the many differences that emerged out of the early critical work of James and Howells, none was more significant than the ways each regarded America and its postbellum potential as a literary subject. While both artists

---

12. Edwin H. Cady, *The Road to Realism: The Early Years, 1837–1885, of William Dean Howells,* 221.

clearly and forcefully broke with their literary predecessors, James also broke away, literally and figuratively, from the domestic American scene. In an 1867 letter to his friend Thomas S. Perry, Henry James eloquently summed up his reasoning on the issue:

> we young Americans are (without cant) men of the future. I feel that my only chance for success as a critic is to let all the breezes of the west blow through me at their will. We are Americans born—*il faut en prendre son parti.* I look upon it as a great blessing; and I think that to be an American is an excellent preparation for culture. We have exquisite qualities as a race, and it seems to me that we are ahead of the European races in the fact that more than either of them we can deal freely with forms of civilization not our own, can pick and choose and assimilate and in short (aesthetically etc.) claim our property wherever we find it. To have no national stamp has hitherto been a defect and a drawback, but I think it not unlikely that American writers may yet indicate that a vast intellectual fusion and synthesis of the various National tendencies of the world is the condition of more important achievements than any we have seen. We must of course have something of our own—something distinctive and homogenous—and I take it that we shall find it in our moral consciousness, our unprecedented spiritual lightness and vigour. In this sense at least we shall have a national *cachet.*—I expect nothing great during your lifetime or mine perhaps: but my instincts quite agree with yours in looking to see something original and beautiful disengage itself from our ceaseless fermentation and turmoil. (*JL* 1:77)

James clearly felt free to "pick and choose and assimilate" and, in due course, to reject his homeland, which, as this passage illustrates, seemed too young and immature to afford him the literary field he felt he deserved. (Interestingly, this passage also demonstrates that James felt America would, in time, offer the right kind of inspiration to its artists—but he was clearly too impatient to wait for it to bloom during his lifetime.) Correspondingly, James began to trumpet conservative European values and he used his criticism as a way to justify, at least in part, his prejudices (witness the 1875 essay on Balzac, discussed above). His 1879 book-length study, *Hawthorne*, was an outgrowth of this process.

Howells, after a brief stay in Europe during the Civil War, made a conscious decision to stay home and create an identity for himself in New England, the seat of American literary culture. European social values and class distinctions were, for him, as anachronistic as the English writers he condemned: Trollope, Dickens, and Fielding. Howells believed passionately in American freedom and equality, and he saw in his young country unlimited potential for fiction. Consequently, he used his advantageous position as editor of the *Atlantic* to draw attention to his cause. And, after retiring from the position in 1881, he became only more controversial and outspoken. His response to James's *Hawthorne* and his controversial essay "Henry James, Jr." served as early opportunities to articulate what he valued in America as a writer. Howells would shortly enter into the "Realism War," a period during which, as a monthly contributor to *Harper's,* he would provocatively proclaim his literary values from his "Editor's Study" columns, a bully pulpit that would forever change the course of American letters.

3. James's "The Art of Fiction" in Critical Context

Throughout his career, William Dean Howells always considered his friend Henry James a writer of the first rank, and he always thought James the more accomplished of the two. As early as 1866, Howells confided to Edmund C. Stedman that "young Henry James and I had a famous [talk] last evening, two or three hours long, in which we settled the true principles of literary art. He is a very earnest fellow, and I think extremely gifted—gifted enough to do better than any one has yet done toward making us a real American novel" (*HSL* 1:271). As editor of the *Atlantic* (1871–1881), Howells seemed always to be printing or soliciting his friend's work. In contrast to James, who routinely degraded Howells's work in his private correspondence, Howells almost always saw the best in James; he had an uncanny ability both to appreciate James's fiction on its own terms—a cause for which James, in his work as a critic, was forever pleading with his audience—and, perhaps more importantly, to articulate in lucid critical prose that same aesthetic for a reading public often stymied by James's density and weight. In retrospect, then, it perhaps comes as little surprise to find Howells, in his 1882 essay "Henry James, Jr.," loudly declaring realism the school "of the future as well as the present" and Henry James "its chief exemplar . . . ; it is he who is shaping and directing American fiction" (*SLC* 1:322).

Initially, James was not unpleased to be the subject of praise. In an 1882 letter to Isabella Stewart Gardner, he confessed, "Howells's charming article makes me *flush* . . . all over" (*JL* 2:388). But that was before the *London World,* for example, labeled Howells, James, and Charles Dudley Warner the members of an American "Mutual Admiration Society." The *World* went on to ridicule James's "tepid, invertebrate, captain's-biscuit style" before concluding that "Poor old Dickens and Thackeray are kicked out of court. . . . Let us burn our *éditions de luxe,* and fill our shelves with dime copies of *Daisy Miller* or *Their Wedding Journey.*"[1] Months later, then, when the seemingly endless stream of vituperative responses to Howells's article was at its most torrid, James quietly began to distance himself from both Howells and the fray. In February 1883, James wrote to G. W. Smalley:

> I have just been reading in the *Tribune* your letter of Jan. 25, in which you devote a few lines to the silly article in the Quarterly on *American Novels,* etc. It occurs to me that as you apparently have been misled by the author's insinuation that I had contributed to *The Century* an article about Howells, preliminary to his ill-starred amiabilities to me, it is as well I should "just remark" that I never in my life wrote a word about Howells in the *Century,* and had not for years written about him anywhere. I once reviewed one of his early novels—eight years ago—anonymously, in a New York paper. There was an article in the *Century* about Howells written (and signed) by T. S. Perry. The *Quarterly* man . . . doesn't say in so many words I wrote it, but he evidently wishes to convey that impression, by the way the phrase is turned and his talk about mutual admiration, etc.; and the phrasing is disengenuous [*sic*]. Enough, however, about this truly idiotic commotion. (*JL* 2:406)[2]

In his correspondence with Howells, James was naturally more lighthearted. Writing from Boston to Italy, where Howells and his family were traveling, James noted that "articles about you & me are as thick as blackberries—we are daily immolated on the altar of Thackeray & Dickens" (March 20, 1883; *LFL,* 240). Yet, a year later, the "painfully overcharged appreciation from my dear friend Howells" still occupied James's mind (February 22, 1884; *JL* 3:30). An international conversation had begun concerning the novel, and whether he liked it or not, Henry James was at the center of it; it only seemed appropriate, then, for him to enter into the discussion.

He did so in "The Art of Fiction," an essay that marks a conceptual turning point in the development of James's thinking on aesthetic matters. Critics frequently treat the essay as a keystone, a kind of critical "decoder ring" that can help one to contextualize all of the critical writing that followed, most particularly the Prefaces to the New York Edition. Perhaps the most demonstrative example of this approach is found in James E. Miller's

---

1. Quoted in *LFL,* 237n10.
2. James seems to have forgotten, temporarily, that he published not one but two reviews of Howells's *A Foregone Conclusion* in 1875, and that he had also published reviews of Howells's *Italian Journeys* in 1868 and *Poems* in 1874.

edited volume of James's criticism, *Theory of Fiction: Henry James*. Miller begins by reprinting "The Art of Fiction" along with his own outline of the essay's argument. This outline then provides the organizing principle for the book: an exercise, as Miller phrases it, "designed to present the totality of James's views of the art of fiction" by means of "filling out, amplifying, and completing the task [James] merely began in his 1884 essay."[3]

While there is a kind of logic at work in this model—James clearly does introduce a number of ideas in "The Art of Fiction" that inform much of the criticism that followed—the unintended consequence of this approach is to devalue or to ignore the critical work that preceded "The Art of Fiction." If the essay deserves to be noted as a precursor to the later criticism, it also needs to be understood as a manifestation of James's early work, as a culmination of the critical work he had completed between 1865 and 1884. This will be the subject of the second part of this chapter.

In the first part of this chapter, I analyze James's rhetorical strategies throughout "The Art of Fiction." As any reader of the essay knows, it did not appear ex nihilo. Rather, it resulted from a particular series of circumstances that were, for James, both public and personal. The essay is a carefully calculated response not only to Walter Besant, but also to William Dean Howells and to a whole school of English literary critics. "The Art of Fiction" needs to be understood as not only the important theoretical essay that it is, but also as a savvy exercise in the diplomacy of Jamesian aesthetics—and a deliberate effort to reposition James in the public eye.

A Trojan Horse

On April 25, 1884, the Royal Institution in London gathered to hear noted English novelist Walter Besant discourse on "The Art of Fiction." Besant's essay, subsequently published in pamphlet form, was briefly reviewed by the *Pall Mall Gazette* and the *Spectator* in London, while in the United States the *Nation,* the *New York Times,* and the *New York Tribune* fleetingly noted Besant's ideas. Besant's lecture provoked more ripples than waves, but James clearly saw an opportunity; his own "Art of Fiction" appeared in *Longman's Magazine* in September 1884.[4]

James's tone, which he carefully sustains throughout the essay, is that of a humble response to Besant. James is careful to contextualize and summarize various points of Besant's argument, allowing the reader to follow his own

3. James E. Miller, ed., *Theory of Fiction: Henry James,* 28.
4. Mark Spilka, "Henry James and Walter Besant: 'The Art of Fiction' Controversy," 101.

argument without necessarily having read Besant. Given James's premise, this makes perfect sense: he is responding to a lecture, not initiating an argument. His stance, by coyly keeping Besant in the spotlight, allows him to adopt an uncharacteristic pose of humility. Indeed, James is careful, from the very first sentence, to affect meekness:

> I should not have affixed so comprehensive a title to these few remarks, necessarily wanting in any completeness upon a subject the full consideration of which would carry us far, did I not seem to discover a pretext for my temerity in the interesting pamphlet lately published under this name by Mr. Walter Besant. Mr. Besant's lecture . . . appears to indicate that many persons are interested in the art of fiction, and are not indifferent to such remarks, as those who practise it may attempt to make about it. I am therefore anxious not to lose the benefit of this favourable association, and to edge in a few words under cover of the attention which Mr. Besant is sure to have excited. (*LC* 1:44)

Given the international flap in the wake of "Henry James, Jr.," such timidity seems carefully calculated. Indeed, James alludes to Howells's celebrated essay in the second paragraph of "The Art of Fiction," when he feigns surprise that the topic of the English novel is of interest to the public at large: "Only a short time ago it might have been supposed that the English novel was not what the French call *discutable*. It had no air of having a theory, a conviction, a consciousness of itself behind it—of being the expression of an artistic faith, the result of choice and comparison. I do not say it was necessarily the worse for that: it would take much more courage than I possess to intimate that the form of the novel as Dickens and Thackeray (for instance) saw it had any taint of incompleteness" (*LC* 1:44). Although Howells could not have known in advance how "Henry James, Jr." would be received, certainly its bold, authoritative, and occasionally judgmental tone was one reason why certain readers responded with such hostility. James, in "The Art of Fiction," is careful not to repeat the error (even as he playfully nods to Howells's piece).

But James's affected timidity is not only a response to "talk about mutual admiration, etc."; it is also a brilliant rhetorical strategy that allows him to appear shyly to follow up on Besant even while introducing his own aesthetic counterarguments. James continues, noting that the English novel "was, however, *naïf* (if I may help myself out with another French word); and evidently if it be destined to suffer in any way for having lost its *naïveté* it has now an idea of making sure of the corresponding advantages" (*LC* 1:44). By subtly introducing French rhetoric, notes Mark Spilka, "James was helping himself out with more than French words. He was quietly invoking a novel more discussible than the English, a theory more sophisticated" than Besant's. Yet James is careful not to mock or denigrate Besant in any way. James understood Besant's vaunted position as, to quote Mark Spilka, "a register for the national mind." Indeed, Besant had done every literary novelist a favor when he called for England "to consider Fiction as one of the Fine Arts," an idea that was, in 1884, by no means commonplace. In Walter Besant's mouth, however, the idea carried immense cultural weight, which James surely understood. Spilka paraphrases James's hopes: "If he could press strongly and intelligently enough in favor of this newly-arrived commonplace, he could affect the English and American climate for his own kind of fiction; he could educate and enlarge his own limited audience and so insure his own artistic freedom."[5]

And so it is with a temperate call for "discussion" that James begins his argument: "Art lives upon discussion, upon experiment, upon curiosity, upon variety of attempt, upon the exchange of views and the comparisons of standpoints," and while "The successful application of any art is a delightful spectacle, . . . the theory too is interesting. . . . Discussion, suggestion, formulation, these things are fertilising when they are frank and sincere." James seeks to promote "a serious, active, inquiring interest, under protection of which this delightful study may, in moments of confidence, venture to say a little more what it thinks of itself" (*LC* 1:44–45).

James's first topic is relatively benign: a quick dismissal of the traditional *apologia* for the novel, a practice which "is still expected, though perhaps people are ashamed to say it." Trollope, for instance, is an author whose frequent use of the apology is "a betrayal of a sacred office" and "a terrible crime." James's argument is simple: rather than "renounce the pretension of attempting really to represent life," he demands the opposite: "The only reason for the existence of a novel is that it does attempt to represent life." James introduces an analogy to secure his point, that of the "art of the painter and the art of the novelist," which James stresses is "complete. . . . [A]s the picture is reality, so the novel is history." With the introduction of the discipline of history, James actually positions the writing of fiction in a double analogy, which he quickly pursues. A novel ought to "speak with assurance, with the tone of the historian" (*LC* 1:45–46).

At this point, James has introduced two crucial ideas in "The Art of Fiction." First, he gently insists that the novel is mimetic, as objective in its own way as the work of the historian: "To represent and illustrate the past, the actions of men, is the task of either writer, and the only difference that I can see is, in proportion as he succeeds, to the honour of the novelist, consisting

5. Ibid., 104–5; Walter Besant, "The Art of Fiction," 3.

as it does in his having more difficulty collecting his evidence, which is so far from being purely literary." In 1884 this is, of course, a controversial—if not radical—claim; hence James's second crucial idea, which is to construct the "magnificent heritage" of fiction by analogizing it with three of the liberal arts: painting, history, and philosophy. It is a claim James can finally make with some assurance not because he knows it is ultimately correct but because the popular Besant has first introduced it. Besant, James notes, "insists upon the fact that fiction is one of the *fine* arts, deserving in its turn of all the honours and emoluments that have hitherto been reserved for the successful profession of music, poetry, painting, architecture. It is impossible to insist too much on so important a truth." James, in the wake of the public outcry against him and Howells, could not have made such a claim for fear of ridicule or censure, and he knows it. "It is excellent that [Besant] should have struck this note," James modestly observes, "for his doing so indicates that there was need of it, that his proposition may be to many people a novelty" (*LC* 1:47).

With the onus of the claim on Besant, James proceeds to dismantle the popular sentiment that fiction harbors "some vaguely injurious effect upon those who make it an important consideration," as well as the misguided dictum that "Literature should be either instructive or amusing." In a carefully modulated critique of readerly expectations, James dismisses the demand for "virtuous and aspiring characters," the "'happy ending,'" and the overly dramatized novel "full of incident and movement." Citing "this conception of Mr. Besant's of the novel as a superior form," James declares fiction "at once as free and as serious a branch of literature as any other" (*LC* 1:47–49). If readerly expectations are beside the point, and if the novel is totally free, then it is the author who shall decide what form a novel shall take. The reader's role, James quietly suggests, is not to prejudge or to come to a book with narrow expectations, but to come prepared to discover just what form the novel has taken. By keeping the focus on Besant as the initiator of his claim, James has managed to introduce one of his most important ideas: that the reader should grant the artist his donnée.

Interestingly, it is at this point that James offers his first criticism of Besant:

> He seems to me to mistake in attempting to say so definitely beforehand what sort of an affair the good novel will be. To indicate the danger of such an error as that has been the purpose of these few pages; to suggest that certain traditions on the subject, applied *a priori*, have already had much to answer for, and that the good health of an art which undertakes so immediately to reproduce life must demand that it be perfectly free. It lives upon

exercise, and the very meaning of exercise is freedom. The only obligation to which in advance we may hold the novel, without incurring the accusation of being arbitrary, is that it be interesting. (*LC* 1:49)

To be sure, James's reasoning takes a curious bend; the chief criterion for a good novel, "which undertakes so immediately to reproduce life," is that it simply be "interesting." James, who just two paragraphs before this had argued in rather strict formalist terms that "the novel is history" and ought to "speak with assurance, with the tone of the historian," suddenly makes a claim predicated on the most subjective of value judgments. Furthermore, James holds that, "The ways in which it [the novel] is at liberty to accomplish this result (of interesting us) strike me as innumerable, and such as can only suffer from being marked out or fenced in by prescription. They are as various as the temperament of man, and they are as successful in proportion as they reveal a particular mind, different from others." Surely this was not the objective of post-Romantic nineteenth-century historians. James has shifted ground and is no longer arguing for the objective, mimetic novel. Rather, he has begun to articulate its opposite: "A novel is in its broadest definition a personal, a direct impression of life: that, to begin with, constitutes its value, which is greater or less according to the intensity of the impression. But there will be no intensity at all, and therefore no value, unless there is freedom to feel and say" (*LC* 1:49–50).

Scholars have offered a variety of compelling explanations for this shift in "The Art of Fiction." Tony Tanner suggests that James's conception of novelistic truth is grounded in the subjectivity articulated in paragraph five of "The Art of Fiction":

> The "truth" of a novel is now its transcribed fidelity to a personal "impression"—that is, a subjective truth, not usually taken to be the same as more objective "historical" truth, though, to be sure, we now feel that these distinctions do not always seem so secure under closer scrutiny. . . . James recasted or expanded the areas of experience characterizable as "history" until the point that Conrad could aptly describe him as an "historian of fine consciences." James's central intention is, I think, to stress the primacy of the receptive and transformative consciousness.

Tanner makes a solid point; James actually introduced this subjective primacy quite early in "The Art of Fiction," during his brief critique of Trollope, whose overuse of the *apologia* "implies that the novelist is less occupied in looking for the truth (the truth, of course I mean, that he assumes, the premises that we must grant him, whatever they may be)" (*LC* 1:46–47). Tanner remarks, "this off-hand parenthesis is crucial." And surely it is, for it reminds the reader that even as James argues most forcefully for the objective, historical novel, he acknowledges the importance of—perhaps even the primacy of—the subjective.[6]

James's argument thus far in "The Art of Fiction" is more paradoxical than self-contradictory. Dorothy J. Hale goes so far as to argue that such paradoxes are evidence of a critical "ambivalence" that demonstrates "how James strives to preserve the relativity of perspective while also retaining a standard by which to judge artistic achievement." The ambivalence first articulated in "The Art of Fiction," she observes, will resurface in the Prefaces, in which

> James outlines two competing ideals of novelistic authorship: on the one hand, the successful novelist is the one who most transparently expresses his unique "impression" of life; on the other hand, the successful novelist is the one who does not allow his own views to prevent life from making its "impression" on him. In the first case, the novelist is best when he projects his views; in the second, when he refuses to project them.
>
> Once we appreciate this tension between projection and reception in James's account of novelistic point of view, we can better understand why James sometimes describes novel writing as a process of self-expression and other times as a process of recording.[7]

While I find Hale's reading both convincing and helpful, she clearly positions "The Art of Fiction" more as a precursor to James's important late critical work (most notably the Prefaces) and less as a product or outgrowth of his earlier critical work. This is a familiar critical bias, and one to which I shall return in the second part of this chapter.

Having established the importance of an author's subjectivity in the novel, James concludes paragraph five of "The Art of Fiction" by arguing that a text must always be read first on its own terms:

> The form, it seems to me, is to be appreciated after the fact: then the author's choice has been made, his standard has been indicated; then we can follow lines and directions and compare tones and resemblances. Then in a word we can enjoy one of the most charming of pleasures, we can estimate quality, we can apply the test of execution. The execution belongs to the

6. Tony Tanner, "Henry James and the Art of Criticism," 33–34. It should be noted that Tanner's reading of this point favors the revised "Art of Fiction" included in *Partial Portraits* (the text reprinted in *LC* 1). The parenthetical comment Tanner considers "crucial" was added only after Robert Louis Stevenson's 1884 criticism of James in "A Humble Remonstrance," in which Stevenson argues that art cannot compete with the range and diversity of life. See Jones, *James the Critic*, 130–31.

7. Dorothy J. Hale, "James and the Invention of Novel Theory," 84–85.

author alone; it is what is most personal to him, and we measure him by that. The advantage, the luxury, as well as the torment and responsibility of the novelist, is that there is no limit to what he may attempt as an executant—no limit to his possible experiments, efforts, discoveries, successes. (*LC* 1:50)

In the context of its time, this passage is one of the most radical in "The Art of Fiction." James's demands—that the novel be free and interesting, that "the test of execution" be predicated on what is "most personal" to a novelist—are not only responses to Besant, notes Vivien Jones, but to "a whole school of defensively insular critics." In the late nineteenth century, Jones states, "English novel criticism was predominantly pragmatic and insular," not to mention overly prescriptive: "Average Opinion demanded that the novel fulfil certain comfortable conventions." English critics were frequently (and narrowly) preoccupied with "the moral effect of a novel on its reader," judging a novel "according to exclusively external criteria to which the created world must conform." Because the novel was generally regarded as "an inherently inferior genre," critics and readers alike expected the idealized plots and happy endings. A deceptively humble James, proposing his own organic theory of composition, has attacked the very foundations of English novel criticism.[8]

James proceeds, in paragraph six, to respond to a list of "laws of fiction" that Besant proposed in his lecture. Striding his middle course, James can neither dissent nor assent to these laws; rather, he pauses to consider in depth one particular piece of Besant's advice: that a writer should write from her experience. Besant is quite literal, arguing that "a young lady brought up in a quiet country village should avoid descriptions of garrison life," and "a writer whose friends and personal experiences belong to what we call the lower middle class should carefully avoid introducing his characters into Society." Besant concludes, "This is a very simple Rule, but one to which there should be no exception—never to go beyond your own experience."[9] Experience, in this case, is a limiting factor—a catalog of the practical and specific things a writer has done, seen, heard, and so forth. James playfully deconstructs such dogma:

---

8. Jones, *James the Critic,* 112–15. Of course, not all critics agree that James is "attacking" the English critics. Edwin Cady reads "The Art of Fiction" as a kind of tentative middle stance that accepts the right of the romance to exist. James is too universally open to exclude any genre and, Cady suggests, too economically vulnerable to the whims of the market; he literally cannot afford to make too many enemies. Thus Cady reads "The Art of Fiction" as, at best, a limited defense of realism (*The Realist at War: The Mature Years, 1885–1920, of William Dean Howells,* 42–43).

9. Besant, "Art of Fiction," 18.

What kind of experience is intended, and where does it begin and end? Experience is never limited, and it is never complete; it is an immense sensibility, a kind of huge spider-web of the finest silken threads suspended in the chamber of consciousness, and catching every air-borne particle in its tissue. It is the very atmosphere of the mind; and when the mind is imaginative—much more when it happens to be that of a man of genius—it takes to itself the faintest hints of life, it converts the very pulses of the air into revelations. (*LC* 1:52)

Experience, for James, has less to do with the particulars of one's own life; rather, it has everything to do with one's imaginative faculties, with the depths and particular shades of one's subjectivity. "The power to guess the unseen from the seen, to trace the implication of things, to judge the whole piece by the pattern, the condition of feeling life in general so completely that you are well on your way to knowing any particular corner of it—this cluster of gifts may almost be said to constitute experience, and they occur in country and in town, and in the most differing stages of education. If experience consists of impressions, it may be said that impressions *are* experience." James hastens to clarify this point, stressing that he does not intend for his ideas on subjectivity to devalue the artist's responsibility to view the world in a truthful, objectively honest fashion. "I am far from intending by this to minimise the importance of exactness—of truth of detail. One can speak best from one's own taste, and I may therefore venture to say that the air of reality (solidity of specification) seems to me to be the supreme virtue of a novel—the merit on which all its other merits (including that conscious moral purpose of which Mr. Besant speaks) helplessly and submissively depend" (*LC* 1:53). Throughout "The Art of Fiction," James is careful to temper his radical calls for artistic subjectivity with his sense of the novelist's objective responsibilities. The two are, James implicitly argues, conjoined.

James has also begun to address another of Besant's "laws," namely that English fiction should have "a conscious moral purpose."[10] It is a precept James will address more pointedly in the closing pages of his essay, but one notes here that James, in emphasizing form above all, has made a pronouncement familiar to readers of his earliest criticism: that morality in art is irrevocably an aesthetic concern. The issue is seen throughout his early work on French authors (which, for James, included Turgenev). Indeed, for James, the question is exclusively French. They are the writers who let a work create its own morality through its articulation of form; this is precisely what James valued so deeply in Turgenev.

10. Ibid., 29.

What "The Art of Fiction" allows James to do, in part, is to introduce French aesthetic concerns to an Anglo-American audience without mentioning their point of origin. The reasoning here seems obvious: if James were to announce the French origins of his pronouncements, his humble discussion would be over. There was, simply stated, enormous bias in England against the French novel. Again, by beginning with a list of ideas articulated by the respected Walter Besant, James can quietly counterargue using his favorite tools—and can conveniently dispense with citing his, to an English-speaking audience, alien sources. Not that James is merely parroting, or translating, the French at this point; as demonstrated in Chapter 1 of this study, James's French criticism is always an attempt to negotiate between his Anglo-American moral sensibilities and his desire to grant the French writers their aesthetic freedom. But it may not be much of a stretch to suggest that James's carefully planned and expertly executed rhetorical strategy makes "The Art of Fiction" the Trojan Horse of nineteenth-century Anglo-American literary criticism.

In paragraph seven, James widens his critique of Besant's rules, arguing against the general idea of constructing "laws of fiction" in favor of a much more open-ended, organic conception of the novel. "A novel is a living thing," James writes, "all one and continuous, like any other organism, and in proportion as it lives will it be found, I think, that in each of the parts there is something of each of the other parts." James sees no point in quibbling over distinctions between types—the novel of incident versus the novel of character, for example—preferring to reduce his criteria, in this instance, to the simplest possible test: "There are bad novels and good novels, as there are bad pictures and good pictures; but that is the only distinction in which I see any meaning." Incident and character are naturally conjoined in the organic theory of the novel: "What is character but the determination of incident? What is incident but the illustration of character? What is either a picture or a novel that is *not* of character?" James provides a quick example: "It is an incident for a woman to stand up with her hand resting on a table and look out at you in a certain way; or if it be not an incident I think it will be hard to say what it is" (*LC* 1:54–55). Every reader of the fiction will recognize this example as quintessentially Jamesian. And this reminds us again that, for James, "The Art of Fiction" was at heart a deeply personal exercise, a carefully crafted plea for a new aesthetic, an attempt to educate an audience on how to appreciate his fiction.

James's distaste for rigid categories and critical dogma next prompts him to denigrate the question of genre in fiction: "The novel and the romance, the novel of incident and that of character—these clumsy separations appear to me to have been made by critics and readers for their own convenience, and to help them out of some of their occasional queer predicaments, but to have little reality or interest for the producer, from whose point of view it is of course that we are attempting to consider the art of fiction" (*LC* 1:55). The passage is noteworthy for two reasons. First, James's ambivalence regarding genre is not new.[11] On this point, then, "The Art of Fiction" is more closely connected to his earlier critical work, for he would eventually revise this opinion in the 1907 Preface to *The American*. Second, in this passage James once again emphasizes the writer's point of view (in opposition to that of the critic), returning to a point he had first introduced in paragraph five of his essay—namely that the proper consideration of a novel, the "test of execution," must begin with an appreciation of the author's form (*LC* 1:50). Further developing the point, James argues that genre is irrelevant, and he dares cite the French example:

> The French, who have brought the theory of fiction to remarkable completeness, have but one name for the novel, and have not attempted smaller things in it, that I can see, for that. I can think of no obligation to which the "romancer" would not be held equally with the novelist; the standard of execution is equally high for each. Of course it is of execution that we are talking—that being the only point of a novel that is open to contention. This is perhaps too often lost sight of, only to produce interminable confusions and cross-purposes. We must grant the artist his subject, his idea, his *donnée:* our criticism is applied only to what he makes of it. (*LC* 1:56)

James is bolder and more direct here, clearly arguing that the critic must dispense with prescriptive theories that determine in advance what constitutes a good novel.[12] This is one of the most important—and radical—arguments in "The Art of Fiction," and the principle would remain central to James's criticism for the rest of his career.

James can admit the limitations of his criteria, allowing for subjectivity on the reader's part, as well. "Nothing, of course, will ever take the place of the good old fashion of 'liking' a work of art or not liking it: the most improved

11. In Chapter 1 of this study, I use the examples of James's and Howells's 1865 reviews of Dickens's *Our Mutual Friend* in support of this point; James, of course, all but ignores the question of genre in his review, harshly dismissing Dickens's flat characterization (*LC* 1:853–56). In contrast, Howells insists that genre be a consideration in his reading of Dickens (*SLC* 1:55–59). The question resurfaces in Howells's 1880 review of James's *Hawthorne,* in which Howells takes James to task for failing to distinguish between the novel and the romance (*SLC* 1:292–95).

12. As Vivien Jones notes, this idea "is the centre of James's controversy with Besant in its shift of emphasis from external to internal criteria, invalidating prescription at a stroke" (*James the Critic,* 130).

criticism will not abolish that primitive, that ultimate test." James uses Zola as a case in point:

> M. Zola . . . will not reconcile himself to this absoluteness of taste, thinking that there are certain things that people ought to like, and that they can be made to like. I am quite at a loss to imagine anything (at any rate in this matter of fiction) that people *ought* to like or to dislike. Selection will be sure to take care of itself, for it has a constant motive behind it. That motive is simply experience. As people feel life, so they will feel the art that is most closely related to it. This closeness of relation is what we should never forget in talking of the effort of the novel. (*LC* 1:57–58)

The introduction of a specific French novelist—let alone the most controversial novelist of his day—is worth considering closely. By mentioning Zola, James clearly points to the French as the practitioners of the avant-garde novel; as we have noted, French novel theory as James understood and expressed it in his early work on French authors informs much of "The Art of Fiction." Yet he invokes Zola—one of only a handful of specific authors mentioned in this important essay—only as a counter-example, an author who, James believes, does not understand the principle of "the good old fashion of 'liking' a work of art or not liking it."

James's gambit makes sense for two reasons. First, Zola is an easy and rhetorically effective target when one's principal audience is the English critic of the nineteenth century. By arguing that "experience" will guide a reader naturally to select literature "most closely related" to life—that is, to one's own unique perception of it, predicated, in part, on a particular cultural or social viewpoint—James appears to acknowledge (if not validate) English popular opinion regarding Zola. If Zola's fiction does not strike a reader as related to life as she knows it, then the reader will naturally reject the work.

But to reject Zola is not to reject realism, James implies. This is James's second and more subtle point. If a reader rejects an author's donnée, the only proper response is to abstain from comment. In the preceding paragraph, James emphasizes that,

> we do not judge the artist with fairness unless we say to him, "Oh, I grant you your starting-point, because if I did not I should seem to prescribe to you, and heaven forbid I should take that responsibility. . . . [I]t isn't till I have accepted your data that I can begin to measure you. . . . Of course I may not care for your idea at all; I may think it silly, or stale, or unclean; in which case I wash my hands of you altogether. I may content myself with believing that you will not have succeeded in being interesting, but I shall,

of course, not attempt to demonstrate it, and you will be as indifferent to me as I am to you." (*LC* 1:57)

And so James's use of Zola as an example proves to be quite savvy, for while appearing to validate the hostile English response to Zola, James has managed, once again, to reject critical prescription and to privilege the author; the ultimate criterion for judging art is internal. A work must be read as an "organic whole; and since in proportion as the work is successful the idea [the subject] permeates and penetrates it, informs and animates it, so that every word and every punctuation-point contribute directly to the expression" (*LC* 1:60), a critic must judge only after granting the artist her own terms, or judge not at all.[13]

That does not mean James condones Zola. James was always ambivalent about the radical French authors, always torn between granting them their unfettered artistic freedom and preserving his own Anglo-American sensibilities. In "The Art of Fiction," James suggests that if it is the artist's donnée that should govern how a reader responds to a work (if at all), then the burden is on the author to select only the choicest of topics. The subject of a novel "matters, to my sense, in the highest degree, and if I might put up a prayer it would be that artists should select none but the richest." Zola, "who reasons less powerfully than he represents," has erred both in selecting a poor subject and in "thinking that there are certain things that people ought to like" (*LC* 1:57–58). James thus rejects both prescriptive English criticism and French naturalist theory, shifting the terms of the argument from subject to execution, sublimating moral concerns to the question of form: the exclusively internal criteria of the author.[14] This is James's most radical argument in "The Art of Fiction."

The same rhetorical strategy is employed in the closing paragraphs of "The Art of Fiction," wherein James responds to Besant's declaration that English fiction should have a "conscious moral purpose." James gently faults Besant for a lack of clarity in the statement: "it is not very clear whether he be recording a fact or laying down a principle. . . . Will you not

13. It is an idea James would repeat throughout his career as a critic. In his 1889 essay on Guy de Maupassant, for example, James states that "The only excuse the critic has for braving the embarrassments I have mentioned [i.e., presenting a "difficult" French author to a conservative English audience] is that he wishes to perform a work of recommendation. . . . Silence is the best disapproval; and to take people up with an earnest grip, only to put them down, is to add to the vain gesticulation of the human scene. That reader will therefore be most intelligent who, if he does not leave M. de Maupassant quite alone, makes him a present, as it were, of the conditions" (*LC* 2:551–52).

14. One recalls James's 1880 essay on Zola, in which he faulted "not his [Zola's] choice of subject" but "the melancholy dryness of his execution" (*LC* 2:870).

define your terms and explain how (a novel being a picture) a picture can be either moral or immoral? . . . We are discussing the Art of Fiction; questions of art are questions (in the widest sense) of execution; questions of morality are quite another affair" (*LC* 1:62). Once again, James has shifted the terms of debate from subject to execution, from external criteria to internal.

Following this line as he addresses Besant's statement that the "conscious moral purpose" of the English novel is "a truly admirable thing, and a great cause for congratulation," James turns the question around.[15] What Besant considers "truly admirable" and bold others may consider evidence of a "moral timidity" that provokes only "a cautious silence on certain subjects. . . . The essence of moral energy is to survey the whole field, and I should directly reverse Mr. Besant's remark and say not that the English novel has a purpose, but that it has a diffidence." Noting that the predominant audience for the English novel is "young people," James observes "There are certain things which it is generally agreed not to discuss, not even to mention, before young people. That is very well, but the absence of discussion is not a symptom of the moral passion. The purpose of the English novel . . . strikes me therefore as rather negative" (*LC* 1:63). It is, perhaps, James's single strongest pronouncement on the subject.

James begins his conclusion by noting that

> There is one point at which the moral sense and the artistic sense lie very near together; that is in the light of the very obvious truth that the deepest quality of a work will always be the quality of the mind of the producer. In proportion as that intelligence is fine will the novel, the picture, the statue partake of the substance of beauty and truth. To be constituted of such elements is, to my vision, to have purpose enough. No good novel will ever proceed from a superficial mind; that seems to me an axiom which, for the artist in fiction, will cover all needful moral ground: if the youthful aspirant take it to heart it will illuminate for him many of the mysteries of "purpose." (*LC* 1:63–64)

And so James concludes his critique, having once again undercut Besant's position—predicated as it is on critical prescription and a preformed sense of what is moral and correct—and substituted for it his own internally derived sense of standards, shifting the subject as always to internal considerations, to the question of execution. In a final piece of advice, James offers that "the only condition that I can think of attaching to the composition of the novel is, as I have already said, that it be sincere" (*LC* 1:64). For James, this is all one can ask of an artist; morality in art is a question of sincerity in

15. Besant, "Art of Fiction," 29–30.

execution: it is a question of form, to be judged after having read the work in its entirety and only after granting a writer her donnée.[16]

James wrote his essay hoping to spur something of a great public debate on the topic; he hoped to dim the lights of rancor that had been fixed on him in the wake of "Henry James, Jr." and, perhaps, win himself a new audience of admirers. But James may have been too subtle for his own good; "The Art of Fiction" is far more demanding, and far more radical in its arguments, than Howells's "Henry James, Jr." Where Howells had been blunt and forcefully clear, James labored to remain modest in rhetoric and tone. A few months after the essay appeared, James lamented the lack of responses to it. In a letter to T. S. Perry written shortly after the publication of "The Art of Fiction," James complained that "my poor article has not attracted the smallest attention here & I haven't heard, or seen, an allusion to it. There is almost no care for literary discussion here,—questions of form, of principle, the 'serious' idea of the novel appeals apparently to no one, & they don't understand you when you speak of them."[17] When R. L. Stevenson's response to James, "A Humble Remonstrance," appeared in *Longman's* in December 1884, James promptly wrote a gushing letter of thanks to the Scottish novelist for responding to his ideas, initiating a rewarding literary friendship (*JL* 3:57–58).

Of course, the impact of "The Art of Fiction" would be, in time, tremendous. If Walter Besant began the conversation, James ensured that it would continue. And it did: Responses and spin-off discussions were being published as late as 1891.[18] In America, William Dean Howells would shortly take up the fight in the "Editor's Study"; the influence of "The Art of Fiction" is felt in that column from time to time, and it can be sensed as late as 1899 in Howells's "Novel-Writing and Novel-Reading." And James's own work, too, would be changed. In retrospect, with the whole of James's career for the critic to survey, "The Art of Fiction" clearly stands out as a major essay and a turning point in the work of James. Ideas first introduced

16. As Dorothy J. Hale notes, James's "projected morality" in a novel is "a function of the artist's sincerity, her fidelity first to her own perspective and second to the 'mark' made on her by 'experience'" (*Social Formalism: The Novel in Theory from Henry James to the Present*, 24).

17. James, quoted in Jones, *James the Critic*, 133.

18. Spilka notes Besant's and James's essays were eventually published side by side in both England and the United States. This not only promoted a third round of responses (which include Robert Louis Stevenson's "A Humble Remonstrance"), but also initiated a larger discussion that continued up through an 1891 series of essays published in the *New Review*, among which would be Henry James's "The Science of Criticism." Spilka notes that the "era of discussion" began with two 1882 essays: Howells's "Henry James, Jr." in the *Century*, and Stevenson's "A Gossip of Romance" in *Longman's Magazine* (Spilka, "Henry James and Walter Besant," 101).

and articulated in 1884 remained central to James for the rest of his career and were expanded upon, revised, and complicated in several later essays and in the Prefaces to the New York Edition.

Intermingled Relations

But for too many scholars, "The Art of Fiction" has served as a point of departure, rather than the very notable midpoint of a much longer journey. Without stating as much, many scholars, in privileging James's post-1884 critical work, have unwittingly neglected to consider the larger arc of James's development as a critic. "The Art of Fiction" draws heavily from James's earliest work on a range of European critics and novelists.

As we have seen, one of the most radical arguments put forward in "The Art of Fiction" was James's insistence on the openness and the sensitivity of the critic: the willingness of the critic to resist prejudging a work of art and to read the work on its own terms. The origins of this critical stance date to James's 1865 study of Matthew Arnold's *Essays in Criticism*. James appreciated Arnold's "sensitive and generous" approach to criticism, and, most importantly, he found the Englishman "sympathetic" (*LC* 1:712). Arnold taught James to resist the narrow, formalistic approach common among English critics of the time. The influence of James's French mentors, Edmond Schérer and Charles Augustin Sainte-Beuve, is also felt throughout "The Art of Fiction." The spirit of Schérer's intellectual integrity and independence are crucial foundations for the exercise. From Schérer, James learned that one's critical axioms are irrefutably linked to one's moral sensibilities, and that a critic must trust and develop his moral sensibilities, rather than rely on pre-established critical standards. (In other words, one's moral sensitivities create one's critical standards.) Also, James learned from Schérer to think of criticism as a quasi-artistic act: a creative, open-ended form that ultimately afforded the critic the means to articulate his own personal viewpoint. In Sainte-Beuve, James found the disinterested yet sympathetic reader who, avoiding prepackaged critical formulas, acknowledged the deeply personal and always provisional nature of a critical response. Sainte-Beuve also taught James that truth in criticism is always relative. In short, the influence of European criticism, by way of Arnold, Schérer, and Sainte-Beuve, is absolutely vital to "The Art of Fiction."

If James's reviews of fellow critics offered him the opportunity to develop and hone his own critical theories, his reviews of European authors afforded him the opportunity to practice these critical theories. In James's early work on Turgenev and Balzac, one finds important precedents for "The Art of

Fiction." Both Turgenev and Balzac offered a decisive and vivid vision of the world, something unique—something, as James would ultimately phrase it, direct and personal. Both Turgenev and Balzac focused on creating vivid, believable characters, and each placed his characters at the dramatic center of his fiction. James also valued the moral qualities he found in the fiction of Turgenev and Balzac. In Turgenev, James found a model for conjoining artistic form and moral meaning in two regards. First, he felt the Russian's emotionally sympathetic rendering of character appealed to the reader's "*moral* curiosity" (*LC* 2:988). Second, Turgenev's penchant for oblique endings fascinated James (and, as James's own creative work demonstrates, had a profound impact) and served to reinforce the moral value of the work: that is, by resisting explanatory or didactic conclusions, Turgenev forced the reader to determine meaning for himself. In Balzac, morality took on a different hue. Balzac's graphic prose often offended James, yet it was the weight and density of the illusion, the "irresistible force" of the prose that presented a unique moral quality: a measurement of the total effect of the art (*LC* 2:53). Through his study of Balzac, James learned to note but ultimately to look beyond the graphic depiction of controversial subject matter, choosing instead to appreciate the overall conception of form, which (as in Turgenev) became a means of measuring the moral value of the work. In short, from both Turgenev and Balzac James learned the value of "readerly openness," or the willingness to submerge one's self in the world of a writer regardless of subject matter. James promoted this aesthetic for one simple reason: he desired the same from the readers of his own fiction. Clearly, this is one of the ulterior motives behind "The Art of Fiction."

As the case of Balzac proves, the French were always tricky for James; he often struggled to accept their works on the grounds of artistic principle even as he questioned their standards and taste. Such tensions inform his 1880 review of Zola's *Nana,* in which James becomes, uncharacteristically, a de facto apologist for the English novel and the "moral timidity" he would later criticize in "The Art of Fiction." With this 1880 essay in mind, James's use of Zola in "The Art of Fiction" takes on deeper meaning. James's reference to Zola in "The Art of Fiction" is, as we have seen, part of a savvy strategy of playing to his audience's prejudices; yet from the 1880 essay it is clear that James, too, finds the Frenchman's work distasteful. More importantly, if, as I have claimed above, the most radical argument in "The Art of Fiction" comes at the point when James rejects both prescriptive English criticism and French naturalist theory, shifting the terms of the argument from subject to execution, then the 1880 Zola essay operates, one might argue, as an aborted first attempt to realize that argument: James fails to prove his thesis and concludes, rather curiously, by defending the status quo for the English novel. As "The Art of Fiction" demonstrates, James was keen to revise the position.

From this brief review, it should be clear that the roots of James's stance in "The Art of Fiction" can be traced back to his earliest work as a critic. Another crucial transitional piece, and one written closer to "The Art of Fiction," is James's 1883 essay on Alphonse Daudet. Late in the Daudet essay, James quotes Charles Dudley Warner, who had recently argued that "the main object in the novel is to entertain."[19] James, of course, disagrees.

> I should put the case differently: I should say that the main object of the novel is to represent life. . . . The *effect* of a novel—the effect of any work of art—is to entertain; but that is a very different thing. The success of a work of art, to my mind, may be measured by the degree to which it produces a certain illusion. . . . I am perfectly aware that to say the object of a novel is to represent life does not bring the question to a point so fine as to be uncomfortable for any one. It is of the greatest importance that there should be a very free appreciation of such a question, and the definition I have hinted at gives plenty of scope for that. For, after all, may not people differ infinitely as to what constitutes life—what constitutes representation? (*LC* 2:242)[20]

Given that "The Art of Fiction" attempts to negotiate a stance allowing for both the objective and the subjective, James's question in the Daudet essay—"what constitutes representation?"—is important. In the case of Daudet, James expands upon a point first made in his 1875 essay on Balzac, in which James praised the "irresistible force" of Balzac's fiction and the "contagious illusion" that utterly convinced the reader (*LC* 2:53). In 1883, James praises Daudet's work for "its being charged to an extraordinary degree with his temperament, his feelings, his instincts, his natural qualities" (*LC* 2:229). And yet Daudet's particular vision is a direct reflection of his Parisian environment, the world that surrounds him. James notes that Daudet has been called a "modern writer":

> Alphonse Daudet is, in truth, very modern; he has all the newly-developed, the newly-invented, perceptions. Nothing speaks so much to his imagination

---

19. Warner, quoted in James, *LC* 2:241.

20. The question of the novel as entertainment was, for Henry James, not a new one. Indeed, he had addressed the question in his very first published review, an 1864 response to Nassau W. Senior's *Essays on Fiction*. In the review, James noted that Sir Walter Scott's *Waverly* had marked a change in the direction of the novel; where Fielding, Richardson, and Smollett had been arch moralists, Scott went for a different effect: "'Waverly' was the first novel which was self-forgetful. It proposed simply to amuse the reader, as an old English ballad amused him. It undertook to prove nothing but facts. It was the novel irresponsible" (*LC* 1:1202). So much for the novel as entertainment!

as the latest and most composite things, the refinements of current civilisation, the most delicate shades of the actual. It is scarcely too much to say
that (especially in the Parisian race), modern manners, modern nerves,
modern wealth, and modern improvements, have engendered a new sense,
a sense not easily named nor classified, but recognisable in all the most
characteristic productions of contemporary art. It is partly physical, partly
moral, and the shortest way to describe it is to say that it is a more analytic
consideration of appearances. It is known by its tendency to resolve its discoveries into pictorial form. It sees the connection between feelings and
external conditions, and it expresses such relations as they have not been
expressed hitherto. (*LC* 2:229–30)

Clearly, what James values in Daudet is the acute awareness of the ever-
changing French society that surrounds Daudet. This perhaps comes as no
surprise given that evocation of place, or environment, was always a central
concern for James. Daudet's ability to respond to this external world is the
source of his particular charm: "The appearance of things is constantly more
complicated as the world grows older, and it needs a more and more patient
art, a closer notation, to divide it into its parts. Of this art Alphonse Daudet
has a wonderfully large allowance, and that is why I say that he is particularly modern." This observation gives James an opportunity to turn his attention briefly to a crucial difference between English and French criticism:
"[L]ife is, immensely, a matter of surface, and if our emotions in general are
interesting, the *form* of those emotions has the merit of being the most definite thing about them. Like most French imaginative writers (judged, at
least, from the English standpoint), he is much less concerned with the
moral, the metaphysical world, than with the sensible. We proceed usually
from the former to the latter, while the French reverse the process" (*LC*
2:230). Here James articulates precisely what Vivien Jones has noted is the
subtext for James's response to Besant in "The Art of Fiction": the English
critic's habit of imposing, a priori, preestablished moral convictions to the
reading of a text, a practice that necessarily limits the author's "freedom to
feel and say" (*LC* 1:50). And, of course, in this passage on Daudet, James
addresses the paradox of the objective/subjective response to the modern
world. Life may be a matter of surfaces, but art is predicated not merely on
recording those surfaces; rather, art demands that an emotional response, a
subjective response, be conjoined to the act of recording: "the *form* of those
emotions has the merit of being the most definite thing about them." The
work of art is itself the articulation of both objective and subjective responses to the modern world. Daudet's skill at capturing this paradox is precisely what James values most: "Daudet's great characteristic is this mixture
of the sense of the real with the sense of the beautiful. His imagination is

constantly at play with his theme; it has a horror of the literal, the limited; it sees an object in all its intermingled relations—on its sentimental, its pathetic, its comical, its pictorial side" (*LC* 2:231). Daudet embodies precisely what James struggled to articulate both in the 1883 essay and a year later in "The Art of Fiction": the principle that a work of art must provide both "the sense of the real" (the objective) and "the sense of the beautiful" (the subjective). James continued to explore and complicate this paradox in his later writings, but to understand fully what James attempted in "The Art of Fiction," an understanding of what James wrote prior to the 1884 essay is crucial.

What the reader finds, then, in "The Art of Fiction," is a writer not merely responding to Walter Besant and other critics of his time (though he is doing that), a writer not merely articulating a radical aesthetic break with the English novel as it exists in 1884 (though he is doing that), a writer not merely struggling to find the language to express a paradox no other English writer had attempted to define (though he is doing that)—what we find in "The Art of Fiction" is a writer on the crest of an ongoing *personal* discussion that began, for him, with his first published reviews. James's criticism after "The Art of Fiction" would only become more personal, his criteria more idiosyncratic. The culmination of this personal evolution would eventually result in the New York Edition of his works, which would allow James both to revise his own fiction and to craft a series of Prefaces that would, for many critics, stand as his most important contribution to the history of criticism.

II

The Literary Criticism of Henry James and William Dean Howells, 1885–1897

4. Defining the Critic in the "Editor's Study" and "The Science of Criticism"

While the failure of James R. Osgood and Company in May 1885 presented serious difficulties for both Henry James and William Dean Howells, each writer responded differently to the loss of his book publisher. For James, Osgood's bankruptcy was a genuine trial. The publisher had contracted to pay four thousand dollars upon completion of the serial publication of *The Bostonians,* but James never saw the money. Living in London, he was distant from the proceedings, relying on his brother William, Edmund Gosse, and Howells to advise and assist him.[1] Despondent at having lost his highest-paying contract to date, James spent the summer trying to secure a book contract on his own terms. In August, he signed with Macmillan to publish *The Bostonians,* for which he received an advance of only five hundred pounds—just over half of what he had asked. "This year has been disastrous," James wrote to William.[2]

For Howells, the matter played out quite differently. The well-connected

1. Henry James wrote to Howells on May 23, 1885, indirectly asking for information and advice concerning Osgood's failure (*LFL,* 248–49). In addition, William James wrote twice on his brother's behalf to Howells asking for advice on the matter. Apparently, Howells never responded to any of these requests. Howells's silence prompts Michael Anesko to suggest Howells may have deliberately withheld information from both Henry and William James, perhaps for reasons of self-interest (*LFL,* 183–86).

2. Henry James, quoted in *LFL,* 185n32. James had hoped to secure at least an eight-hundred-pound advance for the novel (Anesko, *"Friction with the Market,"* 104). For more on James's difficult attempts to secure a publisher for *The Bostonians,* see Anesko, *"Friction with the Market,"* 101–7.

former editor of the *Atlantic* knew that Benjamin Ticknor, Osgood's former business partner, hoped to contract with both him and James. In June, while James was still casting about for advice and information, Howells negotiated a contract with Ticknor that provided him with both a weekly salary and a book publisher for *The Rise of Silas Lapham,* which was currently appearing serially in the *Century* (*LFL,* 184–85). Ticknor had hoped, of course, to secure contracts for Howells's future work as well.[3] In high demand, Howells played the market expertly; in October, with James Osgood acting as liaison, he signed what he himself called an "incredibly advantageous" contract with Harper and Brothers (*HSL* 3:133). Howells, whom Edwin Cady has called "perhaps the best literary businessman" of his generation, had not merely survived Osgood's failure, he thrived on it, securing the most lucrative publishing contract yet offered to an American author.[4]

Part of that contract stipulated that Howells write a three- to five-page column, to be called the "Editor's Study," for each issue of *Harper's Monthly*.[5] During contract negotiations, Howells initially balked at the suggestion of writing a column: "I was reluctant to undertake the 'Study' in the first instance," Howells noted in an 1891 interview, "[but I] became very much interested in it . . . as I went on. . . . [I had] the finest opportunity ever afforded a man to say what he wanted to say."[6] Howells's hesitancy is understandable; after all, he had resigned as editor of the *Atlantic* in 1881 to devote himself full-time to the writing of fiction. But Howells was never one to miss a splendid opportunity—or miss turning it toward his pecuniary advantage. In the wake of his 1882 essay "Henry James, Jr.," he found himself at the center of an ongoing debate concerning the state of contemporary fiction. His fiction and his opinions on literature had been picked over, debated, criticized, and praised on both shores of the Atlantic. His friend Henry James had further stoked the fires with his influential 1884 essay "The Art of Fiction." The Study was a bully pulpit and the time was right to use it.

One of the most important questions for both Howells and James in this

---

3. Ticknor wrote Howells: "of course you didn't promise anything but we wanted to have everything satisfactory to you & have put ourselves in your hands accordingly" (quoted in *LFL,* 212n30).

4. Cady, *Realist at War,* 2. The Harper's contract secured both a steady income and a long-term publisher for Howells's fiction. In return for one novel a year, Howells would be paid $10,000 annually, plus royalties. In addition, Howells would be paid $3,000 annually to pen a short column for each issue of *Harper's Monthly,* to be called the "Editor's Study." Additional publications would be at top prices: Howells would receive fifty dollars per thousand words for articles in *Harper's Monthly* and thirty dollars per thousand words for articles in *Harper's Weekly* (*HSL* 3:131n1).

5. Hereafter referred to as the Study.

6. Howells, quoted in Spencer H. Coon, "Mr. Howells Talks," 14.

period was the role of literary criticism in the mass-media marketplace. Howells, in the Study, addressed the topic several times. James directly addressed the topic less frequently, always preferring to offer examples before edicts. As literary critics, however, each author felt threatened, to a degree, by the increasing numbers of popular, mass-media book reviewers. Each sought to position himself, in contrast to the "unschooled" reviewers, as rigorous, learned, and professional. In doing so, each sought to create an audience for his own creative and critical work. This chapter examines these efforts, first, by looking at Howells's "Editor's Study" columns that address the question of literary criticism and assessing them in light of his attitudes toward the mass-media marketplace of his day; and second, by examining the same questions in Henry James's essay "The Science of Criticism."

A Symposium of One

"In almost every dwelling of any pretensions to taste there is nowadays a study," William Dean Howells wrote in his first "Editor's Study" column, which appeared in January 1886. Imagine, Howells invites the reader, "the unreal editor, the airy, elusive abstraction who edits the Study" occupying a "fittingly circumstanced" study of his own:

> Heavy rugs silence the foot upon his floor; nothing but the costliest masterpieces gleam from his walls; the best of the old literatures, in a subtly chorded harmony of bindings, make music to the eye from his shelves, and the freshest of the new load his richly carved mahogany table. His vast windows of flawless plate look out upon the confluent waters of the Hudson and the Charles, with expanses, in the middle distance, of the Mississippi, the Great Lakes, and the Golden Gate, and in the background the misty line of the Thames, with reaches of the remoter Seine, and glints of the Tiber's yellow tide.

Within this chamber, the editor invites the reader, "who will always be welcome," to discuss "such matters of literary interest as may come up from time to time." There is but one caveat: "The reader will, of course, not be allowed to interrupt the editor while he is talking. . . . It is meant, in other terms, to make the Study a sort of free parliament, but for the presiding officer only; or, a symposium of one." And this "unreal editor" plans to do some talking: "The editor comes to his place after a silence of some years in this sort, and has a very pretty store of prejudices to indulge and grudges to satisfy, which he will do with as great decency as possible" (*SLC* 2:3–4).

To be sure, this is a playful and enticing opening movement; Howells quite literally sets a stage and, despite the mask of anonymity enforced by the only-too-real editors of *Harper's Monthly,* manages to personalize the account—with the understanding that a sizable share of his audience already knew who was penning the column, as Harper and Brothers had not hesitated to advertise their coup in securing Howells's work. But this opening passage warrants careful consideration; Howells is not merely establishing the tone or atmosphere for his imaginary study, he is also defining the critic's position in society and culture.

In his 1866 essay "Literary Criticism," Howells had defined "Honest criticism" as "at once the attribute and the indication of an educated and refined literary taste." Men of "accomplished mind," Howells felt, were all but duty bound to offer intelligent criticism. Howells's earliest conception of the critic was that of the intellectual aesthete whose "honest, painstaking labor" was performed "for the benefit of all" (*SLC* 1:60–62). The opening of the Study twenty years later demonstrates that Howells still favored that aristocratic vision of the genteel critic. What is noticeably new about the opening movement of the Study is the candidly personal nature of the endeavor; Howells freely admits he has scores to settle. The largest skirmish of the "Realism War," which had really begun in 1882 with "Henry James, Jr.," was about to ensue.

If it were a war, then the literary critics were its foot soldiers. Howells, as former editor of the *Atlantic* and one of the most well-connected and in-demand authors of his day, certainly had a commanding view of the field, and what he saw frustrated him. In his second Study (February 1886) he laments the lack of a serious critical movement in America. "The critics," he notes, "when they are not elders ossified in tradition, are apt to be young people, and young people are necessarily conservative in their tastes and theories." In short, "one might perhaps count our critical authorities upon rather less than the thumbs of one hand." Criticism, in the form of book reviews, takes place from coast to coast in the nation's newspapers and magazines, but it lacks substance and rigor. "There is no critical leadership among us," Howells notes, even as he tries to put matters in the best light. If there is a large amount of criticism being written that collectively touches "every part of [an] author's work," the work will nevertheless "often be deplored as mistaken and of wrong direction or slighter value." Quantity, Howells clearly suggests, does not make up for a lack of quality (*SLC* 2:11–12). Thus Howells modifies his conception of the critic: he must not only be a genteel aristocrat and intellectual aesthete, he must also be aesthetically progressive and selective.

In subsequent columns in the Study, Howells articulated his conception of the critic's proper role in society. In 1866, Howells had argued that the critic's job is "finding what is faulty in a book, and pointing it out to the author and to all authors and readers, for the benefit of all" (*SLC* 1:62). Howells's early conception of criticism privileged its didactic potential; clearly, the critic's audience included artists, including the author of the particular work in question. In July 1886, Howells carefully modifies this assertion: "criticism can . . . do very little toward forming or reforming any writer; if it could, we are painfully aware that we should ourselves be very different from what we are. More and more it must content itself with ascertaining currents and tendencies, and not proposing to direct or stop them; more and more it must realize that it is not a censorship" (*SLC* 2:28). Again, one notes the personal nature of the comment. In the wake of "Henry James, Jr.," Howells had taken the brunt of an enormous amount of negative commentary. Like James, he had been surprised at the vitriol unleashed by his comments. And, like James, Howells stood firm in his artistic and critical opinions. In 1882, shortly after the publication of "Henry James, Jr.," a defiant Howells wrote to Roswell Smith: "I suppose you will have seen that I have stirred up the English papers pretty generally by what I wrote of Dickens and Thackeray in my paper on James. I don't remember just what I said, but so far as they have quoted me, I stand by myself, and should only wish to amplify and intensify the opinions that they object to. I knew what I was talking about, and they don't know at all what they are talking about" (*HSL* 3:43). If Howells had any regrets concerning the essay, it was only for the fact that he had subjected his friend James to unwarranted abuse. "I have been scarcely if at all troubled by the row about me," he wrote to Thomas S. Perry in March 1883, "and have been chiefly vexed because it includes James" (*HSL* 3:57). Howells knew firsthand, then, about critical efforts to reform if not censor authors, and the experience surely contributed to his revised opinion on the critic's role in relation to the author of the work under consideration.

Howells continues in the July 1886 Study by praising two critics whom he feels exemplify "the scientific method" of criticism that should, he suggests, replace the current critical standard of a lone critic voicing "his own mind, which is often but a narrow field" (*SLC* 2:28). In the work of Thomas S. Perry and Hutcheson Macaulay Posnett, Howells lauds the "application of scientific theories to literature." Howells quotes extensively from Posnett, who argues for a progressive literature reflecting the "particular conditions of human character" and "that social instrument language." As for criticism, Posnett argues that "the comparative study of Literature not only opens an immense field of fruitful labor, but tends to foster creative imagination." He further argues against the "old-fashioned worship of imagination" and the "exceptional genius" or "great-man theory" of authorship.[7]

Howells praises "the learning, the sympathy, the logic" of Posnett's critical method—a method that, in contrast to that of the "average romantic critic," favors "principles to impressions in considering literature." Perry and Posnett "stand together in a conscious perception of principles which others have been feeling more or less blindly, and which are really animating and shaping the whole future of criticism" (*SLC* 2:30). The July 1886 Study is notable, then, for two reasons. First, Howells articulates a new conception of the critic as one who resists prescribing to authors what should or should not be written. Second, in contrast to the "average romantic critic" who favors personal impressions as the basis for literary review, Howells calls for a more "scientific" model based on sound principles and, one presumes, more objective criteria.

Howells's new conception of the critic is more cogently articulated in the June 1887 Study. Howells begins by attacking the foundation of contemporary American criticism, whose practitioners are "perilously beset by temptations to be personal, to be vulgar, to be arrogant." For Howells, it is a question of professional rigor, not to mention critical ethics. Following the examples of Perry and Posnett, Howells increasingly favors a scientific criticism: the critic should be objective, tolerant, and principled. In contrast, the "personal" critic "is yet indefinitely far from knowing that in affairs of taste his personal preference enters very little. Commonly he has no principles, but only an assortment of prepossessions for and against." This critic "is not tolerant; he thinks it a virtue to be intolerant" when "it is really his business to classify and analyze the fruits of the human mind as the naturalist classifies the objects of his study, rather than to praise or blame them" (*SLC* 2:51–52).

For Howells, it is a question of pedigree. The American critic "is the heir of the false theory and bad manners of the English school." Critics of both nations are "apt to be amateurish"; furthermore, "it is still the ambition of the American critic to write like the English critic, to show his wit if not his learning, to strive to eclipse the author under review rather than illustrate him. He has not caught on to the fact that it is really no part of his business to exploit himself, but that it is altogether his duty to place a book in such a light that the reader shall know its class, its function, its character" (*SLC* 2:52). Of course, Howells had denigrated the English on several previous occasions. It was his dismissal of Dickens and Thackeray in "Henry James, Jr." that had raised such a firestorm in 1882, much of which had ridiculed Howells and James. In the June 1887 Study, one finds, per-

7. Posnett, quoted in Howells *SLC* 2:29–30.

haps, part of Howells's counterresponse, drawn from his "pretty store of . . . grudges to satisfy."

Not that he places the blame for the current state of American criticism solely at the feet of the English; Howells notes that "our criticism has not improved from the accession of large numbers of ladies to its ranks." Female critics "'know what they like'—that pernicious maxim of those who do not know what they ought to like," and "bring a lively stock of misapprehensions and prejudices to their work." If in the final instance female critics are "more ignorant than malevolent," Howells's gendered comments indicate that his vision of the ideal critic—aristocratic, genteel, intellectual, progressive, and "scientific"—is decidedly patriarchal (*SLC* 2:53).

Midway through the June 1887 Study, Howells shifts from proscribing the existing state of criticism to articulating what he feels the ideal critic ought to do. "He ought, in the first place, to cast prayerfully about for humility, and especially to beseech the powers to preserve him from the sterility of arrogance and the deadness of contempt, for out of these nothing can proceed." To this end, the American critic should look for models outside of England:

> Self-restraint, decency, even politeness, seem to characterize the behavior of critics elsewhere. They may not like an author's work, but they do not for that reason use him with ignominy or insult. . . . All that we now suggest is that the critic need not be impolite, even to the youngest and weakest author. A little courtesy, or a good deal, a constant perception of the fact that a book is not a misdemeanor, a decent self-respect that must forbid the civilized man the savage pleasure of wounding, are what we ask for our criticism, as something which will add sensibly to its present lustre; or, if nothing can do that, will at least approach it to the Continental attitude, and remove it from the English. (*SLC* 2:53–54)

In its call for the reorientation of critical manners and its promotion of the French critical model, this passage distinctly echoes James's "The Art of Fiction." James had quietly invoked both the French critical and artistic models throughout his essay; furthermore, he had suggested that if the critic could not grant the author her premise, or donnée, before offering comment, the proper critical reaction was dignified indifference. James's own calculated humility and mannered rhetoric throughout "The Art of Fiction" had itself offered an ample demonstration of how criticism was above all to be dignified, polite, and genteel; in his call for a more humble and compassionate criticism, Howells follows suit.

Howells also appears to agree with James on the primacy of the writer over the critic. In "The Art of Fiction," James had articulated signal elements of his mature creative aesthetic (for example, demanding complete freedom for the artist in matters of execution), and whatever comments he offered regarding the role of the reader or critic were offered in support of this larger thesis. The critic, James had argued, always worked in response to an artist's work. There is a clear order, or hierarchy: first, the artist produces her work in complete freedom; second, the critic grants the author her don-née before proceeding to comment.

In the June 1887 Study, Howells takes this hierarchy as his starting point and proceeds to codify it with the pseudo-scientific rhetoric he had intro-duced in the July 1886 Study. He implores his fellow critics:

> Consider, dear friends, what you are really in the world for. It is not, ap-parently, for a great deal, because your only excuse for being is that some-body else has been. The critic exists because the author first existed. If books failed to appear, the critic must disappear, like the poor aphis or the lowly caterpillar in the absence of vegetation. These insects may both suppose that they have something to do with the creation of vegetation; and the critic may suppose that he has something to do with the creation of litera-ture; but a very little reasoning ought to convince alike aphis, caterpillar, and critic that they are mistaken. The critic—to drop the others—must perceive, if he will question himself more carefully, that his office is mainly to ascertain facts and traits of literature, not to invent or denounce them; to discover principles, not to establish them; to report, not to create. (*SLC* 2:54–55)

Howells's conclusion, notes Edwin Cady, is that "it is a decorum of tax-onomy which befits the critic."[8] Howells has introduced what one might call the "parasite" model of literary criticism, rigidly codifying the hierarchy implied in "The Art of Fiction."

Howells anticipates the reader in the concluding section of the June 1887 Study when he asks, "Then, are we critics of no use in the world? . . . More than one sober thinker is inclining at present to suspect that aesthetically or specifically we *are* of no use, and that we are only useful historically; that we may register laws, but not enact them. We are not quite prepared to admit that aesthetic criticism is useless, though in view of its futility in any given instance it is hard to deny that it is so" (*SLC* 2:55). Here one sees Howells bumping up against the limits of his conception of criticism's role.[9] He has done so, in part, because of the rhetorical strategy he has employed in his

8. Cady, *W. D. Howells as Critic*, 104.
9. Howells had tested the limits of his critical understanding on at least one previous occa-sion: in his 1867 review of Purnell's *Literature and Its Professors* (*SLC* 1:98–99).

definition of the critic. Scholars have noted that Howells's arguments in the Study frequently take the form of the debate; Howells frequently frames his argument as a simplistic binary, and then employs definition by negation (for instance, realism in contrast to the "romanticistic").[10] There are several reasons why Howells employed such a strategy. First, his conception of his audience as largely feminine and family-oriented demanded that he write clear and decisive commentary. There was no room for Jamesian ambiguity or vagueness. At the same time, Howells wanted to deconstruct his audience's sentimental, romantic prejudices and reconstruct an audience more suited to his own tastes. In a sense, then, Howells—like James—sought to create a new audience for his work. If, in Howells's line of thinking, the "average romantic critic" was a reader who favored personal impressions, then Howells—employing his strategy of definition by negation—believed the "scientific critic" must necessarily articulate principled arguments that lead to logical conclusions (the precise opposite of a "personal impression"). Likewise, as Howells detested the English critical model and its American counterpart, he felt a vital need to articulate a new critical paradigm based on the newest models offered by peers like Perry and Posnett. And, finally, Howells had a deeply personal interest in the matter—the force of personal conviction. If he lamented the lack of critical leadership among American critics, he would both articulate a new "scientific" paradigm and stand as an example of it.

In doing so, Howells ultimately argues against the Jamesian model as he then understood it. James evidenced in his own critical work a tendency first articulated in "The Art of Fiction": to read with a sensitive and generous eye, and above all an awareness of what a given author is attempting in a work. As we have seen earlier in this study, James developed this readerly practice during the first twenty-odd years of his career as a critic. And no one was more attuned to James's unique critical aesthetic than William Dean Howells, who had already criticized it in an 1878 review of *French Poets and Novelists*. Howells had complained James was not "a critic in the systematic sense" and had lamented the "exasperating inconclusiveness" and "somewhat too paradoxical summary" of the work. James, in contrast to the "systematic critic like Saint-Beuve or Matthew Arnold," was merely a "highly suggestive, charming talker." In contrast, Howells had suggested that "pure criticism" should "work out a problem to some conclusion on one side or another" (*SLC* 1:280–81). Howells's 1887 argument for a strictly governed and scientifically objective criticism is an argument against both the mass-media book review and, implicitly, the esoteric judgments of an aesthete like James.

10. Kaplan, *Social Construction*, 15–43.

In June 1887, Howells had essentially shored up his various theories on the role of the critic to produce what was his most articulate statement to date. The ideal critic should be an educated male who employs a genteel, civil, impartial, and scientifically objective tone. He should know his place in the taxonomy of art and criticism and never step outside of its bounds. Conspicuous by its absence is any explicit mention of Howells's earlier conviction concerning the didactic function of criticism; as an artist himself he had become wary of granting the critic too much license. Hence he no longer makes such lofty pronouncements concerning criticism "for the benefit of all" (*SLC* 1:62). In Howells's taxonomy, critics are not permitted to offer prescriptive commentary on aesthetic matters. Rather, courtesy, self-restraint, and perhaps above all humility befit the "scientific" critic.

Howells revisits the topic in the August 1890 Study, in which he addresses the issue of anonymity in literary criticism. He begins by noting that "nearly all current criticism as practised by the English and Americans is bad, is falsely principled, and is conditioned in evil. It is falsely principled because it is unprincipled, or without principles; and it is conditioned in evil because it is almost wholly anonymous." Anonymous criticism, argues Howells,

> is almost wholly an abuse, and we do not confine our meaning here to literary criticism. Now that nearly every aspect and nook and corner of life is searched by print, it is intolerably oppressive that any department of current literature, or of the phase of literature we call journalism, should be anonymous. Every editorial, every smallest piece of reporting, that involves a personal matter, should be signed by the writer, who should be personally responsible for his words. In a free country where no one can suffer for his opinions, no one has a right to make another suffer by them more condemnation than his individual name can carry. Thanks to the interviewer, the society reporter, and the special correspondent, the superstitious awe in which print has been held is fast vanishing; but print still bears too great authority. If each piece of it were signed by the author, its false advantage would be dissipated. (*SLC* 2:143–44)

The passage is, of course, ironic; at the insistence of his editors, Howells wrote the Study anonymously. But the passage is noteworthy for other reasons. First, Howells argues for a new definition of authorship. Rather than effacing the writer as merely "the *Times* representative, or the *Sun* representative, or the *World* representative," Howells wants to assert the writer both professionally and personally. (Howells argues doing so would lessen the "authority" of print media.) As a matter of professional ethics, Howells wants to see the burden of responsibility fall upon the shoulders of the individual critics: "If every interview were signed, so that the public might understand that it was relying upon the accuracy and honesty of this or that reporter, and not upon the good faith of the journal whose management can have no means of verifying the interview, the interviewer would cease to represent anything but himself, and if he were held directly and personally responsible, it would be much to the health of his own soul" (*SLC* 2:145). In essence, Howells wanted to solidify a trend he himself exemplified: the professional author who earns a living by his pen. As Howells's earlier Study columns on literary criticism demonstrate, he sought to professionalize the vocation of criticism by moving it away from the "personal" book review, which he loathed for its lack of professional standards, and toward the learned, polite, and "scientific" model he both championed and represented. At bottom, Howell's argument is with the fundamental nature of the marketplace itself. As Amy Kaplan has noted, Howells's realism can be understood as "a debate . . . with competing modes of representation. Howells, in both his criticism and his novels, asserts realism's truth value not only in its fidelity to real life but in its contest with popular fiction and mass journalism." Howells thus articulates "an argument, not only with older residual conventions, but with emergent forms of mass media from which it gains its power and against which it asserts itself."[11]

Howells's argument with the market is also noteworthy for its deeply personal nature; his call for an end to anonymous criticism is, of course, a request for his own critics to show themselves. By August 1890, Howells had been writing the Study for nearly five years; as scholars have noted, during that time he received a mountain of attention—much of it negative. And though he wrote the Study under the guise of anonymity, its authorship was an open secret.

> If the Study were disposed to be autobiographical it might instance its own fate during the five years of its existence, in which it has practised the invariable courtesy toward persons which is possible with those who treat of methods and principles, and has every month been assailed with personal offense from the whole cry of anonymous criticism; so that in some moments of extreme dismay it has been almost disposed to regard itself as perhaps really an enemy of mankind. But its final conclusion appears to be that anonymous criticism is this enemy, and that the man, or even the young lady, who is given a gun, and told to shoot at some passer from behind a hedge, is placed in circumstances of temptation almost too strong for human nature. (*SLC* 2:146)

One notes that Howells calls attention to his own example of professionalism; and, if one accepts Howells's apparent candor, one senses in the passage a note of exasperation with the combative nature of his position. That

11. Ibid., 13.

Howells felt like a target in the Study is understandable; to be sure, he had invited much of the criticism directed at him, and at times he even reveled in it. In a frequently cited letter to Edmund Gosse, Howells celebrated his work in the Study, declaring that "it's fun, having one's open say again, and banging the babes of Romance about. It does my soul lots of good; and how every number makes 'em dance!" (January 24, 1886; *HSL* 3:152). In February 1887, a cocksure Howells wrote to his father: "As to the things you see about me in the papers, I hope you'll not let them worry you. They are inevitable, because I'm now something of a 'shining mark,' and because in fiction I've identified myself with truth and humanity, which you know people always hate. It will pass, and pretty soon I shall be accepted. My ideas are right" (*HSL* 3:184).

In the August 1890 Study, Howells sounds exasperated by the trial (though not, one hastens to add, less adamant in his opinions). His tone speaks for itself. Anonymous criticism is a "gross and stupid injustice" and a "savage condition . . . an abuse that ought to be as extinct as the torture of witnesses." Anonymous critics "[swoop] down upon [an author] in the dark, panoplied in the authority of a great journal." They "treat [an author] as prey, and strike him into the mire preparatory to tearing him limb from limb" (*SLC* 2:146). If the passage is somewhat hyperbolic, it nevertheless expresses Howells's personal sense of frustration.

But Howells was never one to wallow in his misery. "We ought not to destroy critics," he continues, "we ought to reform them, or rather transform them, or turn them from the arrogant assumption of authority to a realization of their true function in the civilized state." Howells returns to familiar ground, calling for "the gentle, dispassionate, scientific student of current literature" to replace "the arrogant, bullying, blundering pedant, who has come down to our time from the heyday of the brutal English reviewers." He repeats his belief that critics "cannot reform or purify or direct" an author; rather, they should only classify and categorize creative works "as they appear." Howells clarifies his hierarchy by noting that if a book is good, then its author "has learned all that is knowable about it, and every strong point and every weak point in it, far more accurately than any one else can possibly learn them." Conversely, if the book is bad, the author "cannot be taught anything about it from the outside" (*SLC* 2:146–49). Again, the shadow of James is evident—a work is fundamentally a direct personal expression of the artist, and that is its deepest value.

Howells has shifted emphasis and, in doing so, reoriented the critic and his mission. Earlier in the August 1890 Study, Howells had suggested, by means of the tone of his argument, the injurious nature of anonymity in criticism in regards to its effects on an author ("tearing him limb from limb"). He concludes by suggesting that "it is not in the interest of authorship that we urge criticism to throw off its mask, but in the interest of the reading public which is corrupted by the almost inevitable savagery and dishonesty of the anonymous critic" (*SLC* 2:149). The scientific critic's role, in this final example, is to act as a sort of broker between an author and his audience. The author, Howells implies, is ultimately above the critic's reproach; but the public is in need of the critic's insight.

In this August 1890 column of the Study, Howells completes his renegotiation of the terms of his vision of the author, the critic, and their audiences. In 1866, he had called for a criticism that would find "what is faulty in a book, and [point] it out to the author and to all authors and readers, for the benefit of all" (*SLC* 1:62). There was, in this sketchily defined vision, some parity between critic and author; certainly, the critic's role was, in part, to inform the artist of his virtues and faults. In June 1887, he radically revised his stance, denying the critic the power to prescribe to an author and positioning him in a clear-cut hierarchy that effectively rendered the critic a parasite feeding on its author-host; the critic's "office is mainly to ascertain facts and traits of literature, not to invent or denounce them; to discover principles, not to establish them; to report, not to create" (*SLC* 2:55). This revision led Howells to question whether or not criticism was, in fact, even necessary. In August 1890 he repositions the critic as a useful, if perhaps ultimately unnecessary, link between the author and her public.

By August 1890 Howells had taken his revised definition of the critic as far as he would take it in the Study. Between 1866 and 1890, Howells gradually revised his definition of the ideal critic: the critic must be educated, genteel, polite, sophisticated, rigorous, principled, objective (or "scientific"), and willing to assume ultimate responsibility for what he wrote. In short, Howells sought to professionalize the critic's job; he was motivated partly by a desire to assert himself and to legitimize his own vocation as a professional critic. But he was also motivated, as Amy Kaplan and others have shown, by a wariness of the mass media growing exponentially all around him. In contrast to a media market that seemed increasingly unscrupulous and devoid of any sense of professional rigor, Howells sought to define and control the critic's function so as to keep it from devaluing itself beyond rescue. It is perhaps sobering to realize that, in many ways, American society still asks the questions Howells asked over one hundred years ago: what are the standards of our media culture, and who is qualified to critique it?

A Diviner Air

Henry James certainly felt qualified to critique media culture, and he felt equally free to critique the opinions of his friends on the question. The topic of Howells was no exception. James regularly complained of Howells's limitations concerning matters of art and criticism. In an 1884 letter to Grace Norton, for example, he stated that Howells's "simplicity of mind—in artistic and literary questions—seems to me . . . inexpressible" (*JL* 3:33). Matters did not necessarily improve, in James's opinion, with the advent of the "Editor's Study." In an 1888 letter concerning the column, James admonished Howells:

> It seems to me that on occasions you mix things up that don't go together, sometimes make mistakes of proportion, & in general incline to insist more upon the restrictions & limitations, the *a priori* formulas & interdictions, of our common art, than upon that priceless freedom which is to me *the* thing that makes it worth practicing. . . . I am struck with your energy, ingenuity & courage, & your delightful interest in the charming questions. I don't care how much you dispute about them if you will only remember that a grain of example is worth a ton of precept & that with the imbecillity [*sic*] of babyish critics the serious writer need absolutely not concern himself. I am surprised sometimes, at the things you notice & seem to care about. One should move in a diviner air. (*LFL,* 266; *JL* 3:209–10)

If James privately found fault with a great number of Howells's opinions in the Study, he rarely responded publicly. One exception may be in the opening paragraph of James's most important essay on Maupassant. The essay, which appeared in the March 1888 issue of the *Fortnightly Review* (and was later included in *Partial Portraits*), was probably written around the same time as James's aforementioned letter to Howells, and it certainly expresses a similar sentiment: "The first artists, in any line, are doubtless not those whose general ideas about their art are most often on their lips—those who most abound in precept, apology, and formula and can best tell us the reasons and the philosophy of things. We know the first usually by their energetic practice, the constancy with which they apply their principles, and the serenity with which they leave us to hunt for their secret in the illustration, the concrete example." James cautions a writer against wandering into "the dim wilderness of theory. The doctrine is apt to be so much less inspired than the work, the work is often so much more intelligent than the doctrine" (*LC* 2:521). This ambivalence toward aesthetic and critical dictums is responsible for much of the paradoxical tension that propels "The Art of Fiction." But its roots go back even further; as we have seen in Chapter 1 of this study, James learned from his earliest critical mentors—Arnold, Schérer, and Sainte-Beuve—a "horror of dogma," and he proudly cherished it throughout much of his career.

James's condescending dismissal of Howells's work as a critic is, characteristically, bluntly expressed in his personal correspondence. In an 1887 letter to his brother William, he complains:

> [I] deplore the figure that Howells makes every month in his critical department of *Harper*. He seems to me as little as possible of a critic and exposes himself so that I wish he would "quit," and content himself with writing the novel as he thinks it should be and not talking about it: he does the one so much better than the other. He talks from too small a point of view and his examples (barring the bore he makes of Tolstoi) are smaller still. There is, it seems to me, far too much talk around and about the novel in proportion to what is done. Any *genre* is good which has life—which of course is perfectly consistent with the fact that there are some that find it mighty hard to have it and others that one very much prefers to some. (*JL* 3:204)

For most of his career as a critic, James followed his own advice. As a writer of fiction, he preferred to write novels on his own terms and let them, as it were, speak for themselves. As a critic, he preferred to embed his aesthetic and critical arguments within the context of a book review or an overview of a given author. In short, and befitting a novelist who chose to dramatize or show rather than to tell, he preferred examples over dictums. Nearly all of James's important work as a critic prior to the Prefaces takes the form of "case studies," and his points are therefore always contextual.

The Dummies of Criticism

"The Science of Criticism" is a noteworthy exception. In 1891, the *New Review* published a symposium on "The Science of Criticism" featuring contributions from James, Andrew Lang, and Edmund Gosse. In the broadest context, James's "The Science of Criticism" is part of a larger, ongoing conversation on the subject of fiction and literary studies in the late nineteenth century.[12] Howells, as a major figure in that discussion and as one of James's closest confidantes, would naturally be part of James's audience. But James may well have had Howells specifically in mind while writing "The Science of Criticism"; at times, the essay reads like a rejoinder to Howells.

James begins by noting the sheer volume of criticism in the market: "it

12. Also in 1891, the *New Review* published a symposium on "The Science of Fiction," which included essays by Walter Besant, Paul Bourget, and Thomas Hardy. Mark Spilka positions both symposia as part of an ongoing argument that began in 1882 with Howells's "Henry James, Jr." and continued with Walter Besant's and James's respective essays on "The Art of Fiction," among other contributions ("Henry James and Walter Besant," 101).

flows through the periodical press like a river that has burst its dikes. The quantity of it is prodigious." Despite such abundance, James notes, most criticism is wanting in "what one may call literary conduct"—serious, sustained consideration of an author's work. The reason, James explains, is simple: "conditions of contemporary journalism . . . have engendered the practice of 'reviewing'—a practice that in general has nothing in common with the art of criticism. Periodical literature is a huge, open mouth which has to be fed—a vessel of immense capacity which has to be filled." Shifting metaphors, James likens the periodical press to "a regular train which starts at an advertised hour, but which is free to start only if every seat be occupied." In a sharply worded passage reminiscent of his earliest reviews, James satirizes the casual reviewer as a "stuffed mannikin" who merely takes up space on the train so that it can begin its otherwise pointless journey. Returning to the aquatic metaphor with which he began the essay, James notes that "the blocks of *remplissage* are the dummies of criticism—the recurrent, regulated breakers in the tide of talk. They have a reason for being," James snidely notes, "and the situation is simpler when we perceive it" (*LC* 1:95).

James's critique is focused, first, on the nature of the market itself. Criticism is "a commodity" by means of which

> ladies and gentlemen may turn an honest penny by the free expenditure of ink. It gives us a glimpse of the high figure presumably reached by all the honest pennies accumulated in the cause, and throws us quite into a glow over the march of civilization and the way we have organized our conveniences. From this point of view it might indeed go far towards making us enthusiastic about our age. What is more calculated to inspire us with a just complacency than the sight of a new and flourishing industry, a fine economy of production? The great business of reviewing has, in its roaring routine, many of the signs of blooming health, many of the features which beguile one into rendering an involuntary homage to successful enterprise. (*LC* 1:95–96)

Sarcasm aside, James is addressing a vital question. As numerous scholars have noted, the volume of print media in the United States expanded at tremendous rates during the Gilded Age, a fact that presented professional, literary authors like Howells and James with certain challenges. Simply stated, James and Howells—as both creative writers and literary critics—were in competition with the ever-growing masses of reviewers and critics, many of whom were "unschooled": they had neither the aristocratic upbringing and transcultural education of Henry James, nor the thorough-if-not-traditional literary education of the autodidact William Dean Howells. Anyone, it seemed, could offer commentary on any book. Indeed, as James noted, book reviewing was a thriving industry in 1891. The question for professional, literary-minded authors and critics was how best to adapt to the new and changing market.

Howells, as we have seen, worked the situation to his advantage splendidly, capitalizing on the same market demands that nominally threatened him. His lucrative Harper's contract is ample evidence of this fact. "More profoundly than James," notes Michael Anesko, "Howells understood and accepted literature as a social institution; consequently he was more willing to establish himself within a relatively public sphere of literary production and to abide by the normative values it promulgated" (*LFL*, 187). Scholars have debated the extent to which such "normative values" helped or hindered Howells's work.[13] Regardless, Howells always spoke and wrote from his "basis," an economic footing firmly rooted in the marketplace and its demands, to which he willingly assented.

James was neither as market-savvy as Howells nor as keen to establish himself with such a "basis." Ever the free agent and loner in both his personal and professional lives, James would, relatively speaking, resist the market and its demands. Always, he preferred that the market meet him on his own terms—though at times, perhaps, he met it halfway. In an 1889 letter to Howells, for example, he described *The Turn of the Screw* as "an unblushing pot-boiler of a 'ghost-story'" calculated, James suggests, to appeal to the tastes of its *Collier's Weekly* readership (*LFL*, 306). Such comments may strike one as disingenuous, but as any reader of his correspondence can testify, James was not above such strategizing. As numerous scholars have demonstrated, he undertook many literary enterprises—including his failed bid as a dramatist, and the New York Edition—with an eye sharply focused on the market.[14] Generally speaking, however, James loathed the popular press and, at least in part, he wrote his unique, dense prose in proud defiance of it.

The opening paragraph of "The Science of Criticism" can thus be read as a rather cynical assessment of the market for criticism in 1891. The suggestion that popular book reviews and literary criticism ought to be rigorously distinguished was by no means new; Howells had argued the case in his

---

13. See Michael Davitt Bell, *The Problem of American Realism: Studies in the Cultural History of a Literary Idea*; Kaplan, *Social Construction*; and Shi, *Facing Facts*. For a consideration of the impact of normative cultural and social codes on Howells's psyche and creative work, see Crowley, *Black Heart's Truth*.

14. See Anesko, *"Friction with the Market"*; Leon Edel, *Henry James: A Life*; Marcia Jacobson, *Henry James and the Mass Market*; McWhirter, *Henry James's New York Edition*; and Richard Salmon, *Henry James and the Culture of Publicity*.

1866 essay "Literary Criticism," in which he noted that the function of criticism

> is entirely distinct from the mere trade-puff of the publisher, the financial comments of the advertiser, or the bought-and-sold-eulogium of an ignorant, careless, or mercenary journalist. It is equally removed from the wholesale and baseless attacks of some rival publication house, or from the censure which is inspired by political, personal, or religious hatred. So commonly, however, especially in America, is this high function of literary criticism degraded to base uses that we can hardly wonder at the popular incredulity as to its aim and scope. The dignified title of criticism applied to the "book notices" and "literary reviews" of ordinary American periodical literature is simply a misnomer. . . . Criticism is often perverted from being a stern and responsible duty to serve some private feeling or end, to act as a cloak for some entirely alien purpose. (*SLC* 1:60–61)

Howells went on to define "honest criticism" in the terms discussed earlier in this study; he then modified his argument over the course of the "Editor's Study," as noted above. In distinguishing critic from reviewer, then, James is playing an old tune. But that fact itself is significant, for it suggests that in the twenty-five years since Howells wrote "Literary Criticism," the market, or perhaps its audience, had yet to distinguish serious criticism from its less rigorous cousin, the mass-market book review. Or perhaps it merely suggests that the anxieties of the "serious" authors of the day had grown along with—indeed because of—the mass market itself.

The rhetorical questions behind James's cynicism in the first paragraph of "The Science of Criticism" are these: Is there anything the matter with this new and "flourishing industry"? Why not, in good cheer, simply accept the "successful enterprise"? James answers himself in the second paragraph by noting that "certain captious persons are to be met who are not carried away by the spectacle." Rather than shedding light on its subject, the mass-market review seems to do the opposite:

> The vulgarity, the crudity, the stupidity which this cherished combination of the off-hand review and of our wonderful system of publicity have put into circulation on so vast a scale may be represented, in such a mood, as an unprecedented invention for darkening counsel. The bewildered spirit may ask itself, without speedy answer, What is the function in the life of man of such a periodicity of platitude and irrelevance? Such a spirit will wonder how the life of man survives it and, above all, what is much more important, how literature resists it; whether, indeed, literature does resist it and is not speedily going down beneath it. (*LC* 1:96)

James proceeds to catalog "The signs of this catastrophe," which include "the failure of distinction, the failure of style, the failure of knowledge, the failure of thought." In short, we must understand

> that we are paying a tremendous price for the diffusion of penmanship and opportunity; that the multiplication of endowments for chatter may be as fatal as an infectious disease; that literature lives essentially, in the sacred depths of its being, upon example, upon perfection wrought; that, like other sensitive organisms, it is highly susceptible of demoralization, and that nothing is better calculated than irresponsible pedagogy to make it close its ears and lips. To be puerile and untutored about it is to deprive it of air and light, and the consequence of its keeping bad company is that it loses all heart. We may, of course, continue to talk about it long after it has bored itself to death, and there is every appearance that this is mainly the way in which our descendants will hear of it. They will, however, acquiesce in its extinction. (*LC* 1:96–97)

The relationship between critic (or reviewer) and artist is, in James's view, a crucial dynamic on which the very health of literature exists. This paradigm, in which both artist and critic participate to ensure the larger health of the "sensitive organism" that is art, stands in stark contrast to the reductive taxonomy proposed by Howells in the Study. Howells, who saw the critic at best as a middleman between an author and her audience, refused to grant the critic so much agency and control. Clearly, James cannot agree; the "parasite" model proposed by Howells—which sought to ensure the artist's freedom at the expense of the critic's—surely struck James as yet another example of Howells "[insisting] more upon the restrictions & limitations, the *a priori* formulas & interdictions," rather than allowing for openness and freedom.

James counters with a new model for the literary critic. He begins with the French, who exhibit a "dignity of criticism." James praises the French for their taste and their sense of what *not* to review: "The art [of criticism in France] is felt to be one of the most difficult, the most delicate, the most occasional; and the material on which it is exercised is subject to selection, to restriction. That is, whether or no the French are always right as to what they do notice, they strike me as infallible as to what they don't. They publish hundreds of books which are never noticed at all." When the French critic does weigh in, he "goes further than with us. [He] handles the subject in general with finer finger-tips." In contrast, "The bluntness of ours, as tactile implements addressed to an exquisite process, is still sometimes surprising, even after frequent exhibition. We blunder in and out of the affair as if it were a railway station—the easiest and most public of the arts" (*LC* 1:97). James has constructed a binary opposition to emphasize his point; in contrast to the "rough-and-ready reviewing" of America, James points to the mannered French style, which if it attends to far fewer books than the American, notes only the worthiest ones. James here emphasizes culture and taste, privileging the European over the American—the same strategy employed in both his controversial study *Hawthorne* and "The Art of Fiction."

In the most frequently cited passage of "The Science of Criticism," James begins by redefining the critic in elitist terms not dissimilar to Howells's 1866 criteria.[15] Criticism "is in reality the most complicated and the most particular" of the arts. "The critical sense is so far from frequent that it is absolutely rare," James opines, "and the possession of the cluster of qualities that minister to it is one of the highest distinctions. It is a gift inestimably precious and beautiful." But James differs markedly from Howells in that he emphasizes the delicate relationship between art and criticism: "not only do I not question in literature the high utility of criticism, but I should be tempted to say that the part it plays may be the supremely beneficent one when it proceeds from deep sources, from the efficient combination of experience and perception. In this light one sees the critic as the real helper of the artist, a torch-bearing outrider, the interpreter, the brother." James replaces Howells's reductive "parasite" taxonomy with a fraternal paradigm that, if it still positions the critic as subservient to the artist, nevertheless grants the critic increased agency.[16] That the critic is subservient is clear as James depicts the critic in terms sartorial: "When one thinks of the outfit required for free work in this spirit, one is ready to pay almost any homage to the intelligence that has put it on; and when one considers the noble figure completely equipped—armed *cap-à-pie* in curiosity and sympathy—one falls in love with the apparition. It certainly presents a knight who has knelt through his long vigil and who has the piety of his office. For there is something sacrificial in his function, inasmuch as he offers himself as a general touchstone." James's quasi-feudalistic rhetoric further emphasizes the critic's subservience to the artist, but it makes a kind of sense, perhaps, when one understands what James meant by a critic "sacrificing" himself to his cause. James refers to the hierarchy he briefly sketched in "The Art of Fiction," and which he clarifies in "The Science of Criticism." The critic must meet the artist on the artist's terms; the critic must grant the author her donnée before proceeding to comment. If a reader cannot "sacrifice" his agency to

15. That is, criticism as a product of "an educated and refined literary taste" and "an accomplished mind" (*SLC* 1:61).

16. James's fraternal paradigm updates his own, earlier notion that critics were "opposed" to authors (*LC* 2:803–4).

the artist, James had noted in 1884, the proper response was dignified, indifferent silence. So long as the critic is willing to serve the author first, the
critic shall be granted wide powers, but first the critic must submit, "To lend
himself, to project himself and steep himself, to feel and feel till he understands, and to understand so well that he can say, to have perception at the
pitch of passion and expression as embracing as the air, to be infinitely curious and incorrigibly patient, and yet plastic and inflammable and deter-
minable, stooping to conquer and serving to direct—these are fine chances
for an active mind, chances to add the idea of independent beauty to the
conception of success." In James's paradigm, the critic does have the chance
to present "the idea of independent beauty" in his work, but it will be part
of a larger "conception of success" that first depends on the critic's having
fully given himself over—steeped himself—in the artist's production. Only
then is the critic afforded powers on par with those of the artist: "Just in
proportion as he is sentient and restless, just in proportion as he reacts and
reciprocates and penetrates, is the critic a valuable instrument; for in literature assuredly criticism *is* the critic, just as art is the artist; it being assuredly
the artist who invented art and the critic who invented criticism, and not the
other way round." James's criteria are telling: the critic must be "sentient
and restless." He must react, reciprocate, and penetrate. Criticism is a dynamic endeavor in dialogue with art; in this regard, James's paradigm is in
distinct opposition to that of Howells, who argued that the critic's sole office is "to ascertain facts and traits of literature, not to invent or denounce
them; to discover principles, not to establish them; to report, not to create."
Howells's critic, at best, served as a broker between the artist and her public. Clearly, for James, criticism can also be as personal, sensitive, and energetic as fiction itself—but only in the hands of the very few. As in art, in
criticism "the best kind, the only kind worth speaking of, is the kind that
springs from the liveliest experience" (*LC* 1:97–99).

In the conclusion to "The Science of Criticism," James returns to the
quasi-feudalistic imagery in order to reemphasize the hierarchy of artist and
critic. The critic "lives *in* the house" of the artist, "ranging through its innumerable chambers. . . . His life, at this rate, is heroic, for it is immensely
vicarious. He has to understand for others, to answer for them; he is always
under arms. He knows that the whole honor of the matter, for him, besides
the success in his own eyes, depends upon his being indefatigably supple,
and that is a formidable order." James carefully notes that this vicarious subservience is not "a conscious grind" but rather a joy fueled by

the enthusiasm of curiosity. Any vocation has its hours of intensity that is so
closely connected with life. That of the critic, in literature, is connected

doubly, for he deals with life at second-hand as well as at first; that is, he deals with the experience of others, which he resolves into his own, and not of those invented and selected others with whom the novelist makes comfortable terms, but with the uncompromising swarm of authors, the clamorous children of history. He has to make them as vivid and free as the novelist makes *his* puppets, and yet he has, as the phrase is, to take them as they come. (*LC* 1:99)[17]

James wants the critic both to be subservient to the artist and to be afforded equal agency. The critic must take the artist's work as a given, or a starting point, and an articulation or interpretation of that artist's work must always be the critic's chief goal. The critic's freedom is situated in the actual practice of assessing an author's work, and it is in the *practice* of criticism that James affords the critic the freedom to feel and to say: to offer, as James wrote elsewhere, a direct and personal vision. Criticism is thus reconfigured in the rhetoric of art, though James can never wholly free criticism from its fraternal and, perhaps, feudalistic dependence on art.

James emphasizes this point in the final sentence of the essay, in which he returns to one of his most frequently used analogies, that of the painter and his subject: "We must be easy with him [the critic] if the picture, even when the aim has really been to penetrate, is sometimes confused, for there are baffling and there are thankless subjects; and we make everything up to him by the peculiar purity of our esteem when the portrait is really, like the happy portraits of the other art, a text preserved by translation" (*LC* 1:99). James's final image—that of an artist rendering his subject—is curious; the painter-critic's task, in this instance, is to "translate" the "text" for his audience. If one combines the painterly analogy presented in "The Art of Fiction"—the painting as text simultaneously subjective and objective—with the final image presented in "The Science of Criticism," one understands, perhaps, that the Jamesian critic's job is to translate the translation: to offer an interpretation that is at once true to its subject (already a translated text, referencing an objective reality in a subjective, organic form) and a personal expression of the critic. The critical process is analogous to the artistic process, perhaps even mimetic of it, but always at one remove. The artist has the

17. James reiterates this point concerning the critic's "enthusiasm of curiosity" in his 1891 introduction to Rudyard Kipling's *Mine Own People*. The ideal critic should, James argues, have "*à priori,* no rule for a literary production but that it shall have genuine life. Such a critic (he gets much more out of his opportunities, I think, than the other sort,) likes a writer exactly in proportion as he is a challenge, an appeal to interpretation, intelligence, ingenuity, to what is elastic in the critical mind—in proportion indeed as he may be a negation of things familiar and taken for granted. He feels in this case how much more play and sensation there is for himself." James's mention of "the other sort" is a reference to those critics who judge, a priori, "what a writer or a book 'ought,' in the Ruskinian sense, to be" (*LC* 1:1123).

freedom of the entire world, has all his own particular thoughts and sensibilities to draw from. The critic can only respond to the artist's text; it is, by definition, a limited playing field. But within that enclosed domain, James argues, the sensibilities that serve an artist can serve the critic. James's paradigm, like Howells's, presents a hierarchy in which the artist's work is primary. But where Howells constrained the critic and turned him into a glorified list maker, James acknowledges—even demands—that a critic can be as sensitive and insightful, as original and emotive as the artist, so long as that critic is in service to the artist's work.[18]

In the broadest of contexts, James, in "The Science of Criticism," is once again attempting to construct an audience and a market for his own work both as a writer of fiction and as a writer of criticism. As a writer of fiction, he had encountered significant resistance and, more often, indifference. As Howells notes in "Henry James, Jr.," James was difficult to read from the very start, and his readers "had to 'learn to like'" his work; "If we take him at all we must take him on his own ground," Howells instructed, "for clearly he will not come to ours" (*SLC* 1:318–19). James, in arguing for a more sensitive and thoughtful criticism, one in which the critic must be thoroughly steeped in the artist's text, is pleading for critics to meet him on his own ground as a fiction writer. His own fiction is rare and select; he demands a rare and select critic to understand it.

As a critic, James, like Howells, offers himself as a model. His own work as a critic was an attempt to enact the very principles articulated in "The Science of Criticism." In this regard, the essay is a plea for attention and an audience. At its root, James is educating his audience how to read both his fiction and his critical work. His carefully selected criteria for the critic are simultaneously a call to arms for his fellow critics (one imagines James whispering over one's shoulder, "Read in this manner, as I do") and a request that his own work as a critic be valued for enacting these same criteria. "The Science of Criticism" is a crucial essay in the development of James's critical aesthetic, for it reflects the maturation of his early critical practice—as adapted from his self-appointed mentors, Arnold, Sainte-Beuve, and Schérer—and prefigures the complex, self-referential criticism he would offer in the Prefaces.

18. James would slightly revise his position in an 1894 essay on George Du Maurier, in which he distinguishes between the older and newer generations of critics. "The critics of the ancient type" are "those who take their stand on the laws and the suitabilities." In contrast, the new generation of critics "are people who don't enjoy enough till they know *why* they enjoy, and critics so oddly constituted that their sensation amuses them still more even than the work that produces that sensation." These critics are "often reviled for being 'subjective' " (*LC* 1:871). In this slightly amended conception of the critic's role, a reader's subjective "sensation" in reading a text is assigned even greater value than in "The Science of Criticism."

Conclusion

At the height of their powers as both fiction writers and critics in the late 1880s and early 1890s, both Howells and James entered into the "Realism War" with strong opinions concerning the role of the literary critic in the developing mass-media marketplace, a market that consumed both fiction and commentary as quickly as they could be produced. Each author noted the alarming growth of the industry of criticism, and each reacted by distinguishing the literary critic from the mass-media "book reviewer." Each presented his own particular conception of the critic in an effort to promote his own particular brand of literary criticism. And, for each, the critic was a member of the elite.

In the "Editor's Study," Howells clung to his vision of the genteel aristocrat, the learned scholar who wrote for a mass-media public in need of edification. Following Perry and Posnett, Howells developed his conception of the "scientific critic" who read objectively but with courtesy and tact; the critic must be humble and adhere to what Edwin Cady has called a "decorum of taxonomy" in which the critic recognizes and respects his place in the scheme of things. Howells firmly believed that "The critic exists only because the author first existed." The critic's sole office is "to ascertain facts and traits of literature, not to invent or denounce them; to discover principles, not to establish them; to report, not to create" (*SLC* 2:54–55).

Howells so restricted the critic's office that even he was prompted to ask whether or not criticism played any useful function. In essence, he had backed himself into a corner. In seeking to preserve the avant-garde artist's freedom, he had restricted the critic nearly to the point of paralysis. In the final instance, he could grant the critic a useful role only "in the interest of the reading public" (*SLC* 2:149); he argued that if criticism dropped its mask of anonymity and became a personal endeavor, more critics would follow the professional model of the "scientific critic." But his paradigm remained restrictive and problematic.

James, as both a critic and a writer of fiction, always preferred an example to a treatise. Accordingly, his theories of critical practice were enacted in his reviews. "The Science of Criticism" is a rare exception. While essentially agreeing to the hierarchy implied in his own essay "The Art of Fiction" and further codified by Howells in the Study, James reconfigures the critic as an artist in his own right; good criticism is predicated on thought, feeling, and personal experience—the criteria James demands from the artist in "The Art of Fiction." In "The Science of Criticism," James argues that the critic's job, while "immensely vicarious," is nevertheless as rigorous and demanding as the artist's job—and its most excellent practitioners are equally rare.

James envisions a kind of "limited freedom" for a critic: the freedom to feel and to say, but only so long as the critic's aim and motive are the elucidation of an artist's text. James's paradoxical stance affords the critic freedom, but not at the expense of the artist, who must always remain primary. James saw art and criticism as dynamically related: art was a sensitive organism and criticism could help or hinder it—even drive it to extinction. Art needed inspiration and support, it needed a learned audience. In "The Science of Criticism," James presented a paradigm promoting the health and development of both art and criticism.

In their writings on the topic of the literary critic, both Howells and James responded to a mass-media marketplace that challenged their status as professional authors. At the broadest of levels, each sought to create an audience for his own work, to train an army of critics to read his fiction on its own terms, and to appreciate his work as a literary critic. By distancing themselves from the "popular book reviewer" they positioned themselves as examples of the finest model available: the learned, sensitive, thoughtful critic through whom the humble reader could learn to appreciate a new brand of prose.

5. "The Honest Daylight about Us"

Social, Ethical, and Moral Concerns in the Criticism
of Howells and James, 1886–1895

William Dean Howells was a man of startling contrasts. In September 1886, a mere nine months into the "Editor's Study," he blithely celebrated "the large, cheerful average" of Americans and invited his fellow novelists to focus on "the more smiling aspects of life, which are the more American" (*SLC* 2:35–36). Some five years later, a very different Howells lamented an American society in which "the toiler is socially nothing" and "the condition of ninety-nine workmen out of every hundred" is "hopeless" (*SLC* 2:193). Howells resigned the Study shortly thereafter, discouraged and weary from his self-imposed campaign to promote realism.

What happened in the five years between those two columns—one very near the beginning of the Study, and one very near its completion—was the kind of radical awakening one typically associates with the young or the ungrounded. Howells was neither: in his early fifties, he was a celebrated author and editor. He moved among the top echelons of society, the friend of poets and presidents, confidante to both Mark Twain and Henry James. In possession of the most lucrative publishing contract ever offered to an American writer, he enjoyed the kind of security and economic well-being most authors—even by today's standards—could only dream about.

Yet Howells was restless and alert. During his tenure in the Study, he was greatly concerned by the changing social and ethical questions of the day and their relation to literature. Generally speaking, one can chart his development from naive optimism and good cheer (the "more smiling aspects of life") toward a less optimistic, more ambiguous, and finally more contentious social vision. He was affected both by the literature he read and by the cultural and historical events of his time. For instance, Tolstoy's Christian ethics became a major influence during this period, as did the Haymarket Riot and its aftermath. Howells focused on a socially oriented morality, arguing for a didactic fiction that would at once reflect the "true" nature of society and seek to influence it for the common good. He was rarely more impassioned, intense, and exciting than when he addressed these questions.

In Howells's critical writings from this period, the questions of social and ethical concerns essentially centered around two areas: first, the question of propriety, or the sense of social mores and taste in art; for Howells questions of literary standards and taste were irrevocably questions of social ethics. Second, the question of audience and the artist's relation to the literary market. Perhaps not surprisingly, these two concerns informed one another. As this chapter will demonstrate, Howells's arguments for propriety in fiction are simultaneously assessments of the working author in a business marketplace.

In contrast, Henry James became increasingly fascinated with questions of subjectivity and personal artistic practice. Morality in literature remained a vital question for him, but only as it related to an individual artist's ability to present a unique aesthetic vision. Indeed, for James, morality in literature became a measure of the individual artist's ability to convey that unique vision.

The More Smiling Aspects of Life

If ever there was a quote that suffered from being taken out of context, it is Howells's "smiling aspects of life" passage. Although the scholarly hubbub surrounding this comment has quieted with time, it behooves any serious student of Howells's criticism to understand the legacy of this quote and its origins, which are multiple and complex. Howells wrote, revised, and published the comment on three separate occasions and, as we shall see, in three very different contexts: the quote first appeared in the September 1886 "Editor's Study" column; Howells substantially revised and recontextualized it in the first edition of *Criticism and Fiction* (1891); and he contextualized it a third time in the Library Edition of *Criticism and Fiction* (1910).[1] The

---

1. *Criticism and Fiction* (1891) is an edited selection of columns from the first five years of the "Editor's Study" (January 1886–October 1890). The question of how accurately *Criticism and Fiction* reflects Howells's critical thought from the period has long been a contentious question. On the one hand, Kirk and Kirk, in their edited volume *Criticism and*

scholar's first question is to understand each of the three contexts on its own terms. Only then can one argue for a particular text and interpret it.

Howells begins the September 1886 Study praising Dostoyevsky's *Crime and Punishment* and suggesting that, together with Turgenev and Tolstoy, Dostoyevsky confirms "the supremacy of the Russians in modern fiction." In the second part of that Study column, Howells offers a brief biographical sketch of Dostoyevsky and suggests that the Russian was capable of writing his "lurid chapter of human life" because he knew firsthand the difficulties of which he wrote. Howells turns to American literature in part 3, but his argument depends entirely on the context established in parts 1 and 2. Dostoyevsky's difficult life partially explains the nature of *Crime and Punishment;* the novel "was the natural expression of such a life and such conditions," and therefore "it is to be praised only in its place, and its message is to be received with allowances by readers exterior to the social and political circumstances in which it was conceived." An American, Howells argues, simply could not write in such a manner:

> It used to be one of the disadvantages of the practice of romance in America, which Hawthorne more or less whimsically lamented, that there were so few shadows and inequalities in our broad level of prosperity; and it is one of the reflections suggested by Dostoïevsky's book that whoever stuck a note so profoundly tragic in American fiction would do a false and mistaken thing. . . . Whatever their deserts, very few American novelists have been led out to be shot, or finally exiled to the rigors of a winter at Duluth; one might make [nineteenth-century, German-born anarchist] Herr Most the hero of a labor-question romance with perfect impunity; and in a land where journeymen carpenters and plumbers strike for four dollars a day the sum of hunger and cold is certainly very small, and the wrong from class to class is almost inappreciable. We invite our novelists, therefore, to concern themselves with the more smiling aspects of life, which are the more American, and to seek the universal in the individual

---

Fiction and Other Essays, argue that "What realism meant to [Howells] is fully expressed in *Criticism and Fiction*" (3). On the other hand, Everett Carter and Edwin Cady both argue that *Criticism and Fiction* was hastily prepared and poorly edited, and that the original columns of the Study best reflect Howells's critical thought from the period. In the final instance, argues Cady, "one cannot accept" the "deadly damage done to Howells's thought and prose" in *Criticism and Fiction* (*W. D. Howells as Critic,* 75). More recently, Donald Pizer has argued that *Criticism and Fiction* is an accurate—if somewhat narrow—reflection of Howells's critical thought. Pizer too, however, suggests that the original columns of the Study constitute the preferred text, as they best demonstrate the breadth of Howells's critical concerns during the period. (I concur with Pizer on this question.) For more on this question, see Cady, *W. D. Howells as Critic,* 74–76; Carter, *Howells and the Age of Realism,* 185–90; Kirk and Kirk, *Criticism and Fiction and Other Essays,* 3–8; and Pizer, introduction, *SLC* 2:xviii–xix.

rather than the social interests. It is worth while, even at the risk of being called commonplace, to be true to our well-to-do actualities; the very passions themselves seem to be softened and modified by conditions which cannot be said to wrong any one, to cramp endeavor, or to cross lawful desire. (*SLC* 2:32–36)

Clearly, the "invitation" to the American novelist is issued on behalf of American society in general (not solely Howells). In the broadest of senses, Howells is voicing a long-established tenet of Gilded Age realism: that the novelist ought to respond to the perceived conditions of his society (in this case, "our well-to-do actualities"). Howells's comments on American life in this passage may be critiqued—and shall be, below—but one must first understand the relative context in which he offered the observation.

In the 1891 edition of *Criticism and Fiction,* the "smiling aspects of life" comment is offered not in the context of Dostoyevsky, but in the context of a larger discussion concerning the differences between the English and the American novel (which, interestingly, follows a discussion of Henry James in the preceding section). Section 21 of *Criticism and Fiction* begins with a lengthy quotation from English critic Eilian Hughes, who concedes the current dominance of American fiction while noting that "The strength of the American novel is in its optimistic faith."[2] Howells concurs, praising the "superior freshness and authenticity" of the American novel while maligning the "love of the passionate and the heroic" in the English novel, which Howells finds "crude and unwholesome." It is the question of the realist novel versus the sentimental romance, a frequent topic of debate in the Study. Howells proceeds to explain why the American novel, in contrast to the English, promotes the "optimistic faith" noted by Hughes. It is a question of relative cultural values: "the American who chooses to enjoy his birthright to the full, lives in a world wholly different from the Englishman's, and speaks (too often through his nose) another language: he breathes a rarefied and nimble air full of shining possibilities and radiant promises which the fog-and-soot-clogged lungs of those less-favored islanders struggle in vain to fill themselves with" (*SLC* 2:334–35). American literature, Howells argues, "is all alive with the keenest interest for those who enjoy the study of individual traits and general conditions as they make themselves known to the American experience." This explains American optimism: "Our novelists, therefore, concern themselves with the more smiling aspects of life, which are the more American, and seek the universal in the individual rather than the social interests. It is worth while, even at the risk of being called

---

2. Hughes, quoted in *SLC* 2:334.

commonplace, to be true to our well-to-do actualities; the very passions themselves seem to be softened and modified by conditions *which formerly at least* could not be said to wrong any one, to cramp endeavor, or to cross lawful desire" (*SLC* 2:335–36; emphasis mine).

Howells has made two noteworthy changes to the passage; first, he has removed the "invitation" phrase, thereby clarifying his point—novelists respond to perceived social conditions—in language less open to misinterpretation. (Some readers mistakenly assume that Howells employs the "royal" we in the 1886 column, as if he were personally extending the invitation.) Howells makes an assessment concerning American authors in relation to English authors, and, as had James seven years earlier in "The Art of Fiction," he cleverly does so under the guise of explaining a point first introduced by an English critic.[3] Second, Howells, with the addition of the phrase "formerly at least," acknowledges that American life is less fair and just than he had naively proclaimed in 1886. Clearly, the context and meaning of the revised statement differs substantially from the original column in the Study.

The context for the 1910 Library Edition of *Criticism and Fiction* is different again. In section 20 of that volume, Howells discusses the varieties of the romance novel: Hawthorne, "the great master of the romance," and his incomparable *Scarlet Letter* and *Blithedale Romance,* which Howells gently suggests might be "novels rather than romances": the "fantastic romance," à la *Frankenstein;* and the "historical romance," which, Howells quips, "might be reopened with advantage to readers and writers who cannot bear to be brought face to face with human nature, but require the haze of distance or a far perspective, in which all the disagreeable details shall be lost. There is no good reason why these harmless people should not be amused, or their little preferences indulged." Long after the "Realism War" had been fought and, by his own admission, lost, Howells softens his stance on the issue.[4] For his part, however, he insists (as he did in the May 1886 Study from which much of this passage is taken) that the romance "belongs to the decorative arts, and though it has a high place among them, it cannot be ranked with the works of imagination."[5]

Employing only the slimmest of transitions, section 21 abruptly changes

3. Howells's rhetorical strategy is actually quite sharp; by placing the authority of the observation not on his shoulders but on Hughes's, he positions himself less controversially as someone seeking to clarify and explain the comments of another. The strategy is notable for a subtlety that was absent in Howells's controversial "Henry James, Jr." and perhaps one that he learned from James's "The Art of Fiction."

4. In a 1912 reminiscence, Howells admitted having lost the "Realism War": "my long fight had been a losing fight; I perceive now that the monstrous rag-baby of romanticism is as firmly in the saddle as it was before the joust began, and that it always will be, as long as the children of men are childish" (quoted in Cady, *W. D. Howells as Critic,* 214–15).

5. Howells, *My Literary Passions and Criticism and Fiction,* 250–51.

focus, jumping immediately to the "smiling aspects" passage. The effect is jarring for the reader. Without the benefit of the lengthy contexts established in the previous versions of the passage, the assessment—rendered in language identical to the 1891 edition—seems hapless, offhand, and inconsequential. In the 1910 edition of *Criticism and Fiction,* the assessment lacks the weight and density of context, thus robbing the statement of whatever credence it had in its first two versions.[6]

Few passages from the criticism of William Dean Howells have been more frequently cited than this one. And few passages have elicited a wider range of responses. Beginning with Van Wyck Brooks in *The Ordeal of Mark Twain,* many critics have read the passage as the quintessential example of the genteel, timid, blithe Howells.[7] Others, led by Edwin H. Cady, have argued that the passage has been read out of context and that Howells's reputation as a critic has been unfairly maligned.[8] The history of critical response to the passage is complicated precisely because Howells presented three different versions to the reading public. And while the wording of the passage itself varies only slightly from version to version, the context within which the passage is offered differs widely.

Critics on both sides of the "smiling aspects" issue have been, perhaps, overinsistent in their zeal to malign or to defend Howells on this single point. A much more useful and interesting exercise would be to position the "smiling aspects" quote—in all of its various contexts—within the broader context of Howells's evolving social and literary tastes during the course of the Study and the years immediately following it, years during which Howells underwent fundamental personal, literary, and social changes that profoundly affected his views as a literary critic. Thus it is useful to examine Howells's social and ethical views as they relate to his literary criticism, beginning with a close analysis of the September 1886 Study that contained the "smiling aspects" passage in its first incarnation.

The Large, Cheerful Average

The September 1886 Study was Howells's ninth column in the series and thus serves as an adequate beginning when considering how his social and

---

6. For more on the editorial history of *Criticism and Fiction* and the "smiling aspects" controversy, see Carter, *Howells and the Age of Realism,* 185–90.

7. In addition to Brooks, H. L. Mencken and Sinclair Lewis were among the most outspoken critics of Howells in the 1920s and 1930s. Their influential opinions were largely responsible for the decline of Howells studies in the mid-twentieth century (when, nurtured by the New Critics and Leon Edel, James studies first bloomed). For more, see Edwin H. Cady and David L. Frazier, eds., *The War of the Critics over William Dean Howells.*

8. Scholars in this camp also include William Alexander and Everett Carter.

ethical views, as they relate to his literary criticism, evolved over the course of the Study. And it is in this light I would like to read the column: as a point of departure. Howells, as a critic, changed drastically during the years he wrote the Study in regard to his social and ethical views.

A close examination of part 3 of the September 1886 Study might pick up from the point at which Howells mentions "the more smiling aspects of life," for it is in the lines that follow the "invitation" that Howells's idealism reaches its peak:

> Sin and suffering and shame there must always be in the world, we suppose, but we believe that in this new world of ours it is mainly from one to another one, and oftener still from one to one's self. We have death too in America, and a great deal of disagreeable and painful disease, which the multiplicity of our patent medicines does not seem to cure; but this is tragedy that comes in the very nature of things, and is not peculiarly American, as the large, cheerful average of health and success and happy life is. It will not do to boast, but it is well to be true to the facts, and to see that, apart from those purely mortal troubles, the race here enjoys conditions in which most of the ills that have darkened its annals may be averted by honest work and unselfish behavior. (*SLC* 2:36)

Even when read most generously in its original context—the placidity of the average American life relative to the suffering of Dostoyevsky—this passage seems hyperbolic in its optimism, not to mention more than a little naive.

To be fair, Howells's comments probably did hold true for at least one group of Americans: the educated, white, largely feminine middle-class readership that constituted the bulk of the *Harper's Monthly* audience. And Howells was always keenly aware of that audience, frequently writing to them or for them. But even with this slender caveat in mind, the September 1886 Study reveals a blind side to Howells's conception of American society and history. Rarely, for example, did Howells seem more socially and racially naive than when he wrote, in the following paragraph, that accounts of Harriet Tubman and the Fugitive Slave Act read to him like ancient history: "We can hardly imagine such things now for the purposes of fiction; all troubles that now hurt and threaten us are as crumpled rose leaves in our couch" (*SLC* 2:36).[9]

It is perhaps for this very reason, because of this sense of middle-class insulation and detachment, that Howells points to the deeper lesson to be

9. Howells is referring specifically to Tubman's life as recounted in Sarah Bradford's *Harriet: The Moses of Her People* (1886).

learned by reading Dostoyevsky: all people, "and especially our novelists," can read him "to advantage" for he "teaches in every page patience, merciful judgment, humble helpfulness, and . . . brotherly responsibility." This is the novelist's "obligation" (*SLC* 2:36). In the brief concluding section of the September Study, Howells quotes a lengthy passage from Vernon Lee's *Baldwin* reiterating this point (novelist as shaper of social mores), and concludes with Lee's assessment that the "chief use of the novel" is "To make the shrewd and tolerant a little less shrewd and tolerant, to make the generous and austere a little more skeptical and easy-going."[10] This assessment of the novelist's "obligations"—to teach strong morals and ethics—was not new. Howells had long believed that the novelist's didactic responsibilities included educating his audience on moral and ethical matters. In 1873, for instance, he had praised Turgenev's "deep moral earnestness" and the way in which a novel like *Dimitri Roudine* taught readers "a merciful distrust of our own judgments" (*SLC* 1:207, 219). Howells's final comments, in September 1886, are a reiteration of points long held dear. And he would forever hold them dear; he would always believe strongly in the didactic responsibilities of the novelist.

While Howells's strong beliefs in this regard lent the Study a convincing tone of authority and enriched his prose with the power of conviction, these beliefs also prompted him to be at his most prescriptive and dogmatic. In the April 1887 Study, for example, he lashes out at the sentimental novel: "If a novel flatters the passions, and exalts them above the principles, it is poisonous; it may not kill, but it will certainly injure; and this test will alone exclude an entire class of fiction." Such fiction is "innutritious" and can "clog the soul with unwholesome vapors of all kinds" that will ultimately "weaken the mental fibre" of the reader. In a passage that echoes Reverend Sewell's comments in chapter 14 of *The Rise of Silas Lapham*, Howells argues against the sentimental novel and its distortions of love, sacrifice, and devotion. An author, he suggests, is all but obligated to present a truer, more accurate picture of human relations:

> no one hereafter will be able to achieve greatness who is false to humanity, either in its facts or its duties. The light of civilization has already broken even upon the novel, and no conscientious man can now set about painting an image of life without perpetual question of the verity of his work, and without feeling bound to distinguish so clearly that no reader of his may be misled, between what is right and what is wrong, what is noble and what is base, what is health and what is perdition, in the actions and the characters he portrays. (*SLC* 2:44–45)

10. Lee, quoted in *SLC* 2:37.

The "conscientious" artist will therefore willingly shoulder these ethical and didactic responsibilities. Correspondingly, critics must "demand" that authors meet these idealistic standards. The critic's first question of a book should be, "Is it true?—true to the motives, the impulses, the principles that shape the life of actual men and women? This truth, which necessarily includes the highest morality and the highest artistry—this truth given, the book *cannot* be wicked and cannot be weak; and without it all graces of style and feats of invention and cunning of construction are so many superfluities of naughtiness" (*SLC* 2:45–46).

For Howells, the campaign to promote realist fiction was simultaneously a moral and ethical campaign. Implicit in his aesthetic argument is the belief that there is an objective reality to capture and reproduce in art, a reality that includes a stable, universal moral code.[11] For Howells, the aesthetic and the moral are thereby fused. "Morality penetrates all things," he wrote in the November 1886 Study, "it is the soul of all things." Realist fiction, by means of rigorous verisimilitude, should portray only that which is "true to the motives, the impulses, the principles that shape the life of actual men and women." And the author, in capturing these truths, should depend on his conscience "to distinguish . . . clearly" between "what is right and what is wrong, what is noble and what is base, what is health and what is perdition," because these are "the principles that shape the life of actual men and women" (*SLC* 2:40, 45–46).

However radical Howells's aesthetic arguments may have been in his day, his moral and ethical assumptions were in step with the times. Everett Carter notes that Howells's sense of the "deep moral purpose" of fiction was predicated on three ideas: "that life, social life as lived in the world Howells knew, was valuable, and was permeated with morality; that its continued health depended upon the use of human reason to overcome the anarchic selfishness of human passions; [and] that an objective portrayal of human life, by art, will illustrate the superior value of social, civilized man, of human reason over animal passion and primitive ignorance." Carter concludes that Howells's fundamental belief "that social life has value . . . was an unquestioned article of faith during this period." This belief in the value of social life is the bedrock of Howellsian realism and its moral arguments. It is also the basis of a deeper social mission to use art and literary criticism as a means to educate and therefore to unite an increasingly varied audience. Howells's realism "strives to pave a common ground for diverse social classes

---

11. As Everett Carter notes, "The truth the realists were trying to tell . . . was the truth of externalities rather than internalities, truth about the way things looked and the way people acted, an outside kind of truth" (*Howells and the Age of Realism*, 122).

by extending literary representation to 'the other half' while reassuring middle-class readers that social difference can be effaced in the mirror of the commonplace," writes Amy Kaplan. "In Howells's literary criticism, realism emerges as an elaborate balancing act: it reconciles social diversity within an overarching community, assimilates disparate facts to a commonsense morality, and frames a plenitude of details within a coherent form."[12]

These passionate beliefs in the power of fiction would only strengthen as the Study grew older. What would weaken in the coming years was Howells's naive belief in "the large, cheerful average of health and success and happy life" of Americans. Two factors are of prime importance in this regard: first, the Haymarket Riot of 1886 and the hanging of the Chicago anarchists a year later, which would fundamentally redefine his conception of American society; and, second, the ethical works of Leo Tolstoy, which would prompt Howells to question deeply the values and morals of American society.[13]

Haymarket

On May 4, 1886, a small anarchist contingent called an open-air public meeting in Chicago's Haymarket Square to protest recent police brutality. When Chicago police officers forcefully moved to disperse the crowd, a dynamite bomb was thrown, killing one police officer and wounding several more. In the media frenzy that followed, the Haymarket Riot became a polarizing issue.[14] The general public, frightened by the seemingly sudden outburst of labor unrest, demanded justice. Eight known anarchists were charged with the murder of the slain police officer. Despite a lack of evidence connecting them with the crime—some were not even present at the riot—the

12. Ibid., 157; Kaplan, *Social Construction*, 46.

13. It should be stated that the Haymarket affair and the works of Tolstoy are by no means the only factors involved in Howells's reconsideration of American society and values; they are merely two of the largest and most obvious influences. As the biographies by Cady and Lynn both demonstrate, during this period Howells felt the impact of a wide range of events and circumstances, including matters social (e.g., Howells's visits to the factories of Lowell, Massachusetts, while writing *Annie Kilburn*) and domestic (e.g., the illness and death of his daughter Winifred; the invalidism of his wife shortly thereafter; and his own recurring bouts with depression). For the purpose of this study, which focuses on the development of Howells's critical perspective, I take Haymarket and Tolstoy as representative of this wider range of influences; I direct the reader to the biographies for more extensive information. See Cady, *Road to Realism* and *Realist at War;* and Lynn, *American Life.*

14. According to Amy Kaplan, the Haymarket Riot inspired a "middle-class terror of being swallowed up by the outbreak of violence from below" and "crystallized the fear of internal instability and change in the external threat of class warfare" (*Social Construction*, 45).

men were hastily tried and, in August 1886, convicted of murder. After a series of lengthy and ultimately unsuccessful appeals, one man committed suicide in his jail cell. Three of the men were sentenced to lengthy prison terms. But on November 11, 1887, four innocent men were hanged.[15]

As biographers and scholars have demonstrated, Howells was deeply affected by the Haymarket affair. Beginning in August 1887, he began writing friends, editors, and politicians in an effort to prevent the executions. On November 4, the *New York Tribune* published a letter publicly calling upon the governor of Illinois to commute the anarchists' death sentence to life in prison (*HSL* 3:199).[16] Howells's firm public stand on the issue was a risky move, considering the public hysteria at the time, and he was widely criticized.[17] The Haymarket affair and its unfortunate aftermath punctured Howells's naïveté concerning American society; it forced him to realize that gross inequalities existed in America and that justice was not always evenly dispensed. "You'll easily believe that I did not bring myself to the point of openly befriending those men who were civically murdered in Chicago for their opinions without thinking and feeling much," Howells wrote to Hamlin Garland shortly after the executions, "and my horizons have been indefinitely widened by the process." For example, he confessed to Garland, he felt himself open to new economic and social theories, though he sensed his own limitations: "I am still the slave of selfishness, but I no longer am content to be so. That's as far as I can honestly say I've got" (*HSL* 3:214–15).

Through his study of the Haymarket affair, Howells was also exposed to socialist theory, to which he became deeply sympathetic. "I incline greatly to think our safety and happiness are in that direction," he wrote to his father in 1888, "though as yet the Socialists offer us nothing definite or practical to take hold of. They mostly show us a general theory, with no immediate steps leading to it" (*HSL* 3:216). He would forthwith integrate his newfound perspectives on American society into his two most socially oriented realist novels, *Annie Kilburn* and *A Hazard of New Fortunes,* and into his work as a critic. Howells would always remain an optimist, but he would

15. In June 1893, Governor Altgeld of Illinois pardoned the surviving anarchists, citing insufficiency of evidence for the crime. Carter, *Howells and the Age of Realism,* 179–85; Lynn, *American Life,* 288; Shi, *Facing Facts,* 182–84.

16. A second letter to the *Tribune,* written the day after the execution, is even more impassioned and contentious. The letter was never published, however, probably because Howells did not actually submit it (November 12, 1887; *HSL* 3:201–4). Michael Anesko claims the letter "testifies to a vital link between [Howells's] literary and social priorities. What Howells demanded of the artist (truthful treatment of material) was precisely what he expected of a court of law or any other democratic institution (a proper regard for the evidence)" (*LFL,* 192).

17. Alexander, *Realist as Humanist,* 83–93; Cady, *Realist at War,* 69–80; Carter, *Howells and the Age of Realism,* 179–85; Lynn, *American Life,* 288–92.

never again believe so wholeheartedly in "the large, cheerful average of health and success and happy life" of Americans.

While Howells never directly addressed the Haymarket affair in the Study, its influence is occasionally felt—perhaps most palpably in the March 1888 issue. Reviewing H. C. Lea's *History of the Inquisition of the Middle Ages,* Howells notes that,

> the primitive passions which stirred the heart of the Cave Dweller . . . still animate civilization in its social, commercial, and political rivalries and competitions. . . . We need not go far afield for exemplifications; if we cannot find them in our own hearts, we may see them in the lives of our neighbors all round us. . . . [The Inquisition] flourished up from the profoundest depths of our common human nature, from the roots of greed and hate and fear that take hold on hell in every Protestant and Anglo-Saxon heart to-day as firmly as in the dark ages and the Latin races. Wherever one man hates another for his opinions, there the spirit of the Inquisition is as rife as ever. (*ES,* 124)

While the "mission" of the Study was first and foremost to discuss literary matters, this passage exemplifies the subtle way in which Howells integrated his social and ethical arguments with his ostensibly literary discussions.[18]

After he resigned the Study in 1892, Howells became even more outspoken on social and ethical questions, publishing a series of social essays that perhaps best exemplify his increasingly sophisticated views of society. In the 1895 essay "The Nature of Liberty," for example, Howells examines the tenuous connections between liberty and economic stability—a question at the very heart of the Haymarket incident. The essence of liberty is choice, Howells argues, and the essence of choice is freedom. Freedom is not a theoretical question; it is "a social affair, a pecuniary affair, an economic affair." Freedom is the ability to work and negotiate the marketplace: a man "is a free man if he has the means of livelihood, and is assured in their possession; if he is independent of others. But if he is dependent upon some other man for the means of earning a livelihood, he is not free." Nevertheless, "the richer man is always freer than the poorer man." By this account, it follows that

> liberty and poverty are incompatible; and, if the poverty is extreme, liberty is impossible to it. We pretend otherwise, such of us as are not so directly

---

18. One reason Howells did not directly address the Haymarket affair in the Study probably had to do with his employers; for example, George William Curtis, editor of *Harper's Weekly* and an influential member of the Harper's firm, maintained an official editorial policy against the anarchists (Alexander, *Realist as Humanist,* 83).

oppressed by the conditions; but those who feel the burden know better. From time to time they express their dissent in their uncomfortable way, but, tacitly or explicitly, they always dissent from our optimistic pretense. It is possible that the American who earns his bread in the sweat of his brow and votes with his party has known all along that he was not the sort of sovereign we fancied him.

The violent unrest which we call labor troubles is nothing more nor less than an endeavor for the liberty which the working classes think they see the employing classes possessed of. It seems to be a question of more wages with them, and primarily it is a question of more wages, but ultimately it is a question of more power, more ease, more freedom. It is a question of business, of the means of livelihood; and how to secure every man in the means of livelihood, and so guarantee equal freedom to all, is the great problem for statesmanship to solve.

These problems cannot be solved quickly, or easily. Howells concludes: "In the meantime the fact remains that liberty is for those who have the means of livelihood." Howells's leftist sympathies are in strong evidence in "The Nature of Liberty." His awareness of the complex economic forces behind class divisions and labor strikes inform a social theory that, if it lacks depth and rigor, is without question a world apart from the gross naïveté of September 1886. Gone forever, it seems, is the Howells who believed in the "large, cheerful average" of Americans.[19]

Tolstoy

The second major factor that prompted Howells to expand and complicate his social and ethical vision in his literary criticism was the work of Leo Tolstoy. The Russian nobleman "is precisely the human being with whom at this moment I find myself in the greatest intimacy," Howells wrote, "not because I know him, but because I know myself through him." While Tolstoy's fiction was certainly important to Howells, the ethical works *What to Do?*, *My Religion*, and *My Confession* had a deep impact on him. "As much as one merely human being can help another I believe that he has helped me," Howells testified; "he has not influenced me in aesthetics only but in ethics too, so that I can never again see life, in the way I saw it before I knew him."[20]

19. Howells, "The Nature of Liberty," 404–5, 408–9.
20. Howells, introduction to *Sebastopol*, 5; Howells, *My Literary Passions*, 250. Scholars have long understood the power and influence of Tolstoy's Christian ethics on Howells's social views and on his fiction (most notably *Annie Kilburn*). For the standard account of Tol-

Howells first notes Tolstoy's *My Religion* in the April 1886 Study, where he admits that the Russian's argument to embrace the Christian life immediately, to give up one's wealth and to live and work among the poor after the manner of Christ, "[gives] one pause, but probably an average American humorist could dispose of his arguments in a half-column funny article" (*SLC* 2:17). In the July 1887 Study, however, Howells admits Tolstoy's *Que Faire? (What to Do?)* has unsettled him. Its renunciatory argument, while cogent and clear, is difficult to embrace: "We will own that we do not like the prospect. . . . *Que Faire* is another of those Russian books which have given some people the impression that Russia cannot be an agreeable country to live in. Like the rest of Russian literature, it seems intended to direct the mind to uncomfortable subjects, to awaken harassing thoughts in it. . . . After reading it you cannot be quite the same person you were before; you will be better by taking its truth to heart, or worse by hardening your heart against it." Howells soberly concludes: "whatever may be said in ridicule or argument, it cannot be denied that the life [Tolstoy] is living is in literal fulfilment of the teachings of Jesus Christ"; furthermore, it is "impossible for one to regard [the book] without grave question of the life that the rest of us are living" (*SLC* 2:58–59).

Howells's growing unease with Tolstoy is evidence of how seriously he regarded the Russian's argument. In an April 1887 letter to his father, written as he was preparing to draft the July 1887 Study,[21] Howells's discomfort is palpable: "I am just reading one of Tolstoi's books [*Que Faire?*]—on poverty, and prosperity's responsibility for it,—and I confess it makes me very unhappy. His remedy is to go into the country, and share the labor of his peasants—to forego luxury and superfluity; but I don't exactly see how this helps, except that it makes all poor alike, and saves one's self from remorse. It's a terrible question. How shall it ever be answered? . . . When I think of it, my pleasure in possession is all spoiled" (*HSL* 3:186). The unease is again evidenced in an 1887 letter to Edward E. Hale, wherein Howells admits that Tolstoy's

> ethical books . . . have made me unhappy. They have shown me the utter selfishness and insufficiency of my past life, without convincing me that Tolstoi offers quite the true solution. To work for others, yes; but to work

---

stoy's influence on Howells, see George N. Bennett, *The Realism of William Dean Howells, 1889–1920*, 164–71. See also Alexander, *Realist as Humanist*, 61–110; Sarah B. Daugherty, "Howells, Tolstoy, and the Limits of Realism: The Case of *Annie Kilburn*"; Cady, *Realist at War*, 7–10; and Lynn, *American Life*, 282–304.

21. Howells typically wrote his Study columns two to three months prior to their publication date (Carter, *Howells and the Age of Realism*, 187–88).

with my hands, I'm not sure, seeing that I'm now fifty, awkward and fat. . . .
I'm afraid Tolstoi doesn't value amusement enough in a world that seems
to get very wicked without it. I'm afraid also that this fear is a sneaking love
of the world anyway in me.

But Tolstoi has freed me in flooring me. Never again can I be a snob; my
soul is at least my own henceforth. (*HSL* 3:189)

If Tolstoy disturbed Howells, he also prompted him to examine rigorously many dearly held convictions. In the March 1888 Study, Howells
notes that reading both Zola's novel *La Terre* and Tolstoy's play *The Power
of Darkness* compelled him to question what a reader ought to do or think
when confronted with narratives depicting the "hideous shames and
crimes" of society. "Whether much is done to help those whose life is depicted in fiction is a question which no one yet is qualified to answer,"
Howells notes, adding that "fiction has only so very recently assumed to
paint life faithfully, and most critics still claim that it is best for it not to do
so." He cites the examples of Emile Erckmann and Alexandre Chatrain, whose
stories "have had the effect of weakening the love of military glory in the
French people." He notes, too, Albert Bitzius, whose *Bauernspiegel* (1837)
is "claimed to have wrought a great reform in the manners and morals of
the Bernese peasants. . . . But we suspect that fiction, like the other arts, can
only do good of this kind indirectly; when it becomes hortatory, it is in danger of becoming dull, that is to say, suicidal" (*SLC* 2:85). If these thoughts
do not repudiate his April 1887 claim concerning the obligations of the
artist—the "conscientious" author is "bound to distinguish so clearly that
no reader of his may be misled, between what is right and what is wrong,
what is noble and what is base, what is health and what is perdition, in the
actions and the characters he portrays" (*SLC* 2:45)—then Howells at least
complicates the conception.

The idea is further complicated in the October 1890 Study. Reading Tolstoy's *The Kreutzer Sonata* has, in part, prompted Howells to question the
ultimate value of art as a means of teaching or reflecting moral understanding: "The moral superiority of good art of any kind is in its truth, but we
can have truth without any art whatever. It is well to keep both of these
points in mind, the one that we may be good artists, and the other that we
may be modest about it. There is danger to man, who is first of all a moral
being, in setting up merely an aesthetic standard of excellence, and endeav-
oring for that, or in making the good of life consist of aesthetic enjoyment,
which is really only one remove from sensual enjoyment." While Howells
still believes passionately in his realist aesthetics, he is less certain that art of
any kind is an effective means of conveying moral and ethical values. "Ruskin
observed long ago that the best people he had ever seen knew nothing and

cared nothing about art," he quietly notes, "and Tolstoï noticed among the literati of St. Petersburg that those who had the true theory of fiction were no better men than those who had the false theory" (*SLC* 2:156). Art, Howells is gradually coming to understand, holds at best a limited capacity to shape society, to shape social and ethical questions. It would be a mistake to champion "merely an aesthetic standard of excellence" or to promote "aesthetic enjoyment" exclusively. If social and ethical questions are simply too big to be handled by art alone, then Howells must question, perhaps for the first time, the final value of art. If Howells is not ready to follow Tolstoy in wholly abandoning the artistic practice, he is at least willing to rethink the overearnest, grandiose claims for art he made prior to reading Tolstoy.

It is perhaps because Howells saw the limited potential of art as a means for handling larger social questions that he turned, for a time after completing the Study, to the writing of social essays. Several of these essays bear the imprint of Tolstoy's social vision. For example, in "Are We a Plutocracy?" Howells begins with the post-Haymarket observation that "financially, industrially, economically, we are not a nation, a people, a solidarity, but a congeries of 'infinitely repellent particles'" and that "economically we are all at war with another." Howells goes so far as to argue that "business can never be democratically transacted" because "Every private business is at war not only with every like business, but is at war within itself between the employer and employee, the wage-giver and the wage taker." Positioning the ideals of democracy against the inherent greed of a plutocracy, Howells argues that if America is a plutocracy, the rich alone are not to blame: "a plutocracy is not so much, or not so merely, the rule of the moneyed class as it is the political embodiment of the money-making ideal; and the mass who have no money at all may cling as fondly and worshipfully to this ideal as the class who have millions of money." The question becomes less political and more behavioral: a plutocrat is defined by his attitude toward wealth. Howells is not against capitalism per se; rather, he resents any person who seeks to profit: "the man who pays wages with the hope of profit to himself is a plutocrat, and the man who takes wages upon such terms, believing them right, is in principle a plutocrat; for both approve of the gain of money which is not earned." Indeed, Howells maligns the plutocrat at every level in society; he has as little sympathy for striking laborers motivated principally by greed as he does for the rich man and concludes his argument by stating simply that "If we have a plutocracy, it may be partly because the rich want it, but it is infinitely more because the poor choose it or allow it."[22]

---

22. Howells, "Are We a Plutocracy?" 186, 188–91, 196. Although he would not have recognized the term, Howells here seems to anticipate Antonio Gramsci's concept of "hegemony": the widespread interiorization of dominant cultural ideologies, even by those who are the victims of such ideologies.

Resting on a hazy distinction between the plutocrat who "makes" his money and the democratic capitalist who "earns" it, Howells's argument in "Are We a Plutocracy?" lacks rigor and sophistication. What is important in this context, however, is that Tolstoy's renunciatory Christian ethics resonate throughout the argument. But where Tolstoy held that one should renounce all wealth and live as an equal among the poorest of the poor, Howells suggests one need not give up all wealth—only that portion of one's profit that is, by Howells's account, unjustly taken or received. The question of plutocracy, in Howells's eyes, is principally an ethical question, and it will only be solved when the attitudes and ethics of society are reformed. "Are We a Plutocracy?" is therefore an important example of Howells's larger campaign to correct society's ills. Daniel H. Borus has noted that in the essay "Howells stressed both the ideational causes for the breakdown of prior social unity and the hope that the reconciliation could be achieved through a return to a common code of conduct." "Are We a Plutocracy?" with its implicit plea to renounce greed and avarice, acts in concert with the broader objectives of Howellsian literary realism as identified by Amy Kaplan: Howells "envisioned realism as a strategy for containing social difference and controlling social conflict within a cohesive common ground."[23] In his fiction he emphasized the development of character; one might argue that he emphasized the same thing in his literary criticism and social essays, albeit in a slightly different sense of the phrase.

This humanist sentiment informs two other social essays from the period. The title of one, "Equality as the Basis of Good Society," speaks for itself. Tolstoy stands just behind Howells when the latter argues that social inequality—and in particular class inequality—is the root problem behind most ills of society. And Tolstoy practically drips from the pages of "Who Are Our Brethren?" wherein Howells promotes Christian fraternity, a "supernatural brotherhood" which, fully realized, would provide "a refuge from all . . . woes" and would promote a truly equal society.[24]

This humanist sentiment is evident throughout much of *Impressions and Experiences,* Howells's 1896 collection of personal and social essays. In "Police Report," Howells compassionately examines the victims of drunkenness, bodily violence, thievery, and prostitution. If the aim of the petty court system is to reform the offenders, Howells bemoans the "apparent futility" of a system that "does no good" whatsoever. Abject poverty is the focus of "An East-Side Ramble," in which Howells surveys New York's Jewish quar-

23. Borus, *Writing Realism,* 169; Kaplan, *Social Construction,* 23.

24. Howells, "Equality as the Basis of Good Society"; Howells, "Who Are Our Brethren?" 934. For more on this topic, see Robert L. Hough, *The Quiet Rebel: William Dean Howells as Social Commentator.* It is worth noting that these idealistic social essays were written just after Howells had published his utopian social romance *A Traveler from Altruria.*

ter. He concludes the essay by likening the plight of the very poor to slaves, and the slumlords to slaveholders; as with slavery, one cannot trust the situation to right itself: "Nothing but public control in some form or other can secure [the poor] a shelter fit for human beings." Other socially informed essays in *Impressions* include "Tribulations of a Cheerful Giver," which examines charity, poverty, and the conscience of the giver, and "Glimpses of Central Park," which examines the unequal distribution of wealth in the United States and revisits Howells's thesis that the United States is essentially a plutocracy. These essays all bear a strong imprint of Howells's newly minted social views, and they demonstrate that, throughout the 1890s, Howells explored his fresh take on society in a range of venues that included fiction, literary criticism, and the personal and social essay.[25]

In closing, one hastens to emphasize that the reconfiguration of Howells's artistic and critical horizons was not, of course, due solely to the impact of Tolstoy and the Haymarket affair. But the effects of both on Howells's critical output during his tenure in the Study are indicative of the kinds of major changes his theories underwent during the period. An examination of selected literary essays from the Study will show how they reflect Howells's developing social, ethical, and moral views as they appeared in his literary criticism and aesthetic arguments.

The Honest Daylight about Us

The September 1887 Study, written shortly after Howells's review of Tolstoy's *Que Faire?* in July of that year, is an excellent starting point for examining Howells's changing social and ethical views. It was probably composed sometime in late June or early July; shortly thereafter, Howells began his earnest campaign to save the Chicago anarchists from execution.[26] The September 1887 Study demonstrates both the growing influence of Tolstoy and Howells's mounting disquiet with the society he saw around him.

While discussing the question of "popularity as a test of merit in a book,"

---

25. Howells, *Impressions and Experiences*, 68, 110, 111–39, 166–80. In their original form, "Police Report" and "Tribulations of a Cheerful Giver" both antedate Howells's knowledge of Tolstoy, demonstrating that the roots of Howells's humanism run far back. ("Police Report," however, was revised prior to its 1896 republication.) Howells, "Police Report," *Atlantic Monthly* 49 (January 1882): 1–6; "Tribulations of a Cheerful Giver," *Century* 50 (June–July 1895): 181–85, 417–21. See also Alexander, *Realist as Humanist*, 15–19, 152.

26. Due to family medical concerns, Howells was not able to begin his campaign before August 1887 (Lynn, *American Life*, 289–90). According to the extant correspondence, Howells began writing to friends and circulating information concerning the case on August 10, 1887 (*HSL* 3:193 and passim); during the following six months, he wrote dozens of letters in an effort to win pardons for the convicted men.

Howells notes that even the well-educated "literary elect" make poor choices: "It is the habit of hasty casuists to regard civilization as inclusive of all the members of a civilized community; but this is a palpable error. . . . In fact, no man can be said to be thoroughly civilized or always civilized; the most refined, the most enlightened person has his moods, [and] his moments of barbarism." Once in a while, Howells admits, every person is wont

> to find relaxation in feeling—feeling crudely, grossly, merely. For once in a way there is no great harm in this; perhaps no harm at all. It is perfectly natural: let them have their innocent debauch. But let us distinguish, for our own sake and guidance, between the different kinds of things that please the same kind of people; between the things that please them habitually and those that please them occasionally; between the pleasures that edify them and those that amuse them. Otherwise we shall be in danger of becoming permanently part of the "unthinking multitude," and of remaining puerile, primitive, savage. We shall be so in moods and at moments; but let us not fancy that those are high moods or fortunate moments. If they are harmless, that is the most that can be said for them. They are lapses from which we can perhaps go forward more vigorously; but even this is not certain. (*ES*, 95)

Howells is ostensibly discussing the reading habits of the "literary elect," but the open-ended nature of his comments clearly resonates in broader social contexts—contexts that, in the summer of 1887, Howells was beginning to address directly. A growing note of pessimism is clearly discernible in the passage. One also notes how Howells conflates the literary and the social, reinforcing the notion that for him questions of literary standards and taste were irrevocably questions of social ethics. It is a point noted by recent scholars. "Drawing a parallel between the experience of reading and the conduct of social life," writes Daniel Borus, "realists hoped that realism would also serve as a reminder to the nation of the possibilities of democracy in political and social life. They regarded their fiction as a form of political intervention designed to repair the fissures that had run through nearly every aspect of American life."[27]

This notion of a democratic, educative fiction is reinforced later in the September 1887 Study. Howells argues persuasively for the accurate, realistic depiction of character in fiction:

> It appears to us that the opposite position [i.e., the unrealistic depiction of character] is one of the last refuges of the aristocratic spirit which is disap-

27. Borus, *Writing Realism*, 139.

pearing from politics and society, and is now seeking to shelter itself in aesthetics. The pride of caste is becoming the pride of taste; but as before, it is averse to the mass of men; it consents to know them only in some conventionalized and artificial guise. It seeks to withdraw itself, to stand aloof; to be distinguished, and not to be identified. Democracy in literature is the reverse of all this. It wishes to know and to tell the truth, confident that consolation and delight are there; it does not care to paint the marvellous and impossible for the vulgar many, or to sentimentalize and falsify the actual for the vulgar few. Men are more like than unlike one another: let us make them know one another better, that they may be all humbled and strengthened with a sense of their fraternity. Neither arts, nor letters, nor sciences, except as they somehow, clearly or obscurely, tend to make the race better and kinder, are to be regarded as serious interests; they are all lower than the rudest crafts that feed and house and clothe, for except they do this office they are idle; and they cannot do this except from and through the truth. (*ES,* 96)

While Howells had long argued for the didactic role of realist fiction, in this eloquent passage—which he would revise and use as the concluding paragraph of *Criticism and Fiction* (1891)—one again senses the influence of Tolstoy's Christian ethics. Howells wants to reconfigure the arts in general and writing in particular as honest work, a didactic force that, in the spirit of democracy, both humbles and strengthens society "with a sense of . . . fraternity." Howells distances the practice of art from "the aristocratic spirit," positioning it closer to the level of "the rudest crafts" of artisans and laborers. Writing literature is *work*—honest work infused with ethical and social responsibilities.[28]

Howells's broadening social and ethical concerns came into sharper focus in 1888, an important year for the Study. In March, Howells promoted Zola's *La Terre:* "Filthy and repulsive as it is in its facts, it is a book not to be avoided by the student of civilization, but rather to be sought and seriously considered" as a "scientific study of a phase of French life under the Second Empire" (*SLC* 2:84).[29] A month later, he turned his attention to issues of class inequality in a review of Laurence Gronlund's study of the French Revolution, *Ça Ira.* In the course of reviewing Gronlund, Howells quoted twice

28. For more on the postbellum reconfiguration of the author's role in society, see ibid., 27–99. Howells would revisit the idea of the artist as laborer in "The Man of Letters as a Man of Business."

29. Howells's support of Zola provoked yet another round of hostile counterreactions in the American press, including a gentle rebuke from Henry Alden at *Harper's Monthly.* Alden's resistance to Howells would, in the remaining years of the Study, grow significantly. Howells would resign from the Study shortly after Alden blatantly censored him in February 1891 (see Pizer, introduction, *SLC* 2:xvi–xviii).

from Richard T. Ely, an increasingly renowned professor of economics at Johns Hopkins, in favor of socialism (*SLC* 2:86–89). In the June 1888 Study, Howells favorably reviewed Edward Bellamy's socialist utopian romance, *Looking Backward* (*SLC* 2:90–93). And in the December Study, Howells points once again to Tolstoy, "that voice of one crying in the wilderness," as he calls not merely for a new Christmas literature, but for a literature that will permanently embrace the Christian ideals celebrated at the holiday: "all good literature is now Christmas literature. The old heathenish axiom of art for art's sake is as dead as great Pan himself, and the best art now tends to be art for humanity's sake." In the past, the romance novel has idealized "the victims of society" (i.e., the lower classes), quietly overlooking their faults and burnishing their rough spots. Howells demands an unsentimentalized, realistic treatment. "Truth," he continues,

> paints these victims as they are, and bids the world consider them not because they are beautiful and virtuous, but because they are ugly and vicious, cruel, filthy, and only not altogether loathsome because the divine can never wholly die out of the human. The truth does not find these victims among the poor alone, among the hungry, the houseless, the ragged; but it also finds them among the rich, cursed with the aimlessness, the satiety, the despair of wealth, wasting their lives in a fool's paradise of shows and semblances, with nothing real but the misery that comes of insincerity and selfishness. (*SLC* 2:104–6)

Howells argues against romanticist fiction because it presents an idealized, unrealistic depiction of society. An author's choice of narrative genre was therefore more than an aesthetic question; it was a social question. In an increasingly diverse society whose values and principles were challenged, undermined, and exploited, Howells continued to believe in an objective, shared truth about America: he believed that there were fundamental social and ethical values underlying society that, if properly identified and articulated, could repair a fragmented nation.

In the September 1889 Study, Howells's argument takes on added passion because it has become clear to him that the romantic novel is enjoying something of a resurgence in popularity—if, indeed, it ever suffered from diminished popularity. Howells reiterates his argument that new times demand new literary forms: "romanticism was the expression of a world-mood; it was not merely literary and voluntary; it grew naturally out of the political, social, and even economical conditions at the close of the eighteenth century." In contrast, "this is the age of hopeful striving, when we have really a glimpse of what the earth may be when Christianity becomes a life in the equality and fraternity of the race, and when the recognition of all the facts in the honest daylight about us is the service which humanity demands of the humanities, in order that what is crooked may be made straight, and that what is wrong may be set right. The humanities are working through realism to this end" (*SLC* 2:124). Here is one of Howells's most focused and eloquent pleas for a socially informed realism with strong ethical and didactic aims, a fiction that will knit together an increasingly diverse and fragmented society. For Howells strongly believed, as Amy Kaplan has noted, in realism as "a strategy for imagining and managing the threats of social change." Realists like Howells "engage[d] in an enormous act of construction to organize, re-form, and control the social world" in an effort to "negotiate conflict in the narrative construction of common ground among classes both to efface and reinscribe social hierarchies."[30]

For Howells, the question of an artistic genre was only part of the overall equation. The question of which values to define and deploy in one's fiction was not, in the final instance, solely in the hands of the artist. As both a writer of fiction and as a literary critic, Howells was always acutely aware of his audience—of its tastes, its limits, its preferences, and its prejudices. And for Howells as a professional author, considerations of audience were invariably considerations of the marketplace within which he operated. Audience concerns were business concerns. Howells, even as he struggled to join his passionate aesthetic beliefs to his increasingly radical social beliefs, always kept a finger on the pulse of the market and of his audience.

A Matter of Business

Howells's awareness of his audience and the nature of the changing market for literature is superbly evidenced in the June 1889 Study, which addresses the question of propriety in fiction. Howells begins by defending the American novel against the charge of prudishness. "[It] is not really such a prude after all," Howells demurs; rather, it is "more faithfully representative of the tone of modern life" in that it privileges honest, forthright depictions of love, which Howells believes are more common, over "the guilty intrigue, the betrayal, the extreme flirtation even," which he suggests is "the exceptional thing in life" (*SLC* 2:118). Yet Howells, as apologist for the status quo, does not base his justification solely on conservative social mores. Propriety in fiction is also a question of audience:

> the novel in our civilization now always addresses a mixed company, and . . .
> the vast majority of the company are ladies, and . . . very many, if not most,
> of these ladies are young girls. If the novel were written for men and for

30. Kaplan, *Social Construction*, 10–11.

married women alone, as in continental Europe, it might be altogether different. But the simple fact is that it is not written for them alone among us,
and it is a question of writing, under cover of our universal acceptance,
things for young girls to read . . . [and] of appealing to these vivid, respon-
sive intelligences, which are none the less brilliant and admirable because
they are innocent. (*SLC* 2:118–19)

Relative to the French novel, however, Howells believes the American
novel is "truer to life, not only to its complexion, but also to its texture."
Focusing on this higher truth by no means implies that an author must turn
a blind eye to the less pleasant aspects of modern society: "No one will pretend that there is not vicious love beneath the surface of our society; if he
did, the fetid explosions of the divorce trials would refute him; but if he pre-
tended that it was in any just sense characteristic of our society, he could be
still more easily refuted. Yet it exists, and it is unquestionably the material of
tragedy, the stuff from which intense effects are wrought. The question,
after owning this fact, is whether these intense effects are not rather cheap
effects. We incline to think they are." Howells, author of the first novel-
length treatment of divorce in American literature, *A Modern Instance,* pre-
sumably speaks from experience. Nevertheless, he frames the question of
propriety in fiction as one of artistic integrity. An author who refrains from
"cheap effects" must rely on "intellectual equipment" of the highest caliber,
"and then he will succeed only with the highest class of readers." Anyone,
Howells suggests, can write a steamy love intrigue: "He need not at all be a
great author; he may be a very shabby wretch, if he has but the courage or
the trick of that sort of thing." There is a whole class of authors who "have
established themselves in an easy popularity simply by the study of exotic
shivers and fervors" (*SLC* 2:119–20).

In an interesting progression, Howells conjoins his two stated concerns
surrounding the question of propriety in fiction: artistic integrity and audience. Complicating the conception of audience articulated earlier in the essay
(the audience dominated by innocent young girls), Howells argues that
"The manners of the novel have been improving with those of its readers,"
who

have not grown decent without having also grown a little squeamish, but
they have grown comparatively decent; there is no doubt about that. They
require of a novelist whom they respect unquestionable proof of his seriousness, if he proposes to deal with certain phases of life; they require a
sort of scientific decorum. He can no longer expect to be received on the
ground of entertainment only; he assumes a higher function, something
like that of a physician or a priest, and they expect him to be bound by laws

as sacred as those of such professions; they hold him solemnly pledged not to betray them or abuse their confidence.

Sordid topics like adultery and divorce can be treated in fiction, Howells suggests, but an author ought to exercise restraint, maintaining a "true perspective" and "correct proportion" in such matters (*SLC* 2:120–21).

Clearly, Howells's argument thus far is conservative; it justifies the status quo. One imagines it is a chord he knew would resonate with his *Harper's Monthly* readership. Edwin Cady has noted that Howells's motivations in regards to his essays on propriety in fiction were mixed: moral, to a degree, but also "tactical and commercial: he wrote for respectable family magazines, fought for artistic principles to which he thought 'passion' irrelevant—and he knew from hard editorial experience what havoc moral indignation in the readership wreaked upon the subscription list."[31] Yet Howells's analogy to the physician and the priest is noteworthy. It is simultaneously an assertion and a polite request. Howells asserts on behalf of all fiction writers a certain cultural weight and authority, just as James had done in "The Art of Fiction" by comparing the author to the painter and the historian. Howells clearly distinguishes between the literary author who relies on his "intellectual equipment" and the mass-market author who relies on "cheap effects" to secure "an easy popularity." Literature is not mere "entertainment," it is "a higher function." At the same time, Howells gently encourages his audience to revere the serious author, to treat him with high regard. Thus it is a carefully worded plea.

In his conclusion, Howells joins all of his concerns—propriety, audience, and the nature of the market. He begins by noting that it is indeed possible for an American to publish a tale of adultery on a par with *Madame Bovary* or *Anna Karenina,* and that such an author may well meet with great success, but, Howells emphasizes, it would have to be published in book form, for no American magazine would print the story. "[H]ere our novelist must again submit to conditions," Howells notes. "A book is something by itself, responsible for its character, which becomes quickly known, and it does not necessarily penetrate to every member of the household." In contrast,

with the magazine and its serial the affair is different. Between the editor of a reputable English or American magazine and the families which receive it there is a tacit agreement that he will print nothing which a father may not read to his daughter, or safely leave her to read herself. After all, it is a matter of business; and the insurgent novelist should consider the situa-

31. Cady, *W. D. Howells as Critic,* 149.

tion with coolness and common-sense. The editor did not create the situation; but it exists, and he could not even attempt to change it without many
sorts of disaster. (*SLC* 2:122)

The novelist's answer seems obvious: forgo the magazine trade and publish books. But the nature of the publishing market complicates this option:

> in the present state of the book trade it is almost impossible to get an audi-
> ence for an American novel. That seems very likely, but, dear friend, your
> misfortune begins far back of the magazine editor. If you did not belong to
> a nation which would rather steal its reading than buy it, you would be
> protected by an international copyright law, and then you might defy the
> magazines and appeal to the public in a book with a fair hope of getting
> some return for your labor on it. But you *do* belong to a nation that would
> rather steal its reading than buy it, and so you must meet the conditions of
> the only literary form with which stolen literature cannot compete. The
> American magazine much more than holds its own against anything we can
> rob the English of. Perhaps it is a little despotic, a little arbitrary; but un-
> questionably its favor is essential to success, and its conditions are not such
> narrow ones. (*SLC* 2:122)

And so Howells urges the writer to adapt to the market. If one must publish in the magazines to secure one's income, then one must submit to their
restrictions. If one cannot write frankly of adultery in the manner of Tolstoy
and Flaubert in the magazines, one can treat the matter in the more conservative, indirect fashion of an earlier generation: Dickens, Eliot, and Thackeray. In the final analysis, "it is no narrow field [the editor] throws open to
you" (*SLC* 2:123).

The June 1889 Study, which started out as an apology for the status quo,
ends with a rather sharply focused examination of the writer in the marketplace, and with an implicit call for the artist to adapt to that market. It is a
savvy rhetorical strategy: Howells begins by acknowledging—even agreeing
with—the conservative nature of the American novel, but he ends by reconfiguring the boundaries of the argument. The American novel is conservative
not merely because of social mores—though he admits they are important—rather, it is conservative because of market demands and the "realities" of magazine publication. In other words, the issue is not as simple as
writing fiction for young, innocent minds. At heart, the issue revolves around
how the artist negotiates the market. Book publishers and magazine editors
appeal to different markets. Without an international copyright law, the
novelist is all but forced initially to publish his novel serially in the magazines to secure both profit and the rights to his work, and therefore he must
submit to the particular restrictions of that market. To liberate the author

from the demands of the serial market, Howells clearly implies, we must change the law.

The column is not exactly a call to arms; it is something more subtle and carefully crafted than that. While it is one of Howells's most polished rhetorical exercises, it also complicates the frequently held notion that he was morally timid or squeamish. While it is true that he aligns himself with the conservative moral stance of his editors and his audience, he does not argue solely from a moral or ethical viewpoint. Rather, he argues, first, as a working writer with a clear sense of his audience and its tastes, and, second, as a businessman with a keen sense of the market and what it will allow. The June 1889 Study is, in part, a frank and practical view of the nature of the market; it is an assessment of how the publishing market itself creates, promotes, and sustains conservative social mores.

Howells sounds a very different note in his 1895 literary memoir *My Literary Passions*. In a passage on Pope, Howells offers an aside on propriety in literature that ranks as perhaps his most conservative. "The worst of the literature of past times, before an ethical conscience began to inform it, or the advance of the race compelled it to decency . . . leaves the mind foul with filthy images and base thoughts," Howells notes. Expressing concern for young readers, he suggests that

> what is lewd and ribald in the great poets shall be kept out of such editions as are meant for general reading, and that the pedant-pride which now perpetuates it as an essential part of those poets shall no longer have its way. At the end of the ends such things do defile, they do corrupt. We may palliate them or excuse them for this reason or that, but that is the truth, and I do not see why they should not be dropped from literature, as they were long ago dropped from the talk of decent people. The literary histories might keep record of them, but it is loathsome to think of those heaps of ordure, accumulated from generation to generation, and carefully passed down from age to age as something precious and vital, and not justly regarded as the moral offal which they are.

To be sure, the passage is surprising. While there are many examples where the usually pleasant demeanor of Howells gives way to anger, I can think of no other example wherein Howells bluntly calls for the censorship of authors. Of course, it is possible that Howells's sense of his audience dictated the tone of the passage: *My Literary Passions* was written for the female readers of *Ladies' Home Journal*, where the papers were originally serialized (1893–1895). Hence, perhaps, the excessive prudery.[32]

---

32. Howells, *My Literary Passions,* 54–55. Interestingly, later in *My Literary Passions* Howells adopts a more complex (and patently Jamesian) stance, concerning Zola. The French-

In contrast to Henry James, whose relationship to the literary market was quarrelsome at best, Howells understood that the author is always working in a marketplace and, more importantly, he accepted that the market imposes certain conditions on an author. Although Howells never said as much, his arguments demonstrate that he understood the notion of artistic freedom in terms significantly different from those of James. Writing, for Howells, was both business and art. It was for James, too, though James always privileged artistic integrity over market-oriented compromise; he sought, with much less success, to steer and to control the market to meet his artistic demands. One might say Howells was more flexible; or, perhaps he was too easily compromised. Regardless, while he stridently asserted his craft and distinguished his literary output from the mass-media productions he so clearly derided, he was willing to adapt to the market's demands and to exercise his artistic license within the boundaries of the market as he understood it.

An Essential Hardness

Henry James, too, addressed the question of propriety in fiction during this period. In two essays from 1888, he articulated ideas somewhat similar to Howells's on the question. In an essay on French novelist Pierre Loti, James notes Loti's "almost inveterate habit of representing the closest and most intimate personal relations as unaccompanied with any moral feeling, any impulse of reflection or reaction." James complains that Loti's blunt depiction of human passion robs his work of value. Despite the range of subject matter and geographical location, there is something restrictive about Loti's aesthetic: "It occurs to us for the first time that he is partially closed, slightly narrow, he whose very profession it is to be accessible to extreme strangeness, and we feel, as devoted readers, a certain alarm." Indeed, even in *Mon Frère Yves* and *Pêcheur d'Islande*, Loti's two best books, "The part of them that deals with the complicated heart is still the weakest element" (*LC* 2:497, 500).

James lodges similar complaints against Maupassant in an important 1888 essay. Maupassant's admirable tales tend toward the obscene, in James's opinion. "If he is a master of his art and it is discouraging to find what low views

---

man's subject matter is "simply abhorrent, but when you have once granted him his material for his own use, it is idle and foolish to deny his power." Howells concludes that "the books of Zola are not immoral, but they are indecent through the facts that they nakedly represent" and goes on to suggest that "there is but one novelist of our time, or of any, that outmasters him, and that is Tolstoy" (246). Clearly, Howells could grant an author his indecent material when the moral aim of the work remained clear to the reader.

are compatible with mastery, there is satisfaction, on the other hand in learning on what particular condition he holds his strange success." The condition is, James argues, a noteworthy omission: "Maupassant has simply skipped the whole reflective part of his men and women—that reflective part which governs conduct and produces character." James concludes the essay with a reflection on the "erotic element" in literature, asking which is more preferable for a writer—frankly to portray the erotic, or to treat it indirectly if at all? James frames his response in terms of artistic verisimilitude: "The carnal side of man appears the most characteristic if you look at it a great deal; and you look at it a great deal if you do not look at the other, at the side by which he reacts against his weaknesses, his defeats. The more you look at the other, the less the [erotic] . . . will strike you as the only typical one. Is not this the most useful reflection to make in regard to the famous question of the morality, the decency, of the novel? It is the only one, it seems to me, that will meet the case as we find the case to-day" (*LC* 2:547–49). James, speaking the language of artistic integrity, rhetorically tries to steer the reader to accept the conservative Anglo-American standard as "the only one . . . that will meet the case." He simply cannot bring himself to embrace fully the more licentious aspects of Maupassant's fiction, despite their obvious power (much of the essay is an appreciation of the unique power of Maupassant's fiction). And yet, in a masterful conclusion, James is careful not to appear overly restrictive; he wants to avoid the appearance of proposing a dictum:

> Hard and fast rules, *a priori* restrictions, mere interdictions (you shall not speak of this, you shall not look at that), have surely served their time, and will in the nature of the case never strike an energetic talent as anything but arbitrary. A healthy, living and growing art, full of curiosity and fond of exercise, has an indefeasible mistrust of rigid prohibitions. Let us then leave this magnificent art of the novelist to itself and to its perfect freedom, in the faith that one example is as good as another, and that our fiction will always be decent enough if it be sufficiently general. Let us not be alarmed at this prodigy (though prodigies are alarming) of M. de Maupassant, who is at once so licentious and so impeccable, but gird ourselves up with the conviction that another point of view will yield another perfection. (*LC* 2:549)

It is a fine example of James wanting to have an issue both ways. On the one hand, he praises Maupassant for that which is his own, for the art that presents, as James puts it early in the essay, "an essential hardness—hardness of form, hardness of nature." As with Balzac, James is impressed by the force and clarity of Maupassant's aesthetic vision: "the fact with him (the fact of execution) is so extraordinarily definite and adequate" (*LC* 2:522). It

is for these reasons that James can accept, if not overlook, the licentious aspects of Maupassant. Another writer, James suggests in his conclusion, shall
eventually appear who is equally great and who shall write something totally
different, something perhaps less scandalous. James's final comment, then,
is very much in the spirit of "The Art of Fiction": he implicitly calls for each
writer to do what she does best, and for readers to appreciate that fact and
not to ask anything more or less of that artist. But, one hastens to add, he
only does so after not-so-subtly suggesting that a writer ought not to focus
so intently on the erotic.

In the 1888 Loti and Maupassant essays, then, James, like Howells in the
June 1889 Study, presents carefully worded, elaborate arguments that, to
some extent, argue for the moral status quo of the Anglo-American novel.
Without wanting to appear restrictive or dogmatic, James upholds the conservative attitudes of Anglo-American readers even as he argues for complete artistic freedom. The two friends differ, of course, in one important
respect: Howells's argument was a mixture of concerns both moral and
market-oriented; his ultimate criteria for preserving the moral status quo of
American fiction concerned the nature of the marketplace itself. The June
1889 Study expertly conjoins the moral and marketplace threads to create a
complexly woven argument that functions as a complete whole. In contrast,
James gently undercuts—if not contradicts—his own moral argument when
he shifts to the familiar topic of preserving artistic integrity. While this move
may weaken or dissipate the argument's overall effectiveness, it is a familiar
rhetorical signature of James's style. Throughout his career, James held fast
to a "horror of dogma," a critical sensibility adapted from his early mentors
Arnold, Schérer, and Sainte-Beuve. And, as previous chapters in this study
have demonstrated, James remained torn between identifying in principle
with the freedom exhibited by certain European authors and upholding his
own more conservative Anglo-American scruples.

Conclusion

While some of his works of fiction, such as *The Princess Casamassima* or *The
Bostonians,* engaged certain social questions of the day, Henry James, living
abroad in Europe throughout one of the most turbulent periods of social
change in America (1880–1900), remained, as a literary critic, largely silent
on social and ethical questions.[33] And while he did address moral questions

33. James had written a series of essays on British geopolitics in 1878–1879; for the next
two decades he would be, as a critic, publicly silent on issues of society, culture, and politics.
After 1904, however, James became increasingly engaged and wrote more than a dozen essays

as they relate to fiction, he did not stray from the field he had marked out in "The Art of Fiction," privileging artistic freedom and the personal, subjective vision of the individual artist. For William Dean Howells, it was another matter entirely.

While he became measurably less idealistic and naive during the six and a half years he wrote the Study, Howells never surrendered the essential optimism that kept him afloat. In an 1895 review of Max Nordau's *Degeneration,* Howells admits that "the longer I live the more I am persuaded that the problems of this life are to be solved elsewhere, or never." It is the voice of a man weary from battle, but his optimism remains; he is convinced that the artist, as moralist, must educate society:

> It is not by the solution of problems that the moralist teaches, but by the question that his handling of them suggests to us respecting ourselves. . . . What he can and must do ethically, is to make us take thought of ourselves, and look to it whether we have in us the making of this or that wrong; whether we are hypocrites, tyrants, pretenders, shams conscious or unconscious; whether our most unselfish motives are not really secret shapes of egotism; whether our convictions are not mere brute acceptations; whether we believe what we profess; whether when we force good to a logical end we are not doing evil. (*SLC* 2:206)

For a man who struggled throughout much of the late 1880s and early 1890s with both personal and public crises, the passage speaks to his ability to endure and to preserve the essential optimism and humility that inform his work. Howells was never a cynic, but at his most sobered and frank—as in the late Study columns and in essays like "The Nature of Liberty"—he was capable of seeing through the middle-class complaisance and naïveté demonstrated in some of his earlier work. And, more importantly, he was capable of articulating his views in a manner his audience could digest, if not wholly accept.

Throughout his tenure in the Study, Howells believed in the artist as a shaper of social mores. As his own understanding of society deepened and, to some extent, darkened, Howells never wavered in his commitment to his realist aesthetics and his belief that the practice of art could mold, shape, and unite an increasingly fragmented society. His essays on propriety in fiction, including the important June 1889 Study, demonstrate as much. If anything, Howells's exposure to the Haymarket affair and the work of Leo Tolstoy deepened his aesthetic convictions and forced him to reconsider

on a range of topics, as well as his major sociocultural study *The American Scene.* For more, see Henry James, *Henry James on Culture: Collected Essays on Politics and the American Social Scene.*

realism's social and ethical dimensions. "Whether he knew the right answers or not, Howells understood the questions," comments Edwin Cady. "The questions were whether the culture of the West . . . could respond adequately to the challenges of democracy, population density, popular education, industrialization, urbanism, and technological power."[34] For Howells, such questions were always, at their root, personal questions.

Undoubtedly, then, when Howells addressed social and ethical questions in his criticism, he spoke from a position that reflected his own personal convictions. But he also spoke from a position as a businessman, a working writer and editor with one eye on the market and what he felt it could grasp. The June 1889 Study demonstrates a writer keenly aware of both his audience and the literary market in general. Howells's attempt to negotiate his ethical concerns and his marketplace concerns demonstrates his understanding that a writer was simultaneously a molder of social mores and a participant in a marketplace that, to some extent, shaped the work a writer produced. Whether he had the correct answer or not, Howells certainly understood the question.

34. Cady, *W. D. Howells as Critic*, 111.

6. "American Chances and Opportunities"

Criticism and Correspondence II

Throughout much of his career, Henry James felt chronically underappreciated by the reading public. His typical response was haughty disdain. As early as 1872, he complained to his brother William of the public's lack of taste for quality fiction. "To write for the few who have [taste] is doubtless to lose money," he declared, "but I am not afraid of starving."[1] Although James frequently mocked the reading public at large, nevertheless he longed for success. In 1879, while planning *The Portrait of a Lady*—and trying, in advance, to sell the idea of a longer novel to his editor-friend William Dean Howells—James wrote: "I must try & seek a larger success than I have yet obtained in doing something on a larger scale than I have yet done. I am greatly in need of it—of the larger success" (*LFL*, 136; *JL* 2:252).

While such restless ambition spurred James-the-artist throughout his career—in his fiction writing; in his failed bid as a dramatist; and in the most ambitious project of his career, the New York Edition of his selected works—James-the-businessman understood the connections between popularity and market demand. In January 1888, a less obstreperous James voiced a different opinion of his audience when he complained to Howells:

> I have entered upon evil days—but this is for your most private ear. It sounds portentous, but it only means that I am still staggering a good deal under the mysterious & (to me) inexplicable injury wrought—apparently—

1. James, quoted in *LFL*, 33.

upon my situation by my 2 last novels, the *Bostonians* & the *Princess,* from which I expected so much & derived so little. They have reduced the desire, & the demand, for my productions to zero—as I judge from the fact that though I have for a good while past been writing a number of good short things, I remain irremediably unpublished.

As a freelance writer, he feared his lack of popular success might hamper his ability to place his work in the market. "I am condemned apparently to eternal silence," he playfully exaggerated to Howells. "However, I don't despair, for I think I am now really in better form for work than I have ever been in my life, & I propose yet to do many things. . . . Therefore don't betray me till I myself have given up" (*LFL,* 266; *JL* 3:209).

Later that year, a more lighthearted James wrote to Howells to thank him for the generous review of his recent fiction in the "Editor's Study" of October 1888. "You are really very delightful in the October *Harper—*," James begins,

generous & sympathetic beyond my expectations or my deserts. Let me thank you promptly, heartily, joyfully. It's really a strange, startling, reviving sensation to be *understood*—I had so completely got used to doing without it. You console me for all kinds of stupidities & ineptitudes. *They* have been for a long time the only things I look for. Or rather, I don't look for them—I take them for granted. I don't even look *at* them, but go my way now perfectly without annoyance, & only with a certain amount of despair, which is easier to put up with. (*LFL,* 270)

James's pose of indifference strikes one as more than a little disingenuous. He may have expected to be misunderstood, but he always wanted to sell his fiction, even if he knew he could never be a popular success. It is with genuine gratitude, then, that James thanked Howells. In doing so, he sheds further light on his own quarrelsome attitude concerning his audience:

You have washed me down deliciously with the tepid sponge of your intelligence. . . . What you said about the *Reverberator* gave me singular pleasure—so happily have you read in it *all* my pure little intentions. You make me think for a moment that the public might be really a little less idiotic than it is—though tomorrow, no doubt, I shall again perceive that it mightn't. It doesn't matter—the idea is the only thing; on the whole it takes care of itself. One must write for that—to write for the public is to follow the scent of a red herring. (*LFL,* 270–71)

Howells, too, struggled with the American public during this period, though on terms quite different from James. Sales and popularity were less troublesome issues for Howells, who remained a popular, highly visible writer for most of his career. Howells's disenchantment with society resulted from his own personal awakening in the mid-1880s to a host of social and political concerns. His response to James's letter, in October 1888, is telling for what it reveals about his conception of society at large:

> I'm not in a very good humor with "America" myself. It seems to me the most grotesquely illogical thing under the sun; and I suppose I love it less because it wont let me love it more. I should hardly like to trust pen and ink with all the audacity of my social ideas; but after fifty years of optimistic content with "civilization" and its ability to come out all right in the end, I now abhor it, and feel that it is coming out all wrong in the end, unless it bases itself anew on a real equality. Meanwhile, I wear a fur-lined overcoat, and live in all the luxury my money can buy. (*LFL,* 272; *HSL* 3:231)

James had been speaking privately as an author who felt both misunderstood and, to an extent, threatened in his livelihood. Howells's response is that of a concerned citizen—an outgrowth of the radical sociopolitical awakening he was then undergoing in the wake of the Haymarket affair and his readings of Tolstoy, among other factors. At the same time that James became increasingly disaffected with addressing social and political concerns in his fiction, Howells became increasingly engaged with those same concerns, a development that climaxed with his most socially engaged novel, *A Hazard of New Fortunes.*

In a sense, these contrasting personal and artistic trajectories are echoed in certain aspects of James's and Howells's literary criticism during the period 1885–1897. Each writer's opinion of postbellum America as a potential literary subject, for example, could not have been more different. James had, most notably, begun to distance himself from his American literary forebears in *Hawthorne;* his estrangement from America continued to develop and deepen throughout the 1880s and 1890s. During this same period, Howells in a sense became reacquainted with his native ground. After Haymarket and his discovery of Tolstoy, his naive idealism concerning the United States gave way to a more sober, clear-eyed conception of American society and its shortcomings. This new stance necessitated a new way of understanding the nation's literature—and the nation as literary subject.

Throughout this period of profound change, James and Howells continued to read each other's work closely and to comment on it both publicly and privately. Here again, profound differences are in evidence. While remaining close to Howells in his private correspondence, James chose to distance himself publicly from his very American friend in a well-known 1886 essay. Howells, throughout all his own personal and aesthetic changes, remained one of James's closest and most sympathetic readers.

A Puritan Carnival

Henry James's unease with American society was, in the late 1880s, nothing new. He had been living in Europe since 1875. As a critic, he had announced his cultural and aesthetic preferences in scores of essays on French, British, and American authors. His opinions on postbellum America as a literary subject had been clearly articulated in *Hawthorne,* a controversial volume that elicited a fervent response from many critics for its calculated dismissal of American literature. His personal correspondence throughout the 1870s and 1880s gives further evidence of his dissatisfaction with America. Publicly, however, James had not yet spoken his peace. He returned to the topic of literary New England in his 1887 review of James Elliot Cabot's *Memoir of Ralph Waldo Emerson,* an essay which, if it pays scant attention to Cabot's work per se, deeply probes the question of Emerson.[2]

In many ways, the essay is a coda to *Hawthorne;* many of the complaints first registered in 1879 are rearticulated in 1887. James sets the tone early, noting "a singular impression of paleness" in the figure of Emerson, whose "personal history is condensed into the single word Concord, and all the condensation in the world will not make it look rich." Speaking of the public reaction to Emerson's "secession from the mild Unitarian pulpit" as well as to his various essays and addresses, some of which "passed for profane" in their time, James denigrates Emerson's New England audience as "provincial," a phrase employed frequently throughout *Hawthorne.* Indeed, James makes special note of the narrow range of New England society in Emerson's day, which he describes as "a kind of achromatic picture, without particular intensifications."[3] James registers an "impression of a terrible paucity of alternatives" for the man of letters in antebellum New England society, and he suggests that Emerson's signal qualities were in fact a product of this limited environment: "If it be his great distinction and his special sign that he had a more vivid conception of the moral life than any one else, it is probably not fanciful to say that he owed it in part to the limited way in which he saw our capacity for living illustrated. The plain, God-fearing, practical society which surrounded him was not fertile in variations: it had great intelligence

2. James republished the essay under the title "Emerson" in *Partial Portraits.*
3. James's complaints on this topic were not new in 1887. In an 1883 review of Emerson's correspondence with Thomas Carlyle, James notes "what we may call the thinness of the New England atmosphere in [Emerson's] days" (*LC* 1:244).

and energy, but it moved altogether in the straight-forward direction." In contrast, Europe is "a more complicated world," but Emerson was unimpressed by his overseas visits, always preferring the "undecorated walls of his youth" (*LC* 1:250, 253–54).

On this point, James spoke from personal experience. In November 1872, he had personally escorted Emerson on a tour of the Louvre. James had been surprised at Emerson's apparent indifference. "His perception of art is not, I think, naturally keen," he wrote, "and Concord can't have done much to quicken it." James would later confess: "I was struck with the anomaly of a man so refined and intelligent being so little spoken to by works of art. It would be more exact to say that certain chords were wholly absent; the tune was played, the tune of life and literature, altogether on those that remained."[4] For James, Emerson's apparent unworldliness was the result of his New England upbringing, rather than a deliberate rhetorical strategy of national literary chauvinism—and by definition it was narrow and restrictive.

This is clearly the tone implied when James explicates Emerson's conception of the American scholar:

> In truth, by this term he means simply the cultivated man, the man who has had a liberal education, and there is a voluntary plainness in his use of it—speaking of such people as the rustic, or the vulgar, speak of those who have a tincture of books. . . . Moreover an American reader may be excused for finding in it a pleasant sign of that prestige, often so quaintly and indeed so extravagantly acknowledged, which a connection with literature carries with it among the people of the United States. There is no country in which it is more freely admitted to be a distinction—*the* distinction; or in which so many persons have become eminent for showing it even in a slight degree. Gentlemen and ladies are celebrated there on this ground who would not on the same ground, though they might on another, be celebrated anywhere else. (*LC* 1:262–63)

It is a swipe worthy of inclusion in the charged first paragraph of *Hawthorne;* clearly, James in 1887 was not finished distancing himself from his homeland. Speaking of Emerson's audiences in the early nineteenth century, he muses: "In what other country, on sleety winter nights, would provincial and bucolic populations have gone forth in hundreds for the cold comfort of a literary discourse? The distillation anywhere else would certainly have appeared too thin, the appeal too special. But for many years the American people of the middle regions, outside of a few cities, had in the

---

4. James, quoted in Edel, *Henry James: A Life,* 135–36.

most rigorous seasons no other recreation" (*LC* 1:263). James's dismissive tone is not limited exclusively to Emerson. Speaking of Thoreau, Emerson's most famous disciple, James states that

> The application [of Emerson's teachings], with Thoreau, was violent and limited (it became a matter of prosaic detail, the non-payment of taxes, the non-wearing of a necktie, the preparation of one's food one's self, the practice of a rude sincerity—all things not of the essence), so that, though he wrote some beautiful pages, which read like a translation of Emerson into the sounds of the field and forest and which no one who has ever loved nature in New England, or indeed anywhere, can fail to love, he suffers something of the *amoindrissement* of eccentricity. (*LC* 1:265)

Again, James's trivializing, condescending tone clearly echoes *Hawthorne*. James is still keeping antebellum New England literary culture—and indeed most postbellum American literary culture—at arm's length. One notes, too, James's use of the French: a subtle way of aligning himself with the European in contrast to what he perceives as the diminished stature of the very American Thoreau. James's patronizing condescension toward the New England literati climaxes as he bluntly dismisses the legacy of Emerson's generation:

> Nothing is more perceptible to-day than that their criticism produced no fruit—that it was little else than a very decent and innocent recreation—a kind of Puritan carnival. The New England world was for much the most part very busy, but the Dial and Fruitlands and Brook Farm were the amusement of the leisure-class. Extremes meet, and as in older societies that class is known principally by its connection with castles and carriages, so at Concord it came, with Thoreau and Mr. W. H. Channing, out of the cabin and the wood-lot. (*LC* 1:267)[5]

While the final paragraphs of the essay include much praise of Emerson— it is important to remember that James is generally fond of Emerson and praises his work—James cannot resist taking a final, telling jab at Emerson as a writer. Emerson, James notes, "is a striking exception to the general rule that writings live in the last resort by their form; that they owe a large part

5. One wonders if, by association, James is here also distancing himself from Henry James, Sr. Ironically, it was Henry Sr. who was responsible for his son's cosmopolitan upbringing and education. Were the writings of Henry Sr. among the "Puritan carnival" that produced "no fruit"? Henry Jr.'s ambivalent response to the posthumously collected *Literary Remains of the Late Henry James* (1884), edited by William James, offers pause for thought. For more, see Alfred Habegger, "New York Monumentalism and Hidden Family Corpses."

of their fortune to the art with which they have been composed. It is hardly too much, or too little, to say of Emerson's writings in general that they were not composed at all." Emerson "differs from most men of letters of the same degree of credit in failing to strike us as having achieved a style" (*LC* 1:270–71). For James, the question of an author's form is, of course, crucial. As early as 1877, he had noted that "It has been said that what makes a book a classic is its style. We should modify this, and instead of style say *form*" (*LC* 2:730). This emphasis on form as the essential and defining criterion for literary art is the foundation of much of James's aesthetic criticism; for instance, it is at the very heart of "The Art of Fiction." Emerson, then, is a rare exception to James's rule, which is, generally speaking, to privilege form over content.

The continuing need for James to distance himself from America and his literary forebears raises an intriguing question. Certainly, his lack of literary success in America inspired some of his frustration. His most recent efforts in the novel had not done nearly as well as he had hoped. Rather, as Richard Brodhead points out, "*The Bostonians* and *The Princess Casamassima* are the novels that definitively lost James the larger form of the literary reading public of his time." In denigrating Hawthorne and Emerson, James had targeted two of his homeland's most revered literary figures, already canonical mainstays in the late nineteenth century. What he criticized in their work— the narrow scope; the overinsistence, in Hawthorne, on the ideal in contrast to the actual; the lack of form in Emerson; the "provincial" and limited nature of the antebellum American literary landscape—were, like a negative photographic image, precisely the opposite of what James praised in himself. He considered himself sophisticated, a master of form and execution, a literary realist (at least in the 1880s), and an author conversant with the "more complicated world" of European culture and art. Then, of course, there is the anxiety of influence—the argument that James sought to use his critical reassessments of Hawthorne and Emerson as opportunities to sever or obscure lines of influence that were, as Richard Brodhead and other recent scholars have noted, otherwise quite powerful and obvious to the informed reader of James's fiction. Regardless, as "Emerson" makes clear, James felt deeply estranged from America and its literary heritage.[6]

6. Brodhead, *School of Hawthorne,* 165. Brodhead devotes several chapters to the intertextual relationships between the work of Hawthorne and the work of James in all phases of James's career. See also Rowe, *Theoretical Dimensions,* 30–57. One hastens to add that James did not wholly dismiss Hawthorne, Emerson, or Thoreau, or any of the other American writers. Much of *Hawthorne* and the 1877 essay on Emerson contain generous praise of each author's work; for purposes of my argument, I am focusing on selected (if frequent) passages that malign the literary reputations and/or sociocultural environments of these New England writers.

Literary Colonists

Perhaps predictably, Howells's review of Cabot's *Memoir of Ralph Waldo Emerson* differs significantly from James's review, first published in the December 1887 *Macmillan's Magazine*. Howells's review appeared in the February 1888 "Editor's Study." Given the fact that Howells typically composed his Study columns some three months prior to the actual date of publication, it is unlikely that he had seen James's review.[7] Regardless, the two friends could not have been further apart on the question of Emerson.

The contrast is clear from the outset. Howells begins by suggesting that Emerson "was, indeed, so much ahead of his time in his perceptions that we have not yet lived long enough to know how modern they were."[8] He then expands the boundaries of Emerson's influence to include not merely aesthetics, but an all-important humanism: "In humanity, as in his theories of what literature should be to us, Emerson is still the foremost of all our seers, and will be so a hundred years hence." Howells downplays the significance of Emerson's personal reputation for a detached, "intellectual coldness" when meeting strangers, instead urging that the humanistic theory propounded in Emerson's writings is the true example:

> Now we are beginning to know that there is no such thing as Man, that there are only men, but Emerson can, with all his shrinking from men, best teach us how to treat them, with a view to their highest good. . . . To live in the spirit is the lesson of his life as well as of his literature; his whole memory strengthens and purifies. You learn from it that one who lives in the spirit cannot be unfaithful to the smallest rights or interests of others; cannot ignore any private obligation or public duty without shame and pain. (*SLC* 2:78–80)

This comment reconfigures the conventional wisdom concerning the sources of Howells's humanism. As William Alexander notes, "Although Howells's humanism can be traced to his contact with Eliot, Björnson, Turgenev, Tolstoy, and other European writers, a strong case may be made for its simultaneous derivation from a native tradition, emanating for the most part, but not entirely, from New England."[9] Howells's praise of Emerson,

---

7. No extant correspondence exists between James and Howells on this topic. Edwin Cady suggests the February 1888 "Editor's Study" was probably composed in October 1887 (*W. D. Howells as Critic,* 127).

8. It was a point Howells had made, indirectly, in the October 1887 Study. Maligning the "hackneyed plot, scenes, and figures" of the "ordinary English novel," Howells, quoting Emerson, had aligned the "new interests and motives" of the American realist novel with the common, the familiar, and the low (*SLC* 2:68–69).

9. Alexander, *Realist as Humanist,* 7.

then, is not only literary, but moral and ethical. This is of tremendous importance, given that in 1888 Howells was in the midst of his crucial post-Haymarket, Tolstoy-influenced personal awakening concerning ethical and social matters.

Howells conjoins the ethical and the aesthetic later in the February 1888 *Study* when he bridges from Emerson to Whitman and Tolstoy. He praises all three writers for their relative lack of "literary consciousness," an unnecessary element of "literose" complexity that weighs down Thackeray, Dickens, Daudet, and even Zola. Emerson and Whitman, as American writers, represent something of a new order—authors who embrace a disarming if occasionally chaotic (in the case of Whitman) simplicity—the very opposite of the "literose."[10] Howells sees this simplicity as crucial to the development of American literature, declaring,

> We have something worse than a literary past: we have a second-hand literary past, the literary past of a rich relation. We are, in fact, still literary colonists, who are just beginning to observe the aspects of our own life in and for themselves, but who preserve our English ancestors' point of view, and work in their tradition.
>
> Yet the future is ours if we want it, and we have only to turn our backs upon the past in order to possess it. Simplicity is difficult; some of the sophisticated declare it impossible at this stage of the proceedings; but it is always possible to be unaffected, just as it is to be morally honest, to put our object before ourselves, to think more of the truth we see than of our poor little way of telling it, and to prize the fact of things beyond the effect of things. (*SLC* 2:82)

One cannot help but wonder if Howells had his friend Henry James in mind as he wrote these lines; by 1888, James was deep into his quest to write a unique and personal brand of fiction that did nothing if not emphasize form before content, privileging the complex or the "literose" over clarity and simplicity of expression, cherishing "the effect of things" in preference to "the fact of things." Regardless, Howells's passage functions as an apt counterargument to James's assertion that Emerson failed to achieve a distinctive style.

As a whole, the February 1888 *Study* is also important in a broader respect. Edwin Cady suggests that the essay demonstrates a Howells "ready to come to terms with the elder generation" of American romantics.[11] Perhaps

10. Importantly, however, Howells distinguishes between Whitman and Tolstoy regarding the moral effects of their revolutionary writing. While each author is "the same in aesthetic effect," they are "at opposite poles morally." Whitman promotes "a sort of Titanic rapture," while Tolstoy offers "the cry of the soul for help against the world and the flesh" (*SLC* 2:81–82).

11. Cady, *W. D. Howells as Critic*, 127.

Howells was also responding to, and taking up, the call for a distinctly American literature that had its initial utterance in such writers as Emerson, Whitman, and Thoreau. In this regard, Howells's review of Cabot's *Memoir* could not be more different from James's, which articulates the very opposite movement. Whether it be on the level of form and style or on the broader level of literary precedents, James and Howells were literally worlds apart on the question of America as a literary subject.

Common Beauty, Common Grandeur

Howells continued to explore the topic in subsequent Study columns. His increasingly complex and less idealistic view of society and ethical questions during this period prompted him to reassess radically the state of American literature as well as the question of America as literary subject. His evolving opinion of America is demonstrated in the July 1888 Study, which addresses the topic of Matthew Arnold (in his role as critic of American culture) and the question of "distinction" in American society.

Howells begins by considering whether or not Arnold's celebrated social criticisms of American society are fair.[12] He begins by confessing that "Even while we perceive that [Arnold's] observation of our life wanted breadth and depth and finality, we must acknowledge that in its superficial way, and as far as it went, it was mainly just." Howells quickly paraphrases some of Arnold's lighter charges—that many American towns "seem to have been named with less sense and less taste than dogs and horses are named; that our cabs and hotels are expensive"—before jumping to more serious matters:

> Mr. Arnold might have said with some truth that we have not even been equal to our political and economic opportunities; we cannot be particularly proud of our legislatures and administrations; the relations of capital and labor in our free democracy are about as full of violence as those in any European monarchy; we have wasted the public lands which we won largely by force and fraud, and we are the prey of many vast and corrupting monopolies. Perhaps any other Aryan race could have done as well as we have done with our liberties and resources; and if the future is still ours, the present is by no means without its danger and disgrace. (*SLC* 2:94–95)[13]

12. Howells is responding to charges levied by Arnold in his essay "Civilization in the United States."

13. While the mention of the "Aryan race" controlling society is noteworthy and even disturbing, given the tone of the passage I read the phrase more as evidence of Howells's complicity with the culturally normative racialism of the times, and less as an example of overtly malicious racism.

It is one of Howells's sharpest criticisms of the United States in the Study. It bears repeating that in the summer of 1888, Howells, in the wake of the Haymarket Riot and his ongoing readings of Tolstoy, was in the midst of a radical awakening to the ills of American society. This sharply worded comment reflects those changes.

But Howells is not without praise for America. Turning around Arnold's famous quip that America lacks "distinction," he praises America's lack of class discrimination. If "distinction" equals aristocratic snobbery, he suggests, then America does well to lack distinction. Citing the examples of Lincoln, Emerson, and Grant (among others), he states that

> Our notable men, it seems, are notable for their likeness to their fellow-men, and not for their unlikeness; democracy has subtly but surely done its work; our professions of belief in equality have had their effect in our life; and whatever else we lack in homogeneity, we have in the involuntary recognition of their common humanity by our great men something that appears to be peculiarly American, and that we think more valuable than the involuntary assumption of superiority, than the distinction possible to greatness, among peoples accustomed to cringe before greatness. (*SLC* 2:96)

Clearly, Howells praises American culture and society for many of the reasons which prompted Henry James to ridicule it: for its relative lack of Arnoldian "distinction," for its unpretentious demeanor, and for the equalizing effects of democracy. Howells's celebration of American virtues escalates as the column proceeds, as does his earnest and judgmental tone: "The possessor of any sort of distinction, however unconscious he may be of the fact, has somewhere in his soul, by heredity, or by the experience of his superiority, the spark of contempt for his fellow-men; and he is for that reason more deplorable than the commonest man whom his presence brow-beats." His idealization of American democracy reaches its pitch when he declares the United States "a civilization in which there is no distinction perceptible to the eye that loves and values it" (*SLC* 2:98–99). If the first half of that statement ("a civilization in which there is no distinction") seems naive, Howells perhaps rescues himself to a degree by noting that "the eye that loves and values" America may be willing to look beyond (or is simply blind to) the distinctions, Arnoldian or otherwise, that so clearly existed for minorities, women, and the poor in the late nineteenth century. In this instance, Howells's idealism is, perhaps, a result of his over-earnest attempt to revise Arnold's well-known criticism of the United States and, in so doing, to celebrate a cherished American ideal (this is the July Study, after all). But it may be more than that.

In an important progression, Howells argues that

> Such beauty and such grandeur as we have [in America] is common beauty, common grandeur, or the beauty and grandeur in which the quality of solidarity so prevails that neither distinguishes itself to the disadvantage of anything else. It seems to us that these conditions invite the artist to the study and the appreciation of the common, and to the portrayal in every art of those finer and higher aspects which unite rather than sever humanity, if he would thrive in our new order of things. . . . The arts must become democratic, and then we shall have the expression of America in art. (*SLC* 2:99)

This important passage demonstrates, on the one hand, how Howells conjoined his developing social conscience with his fervent aesthetic beliefs. The personal awakening he underwent in the 1880s only solidified—or further radicalized—the realist aesthetics he had favored for over twenty years. In this sense, the passage is a testament to the depth of his aesthetic convictions. On the other hand, there is a slowly mounting sense of overdetermined zeal in the conclusion to the July 1888 Study—and with it, a hint of Howells's youthful naïveté. For example, the call for "the portrayal in every art of those finer and higher aspects which unite rather than sever humanity" echoes an earlier call for the novelist to capture "the more smiling aspects of life, which are the more American." Both passages ask the author to turn a blind eye to other, less desirable, aspects of society in the hopes of uniting an audience of readers otherwise deeply divided. Howells, no matter how much he had learned about American society, still wanted to save it.

The Life of Toil

The joining of social concerns with a corresponding aesthetic vision is at the heart of one of Howells's most important essays on the topic of American literature. In the November 1891 Study—one of his final Study columns, as he would resign four months later—one finds a fully matured Howells, in possession of strong and clearly defined social and aesthetic beliefs. Addressing the question of what constitutes American literature, he begins with the interesting proposition that

> for all aesthetic purposes the American people are not a nation but a condition. They are the old, well-known Anglo-Saxon race, affected and modified by the infusion of other strains, but not essentially changed by these, and not very different from the English at home except in their po-

litical environment, and the vastness of the scale of their development. Their literature so far as they have produced any is American-English literature, just as the English literature is English-European, and it is as absurd to ask them to have a literature wholly their own as to ask them to have a language wholly their own. (*SLC* 2:189)

Howells is, in this column, interested in deconstructing the notion of nationality as a governing ideological force—at least in terms of aesthetics. Rather, one's nationality is a "condition" developed in response to sociocultural factors largely beyond the individual's control. With regard to aesthetics, Howells is interested in moving beyond national boundaries in his search to identify the best artistic criteria. "It appears to us that at this stage of the proceedings there is no such thing as nationality in the highest literary expression," he argues, "but there is a universality, a humanity, which is very much better." Howells believes that "The great and good things in literature now a days are not the national features, but the universal features," and he therefore equates the national with the limited, the esoteric, and the self-serving. (Dare we say the provincial and the anachronistic?) In contrast, the universal is humanistic, compassionate, and caring. Thus he can declare that "The English, who have not felt the great world-movement towards life and truth, are national; those others who have felt it [that is, the Americans, the Russians, and the French], are universal" (*SLC* 2:190). Clearly, his argument thus far is predicated on the Christian humanism he learned, principally, from Tolstoy.

In full Jamesian mode, Howells counsels against applying a priori criteria to literature. In fact, he argues, truly to understand what constitutes American literature, one must look *beyond* art and aesthetics: "the question is not whether this thing or that thing in an author is American or not, but whether upon the whole the author's work is such as would have been produced by a man of any other race or environment." He understands that the question of defining a national literature is too big, too broad to be rigidly codified: "the nationality of a literature is embodied in its general aspect, not in its particular features" (*SLC* 2:190–91). The argument marks a breakthrough for Howells. It is "race or environment" that shapes an author's work, not a predetermined definition of nationality. Thus, Howells implicitly argues, the question of a "national" literature is less a question of the artist's citizenship and is, more precisely, a question of the particular society and culture that shape the author.

"Our critics evidently think that the writers of a nation can make its literature what they like," Howells continues, "but this is a fallacy: they can only make it what the nation likes, involuntarily following the law of environment."

He cites as an example the generalism that American literature "has always been distinguished by two tendencies, apparently opposite, but probably parallel: one a tendency toward an elegance refined and polished both in thought and phrase," and "the other a tendency to grotesqueness, wild and extravagant, to the point of anarchy." He concludes: "Our literature has these tendencies because the nation has them, and because in some measure each and every American has them. It would take too long to say just how and why; but our censors may rest assured that in this anomalous fact exists the real nationality of our literature." Having identified these "two tendencies" of American literature, Howells argues that the critics who promote Whitman as "the representative of our literature" possess at best "a half perception of the truth." Howells admits that Whitman "is expressive of that national life which finds itself young and new in a world full of old conventions and decrepit ideals, and that he is suggestive if not representative of America." But Howells hastens to add that, at best, Whitman—like Twain, Harte, and Cable—"illustrates the prevalence of one of our moods." These may be quintessentially American authors, but the same may also be said of Longfellow, Lowell, James, and Holmes (*SLC* 2:191–92). Howells has introduced, perhaps for the first time in American literature, the argument that society and culture shape an author's sensibilities, and not the other way around. In so doing, he embraces what is generally considered to be a core tenet of American naturalism, namely that human character and behavior—and, by extension, art—are principally shaped by heredity and environment.

It is an argument that Howells would continue to explore in essays after he had finished writing the Study. In an 1895 essay from *Harper's Weekly*, for instance, he argues that

> If [an author's] business is to impart a feeling of life, he must realize more and more that his figures cannot be too intimately inwrought with their environment, or that they cannot be too distinctly shown as an outgrowth of it. The prime condition of their being themselves is that they shall be of their circumstance; whatever projection they have is from their dependence upon each other; and the author when he works artistically works with an instinctive perception that in aesthetics there is no such thing as individuality. Character is interesting, is possible, only as it is affected by character; and the persons of any size group severally appeal to us only in the measure that they are characterized by the surroundings. Otherwise they are merely allegorical types, without vital meaning or value. (*SLC* 2:214)

Here Howells is even more clear about his newly developed argument concerning character in fiction. In a similar vein, he revisits the argument in an 1897 *Harper's Weekly* essay in which he denigrates Lord Byron for his "ignoble" nature and "coarse" personal behavior (certain salacious details of Byron's personal life having recently come to light). "Heredity would account for [Byron] in one case," Howells explains, "and environment would account for him in the other so far that the modern man would be quite willing to leave him to the modern man's God" (*SLC* 2:249). The "modern man's God," one assumes, is the post-Darwinian, naturalist concept of a deity who has set a world in motion but who is no longer interested in or capable of controlling it. What controls or shapes human behavior is, again, heredity and environment. Clearly, Howells's emergent naturalist view of character in both fiction and society had taken root and would continue to inform his work as a critic.

Having established his point concerning heredity and environment in the November 1891 Study, Howells proceeds to address one final question concerning American literature. His tone darkens slightly in section 5 of the column, when he responds to the noted English writer, editor, and anthologist Arthur Quiller-Couch, who has argued that American authors ought to be writing about "the life of toil." Playfully accusing the highly influential Quiller-Couch of ignorance, Howells states that "the American public does not like to read about the life of toil" precisely because "Nearly all the Americans are in their own persons or have been in those of their fathers or grandfathers, partakers of the life of toil." What the American reader wants, he suggests, is

> something select, something that treats of high life, like those English novels which have chiefly nourished us; or something that will teach us how to escape the life of toil by a great stroke of business, or by a splendid marriage. What we like to read about is the life of noblemen or millionaires; that is our romance; and if our writers were to begin telling us on any extended scale of how mill hands or miners, or farmers, or iron puddlers really live, we should very soon let them know that we did not care to meet such vulgar and commonplace people. Our well-to-do classes are at present engaged in keeping their eyes fast shut to the facts of the life of toil and in making believe that the same causes will not produce the same effects here as in Europe; and they would feel it an impiety if they were shown the contrary. (*SLC* 2:192–93)

America's "finest gentilities" care as little for literature as they do for politics, he mockingly proclaims. And the workers already know the life of toil firsthand. Furthermore, the workers

> know that in a nation which honors toil, the toiler is socially nothing, and that he is going from bad to worse quite as if the body politic had no interest in him. . . . [N]o class, and least of all his fellows, would like the life

of a workman shown in literature as it really is, and his condition painted as hopeless as the condition of ninety-nine workmen out of every hundred is. . . . The life of toil! It is a little too personal to people who are trying to be ladies and gentlemen of elegant leisure as fast as they can. (*SLC* 2:193)

Rarely has Howells been this impassioned and direct, rarely this caustic and sarcastic. The November 1891 Study marks both the maturation and the end of his most important period as a literary critic. It was the last Study column to offer the kind of biting social and aesthetic commentary that marked the best years of the Study. In this sense, it is his Parthian shot in the "Realism War." One notes, in the sarcasm of section 5, a hint of the weariness and frustration that, in part, led him to resign the Study. After six years of fighting, the passionate and committed critic who had argued so cogently for realism was exhausted.[14]

This period also marked great change in Howells as a writer of fiction. Having recently published *Annie Kilburn* and *A Hazard of New Fortunes,* two of his most socially engaged novels, both of which examine aspects of "the life of toil" in detail, Howells had completed his major work as a realist. As Amy Kaplan has noted, "*Hazard* both fulfills and exhausts the project of realism to embrace social diversity within the outlines of a broader community, and to assimilate a plethora of facts and details into a unified narrative form."[15] Howells had tried in both his literary criticism (as in the July 1888 Study) and in his fiction to define and unite a divided United States through the practice of realist aesthetics. By 1891, it was clear that American society was more divided and unstable than it had ever been. And realism had quite simply failed to command the scene of art. In fact, the romance novel, which had never really gone away, was enjoying something of a comeback. As a critic, Howells chose to lay down his guns, resigning the Study and its monthly call to arms. As a creative writer, he redirected his attention to new artistic frontiers, exploring psychologically informed fiction in *The Shadow of a Dream* and the socialist-utopian romance in *A Traveler from Altruria.*

The battle had not, however, been fought in vain. Howells, who began his tenure in the Study by inviting American authors to focus on "the more smiling aspects of life, which are the more American," had, by November 1891, arrived at a much more sophisticated and much less naive vision of

14. Of course, the reasons why Howells left the "Editor's Study" are numerous and varied. For instance, as Donald Pizer suggests, Howells was also fed up with the editorial interference of Henry Alden and the editors of *Harper's,* who had grown uneasy with Howells's increasingly radical stands on literature (*SLC* 2:xvi–xviii).

15. Kaplan, *Social Construction,* 63.

American society and its literature. The literature he implicitly calls for in 1891 is one that accurately reflects the culture and society surrounding the individual author. For Howells, this view of society is one in which "the toiler is socially nothing," and the plight of the "hopeless" worker "is going from bad to worse." Given the bias still lingering today around Howells's reputation as a literary critic and as a creative writer, the point bears emphasizing. So does the fact that, in the years that followed, he would promote and champion some of the most important realist and naturalist authors of the day, a well-known list that includes Stephen Crane, Frank Norris, Charlotte Perkins Gilman, Charles W. Chesnutt, and Abraham Cahan (whom Howells personally discovered, assisted in securing a publishing contract, and then unflaggingly supported in print). Without question, Howells occupies a crucial position—both as creative writer and literary critic—in the transition from the genteel realism of the 1870s and early 1880s, to the grittier social realism of the late 1880s and early 1890s, and to the development of American naturalism in the 1890s.

Aberrations of Thought and Excesses of Beer

The essays and correspondence James and Howells wrote to, for, and of one another during this period also reflect their changing opinions about literature and America as a literary subject—and, of course, their opinions of each other. During this time, James published one essay on Howells, an important 1886 overview in *Harper's Weekly*. The essay is a classic example of Jamesian diplomacy, a calculated maneuver designed as much to reposition James in the public opinion as it is to promote the work of his friend. Four years had elapsed since the publication of Howells's "Henry James, Jr.," an essay that, for many readers and critics, cemented the public perception of Howells and James as two of a kind. Deeply uncomfortable with the state of his reputation, James wrote "William Dean Howells" in an attempt to distance himself from Howells and, in so doing, to quiet the opposition once and for all.

James begins by dividing Howells's career into "its early and its later manner," the early work being the poetry and the travel volumes *Venetian Life* and *Italian Journeys*, "those Italian initiations without which we of other countries remain always, after all, more or less barbarians." The "later manner" marks the start of his career as a fiction writer and as editor of the *Atlantic Monthly*, the latter being a "grave complication" that Howells managed "with infinite tact and industry." Howells's tenure at the *Atlantic* was not exactly wasted time; rather, in James's opinion, "They were years of

economized talent, of observation and accumulation. They laid the foundation of what is most remarkable, or most, at least, the peculiar sign, in his effort as a novelist—his unerring sentiment of the American character. Mr.
Howells knows more about it than any one, and it was during this period of
what we may suppose to have been rather perfunctory administration that
he must have gathered many of his impressions of it" (*LC* 1:499–500). The
passage is worth careful consideration. On the one hand, James correctly
praises Howells for his "unerring sentiment of the American character" that
he "knows more about . . . than any one." But the praise is woven into what
is clearly a gentle poke at his friend in his capacity as editor of the most esteemed American literary periodical of its day—a periodical, it hardly requires mentioning, that played a large role in establishing a young Henry
James. James knew as well as anyone that Howells's editorial efforts at the
Atlantic were anything but perfunctory. As the editor, Howells displayed
unflagging zeal, pursuing and promoting a huge number of young and tal-
ented authors; as a critic, Howells wrote numerous reviews and essays that
helped establish the theoretical groundwork of American literary realism.
For James to pass off Howells's editorial work as a "grave complication"
that hampered his creative output may be to some extent true, but to suggest
that Howells was in any respect a perfunctory editor is as gross a misstatement as James would ever make about Howells. The comment is, perhaps,
more indicative of James's growing frustration with editors in general. This,
indeed, is the sentiment implied as he describes the editor's relationship to
the world at large: "His manner of contact with the world is almost violent,
and whatever bruises he may confer, those he receives are the most telling,
inasmuch as the former are distributed among many, and the latter all to be
endured by one" (*LC* 1:500). James, smarting from his pugilistic treatment
at the hands of editors on both shores of the Atlantic, clearly has a bone to
pick with the profession.

James also offers lukewarm praise for Howells's fiction, noting that "He
was still under the shadow of his editorship when, in the intervals of his
letter-writing and reviewing, he made his first cautious attempts in the walk
of fiction. I say cautious, for in looking back nothing is more clear than that
he had determined to advance only step by step."[16] Noting the narrow
range of *Their Wedding Journey, A Chance Acquaintance,* and *A Foregone
Conclusion,* James describes an author who progressed, at least early in his
career, from book to book, lacking in self-confidence:

16. It is a sentiment James had expressed directly to Howells in an 1884 letter; noting his
increasing fondness for the work of the French naturalists, James bluntly told Howells: "I regard you as the great American naturalist. I don't think you go far enough, & you are haunted
with romantic phantoms & a tendency to factitious glosses; but you are in the right path, & I
wish you repeated triumphs there" (*LFL,* 243; *JL* 3:28).

> It is my impression that long after he was twenty he still cultivated the be-
> lief that the faculty of the novelist was not in him, and was even capable of
> producing certain unfinished chapters (in the candor of his good faith he
> would sometimes communicate them to a listener) in triumphant support
> of this contention. He believed, in particular, that he could not make peo-
> ple talk, and such have been the revenges of time that a cynical critic might
> almost say of him to-day that he cannot make them keep silent. (*LC*
> 1:500–501)

To be sure, there is a friendly playfulness in the passage—the gentle (if
highly public) ribbing between close friends. But there is also, perhaps, a
glimmer of envy: the less successful author seeking to tarnish, just slightly,
the reputation of the more successful author. James was a master of disguis-
ing the sour with a thin layer of the sweet; one simultaneously senses that he
himself is playing the role of the "cynical critic" throughout "William Dean
Howells."

Such enigmatic doublespeak is evident a few lines later, when James states
that

> Mr. Howells is literary, on certain sides exquisitely so, though with a sin-
> gular and not unamiable perversity he sometimes endeavors not to be; but
> his vision of the human scene is never a literary reminiscence, a reflection of
> books and pictures, of tradition and fashion and hearsay. I know of no
> English novelist of our hour whose work is so exclusively a matter of paint-
> ing what he sees, and who is so sure of what he sees. People are always
> wanting a writer of Mr. Howells's temperament to see certain things that
> he doesn't (that he doesn't sometimes even want to), but I must content
> myself with congratulating the author of *A Modern Instance* and *Silas
> Lapham* on the admirable quality of his vision. The American life which he
> for the most part depicts is certainly neither very rich nor very fair, but it is
> tremendously positive, and as his manner of presenting it is as little as pos-
> sible conventional, the reader can have no doubt about it. This is an im-
> mense luxury; the ingenious character of the witness (I can give it no
> higher praise) deepens the value of the report. (*LC* 1:501)

Again, these lines warrant careful consideration. James praises the accuracy and authenticity of Howells's literary vision, even referring to Howells, metaphorically, as a painter—an analogy used quite effectively in "The
Art of Fiction" and one that James employed throughout his career. This is
indeed high praise from James, as is his notice of Howells's unconventional
presentation of American life. But James also notes the "tremendously positive" nature of Howells's depiction of America, a phrase that introduces
his critique of Howells's optimism. This is the sentiment behind the carefully worded passage concerning those who "are always wanting a writer of

Mr. Howells's temperament to see certain things that he doesn't (that he doesn't sometimes even want to)." From his earliest published reviews of Howells, James complained that the world described in Howells's work was too narrow and limited—or, in Jamesian parlance, too "little." For now, James is content simply to establish the point; he will return to it later in the essay.

Also, one must carefully consider the final phrase of the passage: "the ingenious character of the witness (I can give it no higher praise) deepens the value of the report." By claiming he can give no higher praise, does James mean only to offer high praise for Howells's work as "witness" to American society? Or does he mean he honestly cannot say anything better about the fiction because of the inherent limitations of Howells's optimism? Howells's fiction may be "as little as possible conventional," and this may be "an immense luxury," but is it enough, in James's opinion, to offset the "tremendously positive" (that is, excessively optimistic) nature of the report? Once again, this passage seems carefully coded. James appears simultaneously to be offering the highest praise and to be placing a boundary on the amount of praise he can award to a "limited" effort such as Howells's. One suspects this enigmatic, paradoxical effect is precisely what James sought in the passage.

James, of course, does not withhold his praise for Howells; in a lengthy and frequently cited passage near the middle of the essay, he proves himself both an astute and a sympathetic reader of Howells's fiction, noting that "His work is of a kind of which it is good that there should be much today."[17] James proceeds to catalog the essential elements of Howells's realist aesthetic in a well-known passage so eloquent it nevertheless deserves to be quoted at length:

> He is animated by a love of the common, the immediate, the familiar and vulgar elements of life, and holds that in proportion as we move into the rare and strange we become vague and arbitrary; that truth of representation, in a word, can be achieved only so long as it is in our power to test and measure it. He thinks scarcely anything too paltry to be interesting, that the small and the vulgar have been terribly neglected, and would rather see an exact account of a sentiment or a character he stumbles against every day than a brilliant evocation of a passion or a type he has never seen and does not even particularly believe in. He adores the real, the natural, the colloquial, the moderate, the optimistic, the domestic, and the democratic; looking askance at exceptions and perversities and superiori-

17. Even this praise can be read as Janus-faced, however, for it implies that Howells is doing the sort of work that many do, whereas James prided himself on being unique.

ties, at surprising and incongruous phenomena in general. One must have seen a great deal before one concludes; the world is very large, and life is a mixture of many things; she by no means eschews the strange, and often risks combinations and effects that make one rub one's eyes. Nevertheless, Mr. Howells's stand-point is an excellent one for seeing a large part of the truth, and even if it were less advantageous, there would be a great deal to admire in the firmness with which he has planted himself. He hates a "story," and (this private feat is not impossible) has probably made up his mind very definitely as to what the pestilent thing consists of. . . . Mr. Howells hates an artificial fable and a *dénouement* that is pressed into the service; he likes things to occur as they occur in life, where the manner of a great many of them is not to occur at all. He has observed that heroic emotion and brilliant opportunity are not particularly interwoven with our days, and indeed, in the way of omission, he *has* often practised in his pages a very considerable boldness. It has not, however, made what we find there any less interesting and less human. (*LC* 1:502–3)

One would be hard-pressed to find a more insightful or sensitive contemporary explication of Howells's realist aesthetic.[18] James's insights in this passage are on par with those Howells offered on James's work in "Henry James, Jr." and reinforce one's sense that the two friends remained, throughout their lives, each other's keenest and most articulate readers. James next examines a dimension of the "considerable boldness" found in Howells's fiction: namely, Howells's depiction of domestic American life. Wondering how it is that Howells has "escaped the imputation of a want of patriotism," James playfully observes that "The manners he describes—the desolation of the whole social prospect in *A Modern Instance* is perhaps the strongest expression of those influences—are eminently of a nature to discourage the intending visitor, and yet the westward pilgrim continues to arrive, in spite of the Bartley Hubbards and the Laphams, and the terrible practices at the country hotel in *Doctor Breen,* and at the Boston boarding-house in *A Woman's Reason*" (*LC* 1:503). Despite James's lighthearted tone, it was a question that truly irked him. In an 1885 letter to Grace Norton, James questioned why the reading public accepted the depiction of American society in *Silas Lapham* when it had visibly shuddered at the portrait offered in *The Bostonians:* "Everyone here [in London] admires extremely the truth and power of 'Silas Lapham,' including myself. But what hideousness of life! They don't revile Howells when he does America, and such an America as that, and why do they revile me? The 'Bostonians' is sugar-cake, compared

18. Anesko has convincingly demonstrated how James, in "William Dean Howells," borrowed—and improved upon—numerous observations first offered by Margaret Oliphant in her 1883 essay "American Literature in England," published in *Blackwood's* (*LFL,* 169–71).

with it" (*JL* 3:106). James's own attempt at an answer constitutes the most famous passage from "William Dean Howells," an allegation from which Howells's legacy has never wholly freed itself:

> This tolerance of depressing revelations is explained partly, no doubt, by the fact that Mr. Howells's truthfulness imposes itself—the representation is so vivid that the reader accepts it as he accepts, in his own affairs, the mystery of fate—and partly by a very different consideration, which is simply that if many of his characters are disagreeable, almost all of them are extraordinarily good, and with a goodness which is a ground for national complacency. If American life is on the whole, as I make no doubt whatever, more innocent than that of any other country, nowhere is the fact more patent than in Mr. Howells's novels, which exhibit so constant a study of the actual and so small a perception of evil. . . . Purity of life, fineness of conscience, benevolence of motive, decency of speech, good-nature, kindness, charity, tolerance (though, indeed, there is little but each other's manners for the people to tolerate), govern all the scene; the only immoralities are aberrations of thought, like that of Silas Lapham, or excesses of beer, like that of Bartley Hubbard. (*LC* 1:503–4)

Arguably, the sentiment expressed in this passage does, more or less, accurately reflect an aspect—perhaps a dominant aspect—of Howells's fiction up to 1886. And James's discomfort with Howells's small perception of evil surely constituted an important part of why he found Howells's work "little." But given the sentiment expressed in James's 1885 letter to Grace Norton—the "hideousness of life" in Howells's *Silas Lapham*—one also wonders if James, for reasons of tone and rhetorical strategy, deliberately emphasizes one (admittedly pronounced) aspect of Howells's fiction in "William Dean Howells" while conveniently overlooking other examples that would complicate his reductive summation.[19]

In closing, James offers two final criticisms of Howells's work. Each complaint is solidly rooted in James's own personal aesthetic of fiction. The broader complaint concerns the general question of style in fiction:

> I should like . . . to allude in passing, for purposes of respectful remonstrance, to a phrase that [Howells] suffered the other day to fall from his pen (in a periodical, but not in a novel), to the effect that the style of a

---

19. A very short and highly selective list of counterexamples to James's reductive assertion might include Bartley Hubbard's not-so-innocent dereliction of his marriage and his violent end in *A Modern Instance* (it was certainly more than an "excess of beer" that destroyed his marriage), the unflagging and destructive greed of Rogers in *The Rise of Silas Lapham*, or the pseudo-Oedipal sexual strategizing rampant in *Indian Summer*.

work of fiction is a thing that matters less and less all the while. Why less
and less? It seems to me as great a mistake to say so as it would be to say
that it matters more and more. It is difficult to see how it can matter either
less or more. The style of a novel is a part of the execution of a work of art;
the execution of a work of art is a part of its very essence, and that, it seems
to me, must have mattered in all ages in exactly the same degree, and be
destined always to do so. (*LC* 1:505)

James's concern with style here is, of course, consistent with his aesthetic
at the time, as evidenced in "The Art of Fiction" and elsewhere. The passage to which he refers is Howells's 1884 review of E. W. Howe's *The Story
of a Country Town,* in the course of which Howells states:

I do not care to praise his style, though, as far as that increasingly unimportant matter goes, it is well enough; but what I like in him is the sort of
mere open humanness of his book. It has defects enough, which no one
can read far without discovering; but, except in the case of Jo Erring [a
principal character in the novel], they are not important—certainly not
such as to spoil any one's pleasure in a fiction which is of the kind most
characteristic of our time, and which no student of our time hereafter can
safely ignore. (*SLC* 1:338–39)

As I believe this passage suggests, the tenor of Howells's review is to overlook certain mismanaged elements of style or form—the overdrawn character of Jo Erring, Howells argues, "finally comes near spoiling the strong,
hard-headed, clear-conscienced story" (*SLC* 1:338)—in deference to its status as a homegrown realist novel. Howells's comment regarding the "increasingly unimportant matter" of style, in this context, functions as a polite
euphemism; the novel, he clearly notes, "has defects enough." The more
important point for Howells is that Howe, a novice novelist, has embraced
realism.

Nevertheless, Howells has made the rather odd claim that style is an "increasingly unimportant matter" in fiction. Without question, James was never
so generous as to overlook a novel's formal blunders in deference to its genre,
realist or otherwise. Form always came first for James, who, in "William Dean
Howells," loftily declares: "I can conceive of no state of civilization in which
[style] shall not be deemed important, though of course there are states in
which executants are clumsy." He then deftly turns the question around to
focus on Howells's own fiction:

I should also venture to express a certain regret that Mr. Howells (whose
style, in practice, after all, as I have intimated, treats itself to felicities which

his theory perhaps would condemn) should appear increasingly to hold composition too cheap—by which I mean, should neglect the effect that comes from alternation, distribution, relief. He has an increasing tendency to tell his story altogether in conversations, so that a critical reader sometimes wishes, not that the dialogue might be suppressed (it is too good for that), but that it might be distributed, interspaced with narrative and pictorial matter. The author forgets sometimes to paint, to evoke the conditions and appearances, to build in the subject. (*LC* 1:505–6)

This is James's second and final complaint concerning Howells, a complaint neatly introduced in an apparently offhand manner with the mention of Howells's two-year-old comment regarding style in fiction. (Hardly a phrase dropped "the other day"—James had clearly noted the occasion.) Importantly, James's complaint regarding Howells's use of dialogue is his first published comment on the topic. In this regard, it is anything but a passing observation; dialogue would remain a concern for the rest of James's career, always an essential consideration in the overall form of a novel.

For example, the issue is at the very heart of James's 1897 critique of George Gissing's *The Whirlpool*. For James, who reminds the reader that "It is form above all that is talent," Gissing serves as the consummate negative example: an author who ignores "the whole question of composition, of foreshortening, of the proportion and relation of parts." Of central concern is Gissing's overuse of dialogue; it "crowds out . . . the golden blocks themselves of the structure, the whole divine exercise and mystery of the exquisite art of presentation." More precisely, Gissing's mismanaged dialogue disrupts the temporal flow of the novel. For James, this is no venial sin. The "novelist's effort" must include a matter of "most difficulty and thereby of most dignity," namely "giving the sense of duration, of the lapse and accumulation of time. This is altogether to my view the stiffest problem that the artist in fiction has to tackle." Dialogue, in its real-time evocation of short scenes lasting only minutes, cannot accurately convey the scope and breadth of time which is the proper domain of the novel. "The picture is nothing unless it be a picture of the conditions," notes James; the novelist, through his foreshortening, selection, and form, must accurately capture the sense of a broad span of time and the feel or sensibility of the "conditions" that inform a scene. Dialogue, which occupies so little space temporally, cannot meet the task: "'Dialogue,' as it is commonly called, is singularly suicidal from the moment it is not directly illustrative of something given us by another method, something constituted and presented" (*LC* 1:1403–4).

Although James does not elaborate on his dissatisfaction with Howells's dialogue in 1886, it is clear from his extended consideration of the topic in

1897 that it constitutes (or would shortly constitute) a crucial dimension of the overall consideration of a novel's form. It is therefore noteworthy that the 1886 Howells essay marks his first public consideration of the issue.[20] One might even speculate that James kept himself from articulating a more extended critique of the issue in "William Dean Howells" in deference to his friend, waiting, perhaps, for another opportunity devoid of such personal connections—though one hastens to add that in the eleven years between "William Dean Howells" and the Gissing essay (one of James's 1897 "London Notes") the issue had surely become more clear and more important to James.

"William Dean Howells" concludes on a tepid note, echoing the tone of the overall essay. It is, of course, a calculated performance from a James who clearly wanted to distance himself publicly from his friend. James confessed as much to Howells in an October 1886 letter, in which he offered

> words of explanation as to the, I fear, rather dry tone of the poor little tribute to your genius in the *Harper* newspaper. That tone, & the general poverty of the article were the result of a desire not to injure you by appearing too much to "return the compliment" of your so generous article about me, in the *Century,* in the past time. I had a horror of appearing too mutual & reciprocal, & cultivated (in your own interest) a coldness which I didn't feel. If I had been more free, I should have twined much fairer garlands round your brow. (*LFL,* 256)

It is interesting that James would suggest he had written "William Dean Howells" in the interest of his friend and former editor. Sadly, Howells's correspondence both preceding and following this letter are not extant, though James does allude, in his letter, to a prior letter in which Howells apparently referred to "William Dean Howells."

Of course, in most of his other personal correspondence with Howells, James voiced more generous opinions. For example, after reading *A Hazard of New Fortunes,* James wrote to Howells to express his "communicable rapture." The novel is "simply prodigious" and, with the noted exception of a lengthy apartment-hunting sequence early in the text, "the whole thing is almost equally good. . . . The life, the truth, the light, the heat, the breadth & depth & thickness of the Hazard, are absolutely admirable" (*LFL,* 275; *JL* 3:281). Perhaps referencing his 1884 assertion that Howells is America's "great American naturalist" (*LFL,* 243; *JL* 3:28), James notes that "You are less *big* than Zola, but you are ever so much less clumsy & really more various,

20. James returned to the issue of dialogue in two important later essays, "The Lesson of Balzac" (*LC* 2:115–39), and the Preface to *The Awkward Age* (*LC* 2:1120–37).

and moreover you & he don't see the same things." James then hints, in characteristically circuitous fashion, at his sense that Howells does not fulfill his own potential: "I won't even compare you with something I have a sort of dim, stupid sense you might be and are not—for I don't in the least know that you might be it, after all, or whether, if you were, you wouldn't cease to be that something you are which makes me write to you thus. We don't know what people might give us that they don't—the only thing is to take them on what they do & to allow them absolutely & utterly their conditions" (*LFL,* 276; *JL* 3:282). In part, James may be hinting that Howells has not fulfilled the role of the "great American naturalist." Or he may be echoing the sentiment expressed publicly in "William Dean Howells," the idea that "People are always wanting a writer of Mr. Howells's temperament to see certain things that he doesn't (that he doesn't sometimes even want to)." He certainly has Howells's "small perception of evil" in mind when he mentions "certain things which make me wonder at your form & your fortune (e.g.—as I have told you before—the fatal colours in which they let *you,* because you live at home—is it?—paint American life; & the fact that there's a whole quarter of the heaven upon which, in the matter of composition, you seem to be consciously—*is* it consciously?—to have turned your back)." Despite these half-articulated reservations, James can assert that

> The novelist is a particular *window,* absolutely—& of worth in so far as he is one; & it's because you open so well & are hung so close over the street that *I* could hang out of it all day long. Your very value is that you choose your own street—heaven forbid that I should have to choose it for you. If I should say I mortally dislike the people who pass in it, I should seem to be taking on myself that intolerable responsibility of selection which it is exactly such a luxury to be relieved of. Indeed I'm convinced that no reader above the rank of an idiot—this number is moderate I admit—can really fail to take any view that's really *shown* them—any gift (of subject) that's really given. The usual imbecillity of the novel is that the showing & giving simply don't come off—the reader never touches the subject & the subject never touches the reader: the window is no window at all—but only childishly *finta,* like the ornaments of our beloved Italy. This is why, as a triumph of *communication,* I hold the Hazard so rare & strong. (*LFL,* 276; *JL* 3:282–83)

This is high praise indeed from James, for whom the principle of selection was always primary. The passage is also interesting in that it prefigures the "house of fiction" conceit in the Preface to *The Portrait of a Lady.* On the whole, this May 1890 letter is an excellent example of how James typically mixed generous praise with gently worded criticism in his personal correspondence with Howells.

The Farthest Departure from the Old Ideal

In his published literary criticism, Howells remained James's most loyal reader and his biggest champion throughout this period. In the April 1887 Study, his first review of James since writing "Henry James, Jr.," Howells unequivocally announces that "We find *no* fault with Mr. Henry James's *Princess Casamassima:* it is a great novel; it is his greatest, and it is incomparably the greatest novel of the year in our language" (*SLC* 2:47). Howells, particularly excited by the fact that the novel addresses the questions of socialism and class inequalities, proceeds to catalog the novel's characters and even gives away the ending. He is even more supportive in the October 1888 Study, bluntly declaring that "it would be futile to dispute [James's] primacy in most literary respects. We mean his primacy not only among fabling Americans, but among all who are presently writing fiction." Noting the tepid reception afforded *The Princess Casamassima,* Howells opines with uncanny foresight: "It is in a way discreditable to our time that a writer of such quality should ever have grudging welcome; the fact impeaches not only our intelligence, but our sense of the artistic. It will certainly amaze a future day that such things as his could be done in ours and meet only a feeble and conditional acceptance from the 'best' criticism, with something little short of ribald insult from the common cry of literary paragraphers" (*SLC* 2:101).

Howells's September 1890 Study, in which he reviews *The Tragic Muse,* ranks among his most insightful work on James. Howells begins with the proposition that James is essentially unclassifiable; he is an artist "who must be called a novelist because there is yet no name for the literary kind he has invented, and so none for the inventor." Narrative, in the hands of James, is something altogether new and different. "To spin a yarn for the yarn's sake," Howells notes, is "wholly impossible to an American of Mr. Henry James's modernity." Rather, "the story could never have value except as a means; it could not exist for him as an end; it could only be used illustratively; it could be the frame, not possibly the picture." Noting the public's growing exasperation with James's difficult fiction, Howells derides readerly expectations that a story be driven by plot and incident, that the novel's conflicts be solved "by a marriage or a murder," and that meaning be spoon-fed "with a moral minced small and then thinned with milk and water, and familiarly flavored with sentimentality or religiosity" (*SLC* 2:151).

In contrast, we have *The Tragic Muse,* "a novel which marks the farthest departure from the old ideal of the novel." Howells praises its moral ambiguities, which strike him as patently modern: "In the nineteenth century, especially now towards the close of it, one is never quite sure about vice and virtue: they fade wonderfully into and out of each other; they mix, and seem to stay mixed, at least around the edges" (*SLC* 2:152). This statement from Howells demonstrates his ever-deepening awareness of the moral complexities of the world around him. Howells, in 1890, is aware of the porous, conditional nature of moral distinctions. He may have been rigid or prudish at other moments, but here he shows that he can celebrate paradox and moral ambiguity in avant-garde art without flinching. Significantly, it was Howells's final comment on James in the Study.[21]

Conclusion

Between 1885 and 1897, Henry James and William Dean Howells remained close personal friends and confidants. After the death of Howells's daughter Winifred in March 1889, James wrote a brief, heartfelt letter of condolence. When Howells responded later that year, he confided that "My wife and I both felt that you had given words to the mute despair and wonder we were in, and had lightened our burden by speaking out its very form and essence for us. My phrase offends me now by its coldness, but indeed none could impart the tender, fond gratitude we felt toward you" (*LFL,* 273–74; *HSL* 3:253).

In a similar fashion, Howells wrote in 1894 to console his friend's wounded sense of stature. "There was a note of unjustified discouragement in your letter," he observes, "which my heart protested against with a promptness that puts my pen to shame. I wished to say to you that so far as literary standing is concerned there is no one who has your rank among us."[22] In a rallying, businesslike manner, Howells suggests journals to which James should submit his fiction. "I am trying to reply to your half-question as to 'American chances and opportunities.' It seems to me that you have only to suggest yourself, and they will rise at you" (*LFL,* 296–97; *HSL* 4:84–85).

Howells's encouragement could not have been better timed. On January 5, 1895, James's play *Guy Domville* opened in London. Following the premier performance, he took the stage to calls of "Author! Author!" only to be met with a curiously mixed reaction. As he later explained to his brother William, "There followed an abominable quarter of an hour during which all the forces of civilization in the house waged a battle of the most gallant,

21. It was not, however, Howells's final word on James for the period covered in this chapter (1885–1897). In 1895, Howells reviewed James's story collection *Terminations* in *Harper's Weekly,* noting positively that "The things for the most part end vaguely, diffusing themselves and ceasing upon the sense without insistence upon a definite intention." He also praises James's "wise and sensitive reticence" (*SLC* 2:225).

22. James's letter, to which Howells is responding, is not extant.

prolonged and sustained applause with the hoots and jeers and catcalls of the roughs [in the theater's gallery], whose *roars* (like those of a cage of beasts at some infernal 'zoo') were only exacerbated (as it were!) by the conflict." It was a humiliating experience that prompted James, a self-described "nervous, sensitive, exhausted author," to abandon the theater and to return to the novel (*JL* 3:508).[23]

James's letter to Howells following the fiasco makes no mention of *Guy Domville,* though he could reasonably assume his friend had read about it in newspapers or heard about it from mutual friends. Speaking of Howells's December letter, James writes, "It lies open before me & I read it again & am soothed & cheered & comforted again. You put your finger sympathetically on the place & spoke of what I wanted you to speak of. I *have* felt, for a long time past, that I have fallen upon evil days—every sign or symbol of one's being in the least *wanted,* anywhere or by anyone, having so utterly failed." By the end of his letter, however, James sounds more upbeat. "I mean to do far better work than ever I have done before. I have, potentially, improved immensely—& am bursting with ideas & subjects" (*LFL,* 298–99; *JL* 3:511–13). Regardless of their creative and aesthetic differences, James and Howells always remained fond friends, and their extant personal correspondence demonstrates their unflagging support for one another.

As critics of America, however, James and Howells continued to grow apart during the period. James, frustrated by winnowing sales and made anxious by a marketplace in which he had increasing difficulty placing his fiction, continued to distance himself from his native country. In "Emerson," as in *Hawthorne,* he depicts a literary culture deficient in opportunities and challenges, peopled by eccentrics and second-rate artists who, in his opinion, would never have loomed so large in Europe as they did in America. James's mixed feelings reflect his own personal frustrations at having failed to establish himself as a successful, popular author in his native country; they also reflect his own state of cultural doubleness as a creative writer (and literary critic) with one foot in Europe and one in America, best known as the author of books, such as *Daisy Miller* and *The Portrait of a Lady,* that represent his divided heart.

For Howells, the United States continued to be a fertile ground for his ever-deepening exploration of what it meant to be an American. In contrast to James, Howells easily came to terms with the antebellum literary generation, celebrating America's lack of European, aristocratic "distinction" in the arts. In this regard, Howells saw both Emerson and Whitman as important literary forebears. At the same time, inspired by an increasingly sophisticated

23. For more on the *Guy Domville* affair, see Edel, *Henry James: A Life,* 402–21.

sense of the society and culture around him, Howells openly embraced a younger generation of authors, including Crane and Norris, who signaled a changing of the guard. Howells, who had studied socialism and embraced it, at least on a philosophical level, saw an America more deeply divided and unstable than ever before; he also saw a land of potential for aspiring artists. Perhaps most important, Howells, as evidenced in the November 1891 Study, came to understand that culture and society shaped an author's sensibilities; in language quite remarkable for its time, he articulated a post-Darwinian argument anticipating certain elements of American naturalist social and aesthetic thought.

As critics of each other, James and Howells functioned in very different capacities. Still smarting from the public tongue-lashing that followed "Henry James, Jr.," James, in "William Dean Howells," publicly distanced himself from his friend and former editor in a calculated, deliberate effort to assert his own aesthetic independence. Typically, James used the opportunity to offer both sharply observed praise and carefully worded criticism of his friend's work, establishing certain benchmarks to which critics have referred ever since. In his personal correspondence with Howells, James was warmer and more supportive, though he never shied from frankly stating his own reservations about Howells's limitations.

In contrast, Howells remained an unflagging supporter of James. Unperturbed by the flap surrounding "Henry James, Jr.," Howells patiently continued to catalog and praise his friend's major achievements in fiction, repeatedly declaring him the most important novelist of the day. Howells remains one of the finest contemporary readers and critics of James; his review of *The Tragic Muse* stands as testament to the sensitivity and openness he brought to the page when reading the increasingly difficult work of his friend. This fact takes on added resonance when one considers that Howells's range as a critic widened tremendously during this period. On the one hand, he could, in the July 1888 Study, call for a very un-Jamesian simplicity of expression in art, celebrating the unaffected and the common. On the other hand, he could, in the September 1890 Study, celebrate Jamesian moral ambiguity, proudly declaring *The Tragic Muse* "the farthest departure from the old ideal of the novel." In a word, Howells shared with James a fundamental appreciation for a well-crafted novel, regardless of genre—further evidence, perhaps, that even as the two critics appeared to move further apart from one another, the two friends remained close.

III

The Literary Criticism of Henry James and
William Dean Howells, 1898–1920

7. The Man of Letters as a Man of Business

Defining the Writer, the Novel, and the Critic
in the Twentieth Century

In December 1899, William Dean Howells read in the *New York Tribune* that his longtime publisher, Harper and Brothers, had gone into receivership. "It was as if I had read that the government of the United States had failed," he later wrote. "It appeared not only incredible, but impossible; it was . . . a misfortune of the measure of a national disaster."[1] It was not the first time that Howells had faced the challenge of a publisher's bankruptcy. He had emerged from the 1885 collapse of James R. Osgood and Company the recipient of the most lucrative publishing contract yet offered to an American author. In 1899, guided by Colonel George B. M. Harvey, both Howells and the House of Harper survived: in September, Howells signed the first of a series of contracts that would, by and large, keep him a Harper author until his death.

The magazine work was an economic necessity. During the nine-month lull between contracts, Howells had experienced a rude awakening: both the *Atlantic* and *Scribner's* had refused to serialize his new novel, *The Kentons*. (Harper eventually published the novel in book form in 1902.) He took the defeats with characteristic dignity, but he did not fail to note the portent. "A change has passed upon things, we can't deny it," he would later remark, in one of his final letters to Henry James. "I could not 'serialize' a story of mine now in any American magazine, thousands of them as

1. Howells, quoted in *HSL* 4:212n4.

161

they are." James's reputation seemed, to Howells, to grow in stature with each passing year. Of himself he wrote: "I am comparatively a dead cult with my statues cast down and the grass growing over them in the pale moonlight" (June 29, 1915; *LFL*, 460; *HSL* 6:80).

Howells, always a keen reader of the rapidly changing literary marketplace, was characteristically prescient. In his final decades, he saw sales of his new work gradually decline. In 1911, a projected thirty-five volume Library Edition of his works stalled after a mere six volumes. The project failed for two principal reasons. First, Howells's publishers—Harper and Houghton, Mifflin—could not come to terms. His earliest, most popular work continued to sell handsomely, and Houghton, Mifflin effectively priced the rights to the early work out of the reach of Harper, whose desire to consolidate Howells's work had pecuniary limits. And these limits were a reflection of the second reason why the Library Edition failed: In 1911, Howells's literary legacy was, at least in the minds of his publishers, already a matter of contention.[2]

Nevertheless, Colonel Harvey and his House of Harper relentlessly capitalized on Howells's cultural cachet. As John Crowley has observed, "The stability of Howells's professional status, which kept him constantly before the public as virtually a trade-mark of the House of Harper, contributed to the perception of his being a fixture in American cultural life." It was during the final two decades of Howells's career that the epithet "Dean of American Letters" was bestowed upon him.[3] Howells, for his part, was never at ease with the cult of personality that grew around him; he frequently felt that the many awards and honors bestowed upon him late in life were unwarranted. After Colonel Harvey organized a gala seventy-fifth birthday party in Howells's honor, to which some four hundred noteworthy guests were invited (including President William Howard Taft), Howells complained to James, "it was all, all wrong and unfit; but nobody apparently knew it, not even I till that ghastly waking hour of the night when hell opens to us" (*LFL*, 454; *HSL* 6:16).

At the heart of Howells's deep discomfort were fundamental questions

---

2. For more on Howells's failed Library Edition, see Anesko (*LFL*, 317–18, 331–39), and Crowley, *Dean of American Letters*, 62–64. Ironically, during a roughly analogous period, Henry James and his agent, James B. Pinker, were able to succeed where Howells had failed: James's New York Edition of his selected works would, in time, help secure his posthumous reputation.

3. Crowley, *Dean of American Letters*, 50. The precise origin of the phrase "Dean of American Letters" is unclear. Edwin Cady argues that "Nobody seems to have been proud enough to claim the paternity of the coinage. It just drifted into casual use" (*Realist at War*, 223). Crowley examines the issue in greater depth but cannot identify a definitive source (*Dean of American Letters*, 45–64).

regarding the rapidly evolving literary marketplace of the twentieth century: a marketplace increasingly defined, he understood, by the force of the advertiser. Both Howells and James explored the effects of a changing marketplace on both the artist and the literary critic in a series of important late essays that address related questions of propriety in fiction and the intersection of aesthetics and ethics in literature.

The Man of Letters as a Man of Business

The question of the artist's relation to the marketplace is most fully explored by Howells in his 1893 essay "The Man of Letters as a Man of Business." Following ideas he first explored in the "Editor's Study," Howells addresses the nexus of art and commerce in the rapidly changing world of publishing. His response is anything but predictable. "I do not think any man ought to live by an art," he provocatively intones. "A man's art should be his privilege, when he has proven his fitness to exercise it, and has otherwise earned his daily bread; and its results should be free to all." Lamenting the "grotesque confusion of our economic being," he suggests that it is both sinful and shameful for the artist to sell his work. "[I]n trying to write of Literature and Business," he confesses, "I am tempted to begin by saying that Business is the opprobrium of Literature." The passage evidences Howells's growing unease with the marriage of literature and business. And if it is a highly idealistic first move in a gambit to distance the "pure and noble" artist from the vulgar marketplace, Howells does not linger in idealism. He frankly confesses that "Literature is Business as well as Art, and almost as soon."[4]

But is the writer actually a businessman? If business thrives on efficiency and regularity of output, then Howells thinks not. He suggests that the very process of writing itself—first drafts followed by slow and painstaking revision, not to mention the author's occasional want for inspiration—all inhibit one's success in the market. Simply put, the artist is not a model of efficient production. "I do not know that I can establish the man of letters in the popular esteem as very much of a business man, after all," he admits. "He

---

4. Howells, *Literature and Life,* 1–2, 4. "The Man of Letters as a Man of Business" appeared first in *Scribner's Magazine* 14 (1893): 429–46. It was subsequently reprinted in *Literature and Life.* While the essay technically antedates the period covered in Part III of this study, I discuss it here because it serves as the introduction to a series of essays on related topics, the bulk of which Howells wrote after 1898. Important, related essays include the March 1890 "Editor's Study" (*ES,* 242–46), and an 1893 autobiographical sketch, "The Country Printer" (*Impressions and Experiences,* 3–34).

must still have a low rank among practical people; and he will be regarded by the great mass of Americans as perhaps a little off, a little funny, a little soft!"[5]

What follows is a very frank and matter-of-fact discussion of the realities of literary publishing, including detailed descriptions of publishing contracts, royalties payments, and other practical matters. This lengthy discussion is, one senses, an effort to differentiate and to demystify the artist, his process, and his product. In this regard, then, Howells could not be more different than James. One finds no lengthy aesthetic abstractions or elaborate metaphors concerning the creative process in "The Man of Letters." This is nuts-and-bolts shoptalk, as down-to-earth as Howells can make it. And his motives are equally clear, for in the final instance Howells wants to deconstruct the notion of the man of letters as a man of business. The publishing business, as Howells so carefully positions it throughout the essay, is necessarily exploitative. It is the domain of the advertiser, who parasitically promotes the product of another man's labor without, in Howells's estimation, contributing anything to the process. In contrast, the artist is "allied to the great mass of wage-workers who are paid for the labor they have put into the thing done or the thing made; who live by doing or making a thing, and not by marketing a thing after some other man has done it or made it. The quality of the thing has nothing to do with the economic nature of the case; the author is, in the last analysis, merely a working-man, and is under the rule that governs the working man's life."[6]

The idealism that began the essay returns in its final paragraphs, when Howells invokes the spirit of Tolstoy's Christian humanism: "I wish that I could make all my fellow-artists realize that economically they are the same as mechanics, farmers, day-laborers. It ought to be our glory that we produce something, that we bring into the world something that was not choately there before; that at least we fashion or shape something anew; and we ought to feel the tie that binds us to all the toilers of the shop and field, not as a galling chain, but as a mystic bond also uniting us to Him who works hitherto and evermore." Howells can admit, however, that most people, and perhaps most of all the working classes, do not share this sentiment. "I will not pretend . . . that the masses care any more for us than we care for the masses, or so much. Nevertheless, and most distinctly, we are not of the classes." The "classes," as Howells defines them, are the wealthy patrons of the arts who, he sarcastically observes, "now and then . . . fancy qualifying

<hr />

5. Howells, *Literature and Life*, 5–6.

6. Ibid., 6–19, 33. The sentiment expressed in this passage goes back at least as far as 1886, when Howells had praised Hutcheson Macaulay Posnett for debunking the "old-fashioned worship of the imagination" and the "exceptional genius" or "great-man theory" of authorship (quoted in *SLC* 2:29–30).

their material splendor or their spiritual dulness with some artistic presence." Despite the fact that the artist "is apparently of the classes; they know him, and they listen to him," the artist is "not of their kind." Rather, "He is really of the masses, but they do not know it, and what is worse, they do not know him." Howells concludes his essay by suggesting that, in the final instance, the artist "will never be at home anywhere in the world as long as there are masses whom he ought to consort with, and classes whom he cannot consort with."[7]

In his attempt to dislocate the artist from the domain of business and the "classes" who control it, Howells ultimately fails to assert that the artist is of "the masses." Despite the earnest tone of "The Man of Letters" and its candid discussion of the practical realities of publishing, Howells's argument suffers from an uneasy and ultimately ambiguous exploration of his own thesis. In his day, Howells was one of the most highly paid and savvy literary businessmen in the market. If he can idealistically assert, in the opening lines of the essay, that "[no] man ought to live by an art," and that art should "be free to all," he undercuts this idealism late in the essay with a smug discussion of the novelist's "money-standing in the economic world." As Howells candidly admits,

> the market for [the novelist's] wares is steadier than the market for any other kind of literary wares, and the prices are better. . . . Another gratifying fact of the situation is that the best writers of fiction, who are most in demand with the magazines, probably get nearly as much money for their work as the inferior novelists who outsell them by tens of thousands, and who make their appeal to the innumerable multitude of the less educated and less cultivated buyers of fiction in book form. I think they earn their money, but if I did not think all of the higher class of novelists earned so much money as they get, I should not be so invidious as to single out for reproach those who did not.

The mercenary tone of the passage acts as a counterweight to the overly ideal aspects of the essay and, together with the paradoxical conclusion concerning the artist who can "never be at home anywhere in the world," suggests that, in the final instance, Howells could not reconcile his own pecuniary and artistic successes with his notion of the idealized artist.[8]

This restlessness has been noted by recent scholars. On the one hand,

---

7. Howells, *Literature and Life*, 34–35.
8. Ibid., 30–31. Howells is more direct in the March 1890 "Editor's Study," when he asserts that "literary men . . . have a right to live comfortably by their art, just as a physician or a minister has a right to live comfortably by his unselfish calling" (*ES*, 243–44). Of course, one notes with some interest the nature of the comparison Howells establishes: he clearly seeks to purchase some of the moral and cultural authority of each profession for the artist.

Lewis Simpson argues that "Howells found it impossible to satisfactorily define the nature of his vocation, or to establish securely his concept of himself
as an American man of letters. Simply put, Howells could never reconcile
his ideal of being a writer in America with the realities—the contingencies—
of being one." Simpson goes on to suggest that if, in "The Man of Letters,"
Howells "remains the idealist of the equalitarian order," his inability "to envision the ideal through the fog of the actual" pushes him close to "the
mood of alienation." Along similar lines, John Crowley places the essay
within the larger context of Howells's biography and concludes that "'The
Man of Letters as a Man of Business' bears traces of Howells's underlying dis-
ease about his own career in relation to his political and moral convictions.
. . . Howells unflinchingly recognized the practical aristocrat in himself as
well as the theoretical socialist." Daniel Borus reads Howells's discomfort in
"The Man of Letters" slightly differently, suggesting that the essay's depiction of the artist is less a portrait of psychological estrangement and more a
figure of change in a rapidly evolving marketplace: "The transition state that
Howells described was not a psychological feeling of complete separation.
The 'homelessness' of the writer was more a professional uncertainty than a
pervasive sense of disconnectedness or alienation."[9]

Simpson, Crowley, and Borus are all correct. In "The Man of Letters,"
Howells's personal sense of alienation (be it greater or lesser) is intimately
connected to, if not a product of, his questioning of the artist's role in the
rapidly evolving literary marketplace of his day—a marketplace that both
perplexed and inspired Howells. Frustrated by his inability to reconcile his
own materialistic success with his aesthetic ideals, Howells attempts to negotiate an idealized middle ground. If his argument trips over its own contradictions, that act speaks to a more complex truth: the professional artist
remains a marketable commodity, potentially well paid but isolated, culturally aligned with no particular social class, and deeply uneasy with the buy-
ing and selling of his art. The essay's failure to cohere is, as Simpson and

9. Lewis P. Simpson, "The Treason of William Dean Howells," 94, 104–5; Crowley, *Dean
of American Letters*, 41; Borus, *Writing Realism*, 152. Crowley points to another key ambiguity in the aforementioned passage of "The Man of Letters": Howells's fuzzy distinction between "earning" and "getting" money (*Dean of American Letters*, 43). Howells's esoteric
economic logic on the topic is exemplified elsewhere; for example, the problem plagues his
1894 social essay "Are We a Plutocracy?" Howells's sense of the distinction between "earning" and "getting" rested on a sentiment most clearly expressed in a 1910 essay called "The
Turning Point in My Life": "Money justly earned is sweet, and its sweetness is quantitative as
well as qualitative; though when the money earned passes immediate need we become insen-
sible to it. That is right; it is a sign from Heaven that we have had enough" (*Criticism and
Fiction and Other Essays*, 360). For more discussion on "The Man of Letters as a Man of Business," see Alan Trachtenberg, *The Incorporation of America: Culture and Society in the Gilded
Age*, 193–96.

Crowley have suggested, a product of Howells's own personal anxieties and unease with his success. But it is also, as Borus argues, a symptom of the professional uncertainties facing the writer at the start of the twentieth century. Howells simply did not have the answers to the questions he posed. But that failure is perhaps less important than the fact that he had the courage and the insight to pose such questions in the first place.

The Supreme Artist of the Twentieth Century

In his later criticism, Howells repeatedly turned his attention to the marketplace and its effect on both artists and literary critics. Of particular interest to Howells was the rapidly evolving world of advertising. In a series of essays, Howells explored an impressive variety of issues surrounding the relationship between art, marketing, and the practice of criticism. In "The Art of the Adsmith," Howells marvels at the prodigious growth of the advertising industry. "[It] can't keep on increasing at the present rate," Howells speculates. "If it does, there will presently be no room in the world for things; it will be filled up with the advertisements of things." Notably, Howells does not rail against the industry, nor does he turn a blind eye. Rather, he asks practical questions about the relationship between advertising and the production of art. Specifically, Howells asks: "how to translate into irresistible terms all that fond and exultant regard which a writer feels for his book, all his pervasive appreciation of its singular beauty, unique value, and utter charm, and transfer it into print, without infringing upon the delicate and shrinking modesty which is the distinguishing ornament of the literary spirit?"[10]

In other words, can advertising accurately and honestly take the measure of art, and convey to the public its value in any meaningful or substantial way—without compromise or detriment to the art? These are not idle questions for Howells; as "The Art of the Adsmith" makes clear, Howells understood that advertising was not only here to stay—it was in direct competition with art. As Howells points out in a mock dialogue with a friend, advertisers "make fifteen or twenty thousand dollars by adsmithing. They have put their art quite on a level with fiction pecuniarily." Howells concedes that advertising perhaps "*is* a branch of fiction"; the aims of advertising, when viewed in a certain light, are not dissimilar from that of the fiction writer. Advertising purports to be true to life, and "discourages the slightest admixture of fable. The truth, clearly and simply expressed, is the best in an ad." Howells humbly notes: Is this not the aim of realistic fiction? The only

10. Howells, *Literature and Life*, 270, 266.

major difference, in this sense, is that, with fiction, "payment tempts [the writer] to verbosity, while in an ad the conditions oblige you to the greatest possible succinctness. In one case you are paid by the word; in the other you pay by the word. That is where the adsmith stands upon higher moral ground" than the fiction writer. Indeed, "The adsmith may be the supreme artist of the twentieth century. He may assemble in his grasp, and employ at will, all the arts and sciences." It seems, Howells concludes, there may be "an indefinite future for advertising" in our culture.[11]

In "The Art of the Adsmith" Howells rather presciently identifies the blurring of distinction between high art and low art, between the commodity in the marketplace and the marketing of that commodity. If fiction is to be both art and entertainment, and the marketing of that art is to be both artful and entertaining, where, Howells asks, does one draw the line between art and advertising? It hardly bears noting that, more than one hundred years later, this is still a vital question in American culture. (One can only speculate what Howells would have made of Andy Warhol's tomato soup cans, but one can hardly imagine him being surprised.) In a sense, Howells sees no practical bounds for advertising. What, he asks implicitly, could possibly stop the force of a medium that could synthesize the force of so many different disciplines and rhetorics—"employ at will . . . all the arts and sciences"?

Howells had, in "The Art of the Adsmith," explained the similarities between art and advertising. He explained the similarities between advertising and the sciences in "Around a Rainy-Day Fire." In this "Editor's Easy Chair" column, Howells's alter ego "the philosopher" explains the recent popularity of "non-literary literature," which relies on stale repetition of themes, plots, characters, and so forth. Howells's philosopher argues that the popularity of this second-rate literature is a result of "the thick spread of our material prosperity," which allows "more people [to be] lettered and moneyed and leisured." Consequently, with more demand for "excitement and amusement" in the form of literature, there are more second-rate books. The increased demand for entertainment is no accident, posits the philosopher. Rather, it is the result of the advertiser having co-opted "the hypothetical method of science. . . . The publishers had hypothesized from the fact of a population of seventy millions, the existence of a body of raw, coarse minds, untouched by taste or intelligence, and boldly addressed the new [and patently inferior] fiction to it. As in many suppositions of science their guess proved true" (*ImI*, 207–13). Advertisers, like scientists, inferred a result from an observable body of data and proceeded to test their hypothesis.

11. Ibid., 269, 271.

Howells has articulated what is now considered a truism of advertising and marketing: audiences are made, not found.

The consequences, for art, are seemingly grave. Authors were once considered special, rare, and select. They were men of genius, touched by the gods. In a marketplace flooded by inferior fiction, Howells's philosopher worries over "the degradation of authorship as a calling, in the popular regard." This is part of a general "transformation of the novelist into the artisan. . . . Literature [has been] degraded from an art to a poor sort of science" in which "A book was concocted, according to a patent recipe, advertised, and sold like any other nostrum" (*ImI*, 209–10). In this, as we shall see below, Howells prefigures some of Henry James's complaints about the changing literary marketplace of the twentieth century. It bears repeating that in this particular column, Howells's mouthpiece is "the philosopher," one of many personae created for the "Editor's Easy Chair." Howells deliberately made a practice of concocting and promoting a wide range of voices for the Easy Chair, and he often put his various voices into dialogue or, sometimes, debate. I wish to stress that the opinions of Howells's philosopher represent, at most, one view of the issue. Howells would— and did—voice other, sometimes contradictory views under the guise of other personae in the Easy Chair.

The Most Modern of the Arts

Finally, Howells was also intrigued by the relationship between advertising and the practice of criticism. Already long made uneasy by what he saw as the essential limitations of the critic's role, Howells, as a careful observer of the marketplace, could not help noticing the relationship between advertising and the runaway best sellers of the early twentieth century—many of which were the romanticistic novels against which he had railed for so long in the "Editor's Study." In a 1901 "Editor's Easy Chair," Howells asks: "Does publicity constitute a sort of newer criticism, and are we to form our opinions of a book from the proclamations of the advertiser, instead of the reasons of reviewers? Is the critic, as we have hitherto had him, to pass, and is the advertiser to come and to stay?" If it is true that "the success of a book itself is a favorable criticism," then it perhaps follows that "the advertiser rather than the critic has always been the arbiter of taste" in the reading public.[12]

Howells treats the nexus of advertising and criticism directly in one of his stronger late essays, a 1911 "Editor's Easy Chair" column entitled "The

12. Howells, *W. D. Howells as Critic*, 355–56.

Functions of the Critic." Here, Howells revisits and revises his long-standing theory of the critic's role in the production and distribution of literary art. He begins by playfully recounting his time in the "Editor's Study," where, when he was not "perpetually thundering at the gates of Fiction in Error," he was "[preaching] Hardy and George Eliot and Jane Austen, Valdés and Galdós and Pardo-Bazán, Verga and Serao, Flaubert and the Goncourts and Zola, Björnson and Ibsen, Tourguénief and Dostoyevsky and Tolstoy, and Tolstoy, and ever more Tolstoy, till its hearers slumbered in their pews." He recounts his work in the Study as "that fierce intolerance, that tempestuous propaganda which left the apostle without a friend or follower in the aesthetic world." The tone is clearly jocular, but it serves to establish his first major concern: literary criticism, now more than ever, appears to be "the sanctuary of the unprincipled, the citadel of the imbecile and immoral." Howells does not spare himself; his earliest work, he notes, was characterized by its haughtiness: "Where our omniscience gave out, we supplied the defect with infallibility" (*SLC* 3:188–89).

This opening movement is familiar rhetoric from Howells. In the June 1887 "Editor's Study," he had defined his own ideal critic as an educated male who practiced a genteel civility and maintained an impartial tone. Howells had also rigidly codified the critic in a problematic taxonomy of art and criticism, so restricting the critic's office that even he was prompted to question the ultimate function of the critic. He had repeated the exercise, with slight modifications to his argument, in the August 1890 Study. "The Functions of the Critic," written some twenty-one years later, essentially confirms Howells's restrictive taxonomy.

What makes "The Functions of the Critic" noteworthy is Howells's increasingly sophisticated understanding of the advertiser's role in the promotion and commodification of art. This awareness provides him with a new context for his critique: the critic's function as a mediator between the artist and the public—a concept Howells had addressed a number of times between 1866 and 1890—has been supplanted by the advertising agent. The taxonomy of art and criticism, Howells understands, has been radically reconfigured:

> Criticism has sat at the feet of Advertising, apparently, which it emulates in both the simplicity and the elegance of its style and the unsparing use of superlatives. . . . After music, advertising is the most modern of the arts, and its advance upon criticism has been indefinitely great. It has become a school in which we may all learn, in the measure of our ability, a habit of shrewd analysis, a lightning swiftness of thought, a diamond brilliancy of diction, and an adamantine poignancy of application, together with an unfailing divination of the public's mental possibilities.

The future course of literary criticism, as Howells sees it, is unavoidable: "the ad-writer's manner and matter are what the people want, and what the critic of the future must study to supply" (*SLC* 3:189–90).

This passage is quite remarkable; Howells understands that the line between "objective" literary criticism and the persuasive rhetoric of the advertiser has blurred irreversibly. And even as he gently mocks the language and rhetorical style of advertising—with its punchy one-liners, use of excessive superlatives, and its feigned objectivity—he understands that this is, unavoidably, the direction in which criticism is headed. Howells, who in 1866 had labored to distinguish "true criticism" from "the mere trade-puff of the publisher, the financial comments of the advertiser, or the bought-and-sold eulogium of an ignorant, careless, or mercenary journalist" (*SLC* 1:60), had lived long enough not only to see the collapse of the distinction, but to be among the first to articulate it.[13]

Nevertheless, Howells attempts to draw a line in the second half of "The Functions of the Critic," distinguishing "the state of criticism among us which may be called static" from "that of the book-noticer [which] may be called dynamic." The thrust of Howells's rhetorical move at this point in his argument seems clear: in the "order of critics," the dynamic book-noticer is the one more subject to the influence of advertising. This practice (of which Howells has never thought highly), having been identified, is to be carefully distinguished from the work of the "static" group that, Howells implies, practices a more rigorous brand of criticism. Howells quickly catalogs the best of the current crop: W. C. Brownell, Georg Brandes, Brander Matthews, and W. L. Phelps, among others (*SLC* 3:189–90).

Howells essentially picks up where he left off in 1890, questioning the use of literary criticism. He notes, first, that "The critic is disabled by the very conditions of his function," and he laments "the practical inutility of criticism. . . . The critic is often quite right, but he is right too late" (*SLC* 3:191–92). At the root of this line of thinking is Howells's 1887 assertion regarding the taxonomy of art and criticism, the notion that "The critic exists because the author first existed." Howells had declared that the critic's "office is mainly to ascertain facts and traits of literature, not to invent or denounce them; to discover principles, not to establish them; to report, not to create." This restrictive paradigm had ultimately led Howells to ask whether critics were, in the final instance, of any use whatsoever (*SLC* 2:54–55). His

---

13. It should be noted that, generally speaking, what Howells refers to as literary criticism throughout "The Functions of the Critic" would be more properly understood by today's reader as the practice of book reviewing, in contrast to the practice of literary scholarship as we generally think of it today. Interestingly, the rapidly evolving schools of literary criticism throughout the twentieth century would effectively pick up Howells's implicit challenge and labor to distinguish their scholarly productions from mass-media book reviews.

1911 complaint concerning the "practical inutility of criticism" is clearly an echo of 1887. Perhaps this is why he refers to the more rigorous school of criticism as "static."

The difference is that, in 1911, Howells proposes a solution to this old dilemma. If "criticism of a thing published is idle," then Howells proposes a "Belles-Lettres Commission": a system of prepublication review and editorial suggestion whereby anonymous critics could be assembled to critique an author's manuscript before it is published. Howells half-heartedly labors to distinguish the services of this "critical trust" or "board of criticism" from the already-existing editorial boards of the trade publishers who, he believes, are motivated principally by greed and profit. In contrast, the Belles-Lettres Commission would "perform the effect of high principle" and judge, Howells would like to believe, only on the highest of aesthetic criteria. Should an author's work be censured, the author would be given the opportunity to respond, providing the author with "an opportunity to teach the court something of true criticism!" (*SLC* 3:192–93). If the idea seems wholly impractical, it does show Howells pondering solutions to his self-imposed dilemma. Howells, who had never felt comfortable with the role or definition of the critic as he understood it, tries, first, to create a space for the critic that would, in his opinion, be truly useful. Second, he tries to "relocate" the critic away from the pernicious influence of advertising. Simply put, in 1911 Howells sees no practical use for the literary critic—the same situation he faced in 1890.[14]

Howells's genius in "The Functions of the Critic" is to recognize and to state unequivocally the growing influence of advertising on the supposedly objective book reviewer. Howells saw the popular book reviewer as a product of and a participant in the burgeoning media culture of the twentieth century, and he clearly understood how the rhetoric of advertising had shaped and would continue to shape the profession. In this media-saturated age of the early twenty-first century, it seems clear that Howells had put his finger directly on the pulse of the matter. His thoughts on the role of the scholarly critic are less cogent. Howells never saw beyond the restrictive taxonomy that he had first introduced in 1887. Ironically, even though Howells in some senses epitomized the notion of the critic as cultural commentator, he always saw the position as subservient to the artist. Nevertheless, "The Functions of the Critic," taken together with a range of other essays written by Howells in his final years, clearly demonstrates his understanding that the

14. As we shall see, Howells's own response to this seeming dead end was to reorient himself as a critic, moving away from the polemic that had characterized the "Editor's Study" and developing a range of rhetorical styles and personae that allowed him to explore a broader range of social and cultural topics that included, but was not limited to, the "literary."

force and influence of advertising in particular—and market forces in general—had already changed the roles of the artist, the art, and the practice of criticism in profound and irreversible ways.

An Immense Omission

Henry James saw things differently. In "The Science of Criticism," James began his examination of the role of the critic by noting the terrific profusion of book reviews in the media. In essence, James felt there were far too many second-rate reviews of second-rate novels, and he pointed to the French critics—who selected a relatively small number of quality books for review—as models. James begins his 1899 essay "The Future of the Novel" in a similar fashion, expressing alarm at the ever-increasing number of new novels being published. "The flood at present swells and swells," he remarks, "threatening the whole field of letters . . . with submersion." The reason for this profusion of books is clear: it is the direct result of the expanded audience, or market, for fiction. "There is an immense public," James remarks, "if public be the name, inarticulate, but abysmally absorbent," and "This public . . . grows and grows each year." In contrast to the unwashed masses, James posits "an admirable minority of intelligent persons who care not" for the popular best sellers of the day; among this group are a select few "who have loved the novel" but "for whom . . . it has become a terror they exert every ingenuity, every hypocrisy, to evade" (*LC* 1:100, 102).

James equates popularity with "the vulgarisation of literature in general." His motive is simple and familiar: he wants to define his own audience—the intelligent, cultivated few—and to restrict his inquiry into the novel's future "to those types [of novels] that have, for criticism, a present and a past." That is, work of enduring quality and depth. This work is invariably not the work read by the ever-expanding reading public. Nor is it the work reviewed by most critics: "The [book] review is in nine cases out of ten an effort of intelligence as undeveloped as the ineptitude over which it fumbles, and the critical spirit, which knows where it is concerned and where not, is not touched, is still less compromised, by the incident" (*LC* 1:103–4).

"The Future of the Novel" demonstrates James's extreme discomfort with a literary marketplace changing and evolving more quickly than he could understand. There is no question that he feels threatened by this developing market. The situation "engender[s] many kinds of uneasiness. The sort of taste that used to be called 'good' has nothing to do with the matter: we are so demonstrably in presence of millions for whom taste is but an obscure, confused, immediate instinct" (*LC* 1:101). It is, perhaps, the observation of an artist who, in the wake of a failed effort to conquer the theater in 1895, feels increasingly frustrated by the readers of his day. And yet, to borrow a phrase from Marcia Jacobson, "James's attitudes are never simple." The Master may have struck an aloof, defiant tone in his literary criticism, but as Jacobson and other scholars have demonstrated, he was a careful student of that same mass market. In his own creative work, he frequently borrowed and brilliantly reinscribed the conventions of contemporary, popular fiction. Therefore, his pose as the haughty aesthete—a "minority artist" as Jacobson has termed it—is best kept in a larger context: James, like Howells, struggled to redefine and reposition himself in response to the ever-changing literary marketplace.[15] James's judgmental tone *is* indicative of his frustration in this regard, but it should not be mistaken for resignation or withdrawal from the scene; rather, "The Future of the Novel"—together with "The Lesson of Balzac," "The New Novel," and, ultimately, the Prefaces to the New York Edition—demonstrates James's ongoing attempt to come to terms with this market. If he appears to reject the "vulgar masses," it is only evidence of his attempt to identify that part of the market that could be his; as we shall see in our discussion of the Prefaces in Chapter 8, James would come to understand his audience with increasing subtlety (even if he ultimately failed to reach it, pecuniarily). In this regard, the Prefaces are a consequence of earlier essays such as "The Future of the Novel" and "The Lesson of Balzac," for it is in these essays that James constructs and explores the persona that pervades much of his late criticism: the aloof, disgruntled literary critic. This "outsider's stance" allows him to explore and analyze the literary marketplace at some remove—with the ultimate aim of identifying and constructing his own audience within that same marketplace.

James understood, of course, that the changing literary marketplace is, necessarily, the product of a larger society and culture. Beginning with the assertion that "the general truth that the future of fiction is intimately bound up with the future of the society that produces and consumes it," James argues that,

> In a society with a great and diffused literary sense the talent at play can only be a less negligible thing than in a society with a literary sense barely discernible. In a world in which criticism is acute and mature such talent will find itself trained, in order successfully to assert itself, to many more kinds of precautionary expertness than in a society in which the art I have named holds an inferior place or makes a sorry figure. A community addicted to reflection and fond of ideas will try experiments with the "story" that will be left untried in a community mainly devoted to travelling and shooting, to pushing trade and playing football.

15. Jacobson, *Henry James and the Mass Market*, 14.

Without experiment and innovation, James suggests, the future of the novel will "more and more define itself as negligible." The "immense variety of life" is visible everywhere; to fail to utilize it is a "great mistake of failing of intelligence" and would be "the only one really inexcusable" error one could make in charting the future course of the novel (*LC* 1:106). In one sense, there is nothing strikingly new in James's culture-shapes-author argument. On a personal level, it was an issue he understood well. James left the United States for Europe because he felt that his homeland offered insufficient opportunity for the artist, and he examined his prejudices in *Hawthorne,* "Emerson," and other critical writings.

James next turns to the question of the Anglo-American novel and its principal audience: "ladies and children—by whom, I mean, in other words, the reader irreflective and uncritical." The question of audience is intimately linked to the related question of propriety in fiction, for the chief threat to the future of the Anglo-American novel as James sees it is its deference to "the inexperience of the young." That is, it has failed to deal frankly with sexual matters. Simply put, "By what it shall decide to do in respect to the 'young' the great prose fable will, from any serious point of view, practically see itself stand or fall." James's own take on this "immense omission in our fiction" is, perhaps, predictable. Thinking of prior "English and American novelists of whom I am fond," he bluntly declares that "I positively prefer to take them as they are." Dickens and Scott "were, to my perception, absolutely right . . . practically not to deal with" sexual matters (*LC* 1:103, 107–8).

James's posture as an apologist for the Anglo-American novel is familiar: One need only look to his 1880 review of Zola's *Nana,* as well as his essays on George Sand and Pierre Loti. But if James has repeatedly acknowledged his own personal limitations on this topic, he has also vigorously defended the freedom of the artist, in principle, to challenge such boundaries. "The Art of Fiction" alone is testament to this much. Throughout "The Future of the Novel," James repeatedly asserts both the need for experimentation as well as the freedom inherent in the form. Echoing "The Art of Fiction," he asserts the novel as "the most comprehensive and the most elastic" of art forms, complete with his frequently employed metaphor of the novel as picture. Despite the popular novel's "precarious" footing, James expresses deep faith in the form: "It can do simply everything, and that is its strength and its life. Its plasticity, its elasticity are infinite. . . . Think as we may, there is nothing we can mention as a consideration outside itself with which it must square, nothing we can name as one of its peculiar obligations or interdictions" (*LC* 1:102, 105). His hope for the future of the novel lies in his faith in the novel's form, its infinite ability to adapt and grow in the hands of its most skilled and gifted artists.

And so it is unsurprising to see James, in the veritable next breath, openly wonder "whether . . . the novel can afford to take things quite so easily as it has, for a good while now, settled down into the way of doing. There are too many sources of interest neglected—whole categories of manners, whole corpuscular classes and provinces, museums of character and condition, unvisited." James notes with some pleasure the possibility that "the revolution taking place in the position and outlook of women" might be the locus of change; women, "for whom the sacrifices have hitherto been supposed to be made," might well break the bubble of propriety in fiction (*LC* 1:108–9). It is an exciting idea, and, in 1899, perhaps a revolutionary one.

"The Future of the Novel" thus concludes somewhat paradoxically. James has ridiculed the evolving literary marketplace and its principal audience. The artist's continued deference to this audience regarding the treatment of sexual matters in fiction, he argues, constitutes a palpable threat to the novelist, who must be free to try any experiment in form. And yet, in the final instance, James himself cannot visualize violating the present boundaries of propriety—though he gently suggests that the next generation of female authors might do just that. Again, there is nothing new in James's stance on the issue. In his many essays on French literature, for example, he vigorously defends and promotes the need for freedom and innovation in art while simultaneously acknowledging his own scruples and marking a boundary he himself cannot cross. To be sure, the essay reinforces the notion that James was deeply discomforted by the emerging literary marketplace of the twentieth century—a market he found difficult to negotiate personally, professionally, and theoretically.

But James's theories on fiction were always best examined and exemplified in relation to a particular author; his finest arguments, with rare exceptions, are always contextual. Not surprisingly, then, his most eloquent examinations of propriety in fiction can be found in a handful of "case study" essays published between 1901 and 1904 and eventually included in *Notes on Novelists*. James's late work on Serao, D'Annunzio, and Zola illustrate not only his final limits on the issue of propriety, but also his most mature attempts to negotiate the issue.

A New Kind of Vulgarity

Characteristically, the 1901 essay on Neapolitan novelist Matilde Serao is a careful examination of the author-in-question's relative strengths and weaknesses. James praises Serao's use of understatement and selection; in *Il Romanzo,* he notes, "we have the real principle of 'naturalism'—a consistent presentment of the famous 'slice of life.'" The novel illustrates the Jamesian principle of selection: "how little 'story' is required to hold us when we get, before the object evoked and in the air created, the impression of the real thing." Nevertheless, the effect of Serao's focus on *passione* "is extraordinarily to falsify the total show and to present the particular affair—the intimacy in hand for the moment, though the moment be brief—as taking place in a strange false perspective, a denuded desert." Serao's characters are known "by nothing but their convulsions and spasms." In the end, argues James, such an approach is a "fundamental mistake" and represents "a new kind of vulgarity." Urging "tact, taste, delicacy, [and] discretion," he suggests that the true lesson of art is in fineness of perception, and in this regard Serao is "not to be trusted at all." The essay concludes with a nod to "dear old Jane Austen," who clearly understood the virtues of "hanging back" and "standing off" from such indelicacies (*LC* 2:963–67).

In the 1904 essay "Gabriele D'Annunzio, 1902," James employs a similar rhetorical strategy. James quickly catalogs D'Annunzio's strengths: "first his rare notation of states of excited sensibility; second his splendid visual sense, the quick generosity of his response to the message, as we nowadays say, of aspects and appearances, to the beauty of places and things; third his ample and exquisite style, his curious, various, inquisitive, always active employment of language as a means of communication and representation." Despite D'Annunzio's strengths, "the only ideas he urges us are the erotic and the plastic, which have for him about an equal intensity," and, therefore, the work lacks "moral beauty" because D'Annunzio's "expression of the personal life [rests] so little on any picture of the personal character and the personal will." Consequently, the "defect" of D'Annunzio's work "is verily that it has no moral sense proportionate to the truth, the constant high style of the general picture" (*LC* 2:910–14, 930).

In the essay's penultimate paragraph, James argues that D'Annunzio's "vulgarity" seriously compromises the work. Unless the erotic is carefully linked to "the rest of life," it becomes an object of interest that can be made "poetically interesting" but is ultimately trivial, artistically. The more interesting question, for James, is how the erotic might affect other dimensions of a fictional character. "What the participants do with their agitation, in short, or even what it does with them, *that* is the stuff of poetry, and it is never really interesting save when something finely contributive in themselves makes it so." But, following his own critical guidelines, James grudgingly grants D'Annunzio his topic, the erotic.[16] Echoing the final lines of his 1888 essay on Maupassant, James concludes "Gabriele D'Annunzio, 1902"

---

16. As if wary of overstepping his bounds, James carefully stakes out his critical turf in "Gabriele D'Annunzio, 1902." Echoing "The Art of Fiction," James reasserts that a critic must "grant [an author] his postulates," or subject. The only question at stake, James insists, is the "treatment of it" (*LC* 2:918).

by musing on the "different issue[s]" and "finer possible combinations" that, in another artist, would yield more palatable results (*LC* 2:942–43).

It is important to emphasize that the essays on Serao and D'Annunzio, relative to some of James's earlier work as a critic, demonstrate a generous critical practice in which James sincerely weighs the strengths and weaknesses of each author's approach. Despite the generous readings, however, James finds that the work of each author is, in the final instance, deeply flawed by an overinsistence on "vulgarity" at the expense of overall artistic depth and intensity. In each essay, James tries to follow his own dictum of granting the artist his or her subject, restricting his inquiry to an examination of the artist's execution or treatment of that subject. But, as the conclusions to both essays suggest, James cannot wholly refrain from implicitly critiquing the subject. In this regard, the essays on Serao and D'Annunzio mark the final limits for James regarding the question of propriety in fiction.

Not so with his 1903 essay on Émile Zola, perhaps the single most surprising reconsideration in James's critical oeuvre. Though he always appreciated the force of Zola's fiction, James had long held up Zola as an example of the unfortunate extremes the French were liable to perpetrate. His 1880 review of Zola's *Nana* is the quintessential example of Jamesian prudery. And, in "The Art of Fiction," James had referenced Zola as an example of an artist who had unwisely tried to force his tastes onto his audience.[17] It is therefore somewhat surprising to find James, in 1903, rediscovering a Zola who was "always there to be had." James humbly admits he must "throw off an oblivion, an indifference for which there are plenty of excuses. We become conscious, for our profit, of a *case,* and we see that our mystification came from the way cases had appeared for so long to fail us" (*LC* 2:871).

James now understands that Zola was radically selective: if he only examined a limited area of human nature, he examined the area that spoke most powerfully to him as an artist. "He was in prompt possession thus of the range of sympathy that he *could* cultivate," and if Zola correspondingly lacked "taste," James notes with some irony that this lack of taste allowed him to penetrate his subject completely: "who cannot see to-day how much a milder infusion of [Zola's 'rank materialism'] would have told against the close embrace of the subject aimed at?" It is the sense of saturation and penetration—the ultimate force of the artist's vision—that James most admires in Zola's best work (which, for James, was *Germinal, La Débâcle,* and *L'Assommoir*). If there is a "sacrifice" to "the common," it is justified by the splendid results: "the sacrifice is ordered and fruitful, for the subject and

17. For more on James's lifelong debt to Zola, see Jones, *James the Critic,* 92–100.

treatment harmonise and work together." Correspondingly, when Zola's work fails, it is "presumptuous . . . without sweetness, without antecedents, superficial and violent, [and] has the minimum instead of the maximum of *value*." Such "inflated hollowness" is, again, the result of Zola's lack of "Taste (deserving here if ever the old-fashioned honour of a capital)" (*LC* 2:879–80, 887–88, 892).

Because the question of propriety is always squarely at the center of James's work on Zola, the nature and depth of the reconsideration articulated in the 1903 essay is noteworthy. If the 1880 essay on *Nana* marks the extreme of Jamesian prudery, the 1903 essay represents an extreme of Jamesian tolerance. In contrast to the essays on Serao and D'Annunzio, the 1903 Zola essay is a model Jamesian exercise: The critic, having fully granted the novelist his subject, assesses whether the individual treatments of that subject succeed or fail, and why. In Zola's best work, James finds the frank depiction of difficult subject matter artistically justifiable. Yet one hastens to add that the essay also demonstrates the increasingly subjective nature of James's critical practice. The final success or failure of Zola's work is a result of the rare nexus of "taste" and "the close embrace of the subject aimed at." If Zola occasionally succeeds, he more frequently fails—as do Serao and D'Annunzio. It is only when this ratio is correct that Zola's work pleases James. Generally speaking, James's late critical work is defined by such increasingly idiosyncratic criteria. This is seen, for instance, throughout the Prefaces to the New York Edition. And it is also seen in the opening sections of James's important essay "The Lesson of Balzac" and in his last major literary essay, "The New Novel," which, when considered together, articulate his final views on the question of the role of the literary critic.

Under a Hedge

Published in 1905, "The Lesson of Balzac" begins with a familiar Jamesian assertion: "criticism is the only gate of appreciation [for literature], just as appreciation is, in regard to a work of art, the only gate of enjoyment." James belittles a literary marketplace that, in his view, represents

> production uncontrolled, production untouched by criticism, unguided, unlighted, uninstructed, unashamed, on a scale that is really a new thing in the world. It is all the complete reversal of any proportion, between the elements, that was ever seen before. It is the biggest flock straying without shepherds, making its music without a sight of the classic crook . . . that has ever found room for pasture. The very opposite has happened from

what might have been expected to happen. The shepherds have diminished as the flock has increased—quite as if number and quantity had got beyond them, or even as if their charge had turned, by some uncanny process, to a pack of ravening wolves.

The disproportionate abundance of second-rate artists to first-rate critics is clearly a matter of grave concern for James. First, it fails to inspire "the critical spirit" and its "educative practice" which, under ideal conditions, would serve to restrain or to restrict the abundance of weaker art. There simply are not enough skilled critics to control the masses of authors; James humorously hopes to find "two or three of the fraternity hiding under a hedge or astride of some upper limb of a tree." Consequently, in the absence of guidance from critics, work of lesser quality is not only present in ever greater abundance: it is a positive threat, "a pack of ravening wolves," that may extinguish the practical utility of criticism altogether (*LC* 2:115–17).

Behind this playful opening section of "The Lesson of Balzac" one finds a rearticulation of the frustration with the marketplace demonstrated in "The Future of the Novel." But one also finds the familiar Jamesian paradigm of the mutually beneficial relationship between author and critic, as sketched out in "The Science of Criticism": the critic depends on the best artists to produce high-quality work; only the best work deserves the attention of the critic, who, in turn, will produce his equally rare and intense criticism; the artist, in turn, benefits from the work of the intelligent critic, who, in his capacity as guide, will inspire the best sort of work from the artist. Art, as personified in "The Science of Criticism," is a delicate and sensitive organism that must be carefully protected and nurtured. In "The Lesson of Balzac," James's point seems clear: criticism is the only bastion of hope for reform or control in a literary marketplace that, in the opinion of James, is very nearly out of control.

James does not hesitate to offer three quick examples of artists "who scarce produce the effect in question [inspiring the 'critical spirit'] at all." George Sand offers "an artistic complexion so comparatively smooth and simple, so happily harmonious, that her work, taken together, presents about as few pegs for analysis to hang upon as if it were a large, polished, gilded Easter egg." James's take on Jane Austen is only slightly less acrimonious. He explains that her posthumous popularity is principally a result of "the stiff breeze of the commercial, in other words of the special book-selling spirit; an eager, active, interfering force which has a great many confusions of apparent value." The "critical spirit," James emphasizes, "is not responsible." Rather, "a sentimentalized vision" is "The key to Jane Austen's fortune with posterity." In a passage noteworthy for its gender-biased condescension—James employs a string of domestic metaphors: a woman's work basket, tapestry flowers, embroidery, etc.—James describes how Austen's "dropped stitches" (that is, sloppy form) have been posthumously regarded as "little touches of human truth, little glimpses of steady vision, little master-strokes of imagination." But it is the case of the Brontës that represents "the highwater mark of sentimental judgment." Their fiction, he notes, is the result of a biographical cause: the rather lonely, dreary life of the sisters. The public has picked up on certain biographical facts and "confound[ed] the cause with the result," resulting in an "intellectual muddle" that James naturally abhors. "Literature is an objective, a projected result," he intones; "it is life that is the unconscious, the agitated, the struggling, floundering cause." The Brontës' posthumous popularity is therefore the result of misplaced sympathy (*LC* 2:117–19).

James's rhetorical strategy is obvious; before addressing the powerful example of Balzac, he wishes to provide counter-examples who are, as he puts it, "but glimmering lanterns" employed "to render the darkness visible" (*LC* 2:119). But why four authors who, then as now, are regarded as important figures in the development of the novel? And why four women? First, these four authors were, in 1905, extremely popular with the reading public. Simply put, these authors occupied precisely the position James wished to occupy, and some measure of professional jealousy may be at work. Sand, after all, had been a frequent subject of inquiry for James, and if he found much to criticize in her work, he also found much to commend. (A Bloomsian anxiety of influence may therefore be another line of tension in this passage.) At the very least, James indirectly expresses his own anxiety regarding how to negotiate the ever-changing literary marketplace. The second question is that of gender; here, the question becomes very complex. James lamented the fact that women constituted the principal audience for the Anglo-American novel; as noted in our discussion of "The Future of the Novel," above, he felt that the very future of the English novel depended on the question of expanding its audience and pushing the boundaries of propriety in fiction. Indeed, he had even gone so far as to suggest that it might be the female novelists who would challenge the standards of the day.

On other occasions, James was less generous. In his 1902 essay on Flaubert, James declares that the English novel's lack of "a beauty of intention and effect" is a result of the fact that "the novel is so preponderantly cultivated among us by women, in other words by a sex ever gracefully, comfortably, enviably unconscious (it would be too much to call them even suspicious,) of the requirements of form." James's point is stark: study not the women authors. "For signal examples of what composition, distribution, arrangement can do, of how they intensify the life of a work of art, we have to go elsewhere" (*LC* 2:333). At the heart of these asides concerning female authors in "The Lesson of Balzac" and the 1902 essay on Flaubert are the familiar Jamesian concerns of form, audience, and authorial production. What is noteworthy is the manner in which James takes issue specifically with female authors. Elsa Nettels demonstrates that this kind of gender-based criticism is prevalent throughout James's criticism. "Early and late in his criticism," writes Nettels, James "made the conventional associations of the masculine with strength and reason, the feminine with weakness and emotion, thereby confirming the inferior status of what he called the 'subordinate sex.'" There is, of course, some irony in this. "In his fiction," Nettels reminds us, "James portrayed women who surpass men in the power to initiate and control action; in his criticism, he maintains the masculine-feminine polarity to guarantee the supremacy of the male artist."[18]

Nettels is right when she indicates how James fell back on the culturally normative gender biases of his day. Nevertheless, James's use of gendered rhetoric is nearly always multilayered. "James had an acute sense of the extent to which his own professional arena was shaped by the presence of women writers and readers," notes Richard Salmon, and James's conflation of gender and the mass market reflects broader concerns about the "democratization" of literature in the late nineteenth century—the rapid growth and expansion of the marketplace—and the changing role of women in contemporary society. Salmon points out that James did not simply "masculinize" himself and "feminize" the marketplace; frequently, it was the reverse: "James himself often assumed the role of a passive, victimized author," or what Marcia Jacobson has termed the pose of the "minority artist."[19] In short, James used gendered language to suit each particular rhetorical occasion. If in some instances James employs decidedly chauvinistic language, in others he "feminizes" himself as a means of accentuating his own sense of displacement (witness the opening of "The New Novel," discussed below). Broadly considered, James's use of gendered rhetoric speaks to a larger set of concerns and anxieties that include the "feminization" of art and culture, the changing nature of the literary marketplace, and James's own personal anxiety at struggling to find a commercially viable position within it.

In "The Lesson of Balzac," then, the rhetorical move of dismissing Sand, Austen, and the Brontës is a blatant attempt to create a division between the "greater" and "lesser" artists, to create a space of appreciation for Balzac. In

18. Elsa Nettels, *Language and Gender in American Fiction: Howells, James, Wharton, and Cather*, 48.

19. Salmon, *Henry James and the Culture of Publicity*, 54; Jacobson, *Henry James and the Mass Market*, 14. See also Alfred Habegger, *Henry James and the "Woman Business"*; and Anne T. Margolis, *Henry James and the Problem of Audience: An International Act*.

so doing, James hopes to illustrate his point concerning the threat of the marketplace relative to the practice of criticism. He revises his paradigm of the relationship between critic and artist in important terms—terms that will, as we shall see, facilitate the self-referential criticism found in the Prefaces to the New York Edition. Similar questions regarding the role of the critic are addressed in James's final major literary essay.

Special, Eccentric, and Desperate

"The New Novel" begins with a tepid assessment of the current literary scene.[20] "[T]he state of the novel in England at the present time is virtually very much the state of criticism itself," he intones, and this is a matter of concern, for "no equal outpouring of matter into the mould of literature, or what roughly passes for such, has been noted to live its life and maintain its flood, its level at least of quantity and mass, in such free and easy independence of critical attention." If the failure of criticism to respond to the current state of the novel is a "responsibility declined in the face of disorder," there are consequences:

> the low critical pitch is logically *reflected* in the poetic or, less pedantically speaking, the improvisational at large. The effect, if not the prime office, of criticism is to make our absorption and our enjoyment of the things that feed the mind as aware of itself as possible, since that awareness quickens the mental demand, which thus in turn wanders further and further for pasture. This action on the part of the mind practically amounts to a reaching out for the reasons of its interest, as only by its so ascertaining them can the interest grow more various. This is the very education of our imaginative life. (*LC* 1:124)

The opening of "The New Novel" is crucial to our final understanding of James's conception of the critic, for it revises the paradigms sketched out initially in "The Art of Fiction," more fully examined in "The Science of Criticism," and, as we have seen, briefly touched on in "The Lesson of Balzac." The critic, painted as deferential and clearly subservient to the artist in 1884, had been transformed, in 1891, to a sympathetic brother-in-arms, though the critic was still clearly positioned in a hierarchy privileging the artist. In "The Lesson of Balzac," James playfully suggested that the critic's

---

20. The essay first appeared in the *Times Literary Supplement* (March 19 and April 2, 1914) under the title "The Younger Generation"; the revised and expanded version presently under consideration appeared in *Notes on Novelists*.

role had become that of the shepherd, or reformatory cultural guide. In "The New Novel," James is less metaphorical: he sees criticism as a kind of legislative body, imposing its system of checks and balances on art so as to encourage high quality and rigorous experimentation.

Yet criticism has failed. In "stale and shrinking waters" sits a disgruntled James, assessing the swelling tide of artistic "stupidity" that surrounds him. The opening movement of "The New Novel" is, in essence, James's "attempt to understand how stupidity could so have prevailed. We take it here that the answer to that inquiry can but be ever the same. The flood of 'production' has so inordinately exceeded the activity of control that this latter anxious agent, first alarmed but then indifferent, has been forced backward out of the gate, leaving the contents of the reservoir to boil and evaporate." The practice of criticism is no longer subservient to that of the artist; criticism is an "activity of control": a cultural authority in and of itself, possessed of its own agency and responsibilities. This paradigm, a modification of the one introduced in "The Lesson of Balzac" and sketched out so briefly in the opening pages of "The New Novel," is not further developed theoretically. Rather, in a classic Jamesian "case study," the theory is applied to a select group of younger novelists. The general picture, he notes, is grim. James laments the "want of observable direction" in the current state of the novel, and he appears to be grasping at straws: "We respond to any sign of an intelligent view or even of a lively instinct." Such condescension sets the tone that pervades the rest of the essay: a select overview touching on a range of authors, including Joseph Conrad, H. G. Wells, Arnold Bennett, Hugh Walpole, and Edith Wharton. The crux of James's complaint with the younger writers is that if they have perfected the art of "saturation," which is to offer the reader "concrete material, amenable for straight and vivid reference, convertible into apt illustration," saturation alone does not "constitute . . . the 'treatment' of a theme." Employing the simile of the squeezed orange, James naturally acknowledges the value of saturation in fiction but stresses that it is only half the formula for successful work. The other half, the "application" of that saturation—essentially, the fine precision of form—is what he finds wanting in the fiction of the new generation (*LC* 1:125–28, 132).

James's case studies in "The New Novel" are uneven. While the essay contains much praise for the younger authors—Wharton, for instance, is lauded for her "artistic economy" and selectivity—it also contains some questionable assessments. James scarcely acknowledges the recently published *Sons and Lovers;* its author, D. H. Lawrence, "hang[s] in the dusty rear" of the current herd. (Given his stance on matters of propriety in fiction, James's ambivalence is, perhaps, understandable.) The discussion of Conrad is restricted to *Chance,* which James critiques for its "special, eccentric, and desperate" narrative style (*LC* 1:154, 127, 148). Curiously, James overlooks some of Conrad's best work, including *Lord Jim*.[21] One can but speculate as to James's reasons, but one suspects that the effort—predicated on James's pose as a "minority artist" assessing a flood of new and popular talent—affords its author the opportunity, albeit indirectly, to promote the aesthetic values embodied in his own work by means of pointing out the perceived shortcomings of other writers.

"The New Novel" is important for three reasons. First, for its brief theoretical rearticulation of the literary critic's "activity of control" in the literary and cultural marketplace, the most liberal, independent definition of the literary critic offered by James. Second, for its example: the bulk of the essay can be read as an attempt to enact this "activity of control." "The New Novel" is a classic Jamesian case study relying on concrete examples rather than on extended theoretical abstraction. Third, "The New Novel" is important because it demonstrates, once again, how James continued to engage the literary marketplace in his later years, analyzing the contemporary scene with keen sensitivity and staking out his own position in relation to it.

The Savage World

Like James, William Dean Howells was deeply interested in the question of propriety in fiction. And, like James, Howells saw Zola as an unavoidable case in point. Prior to 1902, Howells had written only briefly on Zola, an author who, on one occasion, had marked the "wicked end," or terminus, of realism (*ES*, 112). At his most generous, Howells had argued that *La Terre*, though "Filthy and repulsive . . . in its facts," was "a book not to be avoided by the student of civilization, but rather to be sought and seriously considered" for the social problems it so forcefully addressed (*SLC* 2:84). Howells's 1902 essay—published some nine months prior to James's 1903 piece—is his only lengthy consideration of Zola's work, and, with the question of propriety in fiction in mind, is noteworthy for its tone of tolerance.

Importantly, Howells begins his study of Zola with the question of genre, arguing that Zola was "too much a romanticist by birth and tradition, to

---

21. James's antagonism to Conrad is, perhaps, not difficult to puzzle out; Sarah B. Daugherty notes that *Chance* was a commercially successful book written in what some readers have perceived as a Jamesian manner (*Literary Criticism*, 191). Conrad would later write that James's criticism in "The New Novel" made him feel "rather airily condemned" and admitted that "this was the *only time* a criticism affected me painfully" (quoted in *LC* 1:1447n148, lines 20–21). Conrad was not alone. H. G. Wells, whose friendship with James dated to 1898, was deeply offended by "The New Novel." In response, he openly mocked James in the literary spoof *Boon*. James was not amused, and their relationship ended shortly thereafter. For more on Wells and James, see Leon Edel and Gordon N. Ray, eds., *Henry James and H. G. Wells: A Record of Their Friendship, Their Debate on the Art of Fiction, and Their Quarrel*.

exemplify realism in his work." Each of his works is "bound to a thesis" (drunkenness, harlotry, labor strikes, and so forth), whereas "reality is bound to no thesis." Therefore, Zola is perhaps more of an "epic poet" than a novelist (*SLC* 3:65). This point is worth stressing, since in Howells's mind the given genre of a work dictated how he read it. As early as 1865, Howells had argued that "The novelist deals with personages, [and] the romancer with types." Following this line, Howells had defended Dickens's "improbable" characters: "So long as they are not moral impossibilities, we cannot think them exaggerations" (*SLC* 1:55). In pointing out that Zola is a "romanticist," then, Howells essentially argues that Zola's novels are not to be held to realist standards of verisimilitude: "if they are not true to the French fact, [they] are true to the human fact." Howells was always willing to grant the serious romantic author (such as Hawthorne) a larger moral or "human" truth at the expense of absolute verisimilitude. Correspondingly, Howells can allow that "Zola's books, though often indecent are never immoral, but always most terribly, most pitilessly moral. . . . [T]hey may disgust, but they will not deprave" (*SLC* 3:66–67).

In contrast to James, who rationalized Zola's gross depictions of life on purely aesthetic terms, Howells examines Zola principally—though not exclusively—on moral terms.[22] "Zola was an artist," Howells notes, "and one of the very greatest, but even before and beyond that he was intensely a moralist, as only the moralists of our true and noble time have been." Notably, he likens Zola to Tolstoy before concluding that the Frenchman's "success as a humanist is without flaw" (*SLC* 3:68, 71). The 1902 essay on Zola is an important benchmark for Howells; far from prudish, Howells was comfortable with work that violated certain boundaries of taste so long as he saw a justifiable moral purpose in the work. But the question of propriety in fiction was by no means exclusively a moral question for Howells. In his later years, Howells also saw an artistic or aesthetic need for transgressing the limits of propriety in fiction.

For instance, Howells begins "A Case in Point," his 1899 review of Frank Norris's *McTeague,* with the questions of "Whether we shall abandon the old-fashioned American ideal of a novel as something which may be read by all ages and sexes, for the European notion of it as something fit only for age and experience, and for men rather than women; whether we shall keep to the bounds of the provincial proprieties, or shall include within the imperial territory of our fiction the passions and the motives of the savage world which underlies as well as environs civilisation." For Howells, it may well be

---

22. Howells prefigures James on at least one important point: "the condition of every work of art," Howells argues, is that it "must choose its point of view, and include only the things that fall within a certain scope" (*SLC* 3:67). This, Howells argues, Zola did well; as noted above, James makes a similar point in his 1903 essay.

a question of life or death for American literature. "From the very first Europe invaded and controlled in our literary world," he explains. "The time may have come at last when we are to invade and control Europe in literature. I do not say that it has come, but if it has we may have to employ European means and methods." Enter Norris, who is, as Howells notes, a follower of Zola. Norris's great fault is one of imbalance: "Life is squalid and cruel and vile and hateful, but it is noble and tender and pure and lovely, too." If Howells prefers to see more of a balanced view of life, he clearly does not wish to obscure the less appealing side of life Norris depicts. Rather, as Howells notes, such depictions are "the inevitable consequence of expansion in fiction" (*SLC* 3:11–13). "A Case in Point" demonstrates Howells's awareness of the joint nature of audience and propriety—precisely the point James had made in "The Future of the Novel."

Similar issues are at the heart of the 1899 essay "A Question of Propriety," Howells's brief response to the public outrage concerning Henrik Ibsen's *Ghosts,* then playing in New York. Howells offers one of his most liberal readings of propriety in literature, suggesting that *Ghosts* is really no more outrageous than *Hamlet;* both plays "leave the witness in the same sort of uncertainty as to the specific lesson" of the story. Ibsen's frank treatment of incest and congenital syphilis may appear to be more controversial than Shakespeare's depiction of adultery and murder, but such frankness is merely a sign of the times; Ibsen's "'scientific' methods" as a playwright, Howells implies, reflect late-nineteenth-century theories of psychology. In a later age, he speculates, Ibsen's *Ghosts* will be considered no more controversial than *Hamlet* (*SLC* 3:20–21).[23] Along with the essays on Zola and Norris, Howells's comments on Ibsen demonstrate his increasing flexibility and tolerance regarding questions of propriety in literature.

This flexibility and tolerance is again evident in a 1902 "Editor's Easy Chair" column on George Eliot. Howells's consideration of the moral nature of her work gives rise to the observation that

> the authors who deal most profoundly with [moral] problems mostly leave them unsolved, as, for instance, Ibsen does, and it is doubtful whether art can ever do more than life in handling them, or can be more definite with advantage to the witness. Nearly every problem of life is remanded to another life for solution, . . . [and this effect] seems to be the only one that art can successfully study. The greatest achievement of fiction, its highest use, is to present a picture of life; and the deeper the sense of something desultory, unfinished, imperfect, it can give, even in the region of conduct, the more admirable it seems. (*SLC* 3:166–67)

23. Similar sentiments rest at the heart of Howells's longer 1906 essay on Ibsen (*SLC* 3:107–17).

It is clear from this discussion, and from the discussions above, that Howells became increasingly comfortable with both moral ambiguity in literature and the frank depiction of controversial subject matter. Such ambiguity was, in a certain respect, true to life and therefore central to the realist aesthetic as Howells understood it.

It bears emphasizing, however, that Howells remained a moralist. In the 1902 essay on Eliot, he distinguishes major moralists from minor moralists by arguing that major moralists follow the results of "moral wrong," and "show how it causes suffering and misery" to those both immediately and remotely concerned, following the chain of circumstance until "Somewhere the wrong ceases to act" and is "transmuted into the means of good, if not into good itself"; the reader is thereby shown the limitations of evil. (Howells offers *The Scarlet Letter, Crime and Punishment,* and Tolstoy's "Resurrection" as examples of major moral works.) In contrast, minor moral works "leave you to despair as the ultimate condition of wrong" (*SLC* 3:167–68). While Howells does not probe the binary any further, his preference is clear enough.[24]

Like James, Howells was also concerned with the question of the audience for literature and related issues of propriety. He ponders the question in "What Should Girls Read?" wherein he argues that a reader has nothing to fear from even the "profane masterpieces" of world literature (a list that includes Shakespeare, Chaucer, Cervantes, Milton, Goethe, and others). "The things which defile are from within," Howells urges. "While the heart is clean there is little fear that what enters the mind from literature will corrupt the heart or sully it." He therefore concludes that "a girl, if she is a good girl, may read almost anything she likes" (*SLC* 3:236, 240). While this 1902 essay is, for today's reader, laughably chauvinistic and overly prescriptive—at the least, it perfectly exemplifies the normative sexism of its era— "What Should Girls Read?" does confirm the sense of Howells's growing tolerance. In sum, Howells was impressively open to—and comfortable with—the changing tastes in literature; rather than responding to the new literature with shock or distaste, Howells immediately recognized both the aesthetic and moral qualities of the work and praised them accordingly.

A Morality Sane and Simple and Pure

Howells's increasingly catholic tastes, however, did not come at the expense of some of his deepest- and longest-held convictions on the subject of

---

24. Incidentally, Howells finds Eliot "sometimes the one and sometimes the other" (*SLC* 3:168).

art and ethics. He remained deeply committed to what he saw as the ethical and moral obligations of the artist, and even as he saw the need for the expansion of the bounds of propriety in fiction, he also, in his later years, found ample opportunity to reiterate and, in some cases, to gently modify some core beliefs regarding the intersection of art and ethics. A prime example is found in Howells's 1902 essay on Charles Dickens. While Howells had always been generally fond of Dickens, the Englishman's bulky romances did epitomize, in contrast to realism, an outmoded manner of narrative; Howells's gentle swipe at Dickens in the essay "Henry James, Jr." had greatly contributed to the fiery polemic that followed.

In the important final section of the 1902 Dickens essay, we see Howells reassessing Dickens's work in light of his own fully evolved social and ethical perspectives. For example, the pro-socialist Howells notes that Dickens "showed such tenderness for the poor, the common, the hapless and friendless, that one could not read his books without feeling one's heart warm to the author, and without imbibing a belief in his goodness." The Howells who had made peace with Emerson and antebellum New England remarks that "His work made always for equality, for fraternity, and if he sentimentalized the world, he also in equal measure democratized it." And the humanist-moralist can state that "His black was very black, his white was very white, and all his colors were primitive, but he painted an image of life which was not wholly untrue, though it was so largely unlike. In parables, often grotesque and extravagant, he taught a morality sane and simple and pure. Nobody was misled as to what was right and what was wrong by any of his representations of conduct" (*SLC* 3:153). In short, where a younger Howells had seen mostly excesses of idealism, sentiment, and the romanticistic in Dickens, an older Howells sees Dickens as a democratic humanist and as a potent moralist. Howells had broadened the scope of his appreciation for the romance, further evidence of his willingness to reevaluate and reassess his own personal aesthetic standards in light of his evolving moral and ethical beliefs.[25]

In this regard, no author looms larger in Howells's work as a critic than Tolstoy, and in his final major essay on the man, published in 1908, Howells demonstrates his continuing fascination with the powerful example of the Russian's life and work. Howells finds "ethics and aesthetics are one" in Tolstoy. Furthermore, the Russian set a new standard for Howells that permanently impacted his own writing: "His literature both in its ethics and aesthetics, or its union of them, was an experience for me somewhat comparable to the old-fashioned religious experience of people converted at revivals.

---

25. The 1902 essay on Dickens follows Howells's generous reassessments in *My Literary Passions* and *Heroines of Fiction*.

. . . What I had instinctively known before, I now knew rationally. I need never again look for a theme of fiction." But Tolstoy's impact ranged beyond the mere example of a theme or a particular technique. Tolstoy's fiction is "always most spiritual; it is so far from seeking beauty, or adorning itself with style, as to be almost bare and plain. His art is from his conscience, and you feel his conscience in it at every moment. . . . He is never false to his reader because he is never false to himself; it would be foolish to suppose that he could not misrepresent or wrongly color a given motive or action in his tale, but you may trust your soul to him in the assurance that he will not." Howells also appreciates the fact that Tolstoy did not view the world idealistically; Tolstoy "hated the evil in his characters and loved the good, but with an artistic toleration which was also an ethical tolerance of the evildoers" (*SLC* 3:125–30). If Tolstoy shows his reader both good and evil, both beauty and ugliness, Howells especially appreciates the balance exemplified in the work, which he sees as the consummate blend of art and ethics.

Similar sentiments rest at the heart of a 1909 essay, "The Novels of Robert Herrick." Howells begins by noting a paucity of "American novelists of a later generation than Mr. Henry James, who are at once moralists and artists, who set the novel of manners above all other fiction, and who aim at excellence in it with unfailing conscience." Herrick's work meets this latter-day realist criteria, exemplifying "the fulfilment of an ethical impulse effecting itself of truth to life . . . by the study of character, serious [and] self-respectful." Herrick's work promotes moral introspection, prompting the reader to consider "his relations to other men very like himself in their common human nature." Howells had praised Tolstoy's "artistic toleration" in his depiction of evil; he notes a similar virtue in Herrick: "It is the highest privilege of the artist to take not only morally mean and nasty people, but dull and tiresome ones, and by virtue of showing their reality to make them interesting and even fascinating, as Mr. Herrick does." Furthermore, "The novelist takes uncommon lives out of the common life; and if he is wise he shows them as instances, not as examples; but he must make this clear. If he is, like Mr. Herrick, a moralist as well as an artist this is especially his duty" (*SLC* 3:132, 137–38).

In this essay, Howells speaks passionately of the artist's duties and moral responsibilities. In both Tolstoy and Herrick, Howells sees strong examples of fiction that necessarily prompts moral introspection in the reader without sacrificing artistic depth and complexity. Howells does not want a world washed clean of its impurities and evil; rather, he demands that fiction squarely confront evil and ugliness. He only wants to see it done with a sense of balance, or an "artistic tolerance" of extremes. Howells was as uncomfortable with overly idealistic fiction as he was with overly pessimistic fiction. As noted above, this was the essence of his critique of Norris's *Mc-Teague*. Howells was perfectly comfortable with Norris's depiction of the brute, animalistic forces in nature. Norris's failure was in not depicting the other half of the equation: the beautiful, the fair, and the just. It was that thread of optimism, perhaps, that Howells never abandoned.

Conclusion

In Howells's later years he moved away from fiery social polemics in favor of a broader, more open-ended conception of how literature might investigate and convey social and ethical messages. The didactic rhetoric of his early years is, for the most part, absent in his late work as a critic. Rather, Howells values the seamless fusion of aesthetics and ethics in works that prompt moral introspection. Howells was no longer comfortable with the idea that literature could—or should—explicitly instruct or educate its reader. Art, he had come to understand, held only a limited capacity for moral instruction. Art was a better vehicle for moral introspection, for investigation and the raising of difficult questions. This openness, which ripened in Howells's final years, allowed him to embrace writers as diverse and, in their day, as controversial as Henrik Ibsen, Frank Norris, and Émile Zola. It also allowed him to reevaluate some writers he had previously criticized, such as Dickens. As one of the most liberal and progressive literary critics of his generation, Howells's call for the expansion of the bounds of propriety in fiction, coupled with his promotion of Norris, Ibsen, and other avant-garde artists, demands to be recognized for its obvious importance to the development of American literature.

Howells was a keen student of the developing literary market of his day. In "The Man of Letters as a Man of Business," he struggles to define the artist's role in a rapidly developing media society. Howells found himself caught between the practical reality of his own material success in this market and his own liberal social and economic views, which prompted him to idealize and theorize the artist as a working-class hero beyond the reach of gross capitalism. Viewed from the perspective of the twenty-first century, Howells's inability to reconcile these divergent opinions is no fallacy; rather, "The Man of Letters" can be read as an articulation of the paradox of the genteel nineteenth-century author growing fitfully into the twentieth-century literary businessman. In a range of subsequent essays, Howells continued to examine the position of both the artist and the critic in the literary marketplace, paying special attention to the increasingly pernicious effects of the advertiser. These concerns culminated in "The Functions of the

Critic," an important essay that demonstrates both his clear awareness of the increasing force of the advertiser on the literary marketplace and, simultaneously, his inability to envision a new, dynamic role for the literary critic in the twentieth century.

James saw the critic's role in increasingly clear terms. As always, he operated under the aegis that an ounce of example was more valuable than a pound of theory. Leaving aside, for the time being, the titanic example he offered in the Prefaces to the New York Edition, one finds that James's conception of the literary critic continued to evolve and develop, from "The Future of the Novel" right up to his final major literary essay, "The New Novel." James saw the critic's role as an increasingly active one: the critic, in his final estimation, was charged with an "activity of control" that was, ideally, to restrict the flow of second-rate art and to encourage artistic excellence.

Like Howells, James understood that the existing boundaries of propriety in the Anglo-American novel must be challenged in order for the form to develop and expand. On at least one occasion as a critic, James was able to embrace the idea: his 1903 essay on Zola demonstrates that he did find some examples of controversial material artistically justifiable, but as his work on Zola, D'Annunzio, and Serao amply demonstrates, the terms of this appreciation were exclusively—and perhaps narrowly—aesthetic. Unless *passione* could be treated in what James considered an artistically appropriate matter, the issue was best left alone. So, while James understood the eventual need for change, he essentially left the matter for the younger generations to grapple with, content—for once—to side with the status quo.

8. James's Prefaces to the New York Edition

In the wake of his disastrous effort to conquer the theater in 1895, James experienced a late-career crisis that necessarily spilled over into his personal life. Following his decision to quit writing drama, James refocused his attention on fiction. He felt a concurrent need to ground himself, to have a permanent residence. Consequently, in 1899, he purchased Lamb House, in Rye, Sussex. Perhaps not surprisingly, the decision had a direct bearing on his creative work. In a letter to William and Alice James, he declared:

> My whole being cries out aloud for something that I can call my own—and when I look round me at the splendour of so many of the "literary" fry my confrères (M. Crawfords, P. Bourgets, Humphry Wards, Hodgson Burnetts, W. D. Howellses etc.) and I feel that I may strike the world as still, at fifty-six, with my long labour and my genius, reckless, presumptious [*sic*] and unwarranted in curling up (for more assured peaceful production), in a poor little $10,000 shelter—once for all and for all time—*then* do I feel the bitterness of humiliation, the iron enters into my soul, and (I blush to confess it), I *weep!* But enough, enough, enough! I am on firm ground again, and back at work, and the way is clear. (*JL* 4:115)

From the "firm ground" of Lamb House, James would shortly commence the work of his "major phase," dictating his final novels and stories, and engaging in the massive effort of revising selected portions of his creative oeuvre, published as the New York Edition: a final effort by James to root and redefine himself. It was not an easy undertaking; while in the middle of the endeavor, James complained of the "weary grind" of "obscure &

unmeasurable labour" involved.[1] Yet he worked diligently, hopeful that the new edition would bring him the success and notoriety for which he longed.

Scholars are, of course, familiar with the story: sales of the New York Edition were, during James's lifetime, dismal. A heartbroken James died in 1916 thinking the venture yet another failure in his misunderstood, underappreciated career. His sentiments are summed up in a 1915 letter to Edmund Gosse:

> That Edition has been, from the point of view of profit either to the publishers or to myself, practically a complete failure; vulgarly speaking, it doesn't sell. . . . I remain at my age (which you know,) & after my long career, utterly, insurmountably, unsaleable. . . . The Edition is from that point of view really a monument (like Ozymandias) which has never had the least intelligent critical justice done it—any sort of critical attention at all paid it. . . . No more commercially thankless job of the literary order was (Prefaces & all—*they* of a thanklessness!) accordingly ever achieved.[2]

Of course, the New York Edition and its remarkable Prefaces would shortly be rescued from obscurity by Percy Lubbock, R. P. Blackmur, and a host of others. Scholars have been responding to the Edition ever since, and an impressive range of scholarly approaches have been articulated, from New Criticism to biographically centered criticism to Queer Theory. While the Prefaces certainly warrant such attention, the unintended consequence has been to overlook or to ignore the larger context: the Prefaces and their densely woven arguments and observations did not appear ex nihilo. While they can be read as an autonomous whole as per Blackmur and Lubbock, they are perhaps best understood as a product of, a response to, and a revision of the entirety of his previous output as a literary critic. In this regard, the Prefaces can be read as intensely *personal* texts—part of the ongoing personal discussion that was literary criticism for Henry James.

James had always been personally invested in literary criticism. Important essays such as "The Art of Fiction" and "The Science of Criticism" were inspired, in part, by an impulse to teach the reading public—and especially its literary critics—how to appreciate James's difficult fiction. James felt misunderstood and underappreciated, and over time he came to foster a deep ambivalence toward the literary marketplace of his day, which he felt catered to the lowest common denominator. For this reason, James always resisted the impulse to write to an audience on its own

---

1. James, *Selected Letters of Henry James to Edmund Gosse, 1882–1915: A Literary Friendship*, 239.
2. Ibid., 313–14.

terms. "Rather than adapt his art to suit the prevailing desires of the market," notes John H. Pearson, "James stood firm in his devotion to his aesthetic of fiction and sought instead to create desire."[3] James wanted to be read and appreciated, but only on his terms. The Prefaces to the New York Edition are James's attempt to generate desire for a product in a marketplace that, in 1907, showed little interest in an artist whose best-selling works were more than twenty years old.

Henry James sought to create desire in his reader by means of presenting what I call the "figured artist" and the "figured reader." The figured artist is not merely the narrative voice of the Prefaces; it is, rather, a version of Wayne C. Booth's "implied author": an "implied image of the artist" who created the work. This implied author "chooses, consciously or unconsciously, what we read; we infer him as an ideal, literary, created version of the real man; he is the sum of his own choices."[4] Of course, Booth's implied author is a product of fiction; I am arguing here that James, in the Prefaces to the New York Edition, presents to his reader an idealized version of himself: a "figured artist" who is explicitly present throughout the Prefaces. Implicitly present in James's Prefaces is his idealized audience, the "figured reader." James constructs these rhetorical figures in order to create an "economy of desire" in which a seemingly confidential artist-narrator indoctrinates an ideal reader in how to appreciate the art of Henry James. While this rhetorical paradigm is generally familiar to James scholars, few have positioned the Prefaces in relation to James's larger body of literary criticism. Therefore, I shall demonstrate how several key ideas informing James's figured artist and reader in the Prefaces demonstrate the importance of reading the Prefaces contextually with James's other literary criticism. Such an exercise reminds us that, for James, the Prefaces were the product of an entire career; and, as such, they themselves are a revision of a critical theory a lifetime in the making.

We begin our discussion with a careful reading of James's 1907 "Introduction to *The Tempest*." Written concurrently with the early Prefaces, his introduction stages important questions regarding the relationship of the artist to his work and examines how an audience responds to the "figured artist"—issues that resurface in the Prefaces. Next, I examine various strategies used by James to establish and promote his "economy of desire" through establishing and promoting the authority of his figured artist in the Prefaces. This will include contextualizing the Prefaces with "The Lesson of Balzac" and other late-period essays.

---

3. John H. Pearson, *The Prefaces of Henry James: Framing the Modern Reader,* 2.
4. Wayne C. Booth, *The Rhetoric of Fiction,* 71–76 and passim.

The Figure behind the Arras

James begins his "Introduction to *The Tempest*" with the following proposition: "If the effect of the Plays and Poems, taken in their mass, be most
of all to appear often to mock our persistent ignorance of so many of the
conditions of their birth, and thereby to place on the rack again our strained
and aching wonder, this character has always struck me as more particularly
kept up for them by The Tempest" (*LC* 1:1205). One notes his preoccupation with the question of the "conditions of birth" of the works in question,
which is necessarily a question regarding the reader's conception of the author figure. In a sense, the question is quite ordinary: scholars, then as now,
find the paucity of biographical information concerning Shakespeare end-
lessly tantalizing. (*The Tempest* is a particular case in point; some scholars
have theorized that Prospero represents the Bard bidding adieu to his
trade.) But, with the Prefaces to the New York Edition in mind, questions
of the work's "conditions of birth" take on double weight if only because
James addresses that topic throughout a majority of the Prefaces.

For example, most of the Prefaces begin with James relating the "germ"
or trigger that prompted him to begin working on the given fictional text.
James nearly always begins with where he was, and when. This generally
gives way to an account of a particular set of craft-related questions that preoccupied James or gave him trouble with the work, which in turn serves as
a point of departure for his theorizing upon the craft of fiction. One brief
case in point should suffice. *The Portrait of a Lady* was begun in Florence in
1879. The issue at hand "consisted not at all in any conceit of a 'plot'" but
was wholly the question of rendering "a particular engaging young woman,
to which all the usual elements of a 'subject,' certainly of a setting, were to
need to be superadded." This leads to the anecdote concerning Turgenev's
advice regarding character-driven fiction, which in turn becomes a meditation upon rendering a "direct impression or perception of life" via the "artist's
prime sensibility." This leads us directly to the famous "house of fiction"
metaphor. James next relates the difficulties he faced with rendering Isabel:
"If the apparition was still all to be placed how came it to be vivid?" James
realizes what he was "in for—for positively organising an ado about Isabel
Archer." His concerns in this regard are answered in the form of a minor
epiphany: "'Place the centre of the subject in the young woman's own consciousness,' I said to myself, 'and you get as interesting and as beautiful a
difficulty as you could wish.'" After noting his adept use of *ficelles* (though
he does not use the term here) as a means to further render Isabel's fine
state of mind, James concludes the Preface by pointing quite proudly to
Isabel's "extraordinary meditative vigil" before the fireplace: "It is obviously

the best thing in the book, but it is only a supreme illustration of the general plan." Thus James has taken his reader on a fast-paced tour of the "conditions of birth" surrounding his early masterpiece (*LC* 2:1070–84).

This preoccupation with the artistic process accomplishes two things. First, it calls attention to the fact that James wanted to be valued not only for the finished product, but for the labor involved in producing that product. In the Prefaces, "The method of composition is at least as important as the finished work itself," notes John Carlos Rowe, "especially if the 'finish' of the work—its closure as well as its style—is nothing other than this very method objectified." But James's preoccupation with the artistic process also calls attention to the manner in which he presents the figured artist. In contrast to Howells, who in "The Man of Letters as a Man of Business" attempted to align the novelist with the laboring classes, James presents the artist as special, rare, and valuable. John H. Pearson describes James's authorial stance as that of "the heroic artist struggling with complex literary problems and obstacles . . . [who] encourages his reader to attend to authorial performance. The novels and tales then become illustrations of the artist's method and achievement as well as works of art." James wanted to be recognized not only for his product, but also for his process. This is the foundation of the "economy of desire" promoted throughout the Prefaces.[5]

A second function of James's preoccupation with the artistic process is to provide an allegory, or model, for the reader. Time and time again, James emphasizes that the "germ" of the given narrative was merely a starting point; by employing the transformative process of art, James wrought from the crude stuff of life the polished artistic product. Paul B. Armstrong notes the "apparent uselessness" of many details included in James's narrative of creation (e.g., James's recollections of Venice in the Preface to *The Portrait of a Lady*). Such tangential authorial reflections appear not to assist "the reader seeking guidance about how to interpret James's fiction." Or do they? Armstrong argues that such tangents serve an educative purpose, encouraging the reader to move beyond a simplistic reliance on the text (or its author) as the sole source of meaning. Just as James takes his "germ" and improvises freely on it in order to create a work of art, the reader must learn to duplicate "the uses James makes of his germs" by reading the fiction as a text composed of "suggestions emanating from an origin even as we also indulge the liberty to imagine freely about them." Thus the Prefaces serve a rather subtle and indirect function of indoctrinating the reader in *how* to read James.[6]

5. Rowe, *Theoretical Dimensions,* 230; Pearson, *Prefaces of Henry James,* 3.
6. Paul B. Armstrong, "Reading James's Prefaces and Reading James," 134–35.

Armstrong makes a vital point. Despite his plea for readerly attention, James never intended for the Prefaces to be expressly personal or biographical; as we shall see, James differentiates "the artist" from "the man" (that is, the figured artist from the historical James), and he does so for one simple reason: at every point, he wants attention drawn to the art and to its artist. To sell himself as a personality, as a biographical entity, could only distract from this mission. Regarding Alvin Langdon Coburn's illustrations for the New York Edition, James observed that "Anything that relieves responsible prose of the duty of being, while placed before us, good enough, interesting enough and, if the question be of picture, pictorial enough, above all *in itself,* does it the worst of services, and may well inspire in the lover of literature certain lively questions as to the future of that institution" (*LC* 2:1326). Gratuitous biographical or personal information, one imagines James thinking, could only distract from the mission at hand, which was to promote desire in the form of a reconsideration of the fiction. To that end, then, the Prefaces present a version of James the Artist that focuses exclusively on the process and craft of fiction. This is part of the prescriptive and directive mission of the Prefaces; they do not allow the reader to be lost on tangents unrelated to the fictional text. The Prefaces are, at their most base level, designed to create desire for a product.

So who would want such a product? James's idealized reader is always figured implicitly; we sense the reader's qualities indirectly, by means of the criteria presented and promoted by the figured artist. This rhetorical construction, found throughout the Prefaces, was first staged in the "Introduction to *The Tempest.*" For this reason, and given its temporal proximity to the Prefaces, the "Introduction" warrants close scrutiny. In both the "Introduction" and the Prefaces, James promotes in his figured reader an intense desire for the product: the creative text. For example, in the introduction, James implicitly investigates the uses of a reader's curiosity in a creative text's "conditions of birth." If questions of Shakespeare's identity and the biographical or historical sources for his work are maddeningly elusive and therefore a source of readerly discomfort, such questions inevitably lead the reader back to the only thing the reader *does* have, which is the text in question:

> there only, we find that serenity; find the subject itself intact and unconscious, seated as unwinking and inscrutable as a divinity in a temple, save for that vague flicker of derision, the only response to our interpretive heat, which adds the last beauty to its face. The divinity never relents—never, like the image of life in The Winter's Tale, steps down from its pedestal; it simply leaves us to stare on through the ages, with this fact indeed of hav-

ing crossed the circle of fire, and got into the real and right relation to it, for our one comfort. (*LC* 1:1206)

James's figuration of the reader thus begins with an assumed curiosity regarding the figured artist in relation to the work at hand. It is, for James, the question of assessing the "artistic value of the play seen in the meagre circle of the items of our knowledge about it." This "felt need" for biographical context is, for James, a source of "discomfiture" because "The man himself, in the Plays, we directly touch, to my consciousness, positively nowhere: we are dealing too perpetually with the artist, the monster and magician of a thousand masks." At best, the reader can "hover at the base of the thick walls for a sense of him," in a perpetual state of intense curiosity (*LC* 1:1208–9). One notes that the reader is, throughout this description, both in a state of desire *and* grappling with the text.

James's figuration of the artist is more explicit. As the quote above indicates, the artist figure is "as unwinking and inscrutable as a divinity in a temple": a godlike figure out of reach of the mortal reader.[7] Yet there is also a "man" (that is, the historical Shakespeare) to be distinguished from the artist, the "implied author" one senses, indirectly, behind the "thick walls" of art. Interestingly, James argues that—in the case of Shakespeare, at least—the artist consumes the man: "The man everywhere, in Shakespeare's work, is . . . effectually locked up and imprisoned in the artist." The creative process is figured as "a series of incalculable plunges" beginning with "the great primary plunge, made once for all, of the man into the artist: the successive plunges of the artist himself into Romeo and into Juliet, into Shylock, Hamlet," and so forth. This process of submersion—man into the artist; artist into character—is, in the early plays, registered in certain disruptions of form: "the very violence of the movements [i.e., successive plunges] involved troubles and distracts our sight." But "In The Tempest . . . [there] is no violence; he sinks as deep as we like, but what he sinks into, beyond all else, is the lucid stillness of his style" (*LC* 1:1206, 1209). What the figured artist ultimately represents is the work itself. In *The Rhetoric of Fiction*, Wayne Booth reformulates this idea: "Our sense of the implied author includes not only the extractable meanings but also the moral and emotional content of each bit of action and suffering in all of the characters. It includes, in short, the intuitive apprehension of a completed artistic whole; the chief value to which *this* implied author is committed, regardless of what

7. In "The Lesson of Balzac," James playfully refers to his reading of Balzac as "haunting the back shop, the laboratory, or, more nobly expressed, the inner shrine of the temple" of art (*LC* 2:138).

party his creator belongs to in real life, is that which is expressed by the total form."[8] Therefore, for James, the creative work is the purest articulation of both artist and man—each of whom is wholly submerged into that work, though at different removes. And it is for this reason that he sees *The Tempest* as the quintessential example of the process of artistic creation, defined here as "the very act of the momentous conjunction taking place for the poet, at a given hour, between his charged inspiration and his clarified experience: or, as I should perhaps better express it, between his human curiosity and his aesthetic passion" (*LC* 1:1209). In this example, "human curiosity" is the trigger that sets the artist in motion, while "aesthetic passion" is the artistic process and its product: the organically conceived, stand-alone work of art. The trick for any artist, James suggests, is to merge process into product—to shape the product into a perfect articulation of the process itself. This *The Tempest* exemplifies completely: "I can offer no better description of The Tempest as fresh re-perusal lights it for me than as such a surrender, sublimely enjoyed; and I may frankly say that, under this impression of it, there is no refinement of the artistic consciousness that I do not see my way—or feel it, better, perhaps, since we but grope, at the best, in our darkness—to attribute to the author. It is a way that one follows to the end, because it is a road, I repeat, on which one least misses some glimpse of him face to face" (*LC* 1:1210). James emphasizes the sanctity of this process: the artist letting go of not only the trigger or "human curiosity" that prompted him to begin the work, but also the desire to register himself in the work; the work itself, a product of "aesthetic passion," must take absolute precedence. The well-crafted work of art will, itself, engender all the right kinds of curiosity in the reader, who will be ceaselessly drawn back into "the real and right relation" to the work—that is, to grapple with the form of the work itself. The reader, in dealing with the work, trades exclusively with the artist and is forever separated from the man.

James seems to want it both ways. On the one hand, the inability for the reader to access the man by means of a reading of the text, dealing ever with a figured artist as represented more or less explicitly in that text, can be read as a strategy for foregrounding aesthetic questions before questions of biography, history, and so forth. On the other hand, James cannot wholly let go of his hope to find the man figured in the work; he appreciates the "sublime surrender" of the artist as figured in *The Tempest* precisely because he hopes to catch "some glimpse" of the man. If it is a typically Jamesian paradox, it nevertheless begs the question: What did this relentless search for a "glimpse" of the man in the art mean to Henry James?

Vivien Jones argues that James's persistent desire to locate the historical

8. Booth, *Rhetoric of Fiction*, 73–74.

Shakespeare in *The Tempest* demonstrates how James is, to a degree, still a "nineteenth-century critic, [clinging] nostalgically to a hope of reaching 'the Man'" in the creative text.[9] That may be part of it; but James's attempt to locate the man in the text is, perhaps, a stronger, more creative urge on his part to find—or to construct—a figured artist for reasons both critical and personal. (The two were never far apart in James.) For instance, we have seen how, on reading Hawthorne's *Notebooks*, James's "impression of [Hawthorne's] general intellectual power" was "diminish[ed]. . . . They represent him, judged with any real critical rigor, as superficial, uninformed, incurious, inappreciative" (*LC* 1:307–8). James went on, in *Hawthorne*, to use this interpretation of his forebear (the figured artist, Hawthorne) and his New England landscape as an opportunity not only to denigrate America as a literary subject, but, in doing so, to "justify" a personal decision to move to Europe; the idea that "it takes a great deal of history to produce a little literature . . . [and] a complex social machinery to set a writer in motion" (*LC* 1:320) can be read as a declaration by James of his reasons for emigrating. Thus Hawthorne and New England have been constructed—indeed, rather creatively reconfigured—to suit James's own personal needs.

In contrast, James, throughout his various essays on Balzac, constructs an idealized version of the artist who lived exclusively for his craft. Balzac died "at fifty—worn out with work and thought and passion; the passion, I mean, that he had put into his mighty plan and that had ridden him like an infliction of the gods." The quasi-ascetic Frenchman, that "Benedictine of the actual" exemplifies "the lesson that there is no convincing art that is not ruinously expensive." James repeatedly expresses his wonder and admiration for the example of a man so wholly devoted to his craft that he "did *not* live—save in his imagination" (*LC* 2:122, 93, 133, 107). One need not read far in James's letters, autobiographies, or the critical biographies on him to understand that this figured version of Balzac had a profound impact on James (who was, after all, both a lifelong bachelor and the supreme aesthete). Simply put, in the examples of Hawthorne and Balzac—though there are many others that could be examined—this exercise of creating a figured artist out of the work affected James's own sense of what it meant to be an artist. As Ross Posnock puts it, James, in his literary criticism, "projects his own highly personal feelings and thereby turns [these artists] (at least in part) into symbolic figures to which he is, in varying degrees, opposed or in sympathy. In so doing, James partially establishes his identity as artist and man."[10]

This Jamesian paradox—wanting the artistic text read on its own terms,

---

9. Jones, *James the Critic*, 200.
10. Ross Posnock, *Henry James and the Problem of Robert Browning*, 199n4.

while simultaneously allowing for the possibility that the figured artist might be "glimpsed" vis-à-vis the text—is found throughout the Prefaces in James's celebration of the creative process of artistic submersion. The familiar narrative of the "germ" giving way to a discussion of the craft-related issues of the particular work is a recreation or recapitulation of the process. James also celebrates this process in his discussion of revision. In the Preface to *Roderick Hudson,* for example, James the Artist is figured as a godlike "prime creator" reviewing his early work in "a safe paradise of self-criticism." The act of revision cannot merely be a resuscitation of old inspirations and motivations; indeed, James claims to have forgotten them: "The old reasons . . . are too dead to revive; they were not, it is plain, good enough reasons to live. The only possible relation of the present mind to the thing is to dismiss it altogether." Only then is "creative intimacy . . . reaffirmed, and appreciation, critical apprehension, insists on becoming as active as it can" (*LC* 2:1045–46). Revision is not merely revisiting old sources of inspiration; it is a complete and total reconsideration of the work on wholly new terms: a full submersion into the creative process. The artist can never step into the same river twice.

In the Preface to *The Golden Bowl,* revision is an "infinitely interesting and amusing *act* of re-appropriation" because "To revise is to see, or to look over, again—which means in the case of a written thing neither more nor less than to re-read it." James, who had initially balked at the prospect of undertaking the laborious revisions of his early work, found, to his delight, that to reread *is* to revise: "where I had thus ruefully prefigured two efforts there proved to be but one." Rewriting, James emphasizes, is something very different from revising: "What re-writing might be was to remain—it has remained for me to this hour—a mystery" (*LC* 2:1332). Thus James "revised" but did not "re-write" the work in the New York Edition. In the Prefaces, James does not further clarify his point. But, as Philip Horne has shown, the distinction centers around James's role as an "active reader"; he positively grappled with any text that came under his purview (as James's many writer-friends knew only too well).[11] In a 1913 letter to H. G. Wells, James explains: "I am of my nature and by the effect of my own 'preoccupations' a critical, a non-*naif*, a questioning, worrying reader. . . . To read a novel at all I perform afresh, to my sense, the act of writing it, that is of re-handling the subject accordingly to my own lights and over-scoring the author's form and pressure with my own vision and understanding of *the* way—this, of course I mean, when I *see* a subject in what he has done and

11. Philip Horne, *Henry James and Revision,* 47–99. See also Walter Benn Michaels, "Writers Reading: James and Eliot."

feel its appeal to me as one: which I fear I very often don't" (*JL* 4:686). Reading, for James, is an act of appropriation, a hand-to-hand engagement, and this is the spirit behind the conflation of reading and revising in the Prefaces. In sitting down to review his own work, James could hardly help but reenter the creative process.

By conflating the processes of writing and revising, James invites the figured reader into the process of making meaning out of the text. He hopes to incite some sense of connection, some intimacy with the figured artist and, perhaps, the "man" behind the artist. "The 'taste' of the poet is," James argues, "at bottom and so far as the poet in him prevails over everything else, his active sense of life: in accordance with which truth to keep one's hand on it is to hold the silver clue to the whole labyrinth of his consciousness" (*LC* 2:1333). James believes—he insists—that a careful appreciation of the work at hand, of its style and form, will give the reader some sense of the mind of the creator: form, a product of the artist, is an extension of mind; mind is a product of the man. By extension, then, revision and reading—conflated as one process by James—is "a *living* affair" for both author and reader, and the attentive reader can in fact touch the artist's intelligence. If, for the author, "The rate at which new readings, new conductors of sense interposed, to make any total sense at all right, became, to this wonderful tune, the very record and mirror of the general adventure of one's intelligence," then what James is implicitly suggesting is that the reader can share in an appreciation of that intelligence, that growth, that performance. Speaking of the New York Edition as a whole, James asks his reader, toward the end of the final Preface, "What has the affair been at the worst, I am most moved to ask, but an earnest invitation to the reader to dream again in my company and in the interest of his own larger absorption of my sense?" (*LC* 2:1335, 1338). Thus James configures the act of reading as a bridge between man and artist, and, through a process of conflation, between artist and reader, gently insisting that the careful reader can appreciate the sense, the intelligence, and the taste of both artist and man. But in this paradigm, the reader cannot touch the man directly through the work. Like the critic figured in "The Science of Criticism," the reader will always be the attendant to the artist, a respondent, always one step below or removed. Kept at a distance.

But why?

In the "Introduction to *The Tempest*," James suggests that an intimate connection between reader and artist (or the man) might prove fatal for the artist:

> The secret that baffles us being the secret of the Man, we know, as I have granted, that we shall never touch the Man *directly* in the Artist. We stake

our hopes thus on indirectness, which may contain possibilities; we take
that very truth for our counsel of despair, try to look at it as helpful for the
Criticism of the future. That of the past has been too often infantile; one
has asked one's self how it *could,* on such lines, get at him. The figured tapestry, the long arras that hides him, is always there, with its immensity of
surface and its proportionate underside. May it not then be but a question,
for the fulness of time, of the finer weapon, the sharper point, the stronger
arm, the more extended lunge? (*LC* 1:1220)

The passage is remarkable for a number reasons. First, we note James's
dogged insistence on the reader "touching" the Man via the portal of art.
Criticism here is, as always for James, "the only gate of appreciation" (*LC*
2:115), yet the final image of the essay is that of future critics not merely locating or identifying the "hidden" author, but assassinating him. The death
of the author, indeed!

The point gives rise to a fascinating opportunity for conjecture. To be
sure, the authorial stance presented in the Prefaces is anything but "personal." James speaks confidentially, confidingly, even intimately—but only
insofar as the question of artistic production is concerned. At every point,
the reader is directed toward the text at hand; the Prefaces serve as points of
departure, stages on which to prepare a reader for the reading to come. The
Prefaces are educative, prescriptive, didactic. It is James the Artist we hear in
the Prefaces. He is our guide and mentor. James the Man is kept out of sight.
The reason may be, as suggested above, to avoid unnecessary tangents and
distractions: there is nothing in the Prefaces to distract the reader from a
wholehearted appreciation for the work and the Artist. Biographical information could only distract from that.

But another reason for the absence of the Man in the Prefaces could be
hinted at in the image of the assassinated author in the final lines of the
"Introduction to *The Tempest*." The image is quite literally striking, and it
speaks to the anxiety James felt regarding the literary marketplace and its
critics. James felt the artist and the man both needed to protect themselves.
One recalls how James, in "The Science of Criticism," had written of the
"sensitive organism" of art, which "is highly susceptible of demoralization."
He warned that "irresponsible pedagogy," in the form of poor criticism,
could "make [art] close its ears and lips. To be puerile and untutored about
it is to deprive it of air and light, and the consequence of its keeping bad
company is that it loses all heart" (*LC* 1:97). Art and its artists need to be
carefully protected, for poorly executed criticism could kill an artist. Or a
man. And if the man is the first thing submerged into the identity of the
artist, then there can be no artist where there is no man (the source of the

artist's sensibility, taste, and vision). Consequently, the man must and shall remain forever shrouded behind the arras, behind the thick walls of the fortress of art. The somewhat distanced, aloof authorial voice in the Prefaces reflects this set of concerns.

Thus we encounter one of James's richest paradoxes. On the one hand, he was desperately eager at every point in his career to win the attention of a wider audience, both critical and popular. But James was nothing if not proud; success had to be won on his terms. More precisely, he sought to *create* an audience for himself, and he used his literary criticism as a support vehicle for that mission. As we have seen, James adopted the pose of a disgruntled, contentious critic in "The Future of the Novel" and "The Lesson of Balzac," someone apparently disgusted with the swelling, vulgar masses of readers. But his purpose in positioning himself this way was not to reject the changing literary marketplace; rather, it was an attempt to (re)define himself in relation to it. If James could identify those elements of the marketplace that he found lamentable (or flat-out ridiculous), it gave him the opportunity to more clearly define his own brand of fiction—and to "sell" it to his readers. In this regard, the Prefaces are the final, monumental push in a lifelong campaign to educate readers on the virtues of Henry James's fiction.

Yet with each year such popular and critical success seemed further out of reach—a source of great frustration to the ever-ambitious James. An earlier generation of scholars saw the Master's increasingly difficult later manner— and his contentious pronouncements as a critic—and evidence of a kind of withdrawal or a retreat from the literary scene.[12] But more recent scholarship has shown how the later James grew increasingly savvy in his attempts to negotiate the ever-changing literary marketplace. James was anything but isolated or out of touch, and his later criticism—especially the Prefaces— demonstrate a carefully choreographed attempt to carve out a distinct niche. As Richard Salmon has put it, "James's (apparent) distance from the arena of mass culture becomes the sign which allows us to recognize his proximity to it." As Salmon convincingly demonstrates, James understood that the ever-expanding literary marketplace had diversified and specialized; in effect, the savvy author could capitalize on highly specific "target audiences": the sentimental novel, the historical romance, literature for children, and so on. James, in the Prefaces, aims his work at those readers interested in high culture, or refined literary art. Consequently, if James turns away from certain

---

12. Scholars in this camp have largely followed the example of Leon Edel, whose influential biographies of James shaped a generation of readers. See Edel, *Henry James: The Middle Years, 1882–1895; Henry James: The Treacherous Years, 1895–1901;* and *Henry James: A Life.*

audiences—those readers historically associated with "low culture"—it is because he is preoccupied with constructing a different readership. In this regard, then, James is engaged, aware, and keenly sensitive to his intended audience (the "figured reader") and the larger literary marketplace as a whole. The pose of the disgruntled critic in "The Future of the Novel" and "The Lesson of Balzac" gives way, in the Prefaces, to a more inviting persona; James has switched masks—but he is still dancing with his readers.[13]

James's preoccupation with the question of the relationship of the man to his art continued to preoccupy him long after the New York Edition. His final piece of literary criticism was a 1916 preface to Rupert Brooke's *Letters from America*. Brooke, a promising young English poet and an acquaintance of James, died during World War I, leaving behind two volumes of verse and some assorted journalism. Looking back at the short life of Brooke, James confesses to owning "the interest of our learning how the poet . . . has come into his estate, asserted and preserved his identity, worked out his question of sticking to that and to nothing else; and has so been able to reach us and touch us *as* a poet, in spite of the accidents and dangers that have beset this course." Brooke's example seems to prove an "observed law, that the growth and the triumph of the [poetic] faculty at its finest have been positively in proportion to certain rigours of circumstance." James offers a list of examples, including Dante, Milton, Shakespeare, Keats, Shelley, Coleridge, Emily Brontë, Whitman, and others. The various struggles faced by these writers elicit "our affection for the great poetic muse, the vision of the rarest sensibility and the largest generosity we know kept by her at their pitch, kept fighting for their life and insisting on their range of expression, amid doubts and derisions and buffets, even sometimes amid stones of stumbling quite self-invited, that might at any moment have made the loss of the precious clue really irremediable. Which moral, so pointed, accounts assuredly for half our interest in the poetic character" (*LC* 1:747–48). This passage is fascinating when read in light of James's own experiences as an author, particularly the acute personal crisis he experienced after his failed bid as a dramatist in 1895—a "stone of stumbling quite self-invited" if ever there was one—and after the commercial failure of the New York Edition. It suggests that James was very concerned with, first, how an artist survived and thrived under adversity and, second, how a reader could perceive and learn from the example of the artist by means of a careful reading of the work.

James's "Introduction to *The Tempest*" and the thoughts expressed in his preface to Brooke's *Letters from America* both suggest paradigms for under-

---

13. Salmon, *Henry James and the Culture of Publicity*, 5, 58. See also Margolis, *Henry James and the Problem of Audience;* and Jacobson, *Henry James and the Mass Market.*

standing the figured artist in the Prefaces to the New York Edition. James clearly felt that he had invested something of his own personality in the work; James the Man, in his own sense of himself, is submerged into the constructed role as James the (figured) Artist; the role of the figured artist in the Prefaces is to invite or lure the reader to join him in reading (or rereading) the work of his entire career—"to dream again in my company." To do so, James suggests, is to experience a kind of intimate connection. Read in this light, the Prefaces become not merely, as James would famously phrase it in a 1908 letter to Howells, "a sort of plea for Criticism, for Discrimination, for Appreciation on other than infantine lines" (*LFL*, 426), but a more intimate, personal, and eminently *creative* plea for the reader to accompany the Artist, that "monster and magician of a thousand masks," on a tour inside the "thick walls" of the fortress of art.[14]

A Safe Paradise of Self-Criticism

In "The Art of Fiction," James had declared that "We must grant the artist his subject, his idea, his *donnée:* our criticism is applied only to what he makes of it" (*LC* 1:56). James honors his own dictum throughout the Prefaces. The subject of nearly every creative work addressed is taken as a given; there is no analysis of Isabel Archer's failed marriage, no pondering of Kate Croy's motives, no examination of Prince Amerigo's duplicity. At every turn, treatment is foregrounded. James favors close analysis of his now-familiar catalog of preferred, craft-oriented concerns: form, composition, selection, point of view, and characterization. James "is not concerned with telling us what the fiction means," observes John H. Pearson, "instead, he explains how well it is crafted. . . . [H]e is not so concerned about showing us his craft as he is determined to teach us how to read attentively and thereby to appreciate his artistry."[15] The commonly understood explanation for this is that the Prefaces are a didactic exercise designed to indoctrinate a reading public that had been, to that point in James's career, somewhat begrudging and fickle. In order to understand the situation as James perceived it, one must consider the "atmosphere" of the literary marketplace of the early twentieth century.

14. Howells seems to concur with James's idea of the Prefaces as a plea for criticism; in an earlier letter to James, Howells writes admiringly of the way the Prefaces point to the organic, holistic nature of James's work; for Howells, the Prefaces confirm "that you have imagined your fiction, as a whole, and better fulfilled a conscious intention in it than any of your contemporaries" (*LFL*, 423).

15. Pearson, *Prefaces of Henry James,* 69.

As we have seen in previous chapters, William Dean Howells and Henry James held widely different opinions of the literary marketplace. Howells's attempt to position the artist among the working classes as a laborer in "The Man of Letters as a Man of Business" was partly a response to his own material prosperity and success as an author; it was also a response to a changing marketplace in which the author had to negotiate an increasingly complex landscape of business, marketing, advertising, and the burgeoning print media. Within this new social dynamic, Howells wanted to validate the work that he and other writers did in terms the laboring classes would understand. The argument, if not entirely successful, demonstrated that Howells saw the practice of authorship as part of the social and cultural dynamic of production and industry. He wanted to center the practice of art in and among the larger society. The last thing he wanted was to suggest that the artist was removed from the middle or working classes. Consequently, he felt that literature should investigate the pressing social concerns of its time.

Not so Henry James. We have seen how, in both "The Future of the Novel" and the opening paragraphs of "The Lesson of Balzac," James complained of a changing literary marketplace that, in his opinion, championed and promoted all the wrong kinds of art; consequently, James came to equate popularity with "the vulgarisation of literature in general" (*LC* 1:103). This discomfort prompted James to figure himself, in his late criticism, as a "minority artist" who held himself beyond the reach of the vulgar masses. The rhetorical pose of retreat rather cleverly disguises the Master's true aim: not to remove himself from the marketplace, but to approach one corner of it in an increasingly refined and creative manner. His ultimate goal was to construct an audience of readers *from within* the marketplace. This idea is the crucial foundation of the Prefaces, which can be read as a monumental last attempt neither to save nor to reform the public literary marketplace—James felt the situation was beyond rescue—but to create his own space within it, a kind of country-within-a-country. As Sara Blair has noted, part of James's project in the Prefaces involved "locating the work of authorship in the space of a privacy in which forms and values untouched by the marketplace . . . are protected and preserved."[16] As we have seen in the "Introduction to *The Tempest*," James envisioned the artist as a figure hidden behind the "thick walls" of art, out of reach of the vulgar masses and the critics who, he imagined, could "kill" an author.

What James creates for himself in the Prefaces is "a safe paradise of self-criticism" where he, "the artist, the prime creator" can stroll about a "sweet

---

16. Sara Blair, "In the House of Fiction: Henry James and the Engendering of Literary Mastery," 61.

old overtangled walled garden" of his own making (*LC* 2:1045). James invites his readers to enjoy his garden—only, of course, on his terms. We have established that James clearly sought to create desire in the reader for his product (his creative work) by means of presenting a figured artist (rhetorically explicit), who offered a criteria of appreciation, and a figured reader (rhetorically implicit), who would respond positively to that criteria (that is, with desire for the product). An essential part of his rhetorical strategy is the insistence on the *authority* of his figured artist: that is, to promote the idea of a knowing, cultured, sophisticated, and discerning artist who, so the paradigm demands, would instruct the reader in how to share those highly selective and cultivated traits.

Characteristically, James enacts this strategy quite subtly, presenting a multifaceted and complex figured artist. For example, in his capacity as critic in the Prefaces, he does not spare himself. He is quick to point out creative weaknesses, especially in the earlier work. Yet James, ever savvy rhetorically, often twists such instances, finding ways to capitalize on his own weaknesses in an attempt to further bolster the authority of his figured artist. The strongest example of this strategy is found in the very first Preface.

In the Great Shadow of Balzac

Early in the Preface to *Roderick Hudson,* James confesses that his depiction of Northampton, Massachusetts, in the first two chapters of the novel "fails of intensity. . . . To name a place, in fiction, is to pretend in some degree to represent it—and I speak here of course but of the use of existing names, the only ones that carry weight." Therefore, place must be rendered not merely with accuracy, it must also be made essential to the work: a novelist "embarks, rash adventurer, under the star of 'representation,' and is pledged thereby to remember that the art of interesting us in things—once these things are the right ones for his case—can *only* be the art of representing them." The power of place will only be realized if the artist has "a *sense* for it," and "The way in which this sense has been, or has not been, applied constitutes, at all events, in respect to any fiction, the very ground of critical appreciation" (*LC* 2:1043–44).

If James fails to meet his own criteria in *Roderick Hudson,* at least he knows why he made his ill-fated attempt: "one nestled, technically, in those days, and with yearning, in the great shadow of Balzac; his august example, little as the secret might ever be guessed, towered for me over the scene." If Balzac's depictions of provincial French towns in *La Comédie Humaine* inspired James to attempt its American counterpart, then James's artistic immaturity is to blame for the weakly realized result: "The reason was plain: one was not in the least, in one's prudence, emulating [Balzac's] systematic closeness." Balzac only addressed a particular place when he could "make something out of it. To name it simply and not in some degree tackle it would have seemed to him an act reflecting on his general course the deepest dishonour" (*LC* 2:1044–45).[17] The implication is clear: James himself has suffered upon Northampton some such dishonor, reminding us that, for James, morality in fiction was always a question of execution, a question of form, a question of artistic practice.

This anecdote from the Preface to *Roderick Hudson* amply demonstrates James's own capacity for unsparing self-criticism in the Prefaces. The humility is refreshing, perhaps even surprising. Yet the apparent candor masks a savvy rhetorical strategy by which James aligns himself, the figured artist, with a mentor whose values and aesthetic he wants not only to pay tribute to, but to co-opt. James infrequently discusses other writers in the Prefaces; the focus is, for obvious reasons, almost exclusively on himself. Yet Balzac stands at the entry to the Prefaces, casting his "great shadow." The reader is, therefore, perhaps not surprised to find Balzac mentioned, usually in passing, in over a half-dozen of the Prefaces; "the vast example of Balzac" looms again in the closing pages of the final Preface (*LC* 2:1336).[18]

Balzac is, of course, a figure to whom James turned at crucial points in his career as a literary critic. Indeed, Balzac had been there from the first, appearing in 1865 as a cogent counterexample to Harriet Elizabeth Prescott Spofford's novel *Azarian* (*LC* 1:603–13). James's 1875 essay on Balzac— with its lengthy appreciations of the Frenchman's "aesthetic judgment" and "irresistible force"—had been a keystone of his early career as a critic (*LC* 2:49, 53). In a 1902 essay devoted to the Frenchman, James bluntly asserts that "Balzac stands signally apart . . . he is the first and foremost member of his craft." Of particular importance is Balzac's "inner vision . . . for which ideas are as living as facts and assume an equal intensity. This intensity, greatest indeed in the facts, has in Balzac a force all its own, to which none other in any novelist I know can be likened" (*LC* 2:90, 95). Perhaps more than any other figure in James's canon, Balzac's presence is felt throughout

17. James had long valued Balzac's prodigious ability to render place in fiction; in 1875, James had noted that "The place in which an event occurred was in [Balzac's] view of equal moment with the event itself; it was part of the action; it was not a thing to take or to leave, or to be vaguely and gracefully indicated; it imposed itself; it had a part to play; it needed to be made as definite as anything else" (*LC* 2:49–50).

18. Balzac is explicitly named in the following Prefaces: *Roderick Hudson; The American; The Princess Casamassima; The Spoils of Poynton; The Lesson of the Master; The Ambassadors;* and *The Golden Bowl.*

the Prefaces. The reader interested in the rhetorical stance of James's figured artist throughout the Prefaces should study carefully "The Lesson of
Balzac," an important precedent for the Prefaces. "The Lesson" reminds us
that certain aesthetic concerns promoted in the Prefaces—the privileging of
form over subject, for instance—are convictions James learned or co-opted
from his mentors. Interestingly, James explicitly calls attention to his adap-
tation of the aesthetic strategies of his mentors in the Prefaces; indeed, this
is an important part of how James establishes the authority of his figured
artist.

As we have noted, "The Lesson of Balzac" begins with James's assessment of the dismal state of the literary marketplace. If the prime test of
merit in an author is the question of inspiring the critical practice, then
Balzac is king, for he "offers it as no other members of the company can
pretend to do." The single most important thing that James has learned
from Balzac is the importance of the artist's unique vision. Using the analogy of the Poet, James insists that "the Poet is most the Poet when he is
preponderantly lyrical, when he speaks, laughing or crying, most directly
from his individual heart, which throbs under the impressions of life. It is
not the *image* of life that he thus expresses, so much as life itself, in its
sources—so much as his own intimate, essential states and feelings" (*LC*
2:117, 121). This is a reformulation of the artistic subjectivity James had
privileged and promoted in "The Art of Fiction," the "direct, personal vision" he always insisted was essential to any work of art. Balzac, more than
any other writer in James's pantheon, is the wellspring for James's appreciation of the irresistible force of the artist's individual vision; both his 1875
and 1902 essays on the Frenchman demonstrate as much.

In "The Lesson of Balzac," James differentiates and privileges the artist's
force of vision from the subject matter of the individual work of art. The
"individual strong temperament in fiction" is "the color of the air with which
this, that or the other painter of life (as we call them all), more or less unconsciously suffuses his picture. I say unconsciously because I speak here of
an effect of atmosphere largely, if not wholly, distinct from the effect sought
on behalf of the special subject to be treated; something that proceeds from
the contemplative mind itself, the very complexion of the mirror in which
the material is reflected" (*LC* 2:125). This is not to say that James devalued
the question of subject in fiction; in "The Art of Fiction," James had argued
that the subject of a novel "matters, to my sense, in the highest degree, and
if I might put up a prayer it would be that artists should select none but the
richest" (*LC* 1:57). He reasserts this idea in the Preface to *The Ambassadors,*
when he pronounces that "there are degrees of merit in subjects" (*LC*
2:1305). Rather, in "The Lesson of Balzac," James reaffirms a critical stance

that allowed him to bridge the gap between his own relatively conservative Anglo-American scruples and the liberal French artists who had always been more frank and graphic in their depictions of society and human behavior (in particular, the erotic). As we have seen, it was James's appreciation for Zola's "close embrace of [his] subject" (*LC* 2:880) that finally allowed him to overcome his dislike for Zola's choice of subject (a point on which James had, in "The Art of Fiction," criticized the Frenchman). James therefore learned to privilege form over subject not only because he was the supreme aesthete, but also because it allowed him to articulate what he valued so dearly in the French without necessarily condoning their choice of subject, which he would always find measurably discomforting.[19] It is an idea perhaps most eloquently articulated in James's 1902 essay on Flaubert, in which he observes how the example of Flaubert teaches us "that beauty comes with expression, that expression is creation, that it *makes* the reality, and only in the degree in which it *is*, exquisitely, expression; and that we move in literature through a world of different values and relations, a blest world in which we know nothing except by style, but in which also everything is saved by it, and in which the image is thus always superior to the thing itself" (*LC* 2:340). For James, *Madame Bovary* would always stand as the paramount example of a work in which a sordid subject was second to a highly polished style.

Balzac, and the French in general, had long presented James with the delicate question of taste. In 1875, James had found Balzac "morally and intellectually . . . superficial." Balzac's "intellectual atmosphere" was "gross and turbid; it is no wonder that the flower of truth does not bloom in it." Balzac's greedy misers and materialists offended James. Nevertheless, James could ultimately appreciate Balzac's "aesthetic judgment" and the "irresistible force" of his prose (*LC* 2:47, 49, 53). Therefore, when James differentiates Balzac's "effect of atmosphere" from the choice of subject in "The Lesson of Balzac," it is a very old critical and rhetorical strategy that allows James to sidestep the problematic question of choice of subject in favor of probing the question of atmosphere. This point is crucial because James, in the Prefaces, wanted to associate himself only with selected, form-related aspects of Balzac's aesthetic. Clearly, he did not share Balzac's taste in subject matter.

So how, James asks rhetorically in "The Lesson," does a given writer accomplish the task of rendering so powerful an atmosphere in fiction? "It is a

---

19. The privileging of form over content is, of course, a familiar Jamesian preference, articulated on different occasions for different reasons, and often for reasons other than propriety. For example, he would use the strategy in his "Introduction to *The Tempest*" in order to overlook the more trivial plotlines used by Shakespeare (*LC* 1:1212–13).

question," James suggests, "of *penetrating* into a subject." James uses Zola as a quick foil; Zola was powerful, but "had inordinately to simplify— . . . had to leave out the life of the soul . . . and confine himself to the life of the instincts, of the more immediate passions." In contrast to Zola, Balzac's "mystic process of the crucible, the transformation of the material under aesthetic heat, is . . . thanks to an intenser and more submissive fusion, completer, and also finer." Like Zola, Balzac does examine "the commoner and more wayside passions," but manages to do so with "supreme fineness." In the final instance, it is the convincing "effort at *representation*" that allows a novel to succeed: "When saturation fails no other presence really avails" (*LC* 2:127–31). "The Lesson of Balzac" reminds us that James's fascination with form was an old one; therefore, his emphasis on form in the Prefaces is, in this regard, nothing new. Balzac is clearly the prime source of this aesthetic preference, and for James to position his mentor so conspicuously at the beginning and at the end of the Prefaces—and to refer to him so frequently throughout—goes beyond a mere pose of humility. It is an attempt by James to align himself with an artist of the first order.[20]

Such mock deference was not a new strategy for James. As we have previously noted, James's apparent humility and deference to Walter Besant in "The Art of Fiction" was a masterfully executed rhetorical exercise that allowed James to introduce a radical aesthetic argument to a conservative Anglo-American audience. In certain respects, the literary atmosphere for James in 1907 was not significantly different than it had been in 1884. In each era, James faced an audience predisposed to discount him and his work. In 1884, James labored against the atmosphere created by Howells's "Henry James, Jr." In 1907, James labored against a diffident reading public that had failed to embrace his increasingly complex, dense fiction. In 1884, James sought to introduce an aesthetic argument, largely predicated on the French model, that he knew would meet with immediate resistance by Anglo-American readers. In 1907, James sought to promote and champion an aesthetic that the public had, in James's eyes, failed to recognize or value. Read in this light, James's deliberate nod to Balzac in the first Preface can be read as an attempt to borrow authority and cultural weight. At the same time, the mention of Balzac reminds us that the foundations of the aesthetic arguments in the Prefaces run deep—straight back, in this case, to the earliest criticism written by James.

20. While it is James's preoccupation with form and saturation that have preoccupied me in this aside, there are a variety of other important areas in which "The Lesson of Balzac" prefigures the Prefaces. For instance, James discusses both the question of "foreshortening" the novel's "picture"; he also reiterates a familiar complaint regarding the question of dialogue (*LC* 2:136–37); the complaint is restated in the Prefaces to *Daisy Miller* and *The Awkward Age*.

The strategy of acknowledging and co-opting literary authority is repeated in the Preface to *The Portrait of a Lady,* when James credits Turgenev for inspiring his decision to place Isabel Archer at the center of his realist masterpiece. Again, there is a precedent. In an 1874 essay, James had noted the generosity, sympathy, and compassion Turgenev extended to his fictional characters (sensibilities James would later praise in Balzac); James had also noted Turgenev's "preference for a theme which takes its starting point in character" (*LC* 2:977). That James would, in the Preface to the *Portrait,* call attention to the influence of his Russian mentor is not surprising; as with the nod to Balzac in the Preface to *Roderick Hudson,* the mention of Turgenev is clearly an attempt to align himself with a respected author: Turgenev is both a "distinguished friend" and a "beautiful genius," and his anecdote provides James with the "higher warrant" needed to justify focusing the lengthy *Portrait* around a young American naïf (*LC* 2:1073).

Yet the quote from Turgenev is almost certainly not recorded verbatim, given that a quarter of a century had passed since Turgenev would have confided in James. (Also, they would likely have spoken in French.) James co-opts the respected Turgenev, placing his own aesthetic into the Russian's mouth. Of the decision to focus first on character, James "records" Turgenev:

> "To arrive at these things is to arrive at my 'story,'" [Turgenev] said, "and that 's the way I look for it. The result is that I 'm often accused of not having 'story' enough. I seem to myself to have as much as I need—to show my people, to exhibit their relations with each other; for that is all my measure. . . . As for the origin of one's wind-blown germs themselves, who shall say, as you ask, where *they* come from? We have to go too far back, too far behind, to say. Is n't it all we can say that they come from every quarter of heaven, that they are *there* at almost any turn of the road? They accumulate, and we are always picking them over, selecting among them." (*LC* 2:1072–73)

With its emphasis on character-centered fiction, "germs," and the principle of selection, the passage is patently Jamesian. James clearly acknowledges the source of an important aesthetic tenet, thereby bolstering the authority of his own figured artist by means of citing an expert and "translating" the expert into his own parlance, both literally and figuratively.

As these asides on the references to Balzac and Turgenev demonstrate, James strategically aligns two highly respected authors alongside his figured artist in order to bolster the figured artist's authority. He wants to champion and promote his own form-centered, character-driven aesthetic. These concerns—the nature of the artist's authority and his aesthetic—are conjoined in James's discussion of character in the Prefaces.

A Beautiful Infatuation

In "The Lesson of Balzac," James addresses the question of characterization by contrasting Balzac's treatment of Valérie in *Les Parents Pauvres* with Thackeray's treatment of Becky Sharp in *Vanity Fair.* In Balzac, one is fully immersed, or saturated, in character; naturally, this is crucial for James. An intense, deep, and sympathetic depiction of character was always a fundamental Jamesian tenet. Balzac never fails: "There is never in Balzac that damning interference which consists of the painter's not seeing, not possessing, his image." Such a flaw would be fatal for an artist, for "When saturation fails no other presence really avails." Balzac went beyond merely depicting his characters. "'Balzac aime sa Valérie,'" James reminds us, quoting Taine; this affection "show[s] Balzac's extraordinary taste" and rarity of artistic judgment:

> The love, as we call it, the joy in [his character's] communicated and exhibited movement, in their standing on their feet and going of themselves and acting out their characters, was what rendered possible the saturation I speak of. . . . It was by loving them—as the terms of his subject and the nuggets of his mine—that he knew them; it was not by knowing them that he loved.
> He at all events robustly loved the sense of another explored, assumed, assimilated identity—enjoyed it as the hand enjoys the glove when the glove ideally fits. My image indeed is loose; for what he liked was absolutely to get into the constituted consciousness, into all the clothes, gloves and whatever else, into the very skin and bones, of the habited, featured, colored, articulated form of life that he desired to present. How do we know given persons, for any purpose of demonstration, unless we know their situation for themselves, unless we see it from their point of vision, that is from their point of pressing consciousness or sensation?—without our allowing for which there is no appreciation. (*LC* 2:131–32)

This is an extremely important passage for two reasons: first, the idea of an artist "loving" his characters is sensed throughout the Prefaces and, as we shall see, becomes a means by which James establishes the authority of his figured author; second, this passage also indicates a source for the Jamesian "appreciation of alterity," a point to which I shall return, below.

In contrast to Balzac's affection for his characters stands the example of Thackeray. Where Balzac treated his characters with compassion and love, "Thackeray's attitude was the opposite one, a desire positively to expose and desecrate poor Becky—to follow her up, catch her in the act and bring her to shame. . . . The English writer wants to make sure, first of all, of your moral judgment; the French is willing, while it waits a little, to risk, for the sake of his subject and its interest, your spiritual salvation." The question of morality in fiction is thereby conflated with the questions of depiction of character and artistic execution; Balzac is the greater artist because he wanted to get inside the "constituted consciousness" of his characters and did so out of sympathy and compassion. "It all comes back," James concludes, "to that respect for the liberty of the subject which I should be willing to name as *the* great sign of the painter of the first order." Balzac paid utmost attention to "the *conditions* of the creatures with whom he is concerned." In the final analysis, the artist's sympathy for his characters, his keen attention to their social and material conditions, and his respect for the "liberty of the subject" are joined in the crucible of artistic execution and aesthetic form: "the fusion of all the elements of the picture, under his hand, is complete— of what people are with what they do, of what they do with what they are, of the action with the agents, of the medium with the action, of all the parts of the drama with each other" (*LC* 2:132–35). This passage from "The Lesson of Balzac" is a quintessential distillation of several key Jamesian tenets— ideas addressed in depth throughout the Prefaces: questions of form, style, subject, and "saturation," or overall artistic intensity. But, as is clear here, character is of prime importance.

A similar idea is mentioned in James's "Introduction to *The Tempest*." Noting the superficial nature of the subjects of many of the plays (in particular the comedies), James emphasizes that subject is never the primary concern. "Such a thing as The Merchant of Venice declines, for very shame," James opines, "to be reduced to its elements of witless 'story.'" Rather, the critical reader's focus is on language and "personal tone, or in other words brooding expression raised to the highest energy. Push such energy far enough—far enough if you can!—and, being what it is, it then inevitably provides for Character. Thus we see character, in every form of which the 'story' gives the thinnest hint, marching through the pieces" (*LC* 1:1213). James's point in this brief passage—and his larger point in "The Lesson of Balzac"—is that the depiction of character is a top concern of the artist concerned with crafting a polished work. Form is the ultimate criterion for judgment, and character is, without question, the primary element of form with which an artist must be concerned.

In the Prefaces, James reconfigures this long-held aesthetic tenet concerning characterization—learned from both Balzac and Turgenev—and uses it to assert the authority and primacy of his figured artist. For example, James frequently employs gendered or eroticized language regarding character as a means of asserting himself. In the Preface to *The American*, James speaks not merely of "loving" his characters, but of taking physical possession of them:

> A beautiful infatuation this, always, I think, the intensity of the creative ef-
> fort to get into the skin of the creature; the act of personal possession of
> one being by another at its completest—and with the high enhancement,
> ever, that it is, by the same stroke, the effort of the artist to preserve for his
> subject that unity, and for his use of it (in other words for the interest he
> desires to excite) that effect of a *centre,* which must economise its value. Its
> value is most discussable when that economy has most operated; the con-
> tent and the "importance" of a work of art are in fine wholly dependent on
> its *being* one: outside of which all prate of its representative character, its
> meaning and its bearing, its morality and humanity, are an impudent thing.
> (*LC* 2:1068)

Such "personal possession" of one's character is, here, a means by which
the artist establishes and preserves the artistic unity of a text; character becomes the center of the text, the focal point of value employed by the
artist—and by a reader assessing a work of art on aesthetic grounds. And
thus we see that the "intensity of the creative effort to get into the skin of
the creature" on the part of the author is a question of asserting and establishing artistic control.

James employs similar language in the Preface to *The Portrait of a Lady.*
Isabel is an "acquisition" to "grasp" and to hold "in complete possession."
Again, the force of James's creative imagination becomes a source of control: "the imagination . . . detains [the character], preserves, protects, enjoys
it, conscious of its presence in the dusky, crowded, heterogeneous back-
shop of the mind very much as a wary dealer in precious odds and ends,
competent to make an 'advance' on rare objects confided to him, is conscious of the rare little 'piece' left in deposit" (*LC* 2:1075–76). The conflation of the rhetorics of gender, artistic conception, and the marketplace is
striking, and it points to James's very deliberate attempt, in this particular
passage and throughout the Prefaces as a whole, to assert his authority over
his own texts (and his fictional characters) as a means to present a figured
artist firmly in control of his craft. This sense of control would, in turn, elicit
admiration in the idealized reader, who would then naturally desire to read
more fiction by Henry James.

Scholars have noted this conflation of the rhetorics of gender and control
in James's Prefaces. Sara Blair notes that James's appropriation of his characters "serves as a crucial resource in James's performance of a particular
kind of literary authority." Such an act is, in the case of *The Portrait of a
Lady,* deeply ironic; the novel itself challenges many of the culturally normative gender standards of its day. James's assertion of authorial control over
Isabel therefore enacts "the performance of a self-consciously ironic mastery." For Blair, this paradoxical duality suggests that if James "identifies,
and identifies with, the making of women in the domestic sphere . . . he also

exploits this understanding to secure his own access to male and public forms of power."[21]

While Blair is specifically concerned with James's appropriation of his female characters, the authorial practice of control is not restricted by gender. In the Preface to *The Ambassadors,* James employs decidedly homoerotic language as he celebrates "the opportunity to 'do' a man of imagination." As a self-described "handler of puppets," James celebrates the excitement and thrill of the "chance to 'bite'" into a complex character such as Lambert Strether. James celebrates the "excitement" of "pursuit" and the "precious 'tightness'" of such an encounter: "the point is not in the least what to make of [the character and his story], but only, very delightfully and very damnably, where to put one's hand on it" (*LC* 2:1307–8). The rhetoric employed in this passage, and the passage from the Preface to the *Portrait,* demonstrates how James's figured artist establishes his authority by "taking possession" of his characters; the character is subdued and internalized, becoming part of the artist's overall scheme.[22]

But the tone of James's discussion is never cruel or mean-spirited. Rather, following the example of Balzac, James expresses great affection and appreciation for his characters. Dorothy J. Hale notes what she calls James's "appreciation of alterity," which is "an artist's desire to comprehend the identity of an 'other'" through the process of artistic creation. Hale sees this appreciation as an "ethical imperative . . . objectified in the novel's form." The "Artistic wonder" required to create and record the "other" of a fictional character "establishes an economy of relation between viewer and viewed" that, if rendered properly by the artist, demonstrates the artist's "power to make palpable, not just to vivify but to instantiate the authentic identity of the thing that interests him." Hale implicitly argues that this "economy of relation" is, in part, a means of establishing authority for the artist: "the artist's identifactory understanding has the power to turn the object of interest into an artistic subject—and then to recast that subject as a self-expressive art work."[23] The artist has taken the "other" and, through the Jamesian crucible of art, has internalized it and rendered it as part of the subjective vision of the artist. The other is now a crucial aspect of the artist's

21. Blair, "House of Fiction," 60–61, 65.

22. For more on James's use of homoerotic language throughout the Prefaces, see Eve Kosofsky Sedgwick, "Shame and Performativity: Henry James's New York Edition Prefaces." James's ongoing discussion of character is found throughout the Prefaces and is far too complex to address in further detail here. The issue of developing and controlling characters is developed further in the following Prefaces: *The Princess Casamassima; What Maisie Knew; The Spoils of Poynton; The Wings of the Dove;* and *The Golden Bowl.*

23. Hale, "James and the Invention," 82, 86–88.

direct, personal vision. It is an act of artistic compassion, yes—but it is also a performance or demonstration of artistic authority and control.

The Sublime Economy of Art

It is important to emphasize that, under the aegis of character-driven fiction, the problem of asserting control over one's characters is simultaneously the problem of exercising authorial selection and control—artistic discrimination and judgment. This is another strategy by which James asserts the authority of his figured artist. James always wanted to be appreciated for his mind, for the unique quality of his individual temperament. One reason why he repeatedly narrates the progression from "germ" to completed text via the formal process of composition and creation is because it allows him an opportunity to demonstrate, again, his artistic prowess. Rhetorically, James creates opportunities for himself to demonstrate this prowess through the repetition of a binary between "life" and "art." This binary is succinctly laid out in the Preface to *The Spoils of Poynton:*

> Life being all inclusion and confusion, and art being all discrimination and selection, the latter, in search of the hard latent *value* with which alone it is concerned, sniffs round the mass as instinctively and unerringly as a dog suspicious of some buried bone. . . . [L]ife has no direct sense whatever for the subject and is capable, luckily for us, of nothing but splendid waste. Hence the opportunity for the sublime economy of art, which rescues, which saves, and hoards and "banks," investing and reinvesting these fruits of toil in wondrous useful "works" and thus making up for us, desperate spendthrifts that we all naturally are, the most princely of incomes. (*LC* 2:1138–39)

Be he a bloodhound or a banker, the artist is always selective, always plucking from crude life the precious "germ" that may be developed into a story. Life is, in James's "sublime economy," the limitless raw material for the artist. Such a preponderance of material is indeed a blessing; in the Preface to *The Princess Casamassima,* James exhorts his fellow artists to take note of "*this* wisdom—that if you have n't, for fiction, the root of the matter in you, have n't the sense of life and the penetrating imagination, you are a fool in the very presence of the revealed and assured; but that if you *are* so armed you are not really helpless, not without your resource, even before mysteries abysmal" (*LC* 2:1102). Crude material abounds in the chaos of untutored life. The artist must foster and develop his artistic sensibility, for to exercise that sensibility is to impose one's authority over chaos. As James phrased it in a 1915 letter to H. G. Wells, "It is art that *makes* life, makes interest, makes importance, for our consideration and application of these things, and I know of no substitute whatever for the force and beauty of its process" (*JL* 4:770).

From this contrast between "art" and "life," the reader might extrapolate to James's project of revision throughout the New York Edition. John Carlos Rowe has observed that "As a critical reappropriation of his works and his *career*, James's *revision* in the Prefaces is an affirmation of the difference of life and art."[24] Viewed from this perspective, James the Artist has taken the early, crudely wrought material of his youth and refashioned it into a more polished and much-improved state. That certainly is the tenor of the narratives concerning *Roderick Hudson* and *The American*, the earliest novels included in the edition. (Some short fiction antedating *Roderick Hudson* was included in the New York Edition.) Such an insight helps to account for the relatively harsh self-criticism found in those Prefaces.

James's ultimate point with this binary between art and life is to emphasize the burden of choice put upon the author; selection thus becomes a criterion for judgment, a means by which a reader can assess artistic value. This concept is most poignantly developed in the well-known "house of fiction" passage from the Preface to *The Portrait of a Lady*. Here, James emphasizes that the artist must concern himself with, first, selecting a worthy and rewarding subject, and second, finding and developing the best possible "form" for the treatment of that subject. All decisions will ultimately be a reflection of "the artist's prime sensibility, which is the soil out of which his subject springs" (*LC* 2:1074–75). The burden of artistic choice as it relates to form and composition is paramount and omnipresent. To make this point, James frequently employs a painterly metaphor (long a personal favorite, going back at least as far as "The Art of Fiction"). In the Preface to *The Tragic Muse*, James states that "A picture without composition slights its most precious chance for beauty, and is moreover not composed at all unless the painter knows *how* that principle of health and safety, working as an absolutely premeditated art, has prevailed" (*LC* 2:1107). James emphasizes not only the principle of artistic selection, but also the choice and discrimination of the artist, the awareness of the process, the "absolutely premeditated" quality of the artist's imposition of his own particular sensibility. James further emphasizes this act of authorial control in the Preface to *The Spoils of Poynton:*

> [The artist] has to borrow his motive [from life], which is certainly half the battle; and this motive is his ground, his site and his foundation. But after

24. Rowe, *Theoretical Dimensions,* 233.

that he only lends and gives, only builds and piles high, lays together the blocks quarried in the deeps of his imagination and on his personal premises. He thus remains all the while in intimate commerce with his motive, and can say to himself—what really more than anything else inflames and sustains him—that he alone has the *secret* of the particular case, he alone can measure the truth of the direction to be taken by his developed data. There can be for him, evidently, only one logic for these things; there can be for him only one truth and one direction—the quarter in which his subject most completely expresses itself. The careful ascertainment of how it shall do so, and the art of guiding it with consequent authority—since this sense of "authority" is for the master-builder the treasure of treasures, or at least the joy of joys—renews in the modern alchemist something like the old dream of the secret of life. (*LC* 2:1141)

It is the process of artistic creation that James celebrates here and promotes as the vehicle for exercising (and advertising) authorial performance and authority. In the Preface to *The Altar of the Dead,* James celebrates "the process by which the small cluster of actualities latent in the fact reported to [the artist is] reconstituted and, so far as they might need, altered; the felt fermentation, ever interesting . . . that enables the sense originally communicated to make fresh and possibly quite different terms for the new employment there awaiting it" (*LC* 2:1252). The creative process is transformative and personal; it takes the "germ" from crude, unformed life and, as with Balzac's crucible, transforms it into something unique and beautiful. Hence it demonstrates the artist's power and authority.

Of course, the artistic process is not a machine and will not always produce its material on time or in the expected fashion. The artist will occasionally suffer from want of inspiration, which could undermine his authority. James would not have the artist let down his guard. In the Preface to *Daisy Miller,* James suggests that when the artist is "waiting" through a "speculative interval," he should present the mask of "a high and dry, yet irrepressibly hopeful artistic Micawber, cocking an ostensibly confident hat and practising an almost passionate system of 'bluff'; insisting, in fine, that something . . . *would* turn up if only the right imaginative hanging-about on the chance, if only the true intelligent attention, were piously persisted in" (*LC* 2:1276). In short, there is never a time when the author must not at least present the *pose* of authority and determination—even if he occasionally suffers from a lack thereof.

As this brief overview has illustrated, one notices a rhetorical pattern present throughout the Prefaces, a familiar narrative of artistic genesis, production, and selection that James uses to define for himself and his audience the role of the artist as an authority who, out of the crude stuff of life, forges the artistic text. Subject is to be granted; it is a reflection of the artist's unique sensibility and vision—the very soil out of which the process springs. At every turn, it is form that is to be privileged and appreciated. As with the figured artist in the "Introduction to *The Tempest*," we see how, in the Prefaces, James continually directs his reader away from the biographical or historical James and toward an appreciation for James the Artist. It is the artist who undertakes the process of composition and who presents to the reader the finished product, which is a celebration of form and polish. James hopes to present himself as a figure like his mentor Balzac: a monolithic authority and supreme example of art—a heroic figure whom we should not question or defy, but submit to and admire.

Conclusion

"We opened this work with the hope of finding a general survey of the nature and principles of the subject of which it professes to treat." Thus begins Henry James's first published essay, an 1864 review of Nassau W. Senior's *Essays on Fiction*. "Its title had led us to anticipate some attempt to codify the vague and desultory canons, which cannot, indeed, be said to govern, but which in some measure define, this department of literature. We had long regretted the absence of any critical treatise upon fiction" (*LC* 1:1196). Over the course of a career spanning more than fifty years, James set about correcting this lapse in English letters. The Prefaces to the New York Edition are, without a doubt, the culminating performance in his career. James himself sought to accomplish many things in them. In a 1908 letter to Howells, he suggests that they "ought, collected together . . . to form a sort of comprehensive manual or *vade-mecum* for aspirants in our arduous profession" (*LFL*, 426). This is certainly the light in which Lubbock, Blackmur, and many others have viewed them.

Yet the Prefaces are also highly original, creative texts with a clear rhetorical focus. Unable to secure the place and the prestige he desired so deeply from the critics and readers of his day, James took the unusual step of writing the book on himself in an attempt to spur interest and to create desire for his creative work. As the "Introduction to *The Tempest*" demonstrates, James had been mulling over questions of the figured artist and the figured reader during the writing of the New York Edition. In the Prefaces, James constructs a figured artist whose persuasive authority and artistic command were designed to inspire reverence in the ideal reader—and the desire to return to the creative texts in question. Read in this light, the Prefaces are an elaborately choreographed performance by an idealized artist figure with a didactic mission. James is quite specific about what he wants his reader to appreciate: questions of form and execution are always paramount. James references respected mentors such as Balzac and Turgenev in an effort to align his figured artist with firmly established cultural heavyweights. As "The Lesson of Balzac" and his 1902 essays on Zola and Flaubert demonstrate, James had carefully reexamined the sources of his aesthetic preferences in the years leading up to the New York Edition; these influences are found throughout the Prefaces in James's foregrounding of form and character, for example. James's discussions of form and character are a means by which he establishes and promotes the authority of his figured artist—again, in an effort to convince a reading public of the high quality and rich distinction of his fiction. James's references to Balzac and Turgenev also remind readers that the Prefaces were the product of a lifetime of work in literary criticism, and they demand to be read in that broader context.

The Prefaces were, in all of their fascinatingly complex majesty, a deeply personal exercise for James. They stand as a final testament of sorts; after the commercial failure of the New York Edition, James largely retired from the writing of fiction and criticism, penning but a handful of essays and short stories. Ever defiant and proud, James would never surrender, leaving to posterity his hopes for an army of admirers.[25]

25. James, of course, did not quit writing. In his final years, he continued to work on his travel volumes and autobiography, as well as the fiction and criticism mentioned here. He also left one uncompleted novel, *The Ivory Tower,* at the time of his death.

9. Howells's Literary Criticism in the "Editor's Easy Chair" and *Heroines of Fiction*

If there is one area most overlooked in Howells studies, surely it is the final twenty years of the Dean's life; while significant attention has been paid to his early and middle years—admittedly, his most productive period and where one finds the bulk of his best work, both creatively and critically—many scholars have unfairly ignored Howells's twentieth-century work.[1] Yet the Dean maintained an astonishing productivity in his final decades, both as a creative writer and as a critic. Beginning in December 1900, Howells penned the monthly "Editor's Easy Chair" in *Harper's Magazine* until his death in 1920; he never missed a month. And, in addition to numerous volumes of fiction, memoir, and travel writing, he continued to contribute occasional essays to *Harper's Weekly*, the *North American Review*, and other periodicals.

Howells's staunchest defenders have long argued against the unfair dismissal of the Dean's later work as a critic. "It needs to be said, hopefully for the last time," states Edwin H. Cady, "that the tradition of 'the Dean in the Easy Chair'—of a Howells who during these years became bland, weary, chatty, innocuous, inconsequential, 'acquiescent'—does not fit all the facts."

---

1. There are a few noteworthy exceptions: Cady collects more than a dozen of Howells's later columns—and provides lucid editorial commentary—in *W. D. Howells as Critic;* thirty-four essays are included in *Selected Literary Criticism*, vol. 3, ed. Ronald Gottesman; Elsa Nettels's *Language, Race, and Social Class in Howells's America* and *Language and Gender in American Fiction* both examine aspects of Howells's later criticism, in particular the "Editor's Easy Chair"; and John W. Crowley offers an extremely useful overview of the late phases of Howells's career in *Dean of American Letters*.

Ronald Gottesman notes that, between 1898 and 1920, Howells not only "remained faithful to his basic convictions" but demonstrated remarkable flexibility, breadth, and vigor as a critic. While the Dean's many defenders are correct, it is equally true that the quality and the character of the criticism written by Howells after 1900 stands in marked contrast to all of the criticism that preceded it. First, the amount of literary criticism in the strictest sense of the term is a matter of proportion; Gottesman estimates that of the more than four hundred columns written by Howells after 1898, "perhaps 150 are true literary criticism."[2] Why did Howells move away from strictly literary criticism, and to what other styles did he gravitate? As this chapter will demonstrate, Howells grew weary of criticism in the manner he himself had written it in the "Editor's Study." Consequently, the style and tone of the later criticism is decidedly less polemical—though not necessarily any less probing or intelligent. The Dean's eye and pen were drawn elsewhere: to other styles of criticism, to memoir, and to social and cultural essays. As we shall see, Howells pushed at the boundaries of what was considered "literary" criticism in interesting and challenging ways, often blurring the lines of genre in the process.

A survey of some of Howells's best criticism written after 1900 reveals Howells's increasing distaste for literary criticism and links it to the new rhetorical styles adopted in the "Editor's Easy Chair" and elsewhere. Also, several of the essays demonstrate, first, Howells's growing unease with the literary marketplace of the early twentieth century, and, second, his thoughts on the practice and habit of art. Finally, Howells's important but frequently overlooked *Heroines of Fiction* imparts his considerations and opinions of a range of influential British and American authors.[3]

The Uneasy Chair

"Criticism, ever since I filled myself so full of it in my boyhood, I have not cared for," Howells remarked in 1895, "and often I have found it repulsive."[4] Indeed, Howells always maintained a difficult relation to his work as

---

2. Cady, *W. D. Howells as Critic*, 335; Ronald Gottesman, introduction, *SLC* 3:xi–xv.

3. It needs to be emphasized that the purpose of this chapter is but to survey these carefully selected aspects of Howells's later work as a literary critic; I address several other aspects of Howells's later criticism in Chapters 7 and 10 of this study. Due to obvious constraints of space and brevity, there are many dimensions of Howells's later work that must go untreated in the present study. Among these is a more thorough consideration of the whole of Howells's work in the "Editor's Easy Chair."

4. Howells, *My Literary Passions*, 235.

a critic. As we have seen, the young Howells genuinely believed that the work of the critic could be useful and educative. During his tenure in the "Editor's Study" (1886–1892), he gradually revised and reshaped his opinion on criticism until he reached the point where, in 1887, he argued that the critic's "office is mainly to ascertain facts and traits of literature, not to invent or denounce them; to discover principles, not to establish them; to report, not to create" (*SLC* 2:55). It was a restrictive theoretical formulation beyond which he never could progress, as we saw in our earlier reading of "The Functions of the Critic."

Yet, after several years of freelancing, Howells longed for the financial stability and predictability of a fixed income. His 1899 contract with Harper's stipulated that he write a monthly column for *Harper's Monthly,* the "Editor's Easy Chair," commencing with the December 1900 issue. Howells took his seat in what he privately called "the Uneasy Chair" with some grumblings. In a 1900 letter to his friend Thomas Bailey Aldrich, he wrote: "It might have been wiser for me to keep out of that place, but at 63 one likes a fixed income, even when the unfixed is not bad. Essaying has been the enemy of the novelist that was in me. One cannot do both kinds without hurt to both. If I could have held out fifteen years ago in my refusal of the Study, when Alden tempted me, I might have gone on and beat *Silas Lapham*. Now I can only dream of some leisure day doing better." The following spring, Howells wrote to Aldrich in despair: "I hate criticism. . . . I never did a piece of it that satisfied me; and to write fiction, on the other hand, is a delight. Yet in my old age, I seem doomed (on a fat salary) to do criticism and essays. I am ending where I began, in a sort of journalism." Apparently, his discomfort only grew with time. In a 1903 letter to S. Weir Mitchell, he still felt "bound in prosperous slavery to a salary" with Harper's.[5]

Despite these reservations, Howells made the most of his tenure in the "Editor's Easy Chair," reinventing his critical persona—or, rather, personae—in it.[6] The rhetorical stances Howells employed in the Easy Chair were the product of both circumstance and choice. "The Restoration of the Easy Chair by Way of Introduction," the initial column in the series (December 1900), begins with the conceit of Howells retrieving the Easy Chair from a dusty storage vault, only to find that "he confronted in the Easy Chair an animate presence." The chair proceeds to speak with its new occupant, fondly recalling its distinguished predecessors, George William Curtis and Donald G. Mitchell. The chair quotes Curtis at some length, noting the "kind and reasonable mood, the righteous conscience incarnate

---

5. Howells, *Life in Letters,* 2:138, 144; Howells, quoted in Gottesman, introduction, xv.
6. The "Editor's Easy Chair" will hereafter be referred to as the Easy Chair.

in the studied art, the charming literary allusion for the sake of the unliter-ary lesson, [and] the genial philosophy" of Curtis's style, before bluntly ask-ing Howells if he is "fit to take his place." Howells elects to "[evade] this hard question" and turns the subject elsewhere (*ImI*, 3–4).[7]

While there is an unmistakable tone of play and respectful homage in the opening movement of this initial column, Howells clearly acknowledges what he knew his readership at *Harper's Monthly* would be thinking: the tra-dition of the "Editor's Easy Chair" is that of a witty, genial, urbane personal essay—distinctly not the literary pugilism for which Howells had distin-guished himself in the "Editor's Study." As John W. Crowley notes, How-ells's public reputation for "unruly polemics" and "unsound politics" lingered "well into the 1890s."[8] Howells could rightly imagine his audience asking, Is this old firebrand about to step in and tarnish the tradition of the Easy Chair with his blustery arguments and proud denunciations? Howells, by quoting both Curtis and Mitchell, humbly acknowledges his forebears (which, he notes, also included Henry Mills Alden and Thomas Bailey Al-drich). In acknowledging and paying homage to the rhetorical tradition of the Easy Chair, Howells reassures readers that he both knows and will honor the tradition of the column. It is only when the discussion shifts to a consideration of Christmas that the familiar Howells of yore surfaces, with his mention of Tolstoy and Christian charity. But, as he drones on "after the manner of preachers . . . [repeating] himself pitilessly, unsparingly," the fig-urative Easy Chair falls asleep (*ImI*, 11–12). It is the first of many playful self-deprecations that would characterize Howells's tenure in the Easy Chair. The understated tone of the column (compared, at least, to the "Editor's Study") is therefore the result of at least two conditions: first, Howells's willingness to follow, to some extent, the rhetorical precedents of Curtis and Mitchell; and, second, Howells's own weariness with polemical criti-cism, as expressed in his personal correspondence.

The initial column is also important because Howells employs the rhetor-ical conceit of the dialogue, a style he would employ frequently throughout his final years. As if to announce this strategy to his readers, Howells con-cludes the first column by announcing: "It has seemed to the occupant of the Easy Chair, at times, as if he had suffered with it some sort of land-change from a sole entity to a multiple personality in which his several selves conversed with one another, and came and went unbidden." These are not, he insists, the "spirits . . . of Mitchell, of Curtis, [or] of Aldrich," but rather

---

7. *Imaginary Interviews* is a selection of columns from the first ten years of the Easy Chair (1900–1910). As the book title indicates, the columns all employ the style of the dialogue, which will be addressed below.

8. Crowley, *Dean of American Letters*, 2.

are "the subdivisions of his own ego, and as such he has more and more frankly treated them" (*ImI,* 12). This, too, is a deliberate attempt to distinguish his work in the Easy Chair from all of his earlier work as a critic—specifically the "Editor's Study," which began in January 1886 as a "symposium of one." Howells, in the Study, had frankly admitted to owning "a very pretty store of prejudices to indulge and grudges to satisfy" (*SLC* 2:4) and, clearly, he had indulged himself. Howells commences the Easy Chair on a different note; he will employ a markedly different tone—one in keeping with the august tradition of the column—and a different style, one that would allow for a broader range of voices (albeit his own, usually).

The invention of the dialogue form was part of Howells's attempt to test the limits of what criticism could do.[9] While it is true that Howells less frequently employed his earlier style of polemical criticism in the Easy Chair, it is a misstatement to suggest that he abandoned it. He did, on occasion, employ a familiar, straightforward argumentative style when it suited his needs.[10] But, with increasing frequency, Howells sought out other rhetorical modes for expressing his ideas, and the form of the dialogue became a favorite. There are several probable reasons for this. First, the aforementioned distaste for the older style of polemical criticism. Second, on many issues, the increasingly tolerant Howells was of two (or more) minds; the dramatic dialogue allowed him to explore contrasting viewpoints in a manner that, with its reliance on his gift for witty banter and colloquial idiom, kept the reader's interest. Third, in a broad sense, this pursuit of new forms for criticism can be read as part of Howells's ongoing attempt to invent a distinctly American tradition of literature and criticism that is as different as possible from the European models. The American language, including the use of dialect, was always central to Howells's conception of an American literature. "In urging American writers to make their own tradition," Elsa Nettels observes, "Howells was not only writing his declaration of American literary independence; he was affirming a literary philosophy in which political and artistic ideals were inseparable."[11] Howells's pursuit of new forms, including a style of criticism foregrounding conversational American idiom, was one part of an ongoing, lifelong project of American literary independence. But there were other reasons to employ a new style of criticism.

Of equal interest is the fact that Howells often used the dialogue form as a means for probing self-examination and, in many cases, playful self-mockery.

9. James, too, experimented with a dramatic form of literary criticism in "An Animated Conversation" (*LC* 1:66–92).

10. See, for example, the November 1902 Easy Chair concerning George Eliot (*SLC* 3:162–68).

11. Nettels, *Language, Race, and Social Class,* 62.

An excellent example is found in the July 1908 Easy Chair, later reprinted as "Sclerosis of the Tastes." The essay stages a dialogue between the Easy Chair and a "convertible familiar," or alter ego, who had, "at former interviews, been a poet, a novelist, a philosopher, a reformer, [and] a moralist." Beginning with the question of whether or not one, in older age, falls prey to a stiffening of the tastes, Howells's alter ego charges that Howells's efforts "in times past . . . to make others think with you . . . amounted to an effort to make your mental sclerosis infectious, and it was all the worse because, in you, the stiffening of the tastes had taken the form of aversions rather than preferences. You did not so much wish your readers to like your favorite authors as to hate all the others." Howells readily confesses, adding that he failed in his mission: "Our popular failure as a critic is notorious; it cannot be denied. The stamp of our disapproval at one time gave a whole order of fiction a currency that was not less than torrential. The flood of romantic novels which passed over the land . . . was undoubtedly the effect of our adverse criticism." Perhaps, he suggests, one is more inclined to a "sclerosis of the tastes" earlier in life, for in his later years his tastes have widened. While reaffirming his own realist preferences—such "veracities" are "immutable" and persist with "indissoluble tenacity"—Howells nevertheless cites a long list of authors for whom he has developed a recent fondness, including Trollope, Thackeray, Austen, and Dickens. It hardly bears pointing out that a number of these authors (most notably Trollope and Thackeray) had, on other, earlier occasions, represented much that was false in literature. Howells concludes by stating that "the tastes are never so tolerant, so liberal, so generous, so supple as they are" in later life (*ImI*, 22–31).

"Sclerosis of the Tastes" demonstrates Howells's willingness both to critique and to ridicule himself.[12] But it also exemplifies another reason why Howells, in his later criticism, shied away from the polemic of the "Editor's Study." Howells is the first to admit that he lost what later critics would call the "Realism War." Furthermore, he believes he actually might have done more harm than good in the Study: the unintended backlash of his offensive against the romanticistic novel was, ironically enough, to bolster its popularity. Ever on guard against such self-righteous indignation, the septuagenarian Howells had learned a valuable lesson. And he was not keen to repeat his mistakes.

Seeking out new forms of expression, such as dialogue, was one way Howells challenged himself to remake the project of criticism. Other ways included blurring the lines between genres of writing—pushing criticism

---

12. Another fine example of self-deprecation from Howells is found in the May 1911 Easy Chair, "The Functions of the Critic" (*SLC* 3:188–93).

into new territories. One of the more fascinating efforts is the 1914 fantasy novel *The Seen and Unseen at Stratford-on-Avon,* in which Howells addresses a variety of interpretive and biographical issues surrounding Shakespeare. Foremost among these is the ongoing discussion (in the early twentieth century) concerning the authorship of Shakespeare's work. The ghost of Bacon himself discounts the "Baconian" theory in a lengthy diatribe that references recent scholarship and an extended examination of the case of Virgil (of whom even less is known, biographically). While Shakespeare himself downplays lesser accusations, including various petty crimes, as the whims of youth, he is genuinely humble in the face of more substantial issues, such as marital infidelity and the death of his son, Hamnet. When Howells confronts Shakespeare with "Tolstoy's censure of his [Shakespeare's] want of kindness" toward the "English lower classes," the Bard claims "he satirized his own faults in them; and what literature was to do was to join political economy in making men so equal in fortune that there could be no deformity, no vulgarity in them which sprang from the pressure of need or the struggle of hiding or escaping its effects." In short, Shakespeare is a Howellsian humanist: modest, fair-minded, and capable of self-deprecation. He regrets his misdeeds and expresses humility regarding his literary accomplishments. Throughout the novel, Shakespeare speaks in the plain, common idiom of the middle class; there is no air of the "supreme poet" or literary genius.[13] *The Seen and Unseen* is a playful, genre-blurring mix of fiction and criticism that manages to address a surprising number of then-timely critical and biographical issues while playing to Howells's creative strengths.

Another genre-blurring attempt is "Worries of a Winter Walk," an 1897 essay from *Harper's Weekly.* The piece begins in the manner of sociocultural reportage, with an account of poverty under harsh circumstances: the narrator witnesses a small child struggling to carry a bucket of coal in the dead of winter; later, two elderly women quarrel over loose bits of fuel dropped from a coke cart. And while Howells's humanistic compassion is piqued, ultimately it is "the aesthetic instinct" that responds: he quickly sketches out a fictional scenario in which the cart driver falls in love with the granddaughter of one of the old women. Howells imagines two possible endings: in the first, the granddaughter dies; in the second, the granddaughter marries another. (In either case, the cart driver's love is unrequited.) Howells claims he cannot determine which ending is best and leaves the reader to decide.

---

13. Howells, *The Seen and Unseen at Stratford-on-Avon: A Fantasy,* 74. It is interesting to note that Howells's depiction of Shakespeare in *The Seen and Unseen* stands in marked contrast to the supreme aesthete figured in James's "Introduction to *The Tempest.*"

In the final paragraph, Howells acknowledges his different audiences and their probable reactions. There will be those, he knows, who criticize him for failing to help the very real people that he saw and for exploiting them as the subject of art; if he were to write of the poor at all, it should be to "offer my knowledge [of them] . . . for the instruction of those whose lives are easy and happy in the indifference which ignorance breeds in us." At the same time, Howells notes that there are those who "do not want to know about such squalid lives" and who would rather read "about good society." This readership feels that American fiction is "already overloaded with low life" and would rather see more attention paid to the *"grandes dames"* of the aristocracy. The essay ends here, on a tantalizingly indeterminate note.[14]

In "Worries of a Winter Walk," Howells successfully blurs the lines between fiction, social reportage, and literary criticism in an attempt to dramatize the very real conflicts between society, the artist, and the literary marketplace. The rhetorical questions behind the exercise are profound: What, exactly, are the responsibilities of the artist in relation to society? Is literature best seen as a means of "educating" its audience to social inequality? Or should literature provide an escape into bourgeois insulation and detachment? The fact that Howells leaves the reader to decide is a stroke of mastery, for it points to his awareness that it is one's audience that ultimately determines the meaning of a given text. (In this sense, Howells prefigures certain aspects of the reader-response theory of the late twentieth century.) If, as an artist, Howells finds the situation an irreconcilable paradox, he has nevertheless made a fine essay out of the exercise, and "Worries of a Winter Walk" stands as an excellent example of how Howells, in his later criticism, frequently blurred the lines of genre as he pushed literary criticism into new territory.

To conclude, there are three major reasons for the shift in tone and style of the later literary criticism. First, Howells was largely disenchanted with the practice of criticism, both theoretically and personally: he had difficulty envisioning the critic's useful role in the culture and readily admitted his previous attempts to be "notorious" failures; and he resented having to undertake the work for financial reasons. Second, in the Easy Chair he deliberately adopted a style in keeping with the tradition of the column, one that was decidedly less polemical. Third, Howells was interested in testing the boundaries of criticism; he continually sought out new forms and experimented with an impressive range of voices and styles, often blurring the lines of genre in the attempt. He employed the dialogue form with increasing frequency both because it played to certain creative strengths, and because it

14. Howells, *Literature and Life*, 39, 44.

also allowed him to explore multiple sides of an issue in an agreeable, entertaining form.

Reflections of a Veteran Novelist

In August 1908, Howells wrote to Henry James in praise of the Prefaces to the New York Edition, noting especially that he "enjoyed you where you rounded upon yourself, and as it were took yourself to pieces, in your self-censure." The exercise, Howells added, was "full of instruction for me" (*LFL*, 422–23). Initially, Howells planned, in the Library Edition of his works, to emulate James's Prefaces. But after drafting eleven out of a proposed thirty-five, he abandoned the endeavor. As he explained to Frederick Duneka at Harper's,

> I have made a careful experiment of the type in an introduction to A Hazard of New Fortunes, and have convinced my self that I cannot write prefaces for the library edition, much as I would like to meet your wish in the matter. I believe I was right in wishing the volumes to go [before] the public without any word of explanation or comment from me, because they are already most intimately full of me, and are their own explanation and comment. I know that the typical one I have done is well done, but I know also that it is superfluous and impertinent. I cannot pretend to better your judgment as to the advantage of the prefaces with the subscribers, and I only state my insuperable repugnance to them. I not only feel this in regard to them intrinsically, but I feel that I should have the effect of following in James's footsteps, and that with critics this would be a just ground for censure. I know that you do not agree with me on this point, but I count on your kindness to let me have my way, and to let the books go without a personal word from me. (*HSL* 5:276–77)

Howells may have had James's Prefaces and their example of "self-censure" in mind when, in an Easy Chair column on the topic of "Unfriendly Criticism," Howells's alter ego Eugenio flirts with the notion of reviewing his own books:

> [Eugenio] quite rejected the notion, when it came to business, with which he had sometimes played, of an author reviewing his own books, and this apart from his sense of its immodesty. In the course of his experience he had known of but one really great author who had done this, and then had done it upon the invitation of an editor of rare if somewhat wilful perspicacity, who invited the author to do it on the ground that no one else

could do it so well. But though he would not have liked to be his own reviewer, because it was not seemly, he chiefly feared that if put upon his
honor, as he would be in such a case, he must deal with his work so dam-
agingly as to leave little or nothing left of it. He might make the reputation
of a great critic, but in doing execution upon his own shortcomings he
might be the means of destroying himself as a great author. (*ImI,* 300)

Howells's unwillingness to write prefaces to his own work, then, had a variety of motives behind it: modesty, surely, and an artist's pride in asking
that his work stand alone, free from the support of a prescriptive preface;
but, as this passage suggests, Howells may have been unwilling or unable to
critique his work in the manner of James, for fear of showing up his own
weaknesses.

But if Howells never attempted a self-referential vade mecum, he did address a range of related topics throughout his final years. As we have seen,
beginning with his important essay "The Man of Letters as a Man of Business," Howells regularly examined the role of the artist in the marketplace.
In many essays, such as those discussed in Chapter 7 of this study, Howells
maintained a largely objective stance (see "The Art of the Adsmith," for instance). On other occasions, however, Howells used the dialogue format of
the Easy Chair to cross-examine himself in relation to this changing marketplace, and in these essays one senses a growing unease in Howells. On still
other occasions, Howells addressed a range of practical questions concerning the habit and practice of art. Some of these essays were aimed at newcomers to the field; some were the reflections of an elder practitioner of the
art. Taken together, these essays form a special subcategory of Howells's essays on the literary marketplace.

A Normal Hero

In "A Search for Celebrity," Howells stages a conversation between two
of his personae, the "unreal editor" of the Easy Chair and the Veteran
Novelist, who has agreed to answer a series of questions mailed to the Easy
Chair by the author of a book entitled *The Way into Print,* a primer for the
literary aspirant. The questions are predictably narrow, and are asked in the
hopes that the experienced, older generation will share "insider information" with the aspirant, thereby making his way into print that much easier.
The proposition makes the Veteran Novelist edgy and uncomfortable. When
asked to name the "necessary qualifications in the matters of natural ability,
education, life as he sees it and lives it, technical training, etc.," the Novelist

backs away from the question. "No man was ever yet taught any art," he proclaims. "He may be taught a trade, and that is what most versing and prosing is, I suppose. If you have the gift, you will technically train yourself: that is, you will learn how to be simple and clear and honest." The whole topic is cause for distress. "Is it really true," the Veteran Novelist asks, affecting surprise, "that there is a large body of young people taking up literature as a business? . . . And am I, in my prominence . . . an incentive to them to persevere in their enterprises?" The Veteran Novelist, declining to suggest any shortcuts to success, preaches the virtues of hard work: "There is no training that can ever make the true artist's work easy to him, and if he is a true artist he will suspect everything easily done as ill done." In a lengthy passage, the Veteran Novelist, sounding not unlike a stern parent, argues that setbacks, personal defeats, and loss are the making of the artist. "Why should I be so wicked as to help another and a younger man over the bad places? If I could only gain his confidence I should like to tell him that these are the places that will strengthen his heart for the climb" (*ImI*, 189–92).

The Novelist's sermon completed, the Easy Chair suggests that the Novelist has missed the mark. The Novelist has addressed artists, but the true audience for *The Way into Print* are "artisans" and "speculators" who want "a formula for the fabrication of gold bricks." The Veteran Novelist protests; he has never been so mercenary. "Ah, that is what you say!" the Editor counters. "But do you suppose anybody will believe you?" The column ends with the Novelist accusing the Editor of having sat "so long in your cushioned comfort, looking out on the publishing world, that you have become corrupt, cynical, pessimistic" (*ImI*, 192–93).

The column is fascinating; Howells stages a dialogue between two parts of himself: the uncompromising literary artist who, he likes to believe, has never taken any shortcuts or made any compromises, always using the highest aims of literary art and not the whims of the market as his guide; and the persona of the Easy Chair who, as we have shown, represents that part of Howells that played directly to the market and agreed to meet it on its own terms. (And, of course, took home the paycheck.) "A Search for Celebrity" dramatizes one of the issues central to "The Man of Letters as a Man of Business": namely, the uneasy relationship between artist and the marketplace. In both essays, the aims and objectives of each seem essentially irreconcilable—but also irretrievably linked. "A Search for Celebrity" also shows Howells questioning the example he himself had set for the younger generations; even if he had remained true to his art, there would always be those who focused their attention elsewhere—on his demonstrable financial success, for instance. To a large extent, this public perception of Howells was the result of a deliberate campaign by the House of Harper to "sell" Howells as a cultural icon—the "Dean of American Letters." "A Search for Celebrity" addresses some of Howells's discomfort with this new status. Notably, the column ends with the two personae quarrelling; their charges go unanswered, their conflict unresolved.

Howells's personal discomfort with the literary marketplace is evident in other Easy Chair columns. Howells playfully satirizes the generation gap in "A Niece's Literary Advice to Her Uncle," in which the niece demands of her uncle, the Veteran Novelist, a "virile" novel full of epigrammatic passages and palpable "passion." The niece's tastes obviously reflect the sentimental, romanticistic novels of the day; in her youthful energy and enthusiasm, she stands in stark contrast to her uncle, the aged artist who cannot, or will not, meet the demands of this younger reader. The novelist in this column is out of step with more than just his niece's youthful tastes: his books are not advertised or noticed; and, from the gist of the discussion, they are not popular. Worse, producing new work is proving difficult. In the opening paragraph, the niece interrupts her uncle as he struggles with a temporary bout of writer's block. And, after the rapid-fire grilling, the novelist sinks back into his quiet, unproductive torpor (*ImI*, 176–83).[15]

Howells employs a similar conceit in "A Normal Hero and Heroine out of Work," in which he happens upon two fictional characters sitting together on a park bench. The characters, "tastefully dressed" and speaking "grammatically . . . without any trace of accent or dialect," discuss why they have fallen out of favor with the current crop of fiction writers, who want only "impossible circumstances . . . eccentric characters, exaggerated incentives, morbid propensities, pathological conditions, or diseased psychology." The characters are resigned to their fate; they are "commonplace" and out of vogue. Howells, who has been eavesdropping keenly on their conversation, urges upon the characters a strategy to reintroduce them to the market:

> *Not* commonplace. A judicious paragraph anticipative of your reappearance could be arranged, in which you could be hailed as the *normal* hero and heroine, and greeted as a grateful relief from the hackneyed freaks and deformities of the prevalent short story, or the impassioned paper-doll pattern of the mediæval men and maidens, or the spotted and battered figures of the studies in morbid analysis which pass for fiction in the magazines. We must get that luminous word *normal* before the reading public at once,

15. Nettels reads the scene in light of gender and power dynamics: "Although Howells appears to deny his authority by posing as the rueful outmoded writer swept aside by the tide of current fashion, his irony reflects his sense of superiority to the female speaker" (*Language and Gender in American Fiction*, 29).

and you will be rightly seen in its benign ray and recognized from the start—yes! in *advance* of the start—for what you are: types of the loveliness of our average life.

But the characters are spirits, and they cannot hear Howells. These apparitions—figures from the realist novel of the Gilded Age as once written by Howells—are literally out of touch, not to mention unmarketable. The characters resolve to wait patiently for the time when their kind will once again be in demand. Howells is left alone, watching his beloved "normal" characters as they fade into "the mists under the trees" (*ImI*, 245, 248–51).

In both "A Niece's Literary Advice to Her Uncle" and "A Normal Hero and Heroine out of Work," Howells gently mocks the conventions of the sentimental romance then enjoying popularity with the public. In this regard, the columns echo old complaints. More interestingly, each column depicts the novelist as out of touch with the market; in the case of "A Niece's Literary Advice," the novelist is temporarily incapable of any kind of work. And in "A Normal Hero," the novelist's sense of "normal" is patently unmarketable and, therefore, out of reach. A palpable nostalgia for the past informs both columns, as does a certain bitterness over the current state of artistic affairs.

The What and the How in Art

On other occasions, Howells freely discussed the practice of art with his fellow writers and aspirants in an attempt to open it up, to demystify it. Invariably, Howells offered practical, down-to-earth advice. "There is nothing mystical in all this," he writes in "The Editor's Relations with the Young Contributor." It is "a matter of plain, every-day experience. . . . The wonder and the glory of art is that it is without formulas." Howells preaches to novitiate and critic alike in an Easy Chair column on originality and imitation in art (February 1907). Howells begins by insisting that "In either life or art, except at the divine source of both, there is no creation; there is only recreation. Or, we may reverse the paradox and say there are no fathers, only forefathers." Howells writes at length of Tolstoy, who claimed to have learned all he knew of war from Stendhal and the example of *La Chartreuse de Parme* and *Le Rouge et le Noir*. Howells appreciates Tolstoy's frank admission of the debt, but proceeds to use him as a case in point: "what the later artist does is to add his temperament to the example of the earlier, and if he is the greater personality, to become the original when he finds himself." Howells admits that "Not all disciples have had Tolstoy's noble bravery in proclaiming the name of their prophet," and that it would be unrealistic to expect the younger artists to be so forthcoming, especially "in the hour of [their] discipleship." Howells concludes the meditation by shifting the focus back to the artistic practice itself: "After all, what we want is not originality but excellence" in art. Like "The Man of Letters as a Man of Business," "The Editor's Relations" and the February 1907 Easy Chair can both be read as attempts to demystify the artistic process and to render it in frank, honest terms. Howells had no wish to hide behind pretense; he would always seek to define the writer as a laborer, and the work as honest work.[16]

A similar sentiment is evident in "The What and the How in Art." In this 1896 essay, Howells argues that art ought to be aimed at the widest possible audience: "Art is not produced for artists, or even for connoisseurs; it is produced for the general, who can never view it otherwise than morally, personally, partially, from their associations and preconceptions." To write for fellow artists and connoisseurs is a denial of the artist's office, "which [is] to say something clear and appreciable to all sorts of men in the terms of art. . . . I think it a thousand pities whenever an artist gets so far away from the general, so far within himself or a little circle of amateurs, that his highest and best work awakens no response in the multitude."[17] "The What and the How in Art" reveals Howells, on the one hand, laying down his own artistic maxims in the form of meditations and reflections; but it also demonstrates, once again, how Howells could never fully reconcile the aims and objectives of art with the awareness of a growing, general audience for that art. Like James, Howells would always want to win over the largest possible readership without detriment to his work. But where James was steadfastly opposed to compromise in any form, demanding that his readers take him on his own (increasingly difficult) terms, Howells reveals his own hesitations about adopting such a relentless stance; there remained in Howells, until the very end, a democratic ideal of an art that could appeal to all. As "The What and the How in Art" demonstrates, Howells always viewed art in a sociocultural context; the project of realism, as he understood it, was to depict life in accurate, true terms that would appeal to a universal sense of compassion and understanding; inasmuch as Howells valued this social responsibility of art, he felt that art must be readily accessible to the common reader.

As this brief overview indicates, Howells continued to address a range of topics surrounding the role of the artist in the literary marketplace and broader questions about the habit and practice of art.[18] If he chose to avoid

16. Howells, *Literature and Life*, 75; Howells, *W. D. Howells as Critic*, 446–50.
17. Howells, *Literature and Life*, 286–87.
18. Howells also considered the question of artistic genres in his literary essays. In "Some Anomalies of the Short Story," Howells provides an overview of the short story, the novella,

self-referential criticism, and if he never deliberately wrote a vade mecum for aspirants, he nevertheless did offer a series of useful and engaging essays that asked probing questions about the shifting literary mores of his time. Some, like "A Search for Celebrity," address recurring questions about the tensions between the artist and the literary marketplace. "A Niece's Advice" and "A Normal Hero" both suggest that Howells felt, from time to time, out of step with the changing marketplace.[19] Finally, Howells wrote frankly of the process of and habit of art, with an eye toward demystifying the process and making it accessible to the aspirant. Howells always wanted art to be democratic and approachable; there was always a strong educative streak in his criticism, regardless of its form. And this educative focus is seen quite palpably in *Heroines of Fiction*.

Heroines of Fiction

Howells's first book-length literary memoir, *My Literary Passions*, traces his intellectual development as a reader and nascent artist. Written in a warm, accessible style, it is clearly designed to appeal to a general readership familiar with its author.[20] Howells described the book, in a letter to Charles Eliot Norton, as "a mixture of autobiography and criticism" (*HSL* 4:39). It is not, strictly speaking, a volume of literary criticism; as Donald Pizer succinctly puts it, "our interest today [is] more in its revelations of Howells' early years than in its relaxed representation of critical attitudes expressed elsewhere in more insightful form." With *My Literary Passions*, Howells initiated a period of writing literary memoir; he next treated the Boston of his early professional years in *Literary Friends and Acquaintance*, before turning to literary history in *Heroines of Fiction*, a study of female protagonists in the Anglo-American novel.[21] This lengthy work, serialized in *Harper's Bazaar* in 1900–1902, stands as something of an anomaly in Howells's canon of literary texts for reasons of style, rhetorical stance, and purpose.

Howells begins his study of the nineteenth-century heroine, surprisingly

---

and the novel, and tries to explain his sense of how each genre functions in the marketplace (ibid., 110–24). And Howells offers his observations of the state of poetry in the early twentieth century in "The Magazine Muse" (*ImI*, 137–45) and "Some Moments with the Muse" (*ImI*, 236–43).

19. One hastens to add that, if Howells felt out of step, it was not from ignorance. He knew as well as anyone what drove the marketplace of the early twentieth century, and he addressed it, as we have seen here and in Chapter 7, in a range of essays concerning the changing literary marketplace.

20. Originally, the papers were published serially in *Ladies' Home Journal*, 1893–1895.

21. Pizer, introduction, *SLC* 2:xix. I treat the revised, 1910 version of *Literary Friends and Acquaintance* in Chapter 10 of this study.

enough, with Defoe, who "is distinctly of the nineteenth century in the voluntary naturalness and instructed simplicity of his art. . . . He wrote the clearest, purest English, the most lifelike English; and his novels are a self-evident and most convincing fidelity to life" (*HoF* 1:2). Clearly, these are the signal characteristics of nineteenth-century realism; and here, at the opening of this lengthy study, is the book's unstated claim: to compose a critical history of the Anglo-American novel in the context of realism. *Heroines* is a deliberate act of revisionist literary history; it is also an attempt to educate, or to "indoctrinate," its audience. In this regard, it is quite as deliberate, in its own way, as James's Prefaces to the New York Edition.[22]

The nominal thesis of *Heroines of Fiction* is a study the nineteenth-century heroine in the Anglo-American novel. But even this focus is contextualized within Howells's larger realist agenda:

> Many proofs of the fact that a novel is great or not, as its women are important or unimportant, might be alleged. There are exceptions to the rule, but they are among novels of ages and countries different from ours. As we approach our own time, women in fiction become more and more interesting, and are of greater consequence than the men in fiction, and the skill with which they are portrayed is more and more a test of mastery. By this test the romantic novel shows its inferiority, if by no other. . . . Women, above all others, should love the fiction which is faithful to life, for no other fiction has paid the homage and done the justice due to women, or recognized their paramount interest. (*HoF* 1:113–14)

At the center of his argument, always, rests one of Howells's oldest aesthetic tenets: that of the deep, complex, well-rounded fictional character. We note how Howells foregrounds the aesthetic "evolution" of the Anglo-American novel:

> In primitive fiction plot is more important than character; as the art advances character becomes the chief interest, and the action is such as springs from it. In the old tales and romances there is no such thing as character in the modern sense; their readers were satisfied with what the heroes and heroines did and suffered. . . . [Character] . . . is rooted in personality. The novelist of to-day who has not conceived of this is as archaic as any romancer of the Middle Ages in his ideal of art. Most of the novels printed in the last year, in fact, are . . . crudely devised . . . ; and it will always be so with most novels, because most people are of childish imagination.

22. This point of comparison having been noted, there are many significant differences between *Heroines of Fiction* and the Prefaces. Where James is necessarily self-referential, Howells never mentions his own work. And where James is explicitly concerned with form and composition, Howells treats a much broader range of topics, as detailed below.

> The masterpieces of fiction are those which delight the mind with the traits of personality, with human nature recognizable by the reader through its truth to himself. (*HoF* 1:65)

This passage is noteworthy for two reasons. First, it confirms Gottesman's assertion that Howells "remained faithful to his basic convictions" in his later criticism. This strong, clearly articulated realist agenda is the basis of the second and more subtle point, which concerns the rhetorical slant of *Heroines*. Howells is not merely concerned with documenting and explicating his thesis that "a novel is great or not, as its women are important or unimportant." At the deepest level, he is championing, or "selling," his realist aesthetic as the driving force of the Anglo-American novel. The strategy is, at least in part, market-driven: in the face of the popular romance novel, Howells promotes his own aesthetic, educating his audience and promoting his product.

In order to facilitate this market-driven scheme, Howells employs "quotational criticism," the style of a previous generation of scholars, such as Leigh Hunt, Charles Lamb, and Thomas De Quincey. Quotational criticism provides lengthy excerpts from the novels in question, framed by contextual commentary and explication. If, in 1900, quotational criticism was an anachronism, why would Howells employ it in *Heroines of Fiction*? Simply put, the strategy suited Howells's patently educative mission. He would write a lengthy work covering the Anglo-American novel from Defoe to Hardy, but he would be doing so in *Harper's Bazaar*—a predominately female readership not expected to be familiar with every book by every author. In an Easy Chair column entitled "The Advantages of Quotational Criticism," Howells explains that quotational criticism could

> give the ever-increasing multitude of readers a chance to know something of the best literature. If they chose to pursue the acquaintance, very good; if they chose not to pursue the acquaintance, still very good; they could not have made it at all without being somewhat refined and enlightened. . . . [Y]ou could not know a great poet so little as not to be enriched by him. . . . [And] the life into which [the literary acquaintance] fell . . . could never afterward be so common as it was before. (*ImI*, 222)

Howells viewed quotational criticism as the ideal form for a certain audience: namely, the ever-expanding sea of new readers that constituted the book-buying public at the turn of the new century.[23] The project of *Heroines*

---

23. Interestingly, *Heroines of Fiction* is the only book-length example of quotational criticism in the Howells canon. It seems he felt this antiquated style was worth dusting off for this particular project but refrained from using it on any other occasion of which I am aware.

of Fiction is both to introduce these readers to the history of Anglo-American fiction and to indoctrinate them; they are, after all, potential buyers of contemporary realist fiction as written by Howells himself (though he refrains from explicit self-promotion). In pursuit of his agenda, Howells makes a number of interesting discoveries and surprising appropriations.

The Gifted Women

The two great discoveries in *Heroines of Fiction* are Jane Austen and George Eliot.[24] Howells deliberately positions Austen as the capstone of the early tradition of the realist novel: "De Foe, Richardson, Goldsmith, Frances Burney, Maria Edgeworth, Jane Austen: this is the lineage of the English fiction whose ideal is reality, whose prototype is nature" (*HoF* 1:79). Save for Austen, Howells gives cursory attention to them all (for a variety of reasons; for instance, Defoe's heroines are too salacious for inquiry). But Howells devotes three full chapters to Austen, detailing each of her novels and the major female protagonists. In this treatment of Austen—Howells's first lengthy consideration of her work—it is clear that he sees the first full flowering of the realist aesthetic in English letters. An overview of Howells's strategy in his treatment of Austen also reveals deeper dimensions of his educative strategy in *Heroines*.

For Howells, Austen represents everything central to realism. Austen is "the greatest of the gifted women, who beyond any or all other novelists have fixed the character and behavior of Anglo-Saxon fiction. . . . Jane Austen was indeed so fine an artist, that we are still only beginning to realize how fine she was; to perceive, after a hundred years, that in the form of the imagined fact, in the expression of personality, in the conduct of the narrative, and the subordination of incident to character, she is still unapproached in the English branch of Anglo-Saxon fiction" (*HoF* 1:38).[25] Howells moves beyond such generalizations and, stepping into his educative stride, proceeds to explicate the novels. His treatment of *Emma* may stand as a quintessential example of his didactic strategy throughout *Heroines*. The reader is "taught" what to look for and what to value in the fiction. Howells begins, naturally, with character: Emma is "boldly imagined. . . . [It] took supreme courage to portray a girl, meant to win and keep the reader's fancy,

24. By "discovery" I mean only that the study of both Austen and Eliot in *Heroines* stands as Howells's first major consideration of either author. Howells had, of course, read Eliot as a youth and discussed her work in *My Literary Passions*. Austen, however, had been infrequently discussed in Howells's earlier criticism and was not mentioned in *My Literary Passions*.

25. Throughout *Heroines of Fiction*, Howells uses the term "Anglo-Saxon fiction" to mean the English-language novels of both Great Britain and the United States.

with the characteristics frankly ascribed to Emma Woodhouse." Howells catalogs and explicates these characteristics: "she is pretty; not formally, but casually"; Emma "is patronizing and a little presumptuous"; she has "a willingness to shape the future of others without having past enough of her own to enable her to do it judiciously"; in sum, she is "officious and self-confident." Howells offers a range of short, carefully selected quotes from the novel to illustrate his points, all the while emphasizing Austen's focus on the development of character over plot or incident: "the novel of 'Emma' may be said to be hardly more than an exemplification of Emma. In the placid circumstance of English country life where she is the principal social figure the story makes its round with a few events so unexciting as to leave the reader in doubt whether anything at all has happened" (*HoF* 1:66–67). The discussion culminates in a lengthy quote from the novel's famous scene, in which Knightly chides Emma for denigrating Miss Bates. After the quote, Howells offers a brief summary of the key points behind the scene. This general pattern is repeated throughout *Heroines of Fiction* and it is the prime method by which Howells educates, or indoctrinates, his audience.[26]

Of course, part of this didactic focus involved revising the canon, and Howells does not shy from taking the masters to task—again, on his own terms. For instance, aesthetic form is a recurring concern throughout *Heroines;* Austen receives high praise from Howells: "in the high excellencies of symmetrical form, force of characterization, clearness of conception, simplicity and temperance of means, she is still supreme" (*HoF* 1:41). In contrast, Sir Walter Scott is chided for his "loose, inaccurate and ineffectual languaging." Howells, keenly aware of his readers' inherited sympathies, pitches his argument masterfully: "I know that to many it will seem irreverence little short of sacrilege to speak of Scott's work in these terms; but truth is more precious than sentiment, and no harm but much help can come from recognizing the facts. In verse, Scott was a master of diction, compact, clear, simple; in prose, at least the prose of his novels, he was shapeless, tautological, heavy, infirm, wandering, melodramatic and over-literary" (*HoF* 1:109). As this passage demonstrates, Howells did not shy away from dealing out frank and specific criticism in *Heroines* when he saw fit—and, as any

26. One suspects Howells's selections in *Heroines* were, at least in part, driven by the market of the day. For instance, Jane Austen was an enormously popular and best-selling author at the turn of the century; she had been newly "discovered" and her books sold prodigiously. Howells is eager to claim this popular figure for his canon and devotes a large amount of space to her work. That having been said, I do not mean to imply that Howells was not a genuine admirer of Jane Austen. Clearly, he was. But his preoccupation with her work may be driven, in part, by his awareness of her tremendous popularity in the marketplace. The same may be true of Charlotte and Emily Brontë, both of whom Howells treats.

reader of the text will see, he saw fit on a great many occasions. But the criticism is always offered in light of Howells's didactic focus.

The second great "discovery" in *Heroines of Fiction* is George Eliot. *Heroines* includes Howells's first major appraisal of her work, and, as with the discovery of Austen, Howells is delighted to claim Eliot in his canon of realist authors. She is "the greatest talent in English fiction after Jane Austen, but a talent of vastly wider and deeper reach . . . and of a far more serious import" (*HoF* 2:44). Howells charts the growth and increasing complexity of Eliot's characters, singling out *Middlemarch* as

> an immense canvas, thronged with such a multitude of marvellously distinguished and differenced figures, that . . . so richly represents life. . . . It is in its truth to motives as well as results that it is so tremendously convincing. After a lapse of years one comes to it not with a sense of having overmeasured it before, but with the perception that one had not at first realized its grandeur. It is as large as life in those moral dimensions which deepen inwardly and give the real compass of any artistic achievement through the impression received. (*HoF* 2:77)

It is the moral quality of Eliot's work that Howells ultimately praises; he is, for instance, astonished at the complexity and sophistication of the treatment of spousal abuse in *Scenes from Clerical Life*. "It is not ill," Howells remarks, "but it is very well to be confronted with the ugly realities, the surviving savageries, that the smug hypocrisy of civilization denies; for till we recognize them we shall not abate them, or even try to do so. . . . Who can doubt as to the relative value of the pictures? As to the art in them respectively, we almost lose sight of the superiority of George Eliot's in sense of her superior morality" (*HoF* 2:92–93). As we already noted, it was Howells's preoccupation with the moral force of Eliot's work that would inform one of the strongest Easy Chair columns (November 1902), in which Howells asserts Eliot as "one of the greatest moralists who ever lived" (*SLC* 3:166).

Eliot receives the lengthiest treatment of any author in *Heroines*. It is clear that Howells's rediscovery of her work, with its moral authority, ethical rigor, and complex, dynamic characters, was a major occasion.[27] In his later years, Howells demonstrated more than an ability to stay current with

27. Despite Howells's obvious enthusiasm, it bears noting that he is characteristically balanced in his account, offering a succinct catalog of Eliot's faults: "her learning over-weighted her knowledge; her conscience clogged her art; her strong grasp of human nature was weakened by foibles of manner; the warmth of her womanly intuitions failed of their due effect because their sympathies were sometimes hysterical and the intuitions were sometimes over-intellectualized," and her fiction was occasionally pedantic (*HoF* 2:45).

the authors and changing tastes of his day; in the example of his treatment of Austen and Eliot in *Heroines of Fiction,* we see that he continued to read and assess the great authors of the past, continually broadening his understanding of all aspects of literature. But *Heroines* is notable for other reasons as well.

Visionary Conditions

Heroines of Fiction is noteworthy, too, for a few acts of appropriation. Howells had always admired Charles Dickens, but he had always viewed his work as the quintessential example of the romance and had dismissed his characters as grotesques. In *My Literary Passions,* Howells offers his first major treatment of Dickens in nearly thirty years, and there is a notable shift in tone. Howells confesses to having fallen under the spell early on: "While his glamour lasted it was no more possible for a young novelist to escape writing Dickens than it was for a young poet to escape writing Tennyson." Consequently, the young Howells "was compelled, as by a law of nature, to do it at least partially in his way." And despite recognizing that there were certain infelicities of style and a penchant for the grotesque in Dickens's characters, Howells understood that "The base of his work is the whole breadth and depth of humanity itself. . . . His view of the world and of society, though it was very little philosophized, was instinctively sane and reasonable, even when it was most impossible."[28] While not expressly critical in nature, Howells's appreciation of Dickens in *My Literary Passions* marks the beginning of a period of reappraisal; a post-Haymarket Howells saw in Dickens an artist preoccupied with equality, fraternity, and democracy, and this leads to Howells's more probing critical examination in *Heroines of Fiction* (and the important 1902 essay on Dickens, which we examined in Chapter 7).

In *Heroines of Fiction,* Dickens is positioned as a "realescent" author—that is, one "who followed the romancers [and] copied some of their virtues as well as their faults" but who also "brought fiction back to the study of life." Dickens accomplished this "by dint of appealing to our consciences or our sensibilities, and he achieved a moral rather than an artistic triumph in heroines who are for our good rather than our pleasure." These moral and ethical dimensions of character—the deep compassion and sympathy—prompt Howells to claim Dickens as a "realescent" author. Yet Howells does not shy away from naming Dickens's faults, even as he praises the fiction: "[The] author himself falls into pages of hysterical rhythm . . . when he ought to have been writing plain, straight prose; yet there is in all a sense of the di-

28. Howells, *My Literary Passions,* 93, 96–97.

vinity in common and humble lives, which is the most precious quality of literature, as it is almost the rarest, and it is this which moves and consoles" (*HoF* 1:117, 126, 132).

In the end, Howells argues that Dickens's work was too melodramatic, too sentimental, and too theatrical; his characters, with their exaggerated mannerisms and signature tics, strained verisimilitude. Nevertheless, the fiction "was largely and loosely inclusive of life rather than exclusive of it. The impersonation of a quality or a propensity was misrepresentative only as far as it was single. Human nature is never single; . . . [and therefore] his one-sided types are not characters" (*HoF* 1:160). In *Heroines,* Dickens is cast as a catalyst, one who pushed away from the sentimental romance of the early nineteenth century and toward the realist novel. Howells's desire to compose a canonical account of the Anglo-American novel inspires him to appropriate Dickens as a "realescent" author. And Dickens was not the only romancer Howells would claim for his cause.

Ultimately, Hawthorne is the only major American author to be treated in any depth in *Heroines of Fiction.* And, interestingly, it is with the question of nationality that Howells begins his consideration. Playing on the cliché that America is large, crude, and boisterous where England is genteel, refined, and sophisticated, Howells notes with some irony that American fiction,

> owed nothing to English models [and] differed from English fiction in nothing so much as its greater refinement, its subtler beauty, and its delicate perfection of form. While Dickens was writing in England, Hawthorne was writing in America; and for all the ostensible reasons the romances of Hawthorne ought to have been rude, shapeless, provisional, the novels of Dickens ought to have been fastidiously elect in method and material and of the last scrupulosity in literary finish. That is, they ought to have been so, if the obvious inferences from an old civilization ripened in its native air, and the same civilization so newly conditioned under alien skies that it seemed essentially new, were the right inferences. But there were some facts which such hasty conclusions must have ignored: chiefly the fact that the first impulse of a new artistic life is to escape from crude conditions; and subordinately the fact that Hawthorne was writing to and from a sensitiveness of nerve in the English race that it had never known in its English home. (*HoF* 1:161)

The passage is, unmistakably, a playful poke at Henry James's *Hawthorne* and its attack on the "provincial" smallness of antebellum America.[29] But it

---

29. Notably, with his claim to the "greater refinement, . . . subtler beauty, and . . . delicate perfection of form" of the American novel, Howells has turned James's own form-oriented criteria back on James.

also serves as a basis for Howells's first deep consideration of American literature in *Heroines of Fiction*. In Hawthorne, Howells claims a deeper artistic
sensitivity in American literature; he also claims an artistic innovation—a
break with the English model. Following this, he uses the contrast between
Dickens and Hawthorne to distinguish between the romance of the former
and that of the latter:

> Apart from the racial differences of the two writers, there was the widest
> possible difference of ideal in Dickens and Hawthorne; the difference be-
> tween the romanticistic and the romantic, which is almost as great as that
> between the romantic and the realistic. Romance, as in Hawthorne, seeks
> the effect of reality in visionary conditions; romanticism, as in Dickens,
> tries for a visionary effect in actual conditions. These different ideals even-
> tuated with Hawthorne in characters being, doing, and suffering as vitally
> as any we have known in the world. . . . [The] characters of Hawthorne
> speak and act for themselves, and from an authentic individuality compact
> of good and evil. . . . Hawthorne's creations are *persons*, rounded, whole.
> (*HoF* 1:162)

This passage is noteworthy for the sophistication of the distinction between the romance of the two authors; Howells would never speak with
greater subtlety on the subject of the romance. More germane to our discussion, however, is the obvious attempt to claim a realist dimension to
Hawthorne's aesthetic. Where Dickens had been positioned as a "realescent" author whose focus on social, moral, and ethical concerns had helped
to bridge the gap between the romance and the realist novel, it is Hawthorne's emphasis on deep character that prompts Howells to elevate certain characters to the status of quasi-realist protagonists. In *The Scarlet
Letter*, "with the exception of the love-child or sin-child, Pearl, there is no
character, important or unimportant, about which you are asked to make
believe: they are all there to speak and act for themselves, and they do not
need the help of your fancy. They are all of a verity so robust." And *The
Blithedale Romance* "is nearer a novel [that is, realism] than any other fiction of the author. At times we find ourselves confronted there, in spite of
the author, with a very palpitant piece of naturalism." Zenobia is "substan-
tiated with the conscience of a realist to the material as well as the spiritual
vision" and, despite Hawthorne's over-insistence on her exotic hair, she "is
always present to the fancy in a warm reality." In the end, Howells finds
Zenobia "intellectual" and, "emotionally, spiritually, . . . of a coarse fibre,
with even a strain of vulgarity. A certain kind of New England woman, to
specialize a little more than to say American woman, has never been so
clearly seen or boldly shown as in Zenobia; and in her phase of tragedy she

stands as impressively for the nineteenth century as Hester Prynne for the seventeenth in hers" (*HoF* 1:164–65, 175–79).

In *Heroines,* Howells constructs a narrative of the evolution of realism that, beginning with Defoe, leads directly from Austen to Eliot and, eventually, Hardy. Dickens and Hawthorne, ordinarily considered quintessential examples of the romance novel, are appropriated as "realescent" authors whose work helped to propel the novel away from the sentimental romance and toward the realism of the late nineteenth century. It is, to be sure, a provocative thesis. And, to be fair, Howells has his points: Dickens's focus on contemporary social issues and his compassionate, humanistic focus on the poor clearly impacted the realist authors who followed his example; and, indeed, certain characters in Hawthorne are complex and dynamic and therefore can, in a limited sense, be claimed as protorealistic. Read generously, Howells's thesis in *Heroines* might be said to prefigure certain postmodern theories of hybridization and the blurring of aesthetic genres in the literary criticism of the late twentieth century.

But Howells's appropriation of Hawthorne is also highly problematic, and he openly confesses the incongruity: "I must still believe that novelists are great in proportion to the accuracy and fulness with which they portray women; but what really embarrasses me is that I have claimed this pre-eminence hitherto for the realists only, and Hawthorne can scarcely be counted a realist" (*HoF* 1:190). Howells's treatment of Hawthorne is rather remarkable; he downplays or recasts important romantic elements of the work so as to foreground the selected realist criteria that he champions; it is, perhaps, a case of overinsistence, and in the final analysis Howells does not argue the point with any true depth or rigor (perhaps because he knows it will not hold water). Rather, he simply abandons the claim, it would seem, as an esoteric whim. Naturally, this weakens Howells's argument in *Heroines,* a book that ultimately fails in its attempt to construct a convincing, rigorously considered history of the Anglo-American novel.

Nevertheless, Howells has touched on an original and very provocative thesis, even if he cannot fully explicate it. Part of the reason may be the intended audience of *Heroines:* because it was written not for the critics but for the perceived general audiences of *Harper's Bazaar,* and because it was designed to introduce that audience to a wide swath of authors and texts, Howells may have held himself to a less rigorous standard. But *Heroines* purports to be, at least in part, a critical study of the literature, and so Howells's willingness to introduce and leave unresolved such problematic claims as those concerning Dickens and Hawthorne ultimately undermines the text's authority. And this problem of authority—so crucial to any historical study—

is evident in Howells's treatment of social and class issues and, oddly enough, the American novel.

Submission to the Established Order

Throughout much of *Heroines of Fiction,* social or class-based issues are but glancingly noted. Richardson is praised as "a man of a mighty middle-class conscience." Howells explicates, with some pride, the scene in which Austen's Elizabeth Bennet boldly resists a probing Lady Catharine de Burgh. And he chides Amelia Opie's fiction for its class snobbery (*HoF* 1:11, 44–48, 82). In his study of Trollope, however, Howells foregrounds questions of class divisions and social codes. And, contrary to what one might expect, the treatment of class in this instance is surprisingly ambiguous.

Howells begins, of course, with character. After quoting extensively from *The Warden* in his study of Lily Dale, Howells notes that if the psychologically oriented Hawthorne, Tolstoy, or James would have exposed Lily's "naked soul" to the reader, then "it was strictly Trollope's business to show us her soul with its clothes on, for in the world he deals with, the soul as well as the body is clothed, and wears its decorums and conventions as constantly. It is when Trollope shows the soul moving in these that he is most a master." Howells praises Trollope's eye for the foibles of English society, and in particular clerical society: he "wrote so much better of English life than any one except Jane Austen and George Eliot." Yet, unlike Thackeray, who openly mocked his aristocrats, "there is nothing of the satirist in [Trollope]; and he is all the more impressive as a moralist because he contents himself with simply letting us see them as they are. He has no apparent purpose of reforming them. . . . He even imparts a sense of such entire approval of society conditions, such unquestioning fealty to the existing order, that you hardly know whether to admire more the skill with which he portrays it, or the seriousness with which he accepts it and honors it" (*HoF* 2:107–10). The quote is noteworthy for the astute observation of Trollope's authorial stance—compared to Thackeray's, a direct and unbiased presentation of the subject. But Howells goes on to suggest that the reader might "admire" the manner in which Trollope "accepts and honors" the existing social order. A similar ambiguity of sentiment is evident when Howells states that

> the attitude of the characters in all of Trollope's books and the attitude of Trollope himself is one of Asiatic submission to the established order of things, mixed with a strictly Anglo-Saxon freedom of speech concerning it; so that the more democratized American is scarcely more amazed at the one than at the other. No people with less than the English good sense

could prevent their social conditions from working more harm than they do; no people with so much good sense ever abandoned themselves to a status in which the outsider sees no sense at all.

But the law and the gospel of Trollope . . . is that the thing which is must be, and that every one concerned must conform to it in mind and conscience as wisely and decently as possible. It is an immensely frank race, and what Trollope does is to show it with a frankness equalled by that of no other novelist, with a cold-bloodedness, and absence of disagreeable consciousness which almost command respect. (*HoF* 2:116–17)

It is a remarkable statement by Howells; it makes perfect sense that he would note the depiction of "submission" or acquiescence in Trollope's work. Howells's increasingly sophisticated social awareness, developed over the period following the Haymarket affair, had attuned his eye and social conscience to such ideas as never before. What is most interesting are the two moments when Howells notes the admiration and respect that Trollope's work "almost command[s]" in the reader. This does not sound like the pro-socialist Howells of the 1890s. Rather, it is almost as if the aristocratic tendencies in Howells might overtake his social conscience. It is, to be sure, a delicate question. Again, these comments may be a product of Howells's audience in *Heroines of Fiction*—the bourgeois readership of *Harper's Bazaar*.

As a careful observer of his marketplace, Howells was acutely aware of his audience and their sympathies. Occasionally, he even toyed with those sympathies, as he does in a range of social and cultural essays collected in *Literature and Life*. In "The Beach at Rockaway," Howells reports on a visit to the public beach as if checking in from some remote outpost, fully anticipating boorish behavior and public drunkenness. Instead, he finds thousands of polite—if decidedly middle-class—bathers. Nevertheless, his rhetorical pose throughout the essay is that of aloofness and mild disgust. The essay, one suspects, panders to the genteel readers of *Harper's Weekly*. Similar sentiments inform "At a Dime Museum," which examines the curio market and nickel theaters (while gently mocking the highbrow theater of New York, which is more expensive and less entertaining). Howells's sense of play with class is perhaps most palpable in "The Problem of the Summer," which examines the "curse" of the wealthy who are burdened with choosing where to spend their summer holiday. Howells playfully pities these aristocrats, before shifting, in the closing paragraphs, to a passage that, read generously, is a subtle attempt at pricking the readers' consciences by reminding them of those laborers who cannot afford such luxuries. Read less generously, it amounts to a weak and gentle moralizing.[30]

30. Howells, "The Beach at Rockaway" (*Literature and Life,* 161–72), "At a Dime Museum" (ibid., 193–201), and "The Problem of the Summer" (ibid., 216–21). All three essays

What essays like "The Problem of Summer" demonstrate is Howells's keen awareness of his audience and their tastes; this awareness is, at times, palpable in the literary, social, and cultural essays written by Howells. And so, to come back to Howells's treatment of Trollope in *Heroines of Fiction,* the quasi-respect that Howells acknowledges for the social stances implicit in Trollope's fiction may be directed at his readership: the bourgeois, female audience of *Harper's Bazaar.* At the very least, this quasi-respect stands in opposition to some of the more pointedly critical, social, cultural, and literary essays written by Howells during and immediately following his tenure in the "Editor's Study." Arguably, the apparent ambivalence about class in this portion of *Heroines of Fiction* undermines Howells's authority in the text, given its otherwise strong realist slant. Realism, for Howells, ordinarily involved the rigorous probing of the aristocratic conscience, as in such works as *The Rise of Silas Lapham, Annie Kilburn,* and *A Hazard of New Fortunes.* Earlier in *Heroines,* Howells had praised Dickens for steering the novel toward a more socially informed, humanistic realism; the conservative ambiguity hinted at in the passages on Trollope complicates this conception of realism, at least to a degree. But, far and away, the prime weakness of *Heroines* is its failure to accurately assess the American novel.

A Theory Wounding to Our Patriotism

It is clear to any reader of *Heroines of Fiction* that it is principally a history of the British novel. Howells himself calls attention to the fact late in the volume:

> So far in these explorations of Anglo-Saxon fiction, we have come upon only three American novelists [Hawthorne, De Forest, and James], apparently, whose heroines may match with those of the English novelists. Such a fact may be accounted for upon a theory wounding to our patriotism, if we like the pain, or it may be more gratifyingly explained upon the ground that during the past century the English novelists have probably outnum-

---

originally appeared in 1896 as part of Howells's "Life and Letters" series in *Harper's Weekly.* It bears noting that not all of Howells's social essays were jocular and lighthearted; in *Literature and Life* one also finds the remarkable essays "Spanish Prisoners of War" ([1898] 141–53), which humanizes the Spanish soldiers held during the Spanish-American War, and "The Midnight Platoon" ([1895] 154–60), which examines the conscience of the middle and upper classes in the face of abject poverty, hunger, and homelessness in New York City. These, together with the probing social essays contained in *Impressions and Experiences,* demonstrate that Howells, on many occasions, remained a keen and critical observer of society and culture. See also Hough, *Quiet Rebel.*

bered ours quite in the proportion of their representation here. (*HoF* 2:225)

Neither explanation seems sufficient. The argument of paucity seems, especially in the mouth of the catholic Howells, disingenuous—even with the caveat that he restricted the focus of his work to a study of fictional heroines, and that this had forced him to overlook certain American writers like Cooper and Brockden Brown, for example. Perhaps more plausibly, Howells notes that "heroines are subordinate figures" in much of the Western American fiction, and he allows that this fact compromises his thesis, held throughout *Heroines,* that the "supremacy of the heroine in a novel [is] proof of the author's mastery" (*HoF* 2:245). While there may be some merit to this claim regarding Western fiction, it seems more the case that Howells has chosen to ignore or downplay certain writers, especially the female "regionalist" writers. For instance, while Mary Wilkins receives a brief but substantive discussion, Sarah Orne Jewett is mentioned only in passing.

The argument of proportion is hardly more convincing. Despite the large number of major British novelists treated in *Heroines,* Howells treats a sizable number of minor and obscure authors. If there is a disproportionate number of British authors, then, it is apparently by design. In the final chapters, as if to correct this lapse, Howells rushes through a cluster of Americans in a half-hearted attempt to balance his account: Bret Harte, T. B. Aldrich, George W. Cable, Mary Wilkins, and Henry Fuller are all examined. Another dozen or more authors are mentioned in passing. But, in the final analysis, only Hawthorne is treated with the depth or sophistication otherwise reserved for the major British novelists. This is decidedly odd, given the heavy realist slant of *Heroines.* Most curious is the case of Henry James.

Howells's treatment of James is restricted to a brief study of *Daisy Miller.* Howells notes the expert technique in the novella, which "is of course managed with the fine adroitness of Mr. James's mastery; from the first moment the sense of [Winterbourne's and Daisy's] potential love is a delicate pleasure for the reader, till at the last it is a delicate pang." The issue of character is a bit trickier. Howells notes the initial public outcry against *Daisy Miller,* when many Americans perceived James's portrayal of the naive, newly rich girl as derogatory and insulting. Howells argues that Daisy is not a "libel of her nationality" nor "a libel of her sex," but rather a "precious tribute" to a girl's "divine innocence, her inextinguishable trust in herself and others, as the supreme effect of the American attitude toward womanhood" (*HoF* 2:171, 176). It is as generous a reading as James could ever hope for, albeit two decades late.

Why did Howells limit his treatment of James to *Daisy Miller?* One can only speculate. Certainly, the James oeuvre did not lack for heroines; Howells himself catalogs the possible subjects. Perhaps the most convincing possibility is that Howells knew James would be a tough sell with the audience of *Harper's Bazaar*. One perhaps senses as much when Howells insists upon the worth and value of James's work, pitching it as if it were an exquisite commodity: "To enjoy his work, to feel its rare excellence, both in conception and expression is a brevet of intellectual good form which the women who have it prize at all its worth." Like a salesman anticipating a buyer's objection, Howells ridicules the infidels who fail to see James's unique value: "It is because he has worked in a fashion of his own, in regions of inquiry not traversed by the herd of adventurers, and dealt with material not exploited before that he is still to the critical Jews a stumbling block and to the critical Greeks foolishness" (*HoF* 2:165, 168–69). In such passages, one senses a measure of the unease that Howells's readers might have felt toward the difficult James. And this unease may explain why, with the vast range of James's heroines available for examination in 1900, Howells chooses only *Daisy Miller*. The novella had, of course, been one of James's largest successes (though, due to the lack of an international copyright and rampant pirating of the work, James saw little pecuniary reward), and it was certainly one of his most accessible texts. It is also a quintessential example of James's popular "international theme," which Howells praises (even going so far as to demand that James return to the theme, which, in 1900, James seemed to have put aside). Last, *Daisy Miller* is a quintessentially realist text, and Howells knew more than anyone that James had, in some of the more recent work, distanced himself from that aesthetic. Still, one can only puzzle over Howells's decision to choose *Daisy Miller* over, say, *The Portrait of a Lady*.

Inevitably, Howells concludes *Heroines of Fiction* by contrasting the English and the American novels. He frames the discussion in terms of relative social scope: the British novel is broad in social scope but relatively shallow in characterization, whereas the American novel is narrow in social scope but offers greater depth of character. Howells explains: "To put it paradoxically, our [American] life is too large for our art to be broad. In despair at the immense scope and variety of the material offered it by American civilization, American fiction must specialize, and, turning distracted from the superabundance of character, it must burrow far down in a soul or two." Howells offers the example of a deeply "psychological" Hawthorne, who "in the American environment . . . bent his vision inward." Subsequent American novelists have followed Hawthorne's example by subordinating the "practical concerns" to the "psychical": "The usual incidents of fiction have not, in the best American novelists, been the prime concern, but the subliminal effect of those incidents." (Again, the absence of a deeper discussion of James at this point seems a liability.) In contrast, character in the British novel is rooted firmly in social class: "the Englishman feels, thinks, and acts from his class, and when you name his class you measurably state him; after that you have rather to do with what he does than what he is. The result in fiction is a multiplicity of incident and a multitude of persons; and you have breadth rather than depth" (*HoF* 2:261–63).

American writers, Howells suggests, attain their psychological depth "because their characters are unconventionally circumstanced" and "are not in society. . . . American fiction is faithfuller to the average American conditions than if it dealt with people conventionally circumstanced and in society, for most of us are certainly not so, as most equally educated Englishmen certainly are so." Furthermore, there is something restless in the American spirit. Americans "like to travel, to journey and sojourn in far countries, and amidst the outer strangeness to get more intimately at our inner selves. If we are novelists, we like to take our characters abroad . . . and in the resulting isolation to penetrate the last recesses of their mystery, or at least learn that it is not penetrable." Howells offers *Daisy Miller* and *The Marble Faun* as evidence, then suggests that the English, because of their national character, cannot duplicate the effect. "If an English novelist does the same thing," he quips, "the result is not the same; the English environment is inalienable; the characters are continually frittering themselves away in superficial encounter on the native terms, at dinners, and luncheons, and teas, and what not, till there is nothing subliminal left in them." Howells quickly adds, "I could easily take up the foregoing postulate and show it untenably excessive. Nevertheless, I think it has some truth in it" (*HoF* 2:267–68).

In his conclusion, Howells labors to distinguish the American novel from its British counterpart. As such, this portion of *Heroines of Fiction* is part of a larger, ongoing effort made by Howells to assert for America its own tradition. And many of his points are essentially correct: speaking very generally, the American novel was increasingly preoccupied with characters at all levels of society, where the British novel remained preoccupied with the aristocracy. American authors had been increasingly drawn to the "psychological" studies of interiority (and would, in the coming years, become preoccupied with that idea). Properly developed, such a point might have secured Howells a reputation as a prophet of the oncoming high modernism. But, once again, Howells abandons the discussion rather hastily, leaving his thoughts on the American and British novels tantalizingly incomplete. He even cultivates an air of nonchalance: "It is indifferent to me, for the present inquiry, whether the American or the English effect is better" (*HoF* 2:266–67).

It is a rather half-hearted conclusion to what is ultimately an incomplete study of the Anglo-American novel. In its final chapters, the pro-realist agenda of *Heroines of Fiction* fades. Howells's undertreatment of the American novel undermines any sense of balance in the book, and he is unwilling to pursue his most provocative claims. Consequently, the authority of the text is seriously compromised. While the aim of *Heroines*—to indoctrinate the bourgeois readership of *Harper's Bazaar* to a pro-realist history of the Anglo-American novel—breaks exciting new ground for Howells as a critic, he leaves the mission half-realized.

Conclusion

Ultimately, the didactic focus of *Heroines of Fiction* proves a critical liability; perhaps due to his intended audience and his intended purpose, Howells restricts the depth and breadth of his criticism. He is primarily concerned with introducing his readers to the authors in question and exposing them to the work, by means of lengthy quotations from the novels. As we have seen, Howells does offer substantive literary criticism throughout *Heroines*, but these passages tend to be of a concise and focused nature, and Howells avoids the kind of lengthy consideration that a more explicitly critical approach would afford.

Despite these shortcomings, *Heroines* is an important work of scholarship. First, there are the authors he treats. Howells offers thoughtful reconsiderations of heavyweights such as Thackeray and Trollope, ultimately reconfirming opinions that date back to his earliest criticisms of these authors. In the chapters on Dickens and Hawthorne, Howells provocatively appropriates quintessentially romantic writers for his pro-realist agenda; in the case of Dickens, his observations in *Heroines* paved the way for an important 1902 essay. And, most importantly, *Heroines* offers Howells's lengthiest considerations of authors not previously considered in his criticism, such as Austen and Eliot.

Second, *Heroines* is important because of Howells's attempt to recast the history of the Anglo-American novel in realist terms. The assertion of a realist lineage dating back to Austen is a convincing case. Howells's appropriation of Dickens and Hawthorne is exciting and provocative, but it is also problematic; it is tempting to view his arguments as an anticipation of twentieth-century theories of hybridization and the blurring of aesthetic genres. But Howells's own lack of critical rigor undermines his claim. Despite its weaknesses, *Heroines* is an ambitious attempt that is in many regards both surprising and impressive; at the very least, it testifies to the fact that, in his final years, Howells remained intellectually curious and constantly sought new angles, new ideas, and new theories.

Howells also demonstrated his broad range as a critic throughout his twenty-year tenure in the "Editor's Easy Chair," where he adapted the tradition of the witty, urbane social essay to a remarkable range of topics—many of which fall outside the domain of literary criticism. Howells was not explicitly concerned (or particularly interested) in writing only "literary" criticism in his final years; consequently, one finds that his essays frequently cross boundaries, blending genres and shifting between modes of discourse with impressive flexibility.

The allegation that Howells's critical powers weakened in his final years is unfair and overly simplistic. Undeniably, there was a shift away from the polemical criticism of the "Editor's Study"; meanwhile, however, Howells became something of a cultural and social critic, examining, as we have seen earlier, a wide range of topics that included marketing, advertising, politics, social concerns, the function of art in society, and even the generation gap. If he wrote expressly literary criticism less frequently, it was by choice and not because of the winnowing of any talent. And if it can be asserted (for it often is) that James's criticism in the Prefaces to the New York Edition prefigures much of the New Critical method in the twentieth century, then it may be equally valid to claim that Howells, in his late criticism, prefigures the New Historical and culturally centered literary scholarship of the late twentieth century. Just as "literary studies" and the discipline of "English" have, in recent years, moved beyond strict distinctions between literary texts and other types of cultural texts, Howells deliberately blurred the lines between literary and social criticism. He experimented with the language of criticism itself, employing a range of voices, styles, and rhetorical forms such as dialogue in order to find new approaches to the topics that interested him. If the ends were not always successful—though they frequently were—the attempt demands to be recognized, if not praised.

10. On Native Grounds

Criticism and Correspondence III

After the death of his invalid wife, Elinor, in 1910, William Dean Howells and his surviving daughter, Mildred, traveled almost incessantly—to Bermuda, to Europe, up and down the coast of New England. Henry James, on occasion, had to post his letters to Howells in care of his friend's publisher, or to a mutual acquaintance. The more geographically stationary James expressed wonder at his friend's boundless energy. "I saw Howells in London early in the month," James wrote to Edmund Gosse in 1911, "girding himself for Spain even like another conquistador. His capacity to knock about excites my liveliest envy—but clearly it assuages a restlessness in him that makes it a sharp need: if it were all mere elderly fire & flame it would be *too* humiliating—to one's self. But his stoutness & toughness are yet wonderful enough."[1] Despite his peregrinations, Howells's heart and mind were never far from his native country. In his final years as a literary critic, he continued to address the question of America as a literary subject, wrestling to bridge the ever-widening gap between the nineteenth-century America that came of age during and after the Civil War and the very different twentieth-century America that found itself embroiled in the First World War. He saw exciting new opportunities for young writers; he continued to argue for a broad, democratic notion of American literature that embraced the country's ever-expanding range of voices; and he turned his eye occasionally to the past, assessing the work of prior generations.

1. James, *Selected Letters of Henry James to Edmund Gosse*, 255.

James, beset by poor health, traveled less frequently in his final years, though he would make two return trips to the United States: first, a lecture tour in 1904–1905, which also provided the material for *The American Scene;* and, second, to accompany his ailing brother William on his return from Europe in 1910–1911. As a literary critic, James continued to be fascinated by his native country, and he continued to probe the questions of where American literature was headed and what, in his opinion, the most promising subjects would be for the next generation of novelists.

The Question of the Opportunities

In 1898, *Literature,* a weekly supplement to the *London Times,* began publishing an "American Letter" intended to introduce English audiences to currents of thought in the American arts. Henry James begins his first contribution, entitled "The Question of the Opportunities" (March 26, 1898), by noting "the huge, homogenous and fast-growing population" of his native country, a "great common-schooled and newspapered democracy." Acknowledging "the variety of races and idioms" that constitute the ever-changing American public, James nevertheless deems the public "homogenous" because of "the great mill of the language, our predominant and triumphant English." And it is the question of idiomatic language that is first on his list of opportunities for American literature. "What forms, what colours, what sounds may the language take on or throw off in accommodating itself to such a growth of experience," he asks, "what life may it—and most of all may the literature that shall so copiously testify for it— reflect and embody?" (*LC* 1:651–52). The point is surprising not because it is appropriate, but because James asks it in 1898. Several American writers, perhaps most notably Twain and Howells, had been exploring the rich variety of the American language on the page for the better part of two decades.[2] James, who had deliberately avoided rendering colloquial southern American speech in *The Bostonians,* seems quite belated in recognizing this "opportunity."[3]

2. Of course, a variety of lesser-known African American authors had also employed black dialect in their fiction, including William Wells Brown in *Clotel, or The President's Daughter* (1853) and Frances E. W. Harper in *Iola Leroy, or Shadows Uplifted* (1892). For an excellent overview of the question of dialect and realist literature, see Nettels, *Language, Race, and Social Class,* 62–71.

3. Early in the first chapter of *The Bostonians,* James introduces Basil Ransom and notes that his protagonist "came, in fact, from Mississippi, and he spoke very perceptibly with the accent of that country. It is not in my power to reproduce by any combination of characters this charming dialect; but the initiated reader will have no difficulty in evoking the sound, which

Nevertheless, James correctly insists that the sheer size and magnitude of the rapidly expanding nation presents the writer with exciting new opportunities: "It is impossible not to entertain with patience and curiosity the presumption that life so colossal must break into expression at points of proportionate frequency. These places, these moments will be the chances." For James, this represents a kind of literary changing of the guard. New England, which for so long had dominated American literary culture, is of the past. "The American world of to-day is a world of combinations and proportions different from those amid which Emerson and Mrs. Stowe could reach right and left far enough to fill it," he simply notes (LC 1:653–54). For the author of *Hawthorne* and "Emerson"—an expatriate who labored throughout his career to distance himself from New England's literary culture—any expansion of America's literary horizons is an opportunity for celebration.

But James is most prescient when he notes that the role of business in American life is the prime opportunity for the novelist: "the typical American figure is above all that 'business man' whom the novelist and the dramatist have scarce yet seriously touched." Of even greater importance is

> the extraordinary, the unique relation in which [the businessman] for the most part stands to the life of his lawful, his immitigable womankind, the wives and daughters who float, who splash on the surface and ride the waves, his terrific link with civilization, his social substitutes and representatives, while, like a diver for shipwrecked treasure, he gasps in the depths and breathes through an air-tube.
>
> This relation, even taken alone, contains elements that strike me as only yearning for their interpreter—elements, moreover, that would present the further merit of melting into the huge neighboring province of the special situation of women in an order of things where to be a woman at all—certainly to be a young one—constitutes in itself a social position.

James concludes by emphasizing that "the American 'business man' remains, thanks to the length and strength of the wires that move him, *the* magnificent theme *en disponibilité*." The added prospect of exploring the rapidly evolving state of fin de siècle gender relations is a "great double lustre" (LC 1:655–56).

---

is to be associated in the present instance with nothing vulgar or vain. . . . [T]he reader who likes a complete image, who desires to read with the senses as well as with the reason, is entreated not to forget that he prolonged his consonants and swallowed his vowels, that he was guilty of elisions and interpolations which were equally unexpected, and that his discourse was pervaded by something sultry and vast, something almost African in its rich, basking tone, something that suggested the teeming expanse of the cotton-field" (*Novels, 1881–1886*, 804).

"The Question of the Opportunities" is an important essay. With his call for close attention to the American businessman, James all but predicts the works of Dreiser, Dos Passos, and Sinclair Lewis—to say nothing of Adam Verver in *The Golden Bowl*. In so doing, he takes a page from Howells, who had been exploring various aspects of American business in his fiction for the better part of two decades. Likewise, James's recognition of the ripe opportunities inherent in the changing nature of gender relations in America is a prescient observation. In these respects, James proves himself to be, as both a writer and a social commentator, a keen observer of American life.

But his belated call for attention to colloquial American language aptly demonstrates that he was slow to recognize other opportunities long since capitalized upon by the important writers of his generation. One notes with considerable interest, for example, that James never reviewed any of Mark Twain's work—let alone *Adventures of Huckleberry Finn*—and scarcely even mentions his fellow American in his voluminous personal correspondence.[4] Perhaps most telling on this point, however, is James's lukewarm praise of dialect in fiction in his final "American Letter" (July 9, 1898). Observing that "Nothing is more striking, in fact, than the invasive part played by the element of dialect in the subject-matter of the American fiction of the day," he somewhat tentatively suggests that "the needful thing is first to make sure of it, observe and follow it; it may still have unsuspected pearls—for it occasionally deals in these trophies to cast at our feet" (*LC* 1:699). The passage suggests that James remained, at best, uneasy with the prospects of an increasingly local American literature and its reliance on "invasive" dialect.

Such hesitation would not last long; James is anything but ambiguous on the topic of dialect in the Preface to *Daisy Miller*. Here, in the course of meditating on his famous theme of the "international American," James adopts the pose of the interested reader (or perhaps the interviewer) and asks himself why he did not write more fiction set in the United States; specifically, he questions why he did not, like so many other authors, examine the "wild garden of 'unconventional' life" (that is, the lower classes of society, which, up to then, had not been the focus of the novel) and its myriad tongues:

> Why had n't so quickened a vision of the great neglected native quarry *at large* more troubled my dreams, instead of leaving my imagination on the whole so resigned? Well, with many reasons I could count over, there was

---

4. One related point of interest. Despite James's voluminous output as a literary critic and review of contemporary fiction, the absence of minority authors from his list of subjects perhaps speaks for itself. In contrast, Howells regularly championed minority authors, including Paul Laurence Dunbar, Charles W. Chesnutt, and Abraham Cahan.

one that exhaustively covered the ground and all completely answered the question: the reflexion, namely, that the common sign of the productions "unconventionally" prompted (and this positively without exception) was nothing less than the birthmark of Dialect.

James scoffs at "the riot of the vulgar tongue" with its "thick breath" and "ugly snarl." The chance to render American dialect was an opportunity gladly given up; while "thousands of celebrated productions raised their monument . . . to the bastard vernacular," James held back without a second thought. "The monument was there, if one would," he concludes, "but was one to regret one's own failure to have contributed a stone? Perish, and all ignobly, the thought!" (*LC* 2:1279–80). This blunt assertion stands as James's final thought on the topic of dialect in American fiction.

Yet James did celebrate regional American literature in his second "American Letter" (April 9, 1898) as a means, it would seem, to offset a different source of unease. James predicts a certain "movement" in the "international" American novel: "As the novel in America multiplies, it will seek more room, I seem to foresee, by coming for inspiration to Europe; reversing in this manner, on another plane, oddly enough, a great historical fact." James, however, suggests it would be best for the "Western imagination" to stay home:

> This imagination will find for a long time, to my sense—it will find doubtless always—its most interesting business in staying where it has grown; but if there is to be a great deal of it, it must obviously follow the fashion of other matters, seek all adventures and take all chances. Fiction as yet in the United States strikes me, none the less, as most curious when most confined and most local; this is so much the case that when it is even abjectly passive to surrounding conditions I find it capable of yielding an interest that almost makes me dread undue enlargement.

As an example, James offers "a case of saturation so precious as to have almost the value of genius." Hamlin Garland, "the soaked sponge of Wisconsin," demonstrates that "Saturation and talent are, of course, compatible, talent being really but one's own sense and use of one's saturation." James concludes: "The point I for the moment make is simply that in the American air I am nervous, in general, lest talent should wish to 'sail for Europe.' Let me now, indeed, recognize that it by no means inveterately does. Even so great and active a faculty as that of the author of 'The Rise of Silas Lapham' has suffered him to remain, after all, very prosperously at home. On the day Miss Mary Wilkins should 'sail' I would positively have detectives versed in the practice of extradition posted at Liverpool" (*LC* 1:657–58). If

James sounds playful and light here, he is also by his own admission "nervous" and, perhaps, defensive. In urging American authors to stay home, he conveniently ignores his own example, shifting attention to a prosperous (and domestic) Howells. Most curiously, James celebrates the American literary landscape that he had denigrated in *Hawthorne* and "Emerson." To be fair, much had changed in America between 1879 and 1898, but one senses a thinly veiled territoriality throughout the opening section of the April 9 letter. James's American novels, most notably *The Bostonians,* had failed to win a large audience. His literary reputation in 1898, such as it was, rested on "international" works such as *Daisy Miller* and *The Portrait of a Lady.* He would, of course, revisit the theme in all three of his final novels: *The Ambassadors, The Wings of the Dove,* and *The Golden Bowl.* Simply put, James wanted a clear field for his own work, and one senses as much in his urging the Garlands, the Howellses, and the Wilkins-Freemans to stay home.

An Opportunity for American Fiction

On reading "The Question of the Opportunities," Howells wrote James to inform him that "We all greatly liked your first letter (second unseen) in *Literature;* Mrs. Howells copied, for the joy of having it in holograph, apparently, the passage about the 'unmitigable womenkind,' [*sic*] which she thinks supreme, and has already used effectively in putting me to shame for an attempted letter of my own for the same place" (*LFL,* 307; *HSL* 4:171). Howells may well have kept James's letter in mind when he turned his attention to Thorstein Veblen's *The Theory of the Leisure Class,* which he noted in an 1899 essay entitled "An Opportunity for American Fiction."

For the reader familiar with Howells's more socially oriented thought and criticism in the late 1880s and the 1890s, the enthusiasm he shows for Veblen's class analysis comes as little surprise. Howells recognizes the opportunities this new leisure class of "idlers" presents to the artist. "The workers and the idlers of America are essentially the same as the workers and idlers of occidental civilisation everywhere," he notes, "but there is a novelty in their environment peculiarly piquant to the imagination" (*SLC* 3:14). He sees great promise in studying the growing rift between America's leisure class and its working class. For example, in the course of his "evolution," the American aristocrat necessarily

> discovers that he is less and less in his own country, that he is living in a provisional exile, and that his true home is in monarchical conditions, where his future establishes itself often without his willing it, and sometimes

against his willing it. The American life is the life of labor, and he is now of
the life of leisure, or if he is not, his wife is, his daughters and his sons are.
The logic of their existence, which they cannot struggle against, and on
which all the fatuous invective of pseudo public spirit launches itself effect-
lessly, is intermarriage with the European aristocracies, and residence
abroad. Short of this there is no rest, and can be none for the American
leisure class. This may not be its ideal, but it is its destiny.

It is far the most dramatic social fact of our time, and if some man of creative imagination were to seize upon it, he would find in it the material of
that great American novel which after so much travail has not yet seen the
light. It is, above all our other facts, synthetic; it sums up and includes in itself the whole American story: the relentless will, the tireless force, the
vague ideal, the inexorable destiny, the often bewildered acquiescence.
(*SLC* 3:15)

Lamentably, Howells does not expand his thumbnail narrative of American development here. Nineteenth-century America's "relentless will" and
"tireless force" may be relatively easy concepts to grasp, but what, pray tell,
is the "inexorable destiny" of the United States—let alone its leisure class?
And in what ways had the nation settled into an "often bewildered acquiescence"? If Howells does not (or cannot) answer these questions, he suggests
that a novelist could.

To an extent, that novelist would be working with certain known quanti-
ties. Howells holds that the American aristocracy differs little in principle
from the older European patriciate: "It would be hard, in fact, to draw the
line between our leisure class and any aristocracy in the traits of piety, pre-
dacity, courage, prowess, charity, luxury, conservatism, authority, and the
other virtues and vices which have characterised the patricians in all times."
What is different, he notes, is that "hitherto our leisure class has had no political standing." But, Howells believes, that is changing: "The present
proof is in the fact that the industrial classes, with all the means of power in
their hands, are really powerless in any contest with a group of rich men; it
is almost impossible for the people to balk the purpose of such a group; to
undo what money has done has been so impossible, with all the apparatus of
the elections, the legislatures, the courts, that there is hardly yet an instance
of the kind in our history" (*SLC* 3:16). Throughout this essay on Veblen,
Howells maintains a cool, analytic tone. The emergence of an American patriciate comes as no great surprise to him; indeed, to any observer of postbellum America, the rapid rise of industry and the profusion of new wealth
were well understood—even marveled at. Howells himself had, for instance,
explored various aspects of these topics in *The Rise of Silas Lapham, Annie
Kilburn,* and *A Hazard of New Fortunes.* Howells's keen eye for social and
class difference is in sharp evidence throughout the Veblen essay, but, rather

interestingly, his judgmental tone is not. Despite bluntly asserting that "The American life is the life of labor" and rather grimly noting that the workers "are really powerless in any contest with a group of rich men," Howells is not interested in criticizing the leisure class on moral or ethical grounds; rather, he takes their existence as a given and proceeds to mull over the resulting possibilities for the novelist: "This is the most dramatic moment, the most psychological moment which has ever offered itself to fiction; this is the supreme opportunity of the American novelist. . . . A democracy, the proudest, the most sincere, the most ardent that history has ever known, has evolved here a leisure class which has all the distinguishing traits of a patriciate, and which by the chemistry of intermarriage with European aristocracies is rapidly acquiring antiquity. Is not this a phenomenon worthy of the highest fiction?" (*SLC* 3:16–17). Howells, in anticipating the work of authors such as Edith Wharton and F. Scott Fitzgerald, sounds positively prescient throughout the essay on Veblen. But he also sounds uncharacteristically detached. There are no judgments, no exhortations, no appeals to Christian humanism. He treats the leisure class purely on aesthetic grounds and, in so doing, sounds distinctly Jamesian.

In a sense, then, both James and Howells sound a bit like the other in their respective essays on the opportunities for American fiction at the turn of the century. With his newfound interest in colloquial American language, James treads a path long ago broken by Howells. The same might be said for James's call for attention to the American businessman, though he is correct to point to the exciting nexus of gender relations at the turn of the century, with the "New Woman" running head-on into a whole new generation of business tycoons. Howells's observation of America's leisure class is less a celebration of Veblen's influential work and more a call to arms for the next generation of American novelists. Less concerned, in this instance, with social equality or Christian ethics, Howells pleads his case almost purely on aesthetic grounds—a quintessentially Jamesian approach. And Howells's Jamesian echoes were by no means infrequent in his final years.

Novel-Writing and Novel-Reading

Full of personal anecdotes, wit, and warmth, "Novel-Writing and Novel-Reading" is one of Howells's more entertaining essays on the familiar topic of the novel. This comes as no surprise, given that the essay was composed for his lucrative 1899 lecture tour of the American Midwest.[5] But the essay

---

5. Despite finding success with his audiences, Howells's lecture tour proved to be quite a trial. Howells scheduled twenty-five appearances over a ten-week period, but he opted to ex-

is noteworthy for other reasons. First, it reminds us that Howells, long after he had surrendered his position on the front line of the "Realism War," still fervently held to certain core tenets of his aesthetic beliefs. William M. Gibson has gone so far as to argue that the essay is "the fullest, most detailed, most penetrating analysis of the novelist's craft that Howells ever wrote."[6] But Howells does not merely rehash old arguments. The essay is also noteworthy because, with its extended discussions of genre, form, the organic theory of composition, and Howells's reflections on his own creative process, it is Howells's most Jamesian essay. As such, it offers testament to the ongoing influence of James on Howells late in his career.

"Novel-Writing and Novel-Reading" begins with a lucid restatement and reconfirmation of several core tenets of Howells's realist aesthetic. For example, verisimilitude, or "truth to human experience" in fiction, remains "the prime test of a novel. If I do not find that it is like life, then it does not exist for me as art; it is ugly, it is ludicrous, it is impossible." This is a familiar—and typically blunt—Howellsian axiom. But he quickly qualifies "human experience" as "so manifold and so recondite . . . that no scheme can be too remote, too airy for the test. It is a well ascertained fact concerning the imagination that it can work only with the stuff of experience. It can absolutely create nothing; it can only compose" (*SLC* 3:216–17). The language here clearly echoes James's "The Art of Fiction" and its pronouncement that "experience is never limited, and it is never complete" (*LC* 1:52). This pattern—a restatement of a familiar Howellsian tenet modified in light of a Jamesian principle—is seen frequently throughout "Novel-Writing."

For example, Howells certainly borrows a page from James when he discusses his organic theory of composition. "[Each] novel has a law of its own," writes Howells, "which it seems to create for itself. Almost from the beginning it has its peculiar temperament and quality, and if you happen to be writing that novel you feel that you must respect its law. You, who are master of the whole affair, cannot violate its law without taking its life. . . . No more can you change the nature of any character in it without spoiling it." Likewise, the experience of writing each story is unique: "I must strike a new gait, I must get a new pace for every new story. I could issue master from the last, but I must begin prentice with the next." Content and form are also organic: "The events of a real novel grow slowly and necessarily out

ercise a bail-out clause after twenty appearances, citing physical and mental fatigue. For more on the 1899 lecture tour, see Crowley, *Dean of American Letters,* 50–54; Robert Rowlette, "In 'The Silken Arms of the Aristocracy': William Dean Howells's Lecture in Indianapolis, 1899"; Rowlette, "William D. Howells' 1899 Midwest Lecture Tour"; and Thomas Wortham, "W. D. Howells' 1899 Midwest Lecture Tour: What the Letters Tell."

6. William M. Gibson and Leon Edel, eds., *Howells and James: A Double Billing,* 7.

of the development of its characters, and the author cannot fully forecast these" (*SLC* 3:223–24).

The Jamesian quality of "Novel-Writing" reaches its peak when Howells announces that "The old superstition of a dramatic situation as the supreme representation of life must be discarded, and the novelist must endeavor to give exactly the effect of life" (*SLC* 3:228). The "effect" or "sense" of life is a patently Jamesian quality, going back at least as far as "The Art of Fiction," when James called for a "direct personal impression" of experience in the novel and went on to define experience as "The power to guess the unseen from the seen, to trace the implication of things, to judge the whole piece by the pattern, the condition of feeling life in general so completely that you are well on your way to knowing any particular corner of it" (*LC* 1:53). But, in fact, James's praise for the "effect" of a novel goes back to his earliest literary criticism. In his 1875 overview of Balzac, for instance, James praised the "irresistible force" of Balzac's prose. James singled out Balzac's characters, noting a "certain heroic pressure that drives them home to our credence—a contagious illusion on the author's own part. . . . [T]hey seem to proceed from a sort of creative infinite and they help each other to be believed in. . . . This is altogether the most valuable element in Balzac's novels" (*LC* 2:53). For Howells, in "Novel-Writing," to champion the "effect of life" over the mere portrayal of "a dramatic situation" was to reference one of the oldest and most deeply rooted aesthetic tenets held by James.[7]

A third example of the Jamesian influence on "Novel-Writing" concerns Howells's discussion of a novel's form, which he defines as the "outward shape of the inward life of the novel." Howells differentiates between the "autobiographical, the biographical and the historical" novel. Initially, Howells uses each term to address the question of grammatical point of view. In this regard, his divisions are sensible: the autobiographical is the novel written in the first person; the biographical is the novel written in the third-person limited or third-person intimate (in which a third-person narrator is limited to focalizing the thoughts and perceptions of a single character); and the "historical form" is the novel written in the third-person omniscient. Howells next distinguishes the "historical form" from the "historical novel." The term "form" becomes a stand-in for a grammatical point of view, while "historical novel" means "any sort of novel whose material is treated as if it were real history" and in which "the novelist supposes himself to be narrating a series of events, indefinite in compass, and known to him from the original

---

7. Interestingly, Howells is quite candid in assessing his own inability to achieve the aesthetic ideal of rendering the "effect of life" in fiction: "I never can do it, for I was bred in a false school whose trammels I have never been quite able to burst; but the novelist who begins where I leave off, will yet write the novel which has been my ideal" (*SLC* 3:228).

documents" much in the manner of the historian. The difference is that the historian "has got the facts from some one who witnessed them" whereas "the novelist employing the historical form has no proof of them" and "gives his word alone for them." Consequently, the historical form "involves a thousand contradictions, impossibilities" and "There is no point where it cannot be convicted of the most grotesque absurdity" (*SLC* 3:229–30).

This passage constitutes a weakness in "Novel-Writing" for two reasons. First, Howells fails to distinguish clearly between grammatical point of view ("historical form") and the novel as an interaction with the discipline of history (the "historical novel"). Rather, he uses "form" and "novel" interchangeably, thereby clouding the issue unnecessarily. The second and larger problem is with the nature of the contrast Howells constructs; to pit the historian (as an objective recorder of facts) against the creative writer (as a patent fabricator of illusory "facts") is to belabor the obvious. At best, Howells's conclusion—"The historical form, though it involves every contradiction, every impossibility, is the only form which can fully represent any passage of life in its inner and outer entirety" (*SLC* 3:231)—seems an implicit request for the reader to overlook the essential implausibility of the historical novel and to grant the artist his donnée. As such, Howells appears to be echoing yet another key point from James's "Art of Fiction," albeit rather murkily.[8]

While Howells's debt to James in "Novel-Writing" is profound, one hastens to emphasize that the essay does not merely parrot James. In fact, the personal, confidential tone of Howells's piece prefigures the confidential tone of the Prefaces to the New York Edition (and the autobiographies) that James would shortly begin to write. And on at least one major point, Howells remains steadfastly opposed to his friend. Howells clearly distinguishes between three fictional genres: the novel, which is patently realist; the romance, which depicts the allegorical and the ideal; and the "romanticistic," or the sentimental novel (*SLC* 3:218–19). The question of genre had, of course, surfaced previously in the criticism of both Howells and James. The latter had, in "The Art of Fiction," essentially dismissed the question, suggesting that the "clumsy separations" of genre "appear to me to have been made by critics and readers for their own convenience" (*LC* 1:55)—an opinion James did not revise publicly until the 1907 Preface to *The American*. Howells, however, had insisted on recognizing the different genres from as early as 1865. And in an 1880 review of James's *Hawthorne*, Howells

---

8. It is also possible that Howells's strategy of contrasting the historian and the fiction writer is also borrowed from "The Art of Fiction." James had likened the novel writer to the historian in an early portion of his essay (*LC* 1:46–47), whereby he sought to purchase the authority of the established liberal arts for fiction.

made special note of James's failure to distinguish the romance from the realist novel (*SLC* 1:293). "Novel-Writing" contains Howells's lengthiest and most complete discussion of the question of genre.

The Question of Poe

Howells's most surprising Jamesian echo occurred in a 1909 overview of Edgar Allan Poe. As a whole, the essay constitutes a somewhat tentative dismissal. While clearly unsatisfied with the European assessment of Poe's "genius," Howells cannot bring himself to write the man off completely: "I find, indeed, that as a poet, I care more or less for Poe, but as a novelist, large or little, I care scarcely at all. I wish the reader, however, to accept this saying provisionally, for there are possibilities that before I get through here I may take it back, or give it again in modified form." Howells attempts to clarify his position. "Poe is subtle," he writes, "but he is not delicate, he is mysterious, but he is not mystical." To be fair, Howells suggests, one must position Poe against the literary fashion of the day; he was, to an extent, of his times. But so was Hawthorne, whose "truly psychological studies" are of far higher rank. Irving, too, supercedes the best of Poe. "The simple fact is that Poe was as lacking in imagination as he was in sincerity," Howells finally announces, "and that he vainly endeavored to supply his lack with fancy and with science." While praising Poe's "inexhaustible fertility" and "infinite invention," Howells ultimately finds "the curse of unreality is on all his careful plausibility." Simply put, Howells cannot grant Poe his psychological intensity; it always feels forced and strained (*SLC* 3:249–51).

But when Howells tries to temper his judgment, his essay takes a most curious turn. If Poe falls short of genius, he reasons, it is in part because of the literary environment from which he emerged:

> He wrote in an America still abjectly provincial, for a public crudely hungry, and eager for any thing that would fill its famine, but stingy and ungrateful. To live by literature in his time a man must also die by it, and he must suffer the greater torment if he were as ill-starred and ill-conditioned as Poe was in being born to poverty and bred to affluence and then cast off to destitution; if he were at times wildly a drunkard; if he were insanely made up of weakness, pride, viciousness, cruelty and tenderness. What a man like that must have suffered during the eighteen-forties in a poor little vainglorious, self-distrustful country such as this then was! What might he not have been in an older and greater community, with opportunity assured him, unattended by the fear of want! (*SLC* 3:251)

The passage, which could have come straight from James's *Hawthorne* or "Emerson," is almost painfully derivative. For example, the comment regarding what Poe might have accomplished in "an older and greater community" mimics *Hawthorne* in several respects. First, it echoes James's statement that "it takes a great deal of history" and "a complex social machinery to set a writer in motion." Second, it calls to mind James's famous list of what America lacks (*LC* 1:320, 351–52). Finally, the tone of Howells's passage, with its depiction of a provincial and "crudely hungry" public, mirrors the condescending dismissal of antebellum New England that pervades *Hawthorne*. While Howells was frequently at odds with America on social, economic, and political terms, I can think of no other single piece of writing in which he repudiates America as a literary subject in such Jamesian parlance; indeed, he spent most of his career defending his country and its potential as a subject. Consequently, this passage exists as a singular anomaly in an otherwise remarkably consistent area of Howells's critical stances.[9]

Native Grounds

Howells's 1901 review of Barrett Wendell's *A Literary History of America* offers a more balanced opinion of America as a literary subject and, on the whole, is more representative of his final opinion on the topic. Howells's essay is less a survey of American literature than a close reading and sharply worded dismissal of Wendell's book. Howells begins by objecting to Wendell's tone of "superiority" regarding his primary subject, the legacy of literary New England. It is clear to Howells that Brahmins such as Wendell have "outlived the literary primacy of Boston." Echoing James in "The Question of the Opportunities," Howells argues that "A little while ago . . . the air was full of an intellectual life there, which has now gone out of it, or has taken other than literary forms." In the quiet following the passing of the great literary figures of Boston, "the survivor is naturally tempted to question their greatness." It is a time when "the dead are no longer felt as contemporaries, and are not yet established in the influence of classics. . . . Elsewhere, they are still measurably Emerson and Longfellow, Whittier and Holmes and Lowell; but on their native ground, where they lately walked with other men, and the other men are still walking and they not, the other men can hardly fail to ask themselves whether they were not unduly op-

---

9. Howells is, however, consistent in his dismissal of Poe's work. In 1895, Howells had berated Poe for his "bitter, and cruel, and narrow-minded criticisms" of the authors of his day, finally dismissing such "barbarities" as "worthless" (*My Literary Passions,* 119–20).

pressed by a sense of the vanished grandeur" (*SLC* 3:51). Howells paints
Wendell as a second-tier intellectual, incapable of sustaining the "grandeur"
of a literary New England whose heyday is over. The more subtle point is
also duly noted: America's literary center—if there is one in 1901—is elsewhere.

Howells had previously addressed this question in an 1898 essay entitled
"American Literary Centres." Here, Howells argues convincingly for a decentralized American literature and, characteristically, lists a generous number of artists from every corner of the United States. Howells's interest in
and promotion of regional American writing remained steadfast throughout
his later years. In the 1912 essay "The Future of the American Novel,"
Howells argues that "there can be no national American fiction, but only
provincial, only parochial fictions." It is the local, Howells argues, that is to
be treasured: "In fiction, first the provincial, then the national, then the universal; but the parochial is better and more to be desired than either of the
others."[10]

In his review of Wendell's *Literary History,* Howells emphasizes his point
regarding a decentralized American literature, taking the professor to task
for insinuating that Howells, who took over the *Atlantic* from James T.
Fields, deliberately moved the editorial focus of the magazine away from
Cambridge:

> It is ludicrously mistaken to suppose that after Fields left the magazine, it
> ceased to be in sympathy with Harvard. Fields had no special affinity with
> Harvard, and the young Harvard men—it is sufficient to name Mr. John
> Fiske alone—began writing for his successor in greater number than be-
> fore, in proportion to their fitness or their willingness; if there was any
> change it was because Harvard was becoming less literary, and the country
> at large more literary. The good things began to come from the West and
> the South and the Middle States, and the editors took the good things
> wherever they came from. (*SLC* 3:58–59)

As Howells so forcefully suggests throughout this essay, Wendell fails to
grasp the breadth and variety of American literature. While praising certain
aspects of Wendell's appreciation for Bryant, Poe, Longfellow, Twain, and
many others, Howells takes pains to note both the authors and the geographical regions Wendell has overlooked: Bret Harte and James Whitcomb
Riley in the West; Joel Chandler and George Washington Cable in the South;
and, last but not least, "that tendency in the North and East which, widening

10. Howells, "American Literary Centres," in *Literature and Life,* 173–86; Howells, "The
Future of the American Novel," *Criticism and Fiction and Other Essays,* 347.

beyond the trend of the old New England endeavor for ideal excellence, resulted in the distinction of Mr. Henry James's work." (There is no mention
of the fact that Wendell has overlooked Howells, too.) Howells concludes:
Wendell's "subject is not, as I have represented, American literature, but
that episode of our literary history which he calls the New England Renaissance" (*SLC* 3:57, 63).

For Howells, Wendell represents an anachronistic Old School that sees
little work of interest outside of a New England whose flower has so obviously faded. "Yet," notes Howells,

> even as a study of the New England episode of American literature, the
> work is not sympathetic. It is prevailingly antipathetic, with moments of
> kindness, and still rarer and more unexpected moments of cordial respect
> and admiration. Wherever Professor Wendell scents democracy or per-
> ceives the disposition to value human nature for itself and independently of
> the social accidents, he turns cold, and his intellectual tradition gets the
> better of his nature, which seems sunny and light and friendly. Something,
> then, like a patrician view of the subject results. (*SLC* 3:59)[11]

One senses in this passage what Howells values most about American literature: its democratic openness, its compassion and warmth, its breadth
and variety. Indirectly, then, Howells, by roundly criticizing Wendell, celebrates the broad scope of American literature.

In parting, Howells makes one final observation on Wendell's work in regards to the relationship between American and English literature. Howells
faults Wendell for contrasting the two and then "minifying our performance
accordingly." But, Howells contends, American literature is not the equal to
English literature; it is not even a close sibling. The proper relation is that
American literature is the "daughter or the granddaughter of that literature,
or, in terms less flowery, it is a condition of English literature; and it is not
interesting in its equality or likeness to the other conditions, but in its inequality or unlikeness. It has differenced itself from the mother or grand-
mother literature involuntarily, so far as it has differenced itself valuably, and
it is an error either in friend or foe to put it in the attitude of rivalry." If
Howells feels American literature "would fail in that rivalry," he also feels
English literature "would show itself inferior where it was like American literature" (*SLC* 3:62). In essence, Howells argues for a distinct and individual American literary tradition. American and English literatures may have a

---

11. In full Jamesian mode, Howells notes elsewhere that "Wendell's radical disqualification
for his work seems the absence of sympathy with his subject" (*SLC* 3:53).

common ancestry, but each has evolved to the point of being wholly different species.

This marks something of a reversal for Howells on the issue of a national American literature; in the November 1891 "Editor's Study," he had defined Americans as

> the old, well-known Anglo-Saxon race, affected and modified by the infusion of other strains, but not essentially changed by these, and not very different from the English at home except in their political environment, and the vastness of the scale of their development. Their literature so far as they have produced any is American-English literature, just as the English literature is English-European, and it is absurd to ask them to have a literature wholly their own as to ask them to have a language wholly their own. (*SLC* 2:189)

Howells's assertion of a distinct American literature in the 1901 essay on Wendell marks an important development in his thinking on the issue. Howells was aware of the constantly changing society and culture around him; he sought and promoted new opportunities for expression. Howells was impatient with Wendell's stale, patrician view of American letters. In his attacks on Wendell's shortcomings, Howells indirectly points to his own more catholic tastes, a view of American literature that surveys the entire nation and celebrates its diversity and eclecticism. It is a point amply borne out when one surveys just a handful of the American writers Howells promoted in his final years: Stephen Crane, Frank Norris, Charles W. Chesnutt, Abraham Cahan, Paul Laurence Dunbar, and Yiddish poet Morris Rosenfeld.

The Lincoln of Our Literature

Interestingly, Howells himself had been offering his own reflections on literary Boston and the New England Renaissance in a series of papers dating back to 1894. In 1900 these reflections were collected in *Literary Friends and Acquaintance: A Personal Retrospect of American Authorship*. Strictly speaking, the book is not literary criticism but rather literary memoir. The thoughts, reflections, and observations Howells offers are biographical and incidental, rather than rigorously critical and scholarly. Yet the work offers a fascinating insight into how Howells, then in his sixties, looked back on his own youth and literary coming of age amid the figures of the New England Renaissance, nearly all of whom he had known personally. Maintaining a dutiful tone of reverence and admiration for his literary forebears, Howells consistently paints them as generous, affable men who "did not forbid approach" but rather treated all newcomers fairly and "by the rules that govern us with common men." At nearly every turn, Howells praises the American authors for their celebration of domestic virtues and democratic humanism: Howells notes Hawthorne's despite of "the damned shadow . . . of Europe"; he proudly recalls the antislavery stances of Emerson, Thoreau, and George William Curtis; and, despite noting the crudity of his verse, celebrates Whitman as "a sweet and true soul" possessed of "a spiritual dignity." In contrast, the Bohemians in New York are written off as "a sickly colony, transplanted from the mother asphalt of Paris" that failed to produce any substantial work, Howells implies, because it was not patently American in origin. In short, *Literary Friends and Acquaintance* is a celebration of the domestic tradition as Howells defines it, rich in the humanistic, democratic ideals of the common man. It is a legacy he seems keen to share with his fellow Americans.[12]

Yet Howells does offer gentle criticism amid the copious praise. He notes the "intense ethicism" of the writers of the New England Renaissance, who "helplessly pointed the moral in all they did." In their insistent moralizing they were, Howells argues, too much a product of their Puritan past. Furthermore, "It was in poetry and in romance that they excelled; in the novel [that is, realism], so far as they attempted it, they failed. . . . New England yet lacks her novelist, because it was her instinct and her conscience in fiction to be true to an ideal of life rather than to life itself." Howells also gently critiques the style of criticism employed by literary Boston. E. P. Whipple is established, rhetorically, as the case in point: "I doubt if he had any theory of criticism except to find out what was good in an author and praise it; and he rather blamed what was ethically bad than what was aesthetically bad. In this he was strictly of New England, and he was of New England in a certain general intelligence." In the lower-order figure of Whipple, Howells quietly makes a formidable point: for the reader familiar with Howells's opinions on the English criticism of the day—chided for its a priori imposition of moral standards in deference to a Jamesian appreciation of the work on its own formal terms—this passage seems transparent enough.[13]

Finally, at selected points Howells raises the issue of class divisions. This is perhaps most palpably evident when he relates how James Fields revealed to Howells that he had been hired on at the *Atlantic,* in part, because of his background as a printer's apprentice: "the qualification I had as practical

12. Howells, *Literary Friends and Acquaintance,* 32–33, 49, 53–56, 93–94, 67, 62.
13. Ibid., 101–2, 109. On a related note, see Howells's critique of the American heirs to the English style of literary criticism in the June 1887 "Editor's Study" (*SLC* 2:51–56).

printer for the work was most valued, if not the most valued, and that as proof-reader I was expected to make it avail on the side of economy." Howells quietly concludes: "Somewhere in life's feast the course of humble-pie must always come in; and if I did not wholly relish this bit of it, I dare say it was good for me, and I digested it perfectly." This awareness of class differences is, perhaps, obliquely suggested later in the memoir, when Howells notes that as a "young and unknown [author] making my way," he "had to suffer some of the penalties of these disadvantages." Furthermore, literary Boston could be insular: "The life of the place had its lateral limitations," he notes, and "sometimes its lights failed to detect excellent things that lay beyond it." Yet these minor criticisms are couched in what is otherwise a warm, loving remembrance of a generation of literary heavyweights who embraced Howells and, he repeatedly points out, afforded him the opportunity to become the author he is today.[14]

The 1900 edition of *Literary Friends and Acquaintance* ended there, in Cambridge, where it had begun. But in 1910 Howells issued a revised edition that included essays on Bret Harte and Mark Twain. These added chapters alter the scope of the history in profound ways. Like the rest of *Literary Friends and Acquaintance*, "My Mark Twain"—itself a book-length study of a dear, late friend—is written in the familiar, biographical style of the literary memoir.[15] Howells clearly and cogently articulates several signal aspects of Twain's work. First among these is his language itself, so patently American and distinguished by "the Southwestern, the Lincolnian, the Elizabethan breadth of parlance, which I suppose one ought not to call coarse without calling one's self prudish." Twain "used English in all its alien derivations as if it were native to his own air, as if it had come up out of American, out of Missourian ground." Howells proudly announces Twain's staunch hatred of slavery and Southern gentility: "No man more perfectly sensed, and more entirely abhorred, slavery, and no one has ever poured such scorn upon the second-hand, Walter-Scotticised, pseudo-chivalry of the Southern ideal." The point is well taken; like Emerson, Thoreau, and Curtis, Twain stands with the literati as a passionate and democratic humanist. Indeed, in the famous closing sentence of the memoir, Howells ultimately promotes Twain over and above the literati: "Emerson, Longfellow, Lowell, Holmes—I knew them all and all the rest of our sages, poets, seers, critics, humorists; they were like one another and

14. Howells, *Literary Friends and Acquaintance*, 97, 240–41.
15. "My Mark Twain" was first published as "My Memories of Mark Twain" in *Harper's Monthly* 121 (1910): 165–78. The essay was reprinted in book form both in *My Mark Twain: Reminiscences and Criticisms* (1910) and in the 1910 edition of *Literary Friends and Acquaintance*.

like other literary men; but Clemens was sole, incomparable, the Lincoln of our literature."[16]

Yet, prior to that memorable conclusion, Howells has carefully noted—not without humor—both how Twain failed to embrace literary Cambridge on its own terms (witness the Whittier birthday speech) and how literary Cambridge could not immediately embrace Twain: "I do not think Longfellow made much of him, and Lowell made less. He stopped as if with the long Semitic curve of Clemens's nose, which in the indulgence of his passion for finding every one more or less a Jew he pronounced unmistakably racial." The comment is noteworthy not only for its blunt acknowledgement of the anti-Semitism that pervaded some quarters of Cambridge, but because it is the second time Howells mentions this fault in Lowell. In the chapter on Bret Harte, which immediately precedes "My Mark Twain," Howells had noted that Lowell "sumptuously surfeited his passion of finding everybody more or less a Jew by finding that Harte was at least half a Jew on his father's side; he had long contended for the Hebraicism of his name." This, Howells suggests, is part of the reason why Bret Harte never truly fit in in Cambridge. (There were other reasons, Howells acknowledges, not the least of which were Harte's irreverence and patently Western mind-set.) Again, Howells does not belabor the point, but his savvy word choice and the repetition of the fault helps to clarify one of the "lateral limitations" Howells had obliquely hinted at in 1900.[17]

Howells's eloquent praise for his late friend in "My Mark Twain" stands as a benchmark of American literary criticism, and it remains an important text in early Twain studies. But in the context of the 1910 edition of *Literary Friends and Acquaintance* it, along with the chapter on Bret Harte, plays a subversive role in reconfiguring and expanding American literary history. Like Howells himself, who maintained lifelong intimate friendships with both Twain and Henry James, *Literary Friends and Acquaintance* negotiates a middle stance between the patrician tradition of the New England Renaissance and the earthy, often irreverent Western tradition as exemplified by Harte and Twain. *Literary Friends and Acquaintance* is, at heart, Howells's personal testament to the birth of the American tradition as he understood it and, as such, stands in stark contrast to the narrow version promulgated by Barrett Wendell.

16. Howells, *Literary Friends and Acquaintance,* 256, 266, 277, 322. It bears mentioning that some of the points Howells makes about Twain in "My Mark Twain" are ideas he had previously articulated—some in more rigorously critical language—in the seminal 1901 essay "Mark Twain: An Inquiry" (*SLC* 3:37–49).

17. Howells, *Literary Friends and Acquaintance,* 285, 246–47.

A Turmoil of Presences

In their later years, James and Howells remained close friends and avid readers of each other's work. And, as had been the case throughout their early years, each was the other's keenest critic. Howells continued to support his friend unflaggingly. His final major essay on James, "Mr. Henry James's Later Work," appeared in the *North American Review* (January 1903) shortly after *The Wings of the Dove* had been published. Howells begins by noting the difficulties readers have always had with James, and the different kinds of readers he attracts or repels. "Many of his readers," Howells observes, "are also his enemies: they read him in a condition of hot insurrection against all that he says and is; they fiercely question his point of view, they object to the world that he sees from it; they declare that there is no such world, or that, if there is, there ought not to be, and that he does not paint it truly. They would like to have the question out with him personally: such is their difference of opinion that, to hear them talk, you would think they would like to have it out with him pugilistically." The passage is noteworthy. Howells captures the mind-set of certain readers of the day, reminding us that James has never been easy to read, even for those most sympathetic to his work. This quick acknowledgment of James's critics is also a savvy rhetorical strategy. Having granted those readers hostile to James their essential point—James "has his faults," Howells admits—he can sidestep the issue and proceed to offer "almost entirely a study of his merits" (*SLC* 3:80). In so doing, Howells positions himself as a quintessentially Jamesian critic willing to meet his subject on his subject's own ground.

Amid a mock dialogue with a quarrelsome female reader, Howells proceeds to enumerate many of James's signal qualities. If James's characters seem elusive and difficult to grasp, it is because James is "a painter," and "You cannot get behind the figures in any picture. They are always merged in their background." If it is hard to make out just what is going on in a James novel, it is because the author gives you "the color, the light and shade, the delicate *nuances,* the joy of the intimated fact." James "imparts a fact without stating it, approaching it again and again." Like a fine painting, his fiction presents "a turmoil of presences which you could make anything, everything, nothing of as you happened to feel; something going on that you had glimpses of, or were allowed to guess at, but which you were rapturously dissatisfied with, any way." Readers must learn to surrender to an absence of certainty: "it isn't so much what he says—he never *says* anything—but what he insinuates." Indeed, Howells goes so far as to suggest that "it is not well to penetrate every recess of an author's meaning. It robs him of the charm of mystery, and the somewhat labyrinthine construction of Mr. James's later sentences lends itself to the practice of the self-denial necessary to the preservation of this charm. What I feel sure of is that he has a meaning in it all, and that by and by, perhaps when I least expect it, I shall surprise his meaning" (*SLC* 3:82–85). Howells sounds patently Jamesian throughout the passage. James had, of course, introduced the analogy of the painter in "The Art of Fiction" and had returned to it in subsequent essays, including several of the Prefaces. In borrowing the analogy amid a discussion of James's work, then, Howells clearly indicates the important influence James's critical work had on Howells. Howells's willingness to surrender to the felicities of James's style and to forgo certainty is a testament first to his sensitivity as a reader, and second, to the influence of James's work as both literary critic and creative writer.

During his discussion of *The Sacred Fount,* Howells convincingly pleads James's case, emphasizing that the novel's opacity is an aesthetic strength: "why should not a novel be written so like to life, in which most of the events remain the meaningless, that we shall never quite know what the author meant? . . . In the scribbles which we suppose to be imitations of life, we hold the unhappy author to a logical consistency which we find so rarely in the original; but ought not we rather to praise him where his work confesses itself, as life confesses itself, without a plan?" In the final instance, Howells is willing to grant James his every whim, and encourages readers to do the same. Howells argues that *The Awkward Age* and *The Wings of the Dove* "are really incomparable books, not so much because there is nothing in contemporary fiction to equal them as because there is nothing the least like them. They are of a kind that none but their author can do, and since he is alone master of their art, I am very well content to leave him to do that kind of book as he chooses. . . . After all, the critic has to leave authors somewhat to themselves; he cannot always be writing their books for them" (*SLC* 3:87–88). Rarely has Howells sounded more Jamesian than in this passage; he is willing to grant James his donnée and, as a critic, to limit himself to responding to what is on the page, so to speak.

Howells was equally generous in his private correspondence with James. "I must own to you a constantly mounting wonder in myself at your 'way,' and at the fullness, the closeness, the density of your work," he confessed after reading *The Tragic Muse* in the recently issued New York Edition. He added gently, "my own [fiction] seems so meager beside it." Enjoying his rediscovery of James, Howells read *The Bostonians,* a book he had apparently overlooked in 1886. Expressing concern that the novel would not be included in the New York Edition (it was not), Howells pronounces "that it's not only one of the greatest books you've written, but one of the masterpieces of all fiction. Closely woven, deep, subtle, reaching out into worlds that I did not imagine you knew, and avouching you citizen of the American

Cosmos, it is such a novel as the like of has n't been done in our time. . . . I believe I have not been wanting in a sense of you from the first," he concludes, "but really I seem only . . . to be realizing you now" (*LFL*, 437–38; *HSL* 5:294, 307).

Of course, not everyone shared Howells's enthusiasm for James's late manner. After reading "Mr. Henry James's Later Work," an exasperated Charles Eliot Norton—who found James's later style impossibly annoying—wrote Howells and, apparently out of spite or frustration, included a number of James's early letters ridiculing Howells. With admirable equanimity, Howells replied to Norton:

> It was kind of you to include James's early letters to yourself among those Miss Grace is sending me, and I wont pretend I have read them with less interest because of certain allusions to me in them. In a way I think their criticism very just; I have often thought my intellectual raiment was more than my intellectual body, and that I might finally be convicted, not of having nothing *on*, but that worse nakedness of having nothing *in*. He speaks of me with my style, and such mean application as I was making of it, as seeming to him like a poor man with a diamond which he does not know what to do with; and mostly I suppose I *have* cut rather inferior window glass with it. But I am not sorry for having wrought in common, crude material so much; that is the right American stuff; and perhaps hereafter, when my din is done, if any one is curious to know what that noise was it will be found to have proceeded from a small insect which was scraping about on the surface of our life and trying to get into its meaning for the sake of the other insects larger or smaller. That is, such has been my unconscious work; consciously, I was always, as I still am, trying to fashion a piece of literature out of the life next at hand. (*HSL* 5:54)

The reply speaks to Howells's humility and ability to admit his own shortcomings, if not to err on the side of demeaning himself. That he bore no apparent grudge against James is perhaps not surprising, for Norton could hardly know that Howells had, as Michael Anesko aptly notes, "long been accustomed to receiving James's criticism directly from the Master's hand" (*LFL*, 342). Last, the letter eloquently reemphasizes an essential American quality to Howells's efforts—the sense that he always sought to grapple with the question of America in both his fiction and his criticism.

Home-Grown Humanity

While the two friends would write of one another several times in their final years, "Mr. Henry James's Later Work" is the last penetrating critical study written by either author on the subject of the other. After writing the 1886 essay "William Dean Howells," James published only a handful of brief critical assessments of Howells. One such glance is worthy of inspection, however, as it demonstrates that some of James's earliest criticisms of Howells remained concerns throughout his career. Some very familiar charges are at the heart of a short passage in James's final "American Letter" (July 9, 1898). While praising Howells's novel *The Story of a Play* as "admirably light," James suggests that the author "has not cut into the subject quite so deep as the intensity of the experience—for I assume his experience—might have made possible. It is a chapter of bewilderments, but they are for the most part cleared up, and the writer's fundamental optimism appears to have, on the whole matter, the last word. . . . He has perhaps indeed even purposefully approached his subject at an angle that compelled him to graze rather than to penetrate." James unsparingly spells out Howells's particular stylistic faults in a passage that, if intended to serve a particular case, broadens into a more general critique:

> In short I think the general opportunity a great one, and am brought back, by the limits of the particular impression Mr. Howells has been content to give of it, to that final sense of the predestined beauty of behavior on the part of every one concerned—kindness, patience, submission to boredom and general innocent humanity—which is what most remains with me from almost any picture he produces. It is sure to be, at the worst, a world all lubricated with good nature and the tone of pleasantry. Life, in his pages, is never too hard, too ugly, passions and perversities never too sharp, not to allow, on the part of his people, of such an exercise of friendly wit about each other as may well, when one considers it, minimize shocks and strains. So it muffles and softens, all round, the edges of "The Story of a Play." (*LC* 1:700–701)

If this passage is one of James's most bluntly worded assessments of Howells's shortcomings, it is also an echo of long-held opinions. The critique of Howellsian "optimism" offered in 1898 reflects in every significant respect the opinion first articulated in "William Dean Howells." Likewise, the charge that Howells's work was "light" goes back to some of James's earliest published essays on Howells, including his 1868 review of *Italian Journeys* and his twin 1875 reviews of *A Foregone Conclusion*.

James would sing a different song in his final lengthy appraisal of Howells, a 1912 tribute in honor of the Dean's seventy-fifth birthday.[18] The

---

18. The House of Harper, capitalizing on Howells's cultural prestige as the "Dean of American Letters," organized a gala affair whose four hundred guests included President Taft.

tone of this piece is, as would fit the occasion, warm and nostalgic. It is a public celebration of a friendship; there are no opaque passages or subtly coded criticisms. In "A Letter to Mr. Howells," one finds a humble James sincerely thanking Howells for showing him, back in 1866, "a frankness and sweetness of hospitality that was really the making of me, the making of the confidence that required help and sympathy and that I should otherwise, I think, have strayed and stumbled about a long time without acquiring. You showed me the way and opened me the door; you wrote to me and confessed yourself struck with me—I have never forgotten the beautiful thrill of *that*." James professes wonder at Howells's voluminous output over the years—"your heroic consistency and your noble, genial abundance"—and suggests that it was his saturation in American life that enabled him to be so prolific. "For you have had the advantage, after all," James notes, "of breathing an air that has suited and nourished you; of sitting up to your neck, as I may say—or at least up to your waist—amid the sources of your inspiration." Furthermore, James praises Howells for making the most of the opportunities:

> You saw your field with a rare lucidity: you saw all it had to give in the way of the romance of the real and the interest and the thrill and the charm of the common, as one may put it; the character and the comedy, the point, the pathos, the tragedy, the particular home-grown humanity under your eyes and your hand and with which the life all about you was closely interknitted. Your hand reached out to these things with a fondness that was in itself a literary gift and played with them as the artist only and always can play: freely, quaintly, incalculably, with all the assurance of his fancy and his irony, and yet with that fine taste for the truth and the pity and the meaning of the matter which keeps the temper of observation both sharp and sweet. To observe by such an instinct and by such reflection is to find work to one's hands and a challenge in every bush; and as the familiar American scene thus bristled about you, so year by year your vision more and more justly responded and swarmed.

In praising the "temper," or tone, of Howells's work as both "sharp and sweet," James manages simultaneously to praise the more socially penetrating elements of the fiction while perhaps faintly acknowledging the overly "optimistic" quality of the work that he had so cogently pointed out in 1886. Indeed, in the final lines of his tribute, James cannot resist a passing reference to Howells's "incurable optimism" (*LC* 1:507–10).

James's warmth and generosity in "A Letter to Mr. Howells" proved to be par for the course during the birthday celebration. Howells, uncomfortable with the very public attention surrounding the affair, later confessed in a letter to James that "It is at the worst, part of the divine madness of an affair in which I still struggle to identify my accustomed self. . . . [I]t was all, all wrong and unfit; but nobody apparently knew it, not even I till that ghastly waking hour of the night when hell opens to us" (*LFL,* 454; *HSL* 6:16). If the letter expresses Howells's customary self-doubt, it also expresses a growing unease with his status as the Dean of American Letters—a role vigorously promoted by the market-savvy House of Harper.[19]

For his part, James promptly responded to Howells's complaint with a letter noteworthy for its strong tone of encouragement. "How you can take any view of your long career of virtue & devotion & self-sacrifice, of labour & courage & admirable & distinguished production, *but* the friendly & understanding & acceptingly 'philosophic' view, I decline even to lift an eye to comprehending," James intones. "We all fall short of our dreams," he notes authoritatively, "—but of what can you have fallen short unless of some prefiguring *delirium?*" Regarding the "terrible banquet (for I think indeed it must have been terrible)," James acknowledges that "Truly was it an ordeal for you of the 1st water (or I suppose *wine;*) through which, not less clearly, you passed unscathed as to your grace & humour & taste" (*LFL,* 455–56).[20]

If James sounds like a good-natured cheerleader in the 1912 letter, it is perhaps because he understood his friend's capacity for depression. Drawing "from impressions received in long past years," James discussed the topic in a 1903 letter to Grace Norton: "I think, however, that, real as this condition in him is, in a degree, it is yet a thing disconnected, in a manner, from his *operative* self, and that never has been the least paralysing, or interfering, or practically depressing, but on the contrary, very stimulating to endeavour. . . . Still, I've always known that he has a strange, sad kind of subterraneous crepuscular *alter ego,* a sort of 'down cellar' (where they keep the apples of discord) of gloom and apprehension" (*JL* 4:300). That James would mark a difference between Howells's "operative" self and his "subterraneous crepuscular *alter ego*" is telling. James himself suffered from depression

19. None of the many tributary letters was read at the celebration; rather, the letters were published subsequently in the various Harper's magazines, including the *North American Review,* which published James's letter. For a detailed account of the Harper's birthday gala— as well as a convincing account of Howells's role as a commodity in the literary marketplace— see Crowley, *Dean of American Letters,* 45–90.

20. In a letter to T. S. Perry regarding the Harper banquet, James confesses that Perry's report of the evening confirms his own "convictions" regarding the essential vulgarity of his home country: "One of the most irresistible, if not most cherished of these is that the Great Country *que vous savez* has developed the genius for vulgarity on a scale to which no other genius for anything anywhere can hold a candle. But what an awful state of things when a quiet decent honest man like W.D.H. *has* to think he can't under peril of life, do anything but become part of the horror" (*JL* 4:605).

and poor health in his final years, and each condition weakened his capacity for sustained work. Yet it was the solace of work which James longed for; his letters and notebooks offer eloquent testament to this fact.

Howells knew as much and, accordingly, did all he could to encourage his friend. In 1910, James returned to the United States for the final time, traveling with his ailing brother William, who died in August. James's departure for England was delayed by the offer of an honorary degree from Harvard, which he accepted in 1911. Howells, who understood that his friend was impatient to return to his study at Lamb House, wrote to report that he had recently finished a new book, *New Leaf Mills,* and to encourage his friend. "I write and find greater happiness in writing than I ever did," he admits, "and this, my dear old friend, is clumsily leading up to the hope and belief that you will soon begin writing again. You have been miserably interrupted, but you have great things ahead of you to do and to enjoy doing; and you must set yourself to realize this" (*LFL,* 449). Avid readers, keen friends, and regular correspondents—James and Howells provided each other with a lifetime of mutual support that helped fuel two of the most important writers of their period.

Conclusion

In December 1915, Henry James suffered a series of strokes that ultimately led to his death the following February. When Howells received word of his friend's illness, he wrote to James's nephew, Henry James Jr., confessing his sadness. "I cannot say anything," Howells lamented. "He is the last that is left of my earthly world" (*HSL* 6:89).

The editors of *Harper's* invited Howells to write a commemorative essay shortly after James's passing, and he naturally agreed. But the task proved difficult, perhaps because of the intimate nature of the endeavor. Howells never finished his reflections, leaving uncompleted drafts of two essays at the time of his own death in May 1920: an "Editor's Easy Chair" column on Lubbock's edition of James's letters, and an intriguing piece entitled "The American James."[21] If anything, the drafts suggest the ultimate difficulty Howells experienced in trying to sum up a lifelong friendship—not to mention the strenuous task of "reclaiming" an American James. That Howells wished to accomplish the latter seems beyond question; he knew as well as

21. The texts of both essays are reprinted in *LFL,* 469–73. While the texts are without question interesting and valuable, I have decided not to quote from them due to their unrevised and uncompleted status.

anyone that Americans had never really understood James. As he explained in a 1920 letter to T. S. Perry, James's "own countrymen never treated him decently. . . . Never was a great writer so vulgarly hooted at and rejected by his own people" (*HSL* 6:152).

Howells had always understood James, however, and if he never completed the commemorative essays, he could rest easy in the knowledge that no critic on either shore of the Atlantic read or critiqued James with more sensitivity than he himself had done for over fifty years. Howells's ability to read James on the artist's own terms changed and grew along with James's late manner; "Mr. Henry James's Later Work" stands as ample evidence to this fact. Simply stated, Howells proved himself as sensitive and careful a reader as James could ever hope for. In contrast, while James continued to read Howells's later work, the brief critique of *The Story of a Play* suggests that his earliest concerns with Howells's fiction—its "lightness" and overinsistent optimism—remained. In short, James always sensed a lack of depth and sophistication in Howells's work, and he chided his friend for never progressing beyond a certain surface-level polish of style. Nevertheless, he loved and respected Howells, as the glowing tribute for the 1912 birthday dinner clearly shows.

As literary critics, both James and Howells remained fascinated with the question of America as a literary subject. In his "American Letters" James spelled out what he felt were the most promising areas for new writers to explore: colloquial American language; the world of business; and the ever-changing status of gender relations. If he would ultimately reject the use of dialect in fiction, he was customarily prescient in his other observations. Howells's concerns also kept pace with the changing society around him. Inspired by the work of Thorstein Veblen, he rather prophetically suggested that the newly emerged American aristocracy could be a promising subject for literature. Howells had always believed American literature needed to expand and grow to survive. Likewise, the readers of that literature needed to change and adapt. In his review of Barrett Wendell's *A Literary History of America,* Howells lambasted a figure of the Old Order for perpetuating an outmoded and narrow conception of the American literary landscape. In so doing, he argued passionately for a broader, more democratic and inclusive notion of American literature.

Bibliography

Alexander, William. *William Dean Howells: The Realist as Humanist.* New York: Burt Franklin, 1981.

Anesko, Michael. *"Friction with the Market": Henry James and the Profession of Authorship.* New York: Oxford University Press, 1986.

———. *Letters, Fictions, Lives: Henry James and William Dean Howells.* New York: Oxford University Press, 1997.

Armstrong, Paul B. "Reading James's Prefaces and Reading James." In McWhirter, *Henry James's New York Edition: The Construction of Authorship,* 127–37.

Arnold, Matthew. "Civilization in the United States." *Nineteenth Century* 23 (April 1888): 489.

Ballou, Ellen B. *The Building of the House: Houghton Mifflin's First Half Century.* New York: Houghton Mifflin, 1970.

Bell, Michael Davitt. *The Problem of American Realism: Studies in the Cultural History of a Literary Idea.* Chicago: University of Chicago Press, 1993.

Bennett, George N. *The Realism of William Dean Howells, 1889–1920.* Nashville: Vanderbilt University Press, 1973.

Besant, Walter. "The Art of Fiction." 1884. Reprinted in *The Art of Fiction,* by Walter Besant and Henry James, 3–48. Boston: De Wolfe, Fiske & Co., 1885.

Blackmur, R. P., ed. *The Art of the Novel: Critical Prefaces,* by Henry James. 1934. Reprint, Boston: Northeastern University Press, 1984.

Blair, Sara. "In the House of Fiction: Henry James and the Engendering of Literary Mastery." In McWhirter, *Henry James's New York Edition: The Construction of Authorship,* 58–73.

Booth, Wayne C. *The Rhetoric of Fiction.* 2d ed. Chicago: University of Chicago Press, 1983.

Borus, Daniel H. *Writing Realism: Howells, James, and Norris in the Mass Market.* Chapel Hill: University of North Carolina Press, 1989.

Brodhead, Richard H. *The School of Hawthorne.* New York: Oxford University Press, 1986.

Brooks, Van Wyck. "Henry James as a Reviewer." In *Sketches in Criticism*, 190–96. New York: E. P. Dutton, 1932.

———. *Howells: His Life and World*. New York: E. P. Dutton, 1959.

———. *The Ordeal of Mark Twain*. New York: E. P. Dutton, 1920.

Cady, Edwin H. "The Neuroticism of William Dean Howells." *PMLA* 61 (1946): 229–38.

———. *The Realist at War: The Mature Years, 1885–1920, of William Dean Howells*. Syracuse: Syracuse University Press, 1958.

———. *The Road to Realism: The Early Years, 1837–1885, of William Dean Howells*. Syracuse: Syracuse University Press, 1956.

Cady, Edwin H., ed. *W. D. Howells as Critic*, by William Dean Howells. London: Routledge and Kegan Paul, 1973.

Cady, Edwin H., and David L. Frazier, eds. *The War of the Critics over William Dean Howells*. Evanston, Ill.: Row, Peterson, 1962.

Carter, Everett. *Howells and the Age of Realism*. New York: J. B. Lippincott, 1954.

Coon, Spencer H. "Mr. Howells Talks." *Boston Daily Advertiser,* December 26, 1891. Reprinted in *Interviews with William Dean Howells,* ed. Ulrich Halfmann, 14. Arlington: University of Texas Press, 1973.

Crowley, John W. *The Black Heart's Truth: The Early Career of W. D. Howells*. Chapel Hill: University of North Carolina Press, 1985.

———. *The Dean of American Letters: The Late Career of William Dean Howells*. Amherst: University of Massachusetts Press, 1999.

———. *The Mask of Fiction: Essays on W. D. Howells*. Amherst: University of Massachusetts Press, 1989.

Daugherty, Sarah B. "Howells, Tolstoy, and the Limits of Realism: The Case of *Annie Kilburn*." *American Literary Realism* 19 (1986): 21–41.

———. *The Literary Criticism of Henry James*. Athens: Ohio University Press, 1981.

Edel, Leon. *Henry James: A Life*. New York: Harper and Row, 1985.

———. *Henry James: The Middle Years, 1882–1895*. Philadelphia: Lippincott, 1962.

———. *Henry James: The Treacherous Years, 1895–1901*. Philadelphia: Lippincott, 1969.

———. Introduction to *The House of Fiction: Essays on the Novel*, by Henry James, 9–19. London: Rupert Hart-Davis, 1957.

Edel, Leon, and Gordon N. Ray, eds., *Henry James and H. G. Wells: A Record of Their Friendship, Their Debate on the Art of Fiction, and Their Quarrel*. Urbana: University of Illinois Press, 1958.

Exman, Eugene. *The House of Harper: One Hundred and Fifty Years of Publishing*. New York: Harper and Row, 1967.

Fryckstedt, Olov W. *In Quest of America: A Study of Howells' Early Development as a Novelist.* Stockholm: Upsala, 1958.

Gibson, William M., and Leon Edel, eds. *Howells and James: A Double Billing.* New York: New York Public Library, 1958.

Gottesman, Ronald. Introduction to *Selected Literary Criticism,* vol. 3, *1898–1920,* by W. D. Howells, ed. Ronald Gottesman, xi–xx. Bloomington: Indiana University Press, 1993.

Habegger, Alfred. *Henry James and the "Woman Business."* Cambridge: Cambridge University Press, 1989.

———. "New York Monumentalism and Hidden Family Corpses." In McWhirter, *Henry James's New York Edition: The Construction of Authorship,* 185–205.

Hale, Dorothy J. "James and the Invention of Novel Theory." In *The Cambridge Companion to Henry James,* ed. Jonathan Freedman, 79–101. New York: Cambridge University Press, 1998.

———. *Social Formalism: The Novel in Theory from Henry James to the Present.* Stanford: Stanford University Press, 1998.

Halfmann, Ulrich. Introduction to *Selected Literary Criticism,* vol. 1, *1859–1885,* by W. D. Howells, ed. Ulrich Halfmann, xiii–xxiv. Bloomington: Indiana University Press, 1993.

Harper, J. Henry. *The House of Harper: A Century of Publishing in Franklin Square.* New York: Harper, 1912.

Hawthorne, Nathaniel. *Novels: Fanshawe, The Scarlet Letter, The House of the Seven Gables, The Blithedale Romance, The Marble Faun.* Ed. Millicent Bell. New York: Library of America, 1983.

Horne, Philip. *Henry James and Revision.* Oxford: Oxford University Press, 1990.

Hough, Robert L. *The Quiet Rebel: William Dean Howells as Social Commentator.* Lincoln: University of Nebraska Press, 1959.

Howells, William Dean. *Annie Kilburn.* New York: Harper, 1889.

———. "Are We a Plutocracy?" *North American Review* 158 (February 1894): 185–96.

———. *A Chance Acquaintance.* Boston: Osgood, 1873.

———. *Criticism and Fiction and Other Essays.* Ed. Clara Marburg Kirk and Rudolf Kirk. New York: New York University Press, 1959.

———. *Dr. Breen's Practice.* Boston: Osgood, 1881.

———. *Editor's Study.* Ed. James W. Simpson. Troy, N.Y.: Whitston, 1983.

———. "Equality as the Basis of Good Society." *Century* 51 (November 1895): 63–67.

———. *A Foregone Conclusion.* Boston: Osgood, 1875.

———. *A Hazard of New Fortunes.* New York: Harper, 1890.

———. *Heroines of Fiction*. 2 vols. New York: Harper, 1901.

———. *Imaginary Interviews*. 1910. Reprint, New York: Greenwood, 1969.

———. *Impressions and Experiences*. 1896. New York: Harper, 1909.

———. *Indian Summer*. Boston: Ticknor, 1886.

———. Introduction to *Sebastopol*, by Leo Tolstoy, 5–12. New York: Harper, 1887.

———. *Italian Journeys*. New York: Hurd and Houghton, 1867.

———. *The Kentons*. New York: Harper, 1902.

———. *Life in Letters of William Dean Howells*. Ed. Mildred Howells. 1928. Reprint, 2 vols., New York: Russell and Russell, 1968.

———. *Literary Friends and Acquaintance: A Personal Retrospect of American Authorship*. 1900 and 1910. Reprint of the 1910 edition, ed. David F. Hiatt and Edwin H. Cady, Bloomington: Indiana University Press, 1968.

———. *Literature and Life*. 1902. Library Edition. New York: Harper, 1911.

———. *A Modern Instance*. Boston: Osgood, 1882.

———. *My Literary Passions*. New York: Harper, 1895.

———. *My Literary Passions and Criticism and Fiction*. Library Edition. New York: Harper, 1910.

———. *My Mark Twain: Reminiscences and Criticisms*. New York: Harper, 1910.

———. "My Memories of Mark Twain." *Harper's Monthly* 121 (1910): 165–78.

———. "The Nature of Liberty." *Forum* 20 (December 1895): 401–9.

———. *New Leaf Mills: A Chronicle*. New York: Harper, 1913.

———. *The Rise of Silas Lapham*. Boston: Ticknor, 1885.

———. *The Seen and Unseen at Stratford-on-Avon: A Fantasy*. New York: Harper, 1914.

———. *Selected Letters of William Dean Howells*. Ed. George Arms et al. 6 vols. Boston: Twayne, 1979–1983.

———. *Selected Literary Criticism*. Vol. 1, *1859–1885*. Ed. Ulrich Halfmann. Bloomington: Indiana University Press, 1993.

———. *Selected Literary Criticism*. Vol. 2, *1886–1897*. Ed. Donald Pizer. Bloomington: Indiana University Press, 1993.

———. *Selected Literary Criticism*. Vol. 3, *1898–1920*. Ed. Ronald Gottesman. Bloomington: Indiana University Press, 1993.

———. *The Shadow of a Dream*. New York: Harper, 1890.

———. *The Story of a Play*. New York: Harper, 1898.

———. *Their Wedding Journey*. Boston: Osgood, 1872.

———. *A Traveler from Altruria*. New York: Harper, 1894.

———. *Venetian Life*. New York: Hurd and Houghton, 1866.

———. *W. D. Howells as Critic*. Ed. Edwin H. Cady. London: Routledge and Kegan Paul, 1973.

———. "Who Are Our Brethren?" *Century* 51 (April 1896): 932–36.

———. *A Woman's Reason*. Boston: Osgood, 1883.

Jacobson, Marcia. *Henry James and the Mass Market*. University: University of Alabama Press, 1983.

James, Henry. *The Ambassadors*. New York: Harper, 1903.

———. *The American Scene*. New York: Harper, 1907.

———. *The Awkward Age*. New York: Harper, 1899.

———. *The Bostonians*. 3 vols. London: Macmillan, 1886.

———. *Daisy Miller: A Study*. New York: Harper, 1879.

———. *French Poets and Novelists*. London: Macmillan, 1878.

———. *The Golden Bowl*. 2 vols. New York: Scribner's, 1904.

———. *Hawthorne*. London: Macmillan, 1879.

———. *Henry James: Selected Letters*. Ed. Leon Edel. Cambridge: Harvard University Press, Belknap Press, 1987.

———. *Henry James Letters*. Ed. Leon Edel. 4 vols. Cambridge: Harvard University Press, Belknap Press, 1974–1984.

———. *Henry James on Culture: Collected Essays on Politics and the American Social Scene*. Ed. Pierre A. Walker. Lincoln: University of Nebraska Press, 1999.

———. *Literary Criticism*. Vol. 1, *Essays on Literature, American Writers, English Writers*. Ed. Leon Edel and Mark Wilson. New York: Library of America, 1984.

———. *Literary Criticism*. Vol. 2, *French Writers, Other European Writers, the Prefaces to the New York Edition*. Ed. Leon Edel and Mark Wilson. New York: Library of America, 1984.

———. *Notes on Novelists*. New York: Scribner's, 1914.

———. *Novels, 1881–1886: Washington Square, The Portrait of a Lady, The Bostonians*. Ed. William T. Stafford. New York: Library of America, 1985.

———. *Partial Portraits*. London: Macmillan, 1888.

———. *A Passionate Pilgrim*. Boston: Osgood, 1875.

———. *The Portrait of a Lady*. 3 vols. London: Macmillan, 1881.

———. *The Princess Casamassima*. 3 vols. London: Macmillan, 1886.

———. *The Sacred Fount*. New York: Scribner's, 1901.

———. *Selected Letters of Henry James to Edmund Gosse, 1882–1915: A Literary Friendship*. Ed. Rayburn S. Moore. Baton Rouge: Louisiana State University Press, 1988.

———. *Terminations*. New York: Harper, 1895.

————. *The Tragic Muse*. Boston: Houghton, Mifflin, 1890.

————. *The Turn of the Screw*. In *The Two Magics*. London: Heinemann, 1898.

————. *The Wings of the Dove*. 2 vols. New York: Scribner's, 1902.

Jones, Vivien. *James the Critic*. New York: St. Martin's, 1985.

Kaplan, Amy. *The Social Construction of American Realism*. Chicago: University of Chicago Press, 1988.

Kelley, Cornelia Pulsifer. *The Early Development of Henry James*. Rev. ed. Urbana: University of Illinois Press, 1965.

Kirk, Clara Marburg, and Rudolf Kirk, eds. *Criticism and Fiction and Other Essays,* by William Dean Howells. New York: New York University Press, 1959.

Lewis, Sinclair. "The American Fear of Literature." 1930. Reprinted in Cady and Frazier, *The War of the Critics over William Dean Howells,* 153–54.

Lubbock, Percy. *The Craft of Fiction*. New York: Scribner's, 1921.

Lynn, Kenneth S. *William Dean Howells: An American Life*. New York: Harcourt Brace Jovanovich, 1971.

Margolis, Anne T. *Henry James and the Problem of Audience: An International Act*. Ann Arbor: UMI Research Press, 1985.

Matthiessen, F. O. *Henry James: The Major Phase*. 1944. Reprint, New York: Oxford University Press, 1963.

McWhirter, David, ed. *Henry James's New York Edition: The Construction of Authorship*. Stanford: Stanford University Press, 1995.

Michaels, Walter Benn. "Writers Reading: James and Eliot." *Modern Language Notes* 91 (1976): 827–49.

Miller, James E., ed. *Theory of Fiction: Henry James,* by Henry James. Lincoln: University of Nebraska Press, 1972.

Nettels, Elsa. *Language and Gender in American Fiction: Howells, James, Wharton, and Cather*. Charlottesville: University Press of Virginia, 1997.

————. *Language, Race, and Social Class in Howells's America*. Lexington: University Press of Kentucky, 1988.

Pearson, John H. *The Prefaces of Henry James: Framing the Modern Reader*. University Park: Pennsylvania State University Press, 1997.

Pizer, Donald. Introduction to *Selected Literary Criticism,* vol. 2, *1886–1897,* by W. D. Howells, ed. Donald Pizer, xiii–xxi. Bloomington: Indiana University Press, 1993.

Posnock, Ross. *Henry James and the Problem of Robert Browning*. Athens: University of Georgia Press, 1985.

Roberts, Morris. *Henry James's Criticism*. Cambridge: Harvard University Press, 1929.

Roberts, Morris, ed. *The Art of Fiction and Other Essays,* by Henry James. New York: Oxford University Press, 1948.

Rowe, John Carlos. *The Theoretical Dimensions of Henry James.* Madison: University of Wisconsin Press, 1984.

Rowlette, Robert. "In 'The Silken Arms of the Aristocracy': William Dean Howells's Lecture in Indianapolis, 1899." *Indiana Magazine of History* 69 (December 1973): 299–319.

———. "William D. Howells' 1899 Midwest Lecture Tour." Pts. 1 and 2. *American Literary Realism* 9 (1976): 1–2; 10 (1977): 125–67.

Salmon, Richard. *Henry James and the Culture of Publicity.* Cambridge: Cambridge University Press, 1997.

Sedgwick, Ellery. *The Atlantic Monthly, 1857–1909: Yankee Humanism at High Tide and Ebb.* Amherst: University of Massachusetts Press, 1994.

Sedgwick, Eve Kosofsky. "Shame and Performativity: Henry James's New York Edition Prefaces." In McWhirter, *Henry James's New York Edition: The Construction of Authorship,* 206–39.

Shi, David E. *Facing Facts: Realism in American Thought and Culture, 1850–1920.* New York: Oxford University Press, 1995.

Simpson, Lewis P. "The Treason of William Dean Howells." In *The Man of Letters in New England and the South: Essays on the History of the Literary Vocation in America,* 85–128. Baton Rouge: Louisiana State University Press, 1973.

Spilka, Mark. "Henry James and Walter Besant: 'The Art of Fiction' Controversy." *Novel* 6.2 (1973): 101–19.

Tanner, Tony. "Henry James and the Art of Criticism." In *Henry James and the Art of Nonfiction,* 27–57. Athens: University of Georgia Press, 1995.

Trachtenberg, Alan. *The Incorporation of America: Culture and Society in the Gilded Age.* New York: Hill and Wang, 1982.

Wicke, Jennifer. *Advertising Fictions: Literature, Advertisement, and Social Reading.* New York: Columbia University Press, 1988.

Wortham, Thomas. "W. D. Howells' 1899 Midwest Lecture Tour: What the Letters Tell." *American Literary Realism* 11 (1978): 265–74.

Index